Rethinking Knife C

Elaine Williams · Peter Squires

Rethinking Knife Crime

Policing, Violence and Moral Panic?

Elaine Williams
University of Greenwich
London, UK

Peter Squires
University of Brighton
Brighton, UK

ISBN 978-3-030-83741-9   ISBN 978-3-030-83742-6   (eBook)
https://doi.org/10.1007/978-3-030-83742-6

This Palgrave Macmillan imprint is published by the registered company Springer Nature Switzerland AG
The registered company address is: Gewerbestrasse 11, 6330 Cham, Switzerland

Preface and Acknowledgements

Elaine Williams would like to acknowledge and give thanks to the youth practitioners, youth service managers, intervention workers, teachers and young participants from schools and youth centres who contributed their time, support and knowledge to the findings contained in this book. Thanks especially to the ongoing knowledge sharing and collaborative work with Ben Lindsay, Andrez Harriott, Lawrence Russell and Emmanuel Imuere, our discussions and dissatisfactions since 2008 have been a continuous motivation to keep pushing for new understanding in this field. Some of the ideas within this book originally formed part of a Ph.D. completed in the Sociology Department at the University of Goldsmiths. This initial research was made possible thanks to a scholarship from the Economic and Social Research Council and great thanks are expressed to my supervisors Les Back and Kalbir Shukra, whose guidance inspired the framework that underpins this work. Special thanks to Peter, who has been such a pleasure to work with. Peter's uniquely critical interventions in early 'knife crime' literature have been pivotal in my own research and career and to be able to continue this work alongside him has been a great privilege. Thanks also for the momentum Peter and the editorial team at Palgrave maintained throughout the COVID-19 lockdowns that pushed this project forwards and enabled us to bring it together during an otherwise challenging year.

Peter Squires would like to acknowledge the research contributions made by Arianna Silvestri, Roger Grimshaw, Enver Solomon, Richard Garside and Will McMahon, all at the Centre for Criminal Justice Studies, to some of the earlier work featured in this book. Some of the ideas presented here were tested out on students at the University of Brighton and in a couple of seminars, on 'gangs' and on 'knife crime' (an encounter with the 'knife crime industry' but which turned out—perhaps predictably—to be about 'gangs', after all), facilitated by Public Policy Exchange. Thanks also to the editors of the journal British Politics who commissioned the original article 'The knife crime 'epidemic' and British politics' (Volume 4:1) which, by several twists of serendipitous good fortune, became a small stepping-stone towards the book. In a crowded academic market place where journal articles often appear to get few reads, it has been fascinating to receive notifications from Research-Gate of 'reads' topping five figures. No doubt this is chiefly a reflection of the saturating levels of interest in the 'knife crime' phenomenon, even if the critical deconstructionist perspective we bring to it may not be quite that which many expect, an issue addressed already by Elaine. Nevertheless, it underpins our argument that 'knife crime' demands a serious rethinking. Thanks especially to Elaine, who has been a delight to work with—if largely remotely—during the lockdown days of 2020–21, and to our editorial team at Palgrave, Josie Taylor and Liam Inscoe-Jones.

London, UK   Elaine Williams
Brighton, UK   Peter Squires

Contents

List of Figures

Index of Learning Exercises and Study Questions

1

'There Is no Home Office Definition of Knife Crime'

Home Affairs Select Committee, 2009 *Knife Crime*: page 6.

When it Bleeds, it Leads

As we worked on the manuscript for this book, a seemingly relentless catalogue of knife-involved violence, 11 serious stabbings a day (Harper, 2017), was reported across Britain's media. In early December 2019 a man in his forties was fatally stabbed in Hornsey, North London, following a fight. Ten days later, and just five days before Xmas, two men were killed and several others injured following knife attacks in Walthamstow. Although London had gained something of an unwanted reputation as the epicentre of the 'knife crime crisis' (Younge, 2017), journalists described a nationwide phenomenon. On New Year's Day, in Derbyshire, a former head-teacher stabbed his ex-wife and her new lover with a pair of kitchen knives stolen from his mother's house. His frenzied attack left over 100 stab wounds on both victims. On January 6th, in the New Year, an altercation between two homeless men, both of Polish origin, resulted in the 11.30 p.m. stabbing of a sixty-year-old man

© The Author(s), under exclusive license to Springer Nature Switzerland AG 2021
E. Williams and P. Squires, *Rethinking Knife Crime*,
https://doi.org/10.1007/978-3-030-83742-6_1

1

in Clapton, East London. His attacker, 22 years old and of no known address was later charged with murder. In early February a fifty-five-year-old man was stabbed in Berkeley Square, Mayfair, during an attack by three assailants who were attempting to steal an expensive watch, valued at £115,000, he was wearing (Collier, 2020). By contrast, an expensive Gucci bag was the robbery target when a twenty-four-year-old man was fatally stabbed around midnight in Croydon in April.

Two days later an NHS worker, David Gomoh, was attacked by four men as he left his home near the Excel Centre in Newham, London Docklands. At the time, the Centre was hosting the NHS Nightingale C-19 pandemic hospital facility. The attackers, who inflicted eight stab wounds were said to have been wearing medical masks; police described the attack as 'entirely unprovoked' (Dodd, 2020). On the last day of the month, a forty-year-old man stabbed and killed two small children, aged three and nineteen months, at their home in Ilford, East London. In June, in Glasgow, a police officer was stabbed during a knife attack at a city centre hotel. Five other people received knife injuries, two hotel staff and three asylum seekers then resident at the hotel. The incident was concluded when police shot the attacker (Blackall, 2020). In August, a twenty-year-old man, was given a life sentence for an unprovoked fatal knife attack which occurred on the platform of Hillingdon station in North West London. The perpetrator, already on licensed release from HMP Rochester having served half of a four year sentence for an earlier knife attack in Brighton, claimed that the victim, had given him a 'funny look'. The murder weapon was a five and a half inch German military dagger stolen from the London, Warner Bros. film studios where he had briefly worked.

In September, one man was killed and seven others injured during what the police described as a 'ninety minute stabbing spree' of random attacks in Birmingham. Interviewed for the Guardian, paramedics referred to knife attacks as 'not a rare occurrence' while local people described the city as 'unsafe' and 'desensitised' to the violence (Storer, 2020). In October, an eighteen-year-old youth who had fatally stabbed another youth with a 25 cm 'Rambo-style' knife while they were both attending a 'knife awareness' course at Hillingdon Civic Centre, was jailed for life with a minimum term of 18 years recommended by the judge (Cruse, 2020). Finally, in January 2021, a 56-year-old plastic surgeon was arrested for the attempted murder of a 'highly respected' colleague in his own home. The victim was seriously injured following stab wounds to his chest and abdomen (*The Guardian*, Jan 8, 2021).

And so the incidents roll on. Perhaps, taken as individual incidents, they share little in common as regards perpetrators, victims, ages, locations or motives. The one thing they do have in common is the weapon used to inflict the often fatal injuries; the knife—although even knives can vary widely and represent different things: breadknife, penknife, flick knife, 'zombie-knife'. But if we step back from the tragedy and trauma, the individual pain and suffering of bereavement and injury, we can begin to see patterns, similarities and trends. This is to begin to approach knife crime *criminologically*. It is not that we are uninterested in motives, provocations or weapons, just that before we can begin to make sense of the messy world of journalistic detail, or the opinions of police, paramedics, politicians and public, we need to get some grip on the bigger picture, the context. For as Roberts (2021: xv) has argued, 'context yields the full extent of the issue… we should therefore look beyond the knife towards the context'. Just how much knife crime is there? Is it increasing in frequency? What can we discover about the victims and perpetrators? Where is it occurring? And how has this 'knife crime crisis' come about? To be absolutely clear, nothing in this book should be taken to imply that knife violence, or 'knife crime' is not a serious social problem, that stabbings occur with an unacceptable frequency and that addressing the violence associated with knife misuse is an important priority for health, safety and (social and criminal) justice. But the questions we have raised point to fundamental dilemmas in the way that knife crime is understood and responded to. For our analysis tells us that the way in which 'knife crime' is understood ensures that it is responded to rather ineffectively and in ways which largely perpetuate and exacerbate the problem.

'Knife Crime': Recent History, Data and Trends

And yet, for all the recent attention given to it, the use of the label 'knife crime' as a crime category in England and Wales has a relatively recent history. Originally used to describe particular forms of violence in Scotland in the 1990s, when Glasgow gained an unwanted reputation as the 'knife crime capital of Europe' (Kelbie, 2011; Seenan, 2005; Younge & Barr, 2017; WHO, 2002) the term was then revived in the early 2000s to refer to a new violent crime phenomenon appearing in England and Wales. Since then its use has grown so dramatically that this southwards shift of the label has become overlooked. It has become such a matter-of-fact phrase that it now functions as both a collective noun for knife-related offences and an adjective denoting a criminal culture. News headlines commonly reference 'knife crime thugs', 'knife crime teens' or 'knife crime gangs' without justification of the label's meaning or the criteria for its attachment. Government institutions, police, the justice system and scholars, all consistently acknowledge difficulty in establishing a workable, evidence-based definition of 'knife crime' (Eades et al., 2007; Gliga, 2009; Shaw et al., 2011: 267–268; Silvestri et al., 2009; Squires et al., 2008) and yet the phrase continues to be used apparently with great influence and authority. In 2009 the Home Affairs Select Committee report on Knife Crime begins with the caution 'there is no Home Office definition of knife crime', the phrase was adopted by the media and is now popularly used to refer primarily to stabbings but also to the illegal carrying of knives in a public place by young people' (HASC, 2009: para. 4). Arguably, the impact of the label was most strongly felt in the summer of 2008 when national concern over 'knife crime' triggered an extensive authoritarian policing response concentrated upon the streets of London. The government claimed 'knife crime' was their number one priority—more urgent even than terrorism, only a year after London's transport attacks. London's Metropolitan Police (MPS) declared 'war on knife crime', a war that would be fought primarily through controversial stop and search operations facilitated by the extension of policing powers. At the time the MPS admitted their tactics amounted to proactive 'in your face policing' (Edwards et al., 2008), but claimed it was necessary in order to put an end to the 'knife crime epidemic'. In addition to the authoritarian policing responses, the label also became mobilised through high priority intervention schemes and prevention projects targeting young people from 2009 onwards.

Part of our initial focus concerns both the scale and trends concerning contemporary knife-enabled violence, and what appear to be underlying rates of knife carrying and availability. Yet the evidence here is not always straightforward. Available data of violent crime is recognised as particularly susceptible (amongst other factors) to changes in police recording practices as well as changing police activity rates (Brown, 2005), and as our timeline shows (Fig. 1.4) a great deal was happening on this score. Homicide rates have steadily increased since the 1950s, but within these figures killing with a sharp instrument has remained a relatively constant proportion of all homicides including during the decade in which the panic over 'knife crime' first emerged (Eades et al., 2007). Looking at offensive knife use as a percentage of all violent offences from 1997 to 2007 it remained between 5 and 8% throughout the first alleged 'knife crime epidemic' (Eades et al., 2007: 18). And examining the figures covering later phases of concern over 'knife crime' the same picture is revealed—between 2007 and 2017, knife use also remained between 5 and 8% of all violent offences (Allen & Audickas, 2018). Describing knife homicide and violent crime figures in isolation from their proportion of the total is one way in which 'knife crime' data is commonly misrepresented. Furthermore, as we shall see, data on knife-related offences recorded by the police also presents difficulties in interpretation. As our later discussion of the twentieth century 'wounding trends' shows (Figs. 1.5 and 1.6), the weapon in 'knife crime' can be defined as 'any article which has a blade or is sharply pointed' (Allen & Audickas, 2018: 5). Along with knives, recorded offences in 'knife crime' data can include possession or use of broken bottles, glass, screwdrivers and chisels, scissors or sharp sticks.

A further problem with the presentation of 'knife involved' violence is that there is seldom any distinction drawn between the ages of perpetrators or victims or the contexts in which the offences recorded as knife enabled are committed (Allen & Audickas, 2018). Figure 1.1 below shows that although 'knife crime' tends to be overwhelmingly associated with young people, in fact 10–17 year olds represent only around one in five of knife crime perpetrators. The fallback suggestion that the number of youthful knife offenders is rising alarmingly is hardly borne out by the data. Likewise, NHS data on hospital admissions for knife injuries show that knife crime victims aged 18 and under seldom exceed some 15–20% of the total (Shaw, 2019). Although A&E doctors were reported as saying that 'the injuries they were treating were becoming more severe and the victims were getting younger, with increasing numbers of girls involved' the available data does not bear these claims out. A similar analysis covering the years 1997–2008, this time based upon hospital A&E admissions data, found that around eleven per cent of A&E admissions

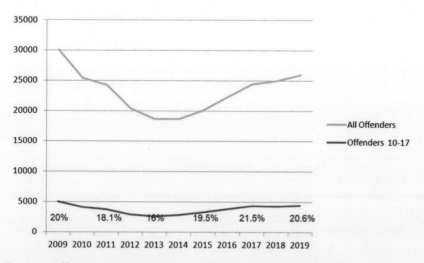

Fig. 1.1   Offences involving knives or offensive weapons: Offenders aged 10–17 as a proportion of all offenders: 2009–2019 (*Source* Ministry of Justice: Knife and offensive weapon sentencing statistics 10 Sept 2020: Table 2A)

for stabbing or cutting injuries involved victims aged eighteen or under (Squires, 2011).[1]

Picking up on the comment regarding female victims of knife crime, another difficulty with the statistics becomes apparent. The presentation of broad 'knife crime' statistics invariably conflates knife-involved incidents arising in a wide variety of contexts including proportions of domestic, intimate partner and adult violence in the home, along with instances of mental health-related violence, suicide threats/attempts, homeless violence, prison violence, bar brawls and even unwitting blade possession offences of small penknives or screwdrivers that were thought to be legal by the carrier (Eades et al., 2007; HASC, 2009: 7). As Cook and Walklate (2020) point out, knives are 'the most commonly used weapon in intimate partner homicide' although knives have generally only 'become an object of fear and panic in England and Wales when used in public by mostly young men on other young men'. Delice and Yasar (2013) draw similar conclusions from their study of women and knife violence in Turkey. Knives are the most frequently employed weapons in cases of intimate partner violence, but until recently, the issue has been little studied. Cook and Walklate centre their discussion on three distinct aspects of the 'knife violence' issue: knives as material and cultural objects, knife violence as a gendered phenomenon and knife violence as a spatial issue.[2] The failure to draw these distinct aspects of knife crime together, they argue, leads to a prioritisation of 'knife' crime as a 'public' problem over its manifestation as an ongoing 'private' one, therefore its gendered and spatialised features remain hidden, thus adding to the failure of policy to tackle 'knife' crime in the round (2020: 1).

---

[1] If anything, the proportion of young people going to A&E with stab wounds was falling over this period, from a high of 12.8 in 1999 to a low of 10.2% in 2006–2007. Nevertheless, with headlines like 'Thousands' of knife crime victims aged 18 or younger' (BBC News, Jan 25, 2017) an impression is reinforced that youth are at the centre of the crisis. Both claims could be true, of course, Fig. 1.1 shows between three to five thousand knife crime offenders sentenced between 2009 and 2019, given the nature of the offence, a roughly equivalent number of victims is likely, but they are far from being the majority.

[2] We discuss certain material and cultural relations associated with knives in chapter 2, while the misleadingly constructed image of knife crime as public violence overwhelmingly occurring between young (black) males is addressed later in this chapter.

The article concluded by considering the extent to which these 'taken for granted and thereby invisible dimensions of "knife" crime sustain an ongoing distinction between public and private violence' and thereby perpetuate dominant 'understandings of who and what counts in relation to fatal violence' (2020: 3). Yet by contrast, on average two women are killed by a partner or former partner every week in England and Wales (ONS, 2019) or, one every three days (Long et al., 2020), while children are far more likely to be killed by a parent than another young person (Silvestri et al., 2009). Having noted that, between 2009 and 2018, 'knives and sharp instruments' were the leading means by which men killed women, the 2020 *Femicide Census* (Long et al., 2020: 37) noted 'men kill women with whatever means they have to hand' and in the home, this was often a knife. The Census report went on to make a more strategic point, while courts had come to interpret young men carrying a knife in public as evidence of 'criminal intent' (Shaw et al., 2011), a man carrying a knife from one room to another would be unlikely to be similarly construed.

But despite adult violence in the home producing a large amount of 'knife crime' data, it is not separated statistically in police records (Allen & Audickas, 2018), and is not considered a dominant context for positivist 'knife crime' research. So when the totals of knife-enabled crimes are conflated together, they may indeed give a misleading impression of a rising profile of knife-enabled violence, as if it were a singular phenomenon. Yet commentaries often fail to disaggregate the distinct trends and the problem, once again, is laid at the feet of young people, gangs and, overwhelmingly, as we shall see, black and minority ethnic communities (Elliott-Cooper, 2021a; Wood, 2010).[3]

The 2018 House of Commons briefing paper on 'Knife Crime in England and Wales' (Ibid.) makes clear from its opening paragraph that crime with sharp instruments is a national concern 'especially as

---

[3] Five years of Hospital A&E injury data (2002–2003 to 2006–2007) show BAME knife victims falling steadily from 43 to 32% of those attending A&E. The figure is undoubtedly disproportionate as regards the BAME population of England and Wales, but the overwhelming majority of knife victims are clearly white. It may be that the duty placed on A&E staff to report stab victims to the police may have impacted the willingness to attend A&E—unless seriously injured. Later in the book we will be addressing the profound racialisation of 'knife crime'.

it impacts particularly upon young people' (Allen & Audickas, 2018: 5). But seven pages of adult inclusive police knife data follow this statement of a youth focus, before a brief and limited presentation of crime survey data with children (Allen & Audickas, 2018: 6–12). These disconnected representations are repeated in a second edition of the Briefing Document published in 2020 (Allen & Kirk-Wade, 2020). In the few places where age analysis is possible this discrepancy of youth-centred concern is further exemplified. The records of disposals given for possession of a knife or offensive weapon reveal the vast majority of offenders are aged over 18 (79%), and that under-18s represent a minority of 16.3% of admissions to hospital for assault by a sharp object. The use of adult knife offence to misrepresent 'knife crime' as a youth phenomenon has become common in official statistics and is often repeated in much positivist research. Due to the lack of appropriate specificity in police data some researchers look to MORI youth surveys (Gliga, 2009) and hospital admission data of knife injuries (Gliga, 2009; Maxwell et al., 2007) to track changes in the rate of knife injury and provide more age specific data (Squires, 2011). But the reliability of some of these sources have also been challenged, they are all caught up in a 'deviance amplification' process we describe later (see Fig. 1.4), whereas MORI often rephrased the questions it asked year by year, responding to growing attention to youth knife carrying (Eades et al., 2007; Shaw et al., 2011: 269–270). Likewise medical staffs were under increasing pressure to record knife injuries, inflating the figures as they increasingly conformed to government recording guidelines (Finch, 2019; Maxwell et al., 2007; Morris, 2009). Although, as we have noted the requirement to report may have had the perverse effect of discouraging violence victims seeking medical help.

As with hospital records, the increased attention and proactive policing responses towards the phenomenon impacts on the data that is then used to measure the problem. The police themselves have acknowledged that increases in stop and search can inflate official knife offence figures (Squires et al., 2008: 20) and the toughening and extension of possession laws targeting knife carrying increases the likelihood of knife offences being committed (Eades et al., 2007). This is especially significant when examining the much discussed self-fulfilling impact of racial disproportionality in stop and search and targeted policing (McCandless et al., 2016; Tiratelli et al., 2018) on the statistical contribution of knife crime data to the calculation of risk in positivist research. It has long been recognised that as a consequence of 'over-policing' and the intensified racialised scrutiny of particular crimes and particular suspects (Long, 2018) the assumption of data as 'fact' itself reproduces the idea that certain crimes are disproportionately committed by young, Black, urban, males (Bowling & Phillips, 2002). By assuming the category of 'knife crime' as fact, despite the lack of accurate data in the context the label describes, positivist approaches contribute to the construction of the phenomenon as a criminality located amongst young, Black, inner-city males. There are a few notable exceptions in the existing field of 'knife crime' research that push against the dominance of such blinkered positivism, some of which we have considered already. A critical analysis of these alternative approaches, in the final section of this chapter, underpins the central argument of our own work.

The Latest Trends

We know that knives are the most frequently employed murder weapon (Brookman, 2005), throughout the ten years to 2019 knives were the murder weapon employed in slightly over a third of recorded homicides, involving both male and female victims. However, knives were not the most frequently employed means of violence overall, punching and kicking are still the most common form taken by interpersonal violence, although these incidents are far less likely to end in fatalities. This goes some way to reinforce the significance of 'weapon effect' in serious violence. The Home Affairs Committee Report of 2009 suggested some of the complications, arising from different sources of data, in even determining whether 'knife crime' was rising or falling, but the absence of a clear crime category further compounded the difficulties (2009: paras. 15–21). That said, the following graph begins with the clearest data and describes the trend for knife homicides over the past ten years. Yet, according to the CSEW (2016), weapons were only used in 21% of violent incidents (although most commonly a knife), and were

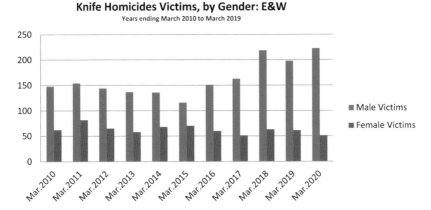

Fig. 1.2 Knife homicide victims, by gender: England and Wales (2010–2019)

more likely to be used in incidents that resulted in no injury (28%) as compared to incidents where an injury resulted (13%). While nearly all of the public, media and political attention given to knife crime appears focussed upon *public* violence, across the decade of the *Femicide Survey*, almost half (47%) of perpetrators killed women with knives and sharp instruments (Long et al., 2020: 37), ONS data likewise revealed that knives were also the most frequently employed weapon in cases of domestic violence (13% of incidents) (Cook & Walklate, 2020; ONS, 2019), further evidence pointing to the significance of knife availability and distinctive violence patterns and locations (Fig. 1.2).[4]

As the graph shows, in most years the number of male knife crime homicide victims is around twice the number of female victims, although this disparity has been growing since 2016, associated with a more general increase in knife-involved violence in recent years (as depicted in the following graph) (Fig. 1.3).

Figures 1.1 and 1.2 both detail a decade's worth of statistics from 2010 to 2011, they already refer to high rates of knife-enabled crime (especially

---

[4] According to Cook and Walklate, 'despite the knife being the weapon of choice in perpetrating (lethal) violence against women… responding to such violence(s) remains obscured and frequently downplayed as a *policy* priority' (2020: 4).

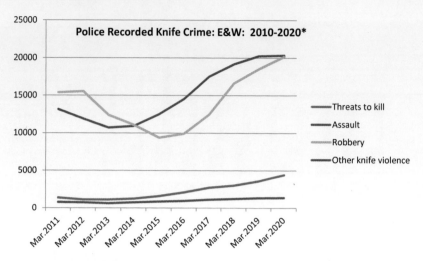

Fig. 1.3 Police recorded 'Knife Crime': 2010–2020 (*Data from Greater Manchester Police are not included in these figures on account of unresolved variations in data recording practices)

assaults and robberies) and over 200 knife homicides annually. Unfortunately such recent data as this, is unable by itself to cast much light on the deeper *origins* of contemporary concerns about knife violence.

Part of the 'knife crime story' we are seeking to uncover in this book concerns the supposed *increasing rate* of knife crime offending and the perceived *increasing seriousness* of the offences committed. Each of these issues—scale, trend and seriousness—point to a set of common assumptions about knife crime in the UK. These assumptions are regularly reflected in media stories suggesting that the problem is becoming worse and that today's violent young perpetrators display an increasing willingness to maim and kill, with a supposed lethal indifference towards the consequences of their violence. Sometimes these developments are given an additional racialised spin, suggesting that the modern youthful propensity to violence and the indifference to hurt represent a uniquely un-British phenomenon, the product of alien, decivilised and inferior cultures (Elliott-Cooper, 2021b).[5] We aim to challenge all of these assumptions. Despite the fact (something we will explore a little further in Chapter 2) that people have been stabbing and cutting one another with sharp and pointed implements for centuries, as Cook and Walklate acknowledge, 'as far as the criminal justice system is concerned, there is no such thing as "knife" crime' (Cook & Walklate, 2020: 3).

There is a major disconnection between media coverage of knife-enabled crimes and their presence in criminal statistics (Squires, 2009a). Indeed, the precise label 'knife crime' first emerged as a supposed new category of crime in the early twenty-first century—even before a statistical evidence base clearly enumerating the scale of knife-enabled violence—existed. The label 'knife crime' is now in regular use, especially in discussions of violent youth crime or 'urban violence'. Functioning as both a noun and (as knife-enabled) an adjective, the phrase refers to singular or collective knife-related acts and offences, as well as a perceived 'knife culture' or an expression of criminal malice. While its meaning is broad and its incidence apparently prevalent, its precise application is narrowed and its connotation specific, concerned especially with the actions of a particular demographic; young, Black, inner-city males. While its matter-of-fact reference infers a common sense meaning, 'knife crime' is nevertheless one of the most used and least understood crime labels in popular parlance. As Elliott-Cooper (2021b: 31) notes, '*knife crime* is not a criminal offence in itself, but an amalgam of already existing offences … by grouping [them] together … the police politician and the press can convey the idea that "knife crime" is new, or is at least worse than anything Britain has seen before'.

In this book, we bring a radical criminological understanding of crime labelling to bear upon contemporary understandings of knife-involved crime. In particular we ask how the label 'knife crime' can itself be understood as a formative part of a wider societal reaction to crime. We draw upon the critical analysis of Stuart Hall and his colleagues, as developed in their important book *Policing the Crisis* (1978), to explore how the consequences of neoliberal social and economic policies, changes

---

[5] That these are highly implausible claims often overlooked despite many first rate histories describing the violent histories of the British and our export of violence via imperial conquest, see for example Sharpe (2016), Brewer and Styles (ed.) (1980), Newsinger (2013).

affecting police policy and operational practice, allied with key reforms to the field of youth justice and an emerging 'new racism', coincided with a resurgent authoritarianism to define a new 'law and order crisis' in which the label 'knife crime' pointed towards a potential solution. While we take the reader through the various stages in this argument, including demonstrating the merits of a critical criminological approach, the rest of the book comprises our attempt to explain and elaborate the previous sentence.

> **Learning Exercise 2: Discussing the Data**
>
> Having looked at the evidence we have presented so far, Figs. 1.1–1.3, what conclusions can be drawn about the nature and extent of knife crime in England and Wales?

Still *Policing the Crisis*

In drawing upon *Policing the Crisis* (1978) we make a direct connection between the social construction and racialised identification of the (legally non-existent[6]) crime of 'mugging' in the 1970s and 'knife crime' in the 2000s. Back in 1978, Stuart Hall and his colleagues analysed the emergence of 'mugging' as a distinct 'moral panic', while providing an in depth explanation of the social and political context in which this occurred. The task of deconstructing the meaning of mugging followed a case (a 'signal crime' of great significance) in which unprecedented severe sentences of ten and twenty years were given to three boys of mixed ethnic background for a violent robbery in Handsworth, Birmingham. It was argued by Hall et al. (1978), that the severe sentences awarded were

---

[6] By 'legally non-existent' we simply mean that 'mugging' was not referenced or defined in any statute of the criminal law. What could not be legally defined could not be accurately counted and, although it was generally taken to refer to personal robbery with violence or intimidation, it was often taken to include any interpersonal theft or assault—especially where the perpetrator was black or mixed race. In effect, it could mean whatever the police, who recorded the offences or the media who reported them, wanted it to mean.

not a response to the individual actions of these particular three boys, but rather to what 'mugging' had come to mean. They were sentences 'intended to have a *social* as well as a punitive impact', allaying the 'fears and anxieties' which the crime had occasioned, reflected in the extensive press coverage, the reactions of local people, experts and commentators, the prophecies of doom which accompanied it, and prompting the mobilisation of the police against certain sectors of the population in the 'mugging areas' (Hall et al., 1978: viii). All of this became wrapped up in the mugging label. From this starting point Hall et al. (1978) argue that 'mugging' should no longer be seen as a fact but rather as a relation—'the relation between crime and the reaction to crime' (ibid.). From this starting point the authors produced a historical and chronological analysis of the emergence and use of the concept 'mugging' in Britain. Their account began by demonstrating the formative role of policing (the 'primary definers') and media reporting (secondary definers) in the amplification of particular crimes and the creation of new criminal phenomena such as 'mugging' and new criminalised identities such as 'black youth' (Gilroy, 1987: 86, 90). Contrary to conventional criminological accounts of how 'mugging' emerged, Hall et al., described the process in structural and sociological terms, occurring in two distinct but developmental phases.

The first stage entailed a period of preparation for 'the war on mugging', this involved a pre-public phrase of intense police mobilisation against particular people in targeted areas, 'above all, groups of black youths' (Hall et al., 1978: 43). This began as a rising profile of incidents involving black suspects and the firming up of core racist assumptions about black criminality (Gilroy, 1987), in due course 'crime, in the form of street disorder and robbery was gradually identified as an expression of black culture' (Gilroy, 1987: 109). More recent research confirms that this process of racialised criminalisation still represents a strong and continuing characteristic of urban crime control (Williams & Clark, 2018), including police stop and search practice (Bowling & Phillips, 2002; Long, 2018), gang interventions (Joseph & Gunter, 2011; Williams, 2015), joint enterprise prosecutions (Squires, 2016; Williams & Clarke, 2020), and police use of force, including both tasers and firearms (Dearden, 2017; Gayle, 2019; Noor, 2018; Siddique,

2018). Furthermore, Elliott-Cooper (2021a: 154) has argued that, along with the MPS Matrix database (Amnesty International, 2018) which disproportionately collated information on the suspected gang affiliations of young black people in London, the statutory duty on health care workers, teachers, housing officers and social workers to report 'signs of violence' displayed by children and young people strongly reflected the requirements in the 'Prevent' anti-terror programme marking a significant step towards the pre-emptive criminalisation of young, and primarily black, young people (Arkwright, 2019; Bradley, 2019). And as we will proceed to demonstrate, many contemporary understandings of 'knife crime' are likewise fabricated upon a similarly racialised foundation.

As Hall et al., demonstrate, the early phase of routine but increasingly intensive police reaction began to promulgate a police definition of 'mugging' (drawing upon American precedents) which was increasingly normalised and accepted. A second and public phase of mobilisation followed, involving 'cases in court, editorials in the papers, official Home Office enquiries about "mugging", a publicly engaged campaign, open warfare' (ibid.), including targeted policing operations, extensive use of stop and search (in London the much discredited 'SUS Law', Section 4 of the 1824 Vagrancy Act [Brogden, 1981; Demuth, 1978] was still in place) and the subsequent appearance of apparently credible statistics revealing how the alleged mugging problem had grown. Since the first phase predated the public panic it went largely unnoticed, it was also obscured from public view as it largely occurred within the 'closed institutional world of the police' (ibid.). Once these two stages have been distinguished, it is clear that in order to understand how and why 'mugging' emerged as the key to unlock the crisis of law and order; it is not just the second stage that requires attention. On the contrary it is vital to explore the hard work undertaken earlier behind the scenes where police constructions of class and race and violence became established as the dominant interpretations of urban criminality. What lay behind this police activism and the broad governmental mobilisation involved? Hall et al. (1978) argue that it is in this question that the origins of the law and order crisis would be found. Accordingly, they proceeded to unravel the construction of mugging, seen first and foremost as a challenge to law and order, invoking moral consensus, public consent and the British way of justice—although persistently ignoring two of the core fault lines (or blind spots) in these cherished ideals, race and class.

According to Hall et al., the state's powerful fabrication of the mugger as 'folk devil' takes place at a crucial historic moment at which a national crisis in the social and legal order occurs. Rooting their analysis in a theory of 'hegemony' deriving from Antonio Gramsci (2005)[7] they depicted racialised street violence as representing a challenge to British notions of consensus, order and justice. For Gramsci, hegemony, referred to the way in which the contradictions and consequences of class (and racial) inequality were maintained but also partially obscured by a dominant culture representing the interests of the ruling social groups as necessary and inevitable social norms and values. Hegemony was said to represent a kind of 'spontaneous consent', a form of ideological conditioning, influencing how citizens thought and acted (Gramsci, 2005). Hall later coined the phrase 'authoritarian populism' (Hall, 1985) to account for the cluster of ideas which claimed that Britain's historical decline, our retreat from Empire, poor economic performance and attendant social problems resulted from immigration. Gilroy in particular attributes the demonisation of black immigrants and the emergence of a surprisingly resilient 'populist politics of race and nation' as a central aspect 'of Britain's attempts to make sense of national decline' (1987: 29, 40–48) and especially 'the British inability to accept the end of empire'. And finally, in Gilroy's observation that, with the exception of the Northern Irish troubles, the British state and society had largely been able to absolve itself from the 'bloodshed and ruthless violence characteristic of decolonization' we have another thread connecting the distant violence of policing the empire to the illusions of security challenged by knife crime today (1987: 57). It is possible to detect a revival of many of these themes in the debates surrounding the Brexit Vote in 2016 (McKenzie, 2017; Winlow et al., 2017) although, in truth, they never entirely went away. Authoritarian populism became internalised as

---

[7] Antonio Gramsci was an Italian Marxist philosopher and founding member of the Italian Communist Party imprisoned by Mussolini's Fascist regime. While incarcerated he wrote many notebooks (*The Prison Notebooks*) addressing questions of power, politics and ideological domination—hegemony. He died in 1937 after 11 years in prison.

a new common sense; for every social problem, there was an identifiable, culpable folk devil. Rising crime was laid at the feet of a new black, urban, underclass which was projected as neither sharing British values nor respecting British laws and institutions.

Hall et al. (1978) argue that it is only by thinking within this particular historical moment that we can begin to appreciate the long historical back-story to mugging and its particular emergence in the 1970s. When the 'mugging' panic first made its appearance in 1972 it embodied all the key features of the British crisis and it leveraged in a new common sense of tough policing and punitive sentencing for law and order management. Mugging both provided a very significant label for the crisis, secured popular approval and thereby pointed towards a solution. In this sense mugging was not itself the crisis, merely a symptom and, by filtering the entire national interest through a single criminal signifier, black street crime, mugging became a solution. It justified and enabled the reassertion of political and police authority, paving the way for the infamous 'Law and Order' general election of 1979 and which has continued to leave an indelible imprint upon British Political culture (Farrall et al., 2017; Hall, 1980).

The kind of constructionist analysis developed by Hall et al. (1978) has been woefully absent from many recent attempts to understand 'knife crime' and its political function as a symbol of 'Black criminality'. Our argument here is that the labelling of 'knife crime', misleadingly and erroneously understood as an overwhelmingly black crime, has come to perform almost exactly the same function as mugging almost fifty years ago. Marx's notion that history repeats itself, although the first time as tragedy, and the second time as farce (1937) could well be true of criminological approaches to knife crime. For with rather few exceptions (Squires, 2009a) existing literature on 'knife crime' tends to focus exclusively upon the later or public stage of the phenomenon when the construction of the label has already taken place while paying less attention to the mobilisation and social construction that preceded first use of the phrase. When Eades et al. (2007) acknowledged the absence of clear 'knife crime' data prior to 2003 this is seen merely as a difficulty to be overcome when seeking to quantify the extent of the problem, rather than evidence of the temporality and fabricated subjectivity of the category itself. The case of 'mugging' demonstrated that the targeting of 'Black crime' provided an opportunity to distract popular attention from the social and economic realities of British decline and instead focus attention upon the scapegoats of empire and late modernity: black Britons. Mugging in the 1970s and 'knife crime' today each play a double role as both decoy and target around which a complex of fears, tensions and anxieties revolve and against which renewed strategies of law and order governance might be deployed. Even as the syntax of British racism is complex and ever changing (Gilroy, 1987; Solomos & Back, 1996), the similarities between the rise of racially defined moral panic in 'mugging' in the 1970s and 'knife crime in the 2000's suggests there is much to be learnt from an investigation of the emerging problem of weaponised youth violence and the pre-public mobilisation around knives and youth and race.

As we have already noted, there are many difficulties involved when attempting to understand what the knife crime data is telling us. In our case, the problem is made worse by virtue of the fact that statistics relating to offences committed with knives only began after the 2001 introduction of the 'knife enabled' category in the police crime recording process. Knife crimes were only consistently reported by the Metropolitan Police from 2003 onwards and, except for cases of homicide, Home Office statistics did not separately identify crimes involving knives until 2007/2008. As will be apparent from our Figs. 1.1 and 1.2, when discussing *recent* 'knife crime' we have focussed upon statistics purely from the past ten years, for which consistent records exist. And, as our knife crime timeline (below) shows we can identify at least three broad phases to the contemporary knife crime crisis, phases defined in part by the discontinuities in the crime data employed to evidence the problem and by the legislative and law enforcement strategies intended to suppress and prosecute knife violence and culminating in the Metropolitan Police 'war on knife crime' from 2007 (Fig. 1.4). The timeline in Fig. 1.4 provides a broad overview of the various phases in the making of the 'knife crime crisis', in order to avoid crowding the chart with too much detail, we present a more focussed timeline taking in just the last ten years (2010–2020) in Fig. 5.1. Figure 5.1 also comprises

'KNIFE CRIME' TIME LINE

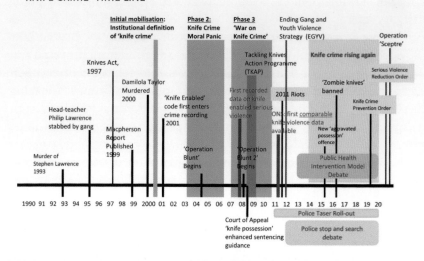

Fig. 1.4 The knife crime timeline 1990–2020

trendlines offering some initial assessment of the impact of knife crime strategies employed so far.

It is clearly significant that it was only from April 2007 onwards, that *national* statistics on the number of offences involving the use of a knife or sharp instrument began to be collated for a selection of serious violent offences, these included (in addition to homicide), attempted murder; wounding or inflicting grievous bodily harm and robbery. The expansion in the range of offences about which data were kept was itself the result of a growing concern about serious youth violence and so-called 'gang related' violence and especially a series of high profile knife-involved murders (Squires, 2009a). The circularity is obvious, the collection of more complete data on knife-enabled crime invariably results in greater law enforcement efforts to tackle knife-involved violence, often resulting in more evidence of the problem being addressed. Two related criminological processes tend to reinforce one another when apparently rising crime trends are under discussion: the first, just alluded to involves the 'deviancy amplification spiral' (Cohen, 1972), the second concerns 'signal crime' analysis (Innes, 2004).

The collection of data on a new series of knife offences illustrates a classic stage in the moral panic or 'deviancy amplification' spiral. In such cases, concern about a new or especially serious type of offending prompts the call (from the public, the media, police and politicians) that more resources be invested to tackle the problem. Furthermore, particular offences, be they especially violent or especially traumatic, sometimes involving more or less 'deserving' (in the eyes of the media) victims, tend to attract greater attention precisely because of the 'signals' they are said to send about risk, safety and contemporary society. As Harding (2020), acknowledges however, not everyone receives the same signals from given events: while middle-aged homeowners might determine not to venture out after dark, teenagers—lacking confidence in police protection—might decide to carry a knife for protection. Surveys repeatedly found that 'self-protection' was the most commonly cited explanation for knife carrying, even as the authorities sought to discourage it (through stop and search and sentencing increases: Hebenton et al., 2010) notwithstanding the ambiguities implicit in such self-report claims (Shaw et al., 2011: 268–270).

Especially prominent 'signal knife crimes' in the modern era have included the racist murder of teenager Steven Lawrence in 1993, although the signals here involved not just knife crime, but also racist violence and police institutional racism. Even though it represents perhaps the most significant and high profile knife crimes of recent times, being prior to the construction of the label itself, this murder was never referred to as a 'knife crime' (this is an issue we develop in later chapters). The murder of head-teacher Philip Lawrence, two years later, when he tried to intervene to prevent a gang attack on a pupil, signalled gang violence, race and the random brutality of knife violence, that a white professional man coming to the aid of one of his pupils could be so casually struck down. Ten-year-old Damilola Taylor was left bleeding to death in the stairwell of a Peckham housing block having been attacked by a number of older youths. Whether he was stabbed, or whether his injuries resulted from falling on broken glass, preoccupied juries in two separate trials, although the case spoke especially of the blighted lives of young black children in Britain's communities of urban despair.

Tyrone Clarke, aged 16, died of multiple stab wounds inflicted when he was attacked by a group of men in Leeds in April 2004. The case connected with the developing race and gang violence narratives developing around knife crime. Tom ap Rhys-Price, aged 31, was 'viciously and gratuitously' stabbed (but when is a stabbing not 'vicious and gratuitous'?) to death *following* a robbery he had resisted in 2006. Rhys-Price was a white, middle-class lawyer although his attackers were described as IC3, young black males, further reinforcing the emerging racialised narrative attaching to knife crime, even though most such offending tends not to be cross racial. A year later 16-year-old Kodjo Yenga was killed in Notting Hill after being approached by a gang of youths. A senior police detective working the case described the killing as 'senseless, meaningless and …despicable'. Yenga had been out walking with his girlfriend. A particular irony of the case, turning the moral panic back upon itself was that, earlier in the week, he had taken part in an MTV interview about knife crime in London. 'Stabbings are getting worse', he had said 'but the media is also making it bigger than what it is' (BBC News 16.3.2007). Then, in 2008, 16-year-old Ben Kinsella, celebrating exam results with friends, became involved in an altercation with three men in a bar in North London. Later that evening when Kinsella was walking home three men confronted him, knocked him to the floor and stabbed him eleven times. The case attracted more than usual attention as Kinsella's half-sister was an actress who had starred in the *Eastenders* TV series, and the incident was a cross racial homicide with a white victim. Bereaved family members established a Trust and website to campaign against knife violence and lobby for knife law reforms. Home Secretary, Jack Straw launched a review of knife crime sentencing shortly afterwards.

The stabbing of Stephen Timms, MP, in 2010 at his constituency surgery and the murder of trooper Lee Rigby in May 2013, by two assailants who first ran him down in a car and then hacked him to death with knives and a cleaver, marked further twists in the knife crime story. More recently this has been followed by further terror-motivated vehicle and knife attacks at Westminster (2017), London Bridge (2017 and 2019), Streatham (2020) and Reading (2020). A total of eighteen victims died as a result of these stabbing attacks, with many more people injured. Six of the perpetrators were shot by police. Many similar Islamist terror attacks have taken place around the world, notably in France, Belgium, Germany, Finland, Holland, Israel, Egypt, Australia, Switzerland and the USA claiming over 43 victims worldwide, although a large proportion of the perpetrators were shot by police, bringing many of the incidents to an end. At Kunming railway station, China, in 2014, eight Xinjiang separatists (six men and two women) randomly attacked passengers with long-bladed knives, cleavers and swords, killing 31 and injuring over 140 until police intervention subdued the attackers. Japan has likewise experienced several 'knife rampage' attacks (although not thought to be terrorism related) between 2002 and 2019 resulting in eighteen people killed and 50 injured.

The signals transmitted by notorious crimes will often be contested and potentially incoherent, but even across the sample of such 'English' murders, 'domestic' and international terrorist attacks and rampage killings, some constants stand out. In the first place, knife killing—stabbing—takes place at very close range, it is 'up close and personal'. Thrusting or slashing a knife into another body takes a kind of strength, intent and determination not required in the case of a single finger pulling a trigger to shoot someone with a firearm. Even if a great deal of youthful knife violence is said to be 'symbolic', intended to 'mark' or scar the face of an opponent rather than genuine attempts to kill (Squires, 2011: 151) the very act of piercing the skin of another person registers an anti-social brutality of intention quite alien to many people. The squeamishness evidenced when watching surgical programmes on TV points to a profound taboo regarding the deliberate cutting of another person's skin; knife violence is a violent and visceral transgression like no other. However, in another sense, when it comes to terrorist-inspired violence, or the kinds of rampage style killings we have referred to above, compared to a firearm, a knife is (fortunately) a rather inefficient weapon to employ. We might say that what it lacks in scale, it makes up for in intimacy (Bourke, 2000) and all the more shocking for that. Indeed, the one thing that, as a killing weapon, the knife has going for it (disregarding all those qualities of the knife (silent, discreet, deadly) celebrated in popular culture),[8] is its widespread availability (Brennan & Moore, 2009; Eades, 2006). There is an important difference here as regards the policing of knives and of guns, however, both of them are seen as 'enablers' of crime and violence, each coining its own distinctive crime type. But while guns can be positioned as 'alien' (or at least as *American* weapons of choice) the tactic of eradicating them can be undertaken quite separately to the policing of violence. Recovering guns can be likened to removing a toxic presence from the community, whereas knives are endemic, common, routine, even useful—every kitchen drawer contains a re-supply. Arguably this lends itself to a more deeply left realist 'community resolution', for policing knives involves policing people's common and historic usages and behaviours (peeling potatoes, slicing bread, cutting vegetables, pruning plants and being 'prepared', just like good boy scouts); whereas policing firearms is partly sustained by supply-side controls to eliminate weapons of intrinsic risk, these are strategies which are nowhere near so feasible in the case of knives.

Furthermore, given the ingenuity shown by inmates in the most secure (prison) environments, fashioning knives—'shivs' or 'shanks'—from the most basic of materials (Lincoln et al., 2006), then approaching knife crime from the supply side is unlikely to offer much purchase on the issue. The problem is primarily social and cultural, a willingness to inflict violence rather than the existence of particular weapons. One of the particular ironies of Britain's 'knife crime crisis' is the fact that it first really 'surfaced' politically as a 'moral panic' around 2004 when significant efforts to restrict illegal firearm availability[9] were appearing to bear results and firearm enabled crime seemed to be falling (Squires, 2014). One argument might be that the rise in knife crime reflected a kind of 'weapon-displacement effect' as firearms became relatively harder to access—a decline in lethality, perhaps, for an increase in availability. But there was no decline in demand. Quite the contrary, for as the dangers associated with urban street life were increasingly accented by the media spotlight on violent killings, the perceived necessity of carrying a weapon

---

[8] Refer to Chapter 2.
[9] Refer to our knife crime timeline Fig. 1.4.

'for protection' was regularly cited by young people when they were surveyed about 'street safety' (Marfleet, 2008; Palasinski & Riggs, 2012; Sethi et al., 2010). Even though more authoritative voices challenged the idea that an offensive weapon could offer any genuine *protection*, insisting instead that weapon carriage simply increased the risks faced by young people,[10] many young people appeared rather unconvinced. Much knife crime propaganda about street violence may well have had entirely counterproductive consequences, prompting and incentivising more young people to carry knives 'for their own protection', a marked weaponisation of street culture, driving up rates of knife possession.

In turn, a direct consequence of the greater attention devoted to the problem is that more instances of the problem are unearthed, more crimes reported and more statistics collected. This cyclical effect is especially marked when police action, such as stop and search operations (for example *Operation Blunt*, I and II), proactively engage with target 'suspect populations' to uncover further cases of illegal knife use and possession: the harder you look, the more you might find (see Fig. 1.5). This might especially be the case where, for example, Hospital A & E departments are incorporated into the crime reporting cycle, mandated to alert police when casualties arrive with suspected stab injuries. In addition to knife crime, a number of recent offence types, perhaps beginning with Hall et al.'s account of the 'mugging panic' in the late 1970s (1978), but also 'joyriding', 'gang-related violence', gun crime, acid attacks and moped-involved offending are susceptible to this cyclical amplification process.[11]

The range of recorded knife offences was further extended in April 2008, to include other violent and sexual offences including threats to kill, causing actual bodily harm (ABH), as well as knife-enabled rape and

---

[10] And, not least, once widespread police 'stop and search' tactics, such as Operation Blunt, were instituted, the additional risk of being found in possession of illegal weapons, leading to arrest and conviction.

[11] A deviance amplification process is often regarded critically in the case of certain offences types. In the case of others, especially hitherto systematically under-reported offences, such as sexual crimes and domestic violence, deviance amplification is often regarded an essential component of taking such offences seriously. The tendency of criminal justice processes to selectively *over-* and *under-* criminalise is a recognised feature of such systems (Vegh-Weis, 2017).

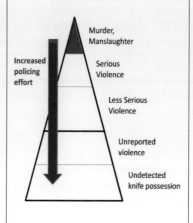

The deviancy amplification model reflects the fact that the most serious violent incidents – homicides - tend to occur less frequently, they are the 'tip' of the iceberg. These represent the 'signal' events which draw in the public and media attention in the first place
When attention is drawn to the new crime, however, much more of it is revealed (serious violence, less serious violence) and a 'crime wave' effect is begun.

The more 'proactive' that policing becomes the more violence comes to light prompting more reporting (and the recording of hitherto unreported violence). Having A&E departments pass details of stabbing victims to the police might also increase recording rates. Finally, increased street policing (stop and search) uncovers hitherto unknown rates of knife possession.

Fig. 1.5 Deviancy amplification model for knife crime

other sexual assaults. At the same time there were a number of changes to the ways in which knife-involved GBH assaults were recorded. The net effect of all these changes is that March 2011 is the first date from which year-on-year comparable statistics for knife-enabled crime are available (Allen & Kirk-Wade, 2020). The knife crime trends extending before need to be treated with great caution, they are often not comparing like with like data across the years, furthermore they are also influenced by the kinds of deviancy amplification processes we have already referred to. In this book, while we might make use of data emerging before 2011, we will always try to draw attention to difficulties in interpreting it. And, it should be recognised, as the knife crime timeline we have developed shows (see Fig. 1.4), even after 2011, important aspects of deviancy amplification continue to influence the production of knife crime data, including the police use of stop and search and the introduction of Serious Violence Reduction Orders (SVRO). Complications such as these are seldom mentioned when media reports, politicians or the police discuss knife crime trends; one of our preliminary objectives in this book is to unravel this aspect of the knife crime story.

Beyond that our aim is to reframe the ways in which knife crime is interpreted and the '*policing of ...*' knife crime constructed as the *solution* to a law and order crisis. As we show in Chapter 3, Knife crime arises at a time when policing had become beset by a series of profound dilemmas. These include questions about police management of public order incidents, which resulted in a partial (perhaps only temporary) rethinking of the policing of the right to protest; police use of lethal force, epitomised by a series of controversial high-profile police shootings and culminating in the shooting of Mark Duggan which, in turn, prompted the 2011 riots (these exposing further operational misgivings about police disorder management); an ongoing debate about disproportionate use of stop and search, which was reflected in a number of ambiguous and fluctuating changes to policy and practice. Finally, the 2008 onset of austerity, followed by policing cuts which, many officers argued, seriously affected the police ability to deliver neighbourhood policing standards. At this juncture, the construction of contemporary knife crime provided both opportunity and justification for a return to a robust form of street policing popular with police, politicians and public alike. Knife crime conferred legitimacy upon tough policing, demanding both new laws and reinvigorated police practices and priorities. Knife crime offered up criminalisation as a solution for the perceived law and order crisis. This decision to criminalise reflects a particular kind of governance choice with particular antecedents and anticipated consequences. In a kind of vicious cycle, criminalisation represents a fairly direct consequence of neoliberal social and economic policies, knife crime thereby becomes a particular means by which neo-liberalism responds to its own law and order crisis—although not the only one (Farrall & Hay, 2010).

Deeper Background; Longer History

Following Hall and his colleagues we have discussed the most recent and proximate causes of the knife crime crisis, during a first 'hidden' phase in which a range of discriminatory policing practices firmed up the 'usual suspect' status of street-socialising young black men. In turn this was recycled through media reporting and the extended circulation of racialised fears and in public and political discourse, and knife crime came of age. But this is not the beginning of the story, knife crime has a long history, knives are one of humanity's oldest weapons and in Chapter two we will explore some of the deeper meanings and uses of knives, a brief history of knife design, knife fighting and the various 'cultures of the blade' that have invested today's weapons with such rich meaning.

But for the moment we are still considering the 'knife crime crisis' of the early twenty-first century, we have identified its various phases, we know when it acquired an internal institutional form and when the 'knife enabled' crime code was first deployed to count offences and we know when the MPS 'war against knife crime' was launched—but when did it all really begin? Figs. 1.6 and 1.7 can be instructive in this respect.

The offence of wounding is defined in Sects. 18 and 20 of the 1861 Offences Against the Person Act, wounding involves an assault that cuts or pierces the skin, so a knife blade or other sharp-pointed object might be used to inflict the harm and commit the offence. Serious wounding is that which is deemed to be 'grievous' or potentially life-threatening. A less serious wounding offence is also provided for, and, as depicted in Fig. 1.7 the differences of scale are very clear. Serious wounding peaks in the year 2000 at just under sixteen thousand offences annually. Wounding, overall, peaks just below two-hundred and fifty thousand offences, some three years earlier. Clearly something changed around 1996–1997, reclassifying offences types and contributing to the dip in

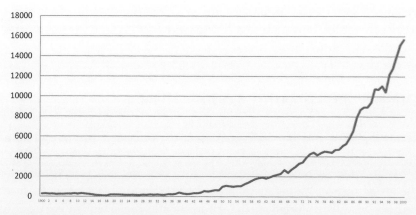

Fig. 1.6 Serious wounding in England and Wales: 1900–2000 (*Source* Offences since 1899, Home Office Dataset)

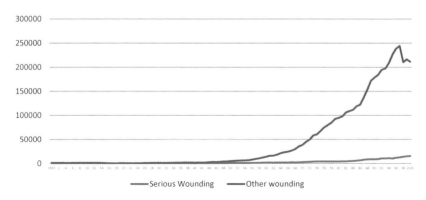

Fig. 1.7 Serious wounding and 'all wounding' in England and Wales: 1900–2000

the trend line at the end of the century. Yet, it does not have to be a knife, a sharpened stick or broken bottle, or a wide array of other tools and implements, might be used to cause wounds. Even so, wounding offences provide our best long-term comparator for today's 'knife crime'. As we have noted already there was no specifically knife-enabled crime identifier for the entire twentieth century, knife-enabled crime statistics were not recorded or kept even after the number of serious wounding offences began to climb increasingly steeply after the century mid-point. It may tell us something that despite the sharper rate of increase after the mid-1980s, discussion of a wounding or stabbing 'crisis'—or even of serious youth violence—never came to a head. From the mid-1980s onwards, it was gun crime, statistically less frequent, but in some respects signalling greater threats, that commanded greater attention (Squires, 2008). In this light, however, the data referred to here pose an important question regarding our contemporary focus on 'knife crime': just how viable is it to tackle violence, one weapon at a time. We will return to this question towards the end of the book.

In fact, the growth trend for wounding closely corresponds with the late twentieth century rates of increase for all recorded crime and for Crime Survey data (CSEW). Both trends peak in the mid-1990s before beginning a two decade decline, although 'serious violence' continues to rise—in part because knife-involved violence represents a significant proportion of this violence, but also because of the greater awareness of violence against women and better recording of domestic violence and intimate violence against women (Walby et al., 2015). So when we ask, when did knife crime begin, what led to the rise in knife crime and what sustained it over a fifty year cycle, we are asking a much wider question about violence and culture in late modern society than just addressing the misuse of knives. This is an enormous question which has preoccupied criminologists for most of the late twentieth century (Radzinowicz & King, 1977; Young, 1999, 2011)—and, of course, the causes of this increase are much debated.

Learning Exercise 3: Accounting for Twentieth Century Violence

Taking account of the crime trends depicted in Figs. 1.5 and 1.6 try to outline the main explanations offered for the growth of this criminal violence throughout the latter part of the twentieth century.

Nevertheless, if we take these twentieth century wounding figures to describe a long-term trend in stabbing and cutting violence (our best proxy for knife crime), then when did knife violence really begin? Even before the unofficial, 'hidden' phase of knife crime where the authorities began to piece together a new focus upon knife violence, wounding trends reveal a fifty year pre-history appearing to begin sometime after the mid-1950s. What happened then? Indeed, what continued to sustain the rising record of violent wounding throughout the latter half of the twentieth century? Interestingly, even tracking back to the 1950s fails to yield the origins of 'knife violence' although new legislation certainly brought a renewed focus upon street weaponry. The *1953 Prevention of Crime Act*, was passed, according to J.L. Edwards, writing in the *Modern Law Review*, 'to grapple with the serious rise in crimes of personal violence' (Edwards, 1953: 482). Introducing the Second Reading of the Bill in the House of Commons, Sir David Maxwell Fyfe, *Secretary of State for the Home Department* had remarked, 'there is so much anxiety about crimes of violence, it would not be right to overlook the deterrent effect on criminals which would be achieved if it were made an offence to be found in possession of an offensive weapon, without lawful reason, in a public place' (Hansard, 26.2.53: 511 c2323).

Edwards provided figures for armed robbery and (malicious and felonious) wounding, from 1938 (immediately preceding WW2) to the late 1940s and early 50s. Although he conceded that 'while it is true that many of these cases did not necessarily involve the use of offensive weapons' (ibid.)—that is to say, there were no clear statistics of widespread weapon use—he flips the rationale of his argument to the more speculative by claiming, 'there is abundant evidence in an increasingly large number of crimes of personal violence, the present-day criminal has no compunction in using a variety of weapons to achieve his purpose' (ibid.). Accordingly, the case for the law is made less by a preponderance of weapons used in violence but rather by the alleged inclinations of a supposedly distinctive type of 'present-day criminals'. It is hard not to see the race and class implications in this formulation of the issue, as Gilroy (1987: 73) has noted, at a time when many commentators argued that black people seemed less criminally involved than the indigenous white population, others noted what they called a specific practice of knife carrying and an enthusiasm for flick knives (1987: 83). It is also interesting how Edwards' accounting for the new legislation corresponds with the wider national mood. Only a few years earlier, the film *The Blue Lamp* (1949) had celebrated policing and social reconstruction after the war (McLaughlin, 2005). The film had launched the media career of everyone's favourite 'bobby', Dixon of Dock Green, and had begun with a cinéma vérité style newsreel adding authenticity to its story and decrying the activities of a new generation of wide-boys and gangsters only too willing to use violence to get what they wanted. The disruptions of wartime conditions were blamed, in part, for the emergence of this new generation of *Lawless Youth* (Grunhut et al., 1948), but so were the media and role models drawn from gangster stereotypes from the USA. Other commentators, however, saw the abolition of corporal punishment for young offenders in the 1948 CJA as part of the explanation (Bailey, 1987) or the emergence of a new focus upon crime prevention (Murray, 2018).

During the second reading of the Bill in the Commons, Maxwell Fyfe *emphasised the support of the police for the new legislation*, 'responsible chief officers of police assure me that a provision of this kind is likely to be of great value in placing a curb on violent crime' (Hansard, 1953: vol.

511 cc 2323–411). Earlier the legislation had been deemed necessary on account of the great 'anxiety about crimes of violence' throughout the country while Edwards, summarising the legislation for the *Modern Law Review*, likewise attributed its appeal to the advocacy of the police 'who believe it will prove of great value in diminishing such crime' (Edwards, 1953: 483).

Many aspects of the House of Commons debate from 1953 anticipated issues arising in more recent debates about knife crime, although discussion about race was conspicuously absent in the 1950s. Two important themes concerned police powers and the widespread utility and availability of legal blades. Some MPs voiced a preference for retaining tough sentencing rather than creating new crimes, conferring greater powers, of stop and search and arrest, upon the police (Hansard, 1953: vol. 511 cc 2384),[12] and shifting the burden of proof of legal possession onto the citizen regarding any object that might be considered a weapon (Hansard, 1953: vol. 511 cc 2375). The Home Secretary was keen to reassure MPs that the Bill was 'not a measure under which law-abiding citizens will be in danger of committing an offence every time they handle something that might be used as a weapon'. And he continued, while ' the principal difficulty, as the House will appreciate, has been to define the term, "offensive weapon" … the carpenter carrying the tools of his trade, the housewife taking home a new chopper, the motorist taking a spanner from his tool kit, a Boy Scout displaying a knife on his uniform, the Highlander wearing his *skean dhu*[13]—all these and a thousand other similar actions will not be interfered with' (Hansard, 1953: vol. 511 cc 2332). Even so, much as parliament wished to prevent

---

[12] For example, Mr. Daniel West, MP, objected to the Bill, in the following terms 'I have some doubt about the provision that the constable may arrest without warrant any person whom he has reason to believe to be committing an offence under this Bill… It seems to me they are a little dangerous and are enlarging the powers of arrest' (Hansard, 1953: vol. 511 cc 2384).

[13] A *skean dhu* is a, now largely ceremonial, single edged dagger, originally employed for a range of purposes including close quarter fighting and cutting and preparing food. Sir Ronald Bell MP., took exception to the Home Secretary's claim that a ceremonial dagger would not be covered by the Bill: 'My right hon. and learned Friend says that a man going to a dance with a skean dhu is not covered by the Bill, but of course he is. What is a skean dhu made for if not to cause bodily injury? It is designed for that. The burden is then squarely put upon the carrier to prove that he is carrying it for a lawful purpose'.

weapon use and crimes of violence and was reluctant to allow a significant extension of police powers of search and arrest, there remained what Lanham (2005: 85) has called an 'uneasy synergy' regarding the personal possession of (defensive) weapons. For while, as Shaw et al. note (2011: 271), 'there has never been an express prohibition on the use of weapons for defensive purposes', it was recognised that 'the use of a weapon in self-defence can prove problematic for the accused if the matter reaches the courtroom' (Murdie, 2003: 316), for it could be taken to indicate an unacceptable degree of criminal intent. For the Home Secretary the dilemma was resolved by explicit reference to the 'certain class of persons' against whom the proposed new legislation was directed:

> there is a large number of people on the fringe of the criminal community who will resort to crime if the opportunity presents itself. Among these, and others with lax standards of conduct, there is a growing tendency to slip a weapon - perhaps a knife or a knuckle-duster - in a pocket. Such a person may get into a quarrel, perhaps after a drink or two, and then the weapon is brought into use. Again, there is the type of young ruffian who, often in a gang with others of the same kidney, sets out to terrorise other people in the neighbourhood. It is primarily against *persons of this type* that the Bill is directed. (HC debates 26 February 1953, c2325. Emphasis added)

Parliamentary attention also focused upon penknives, sheath knives and razors all of which, in the words of the Bill could be *capable* of causing injury, thereby potentially falling within the proposed legislation. Despite the reservations of a number of MPs regarding precisely the types of knives which might be covered by the law and the ambiguities surrounding the 'lawful excuses' which might be given for carrying them, the 1953 Crime Prevention Act passed. In practice the law gave wide situational discretion to the police, allowing them to determine the circumstances and conditions in which lawful carriage of potential weapons might be tolerated and when not. The result was a classic British policing compromise, the police being left free to determine a suspect's status, his intentions and therefore culpability, by reference to *who* was in possession of the alleged weapon. A number of MPs had been concerned about, the seeming elasticity of key concepts in the legislation: such as the vague definition of what might constitute an 'offensive weapon' or the reversal of the burden of proof entailed in the notion of 'lawful excuse' (an accused person had to demonstrate their legitimate purpose in carrying what could be a weapon—Malcolm, 2002: 175). These questions resolved themselves around a police point of view regarding what was 'reasonable' and their confidence in being able to discern the intentions of suspects in advance. This resolution of the question would further coalesce around a familiar construction of 'the usual suspects' (McAra & McVie, 2005; Pantazis & Pemberton, 2009), the primary targets of police attention. In the 1950s this would chiefly be white working class youth, by the late twentieth century attention had largely shifted to young black men (Medina Ariza, 2014; Bowling & Phillips, 2002; Long, 2018). The doctrine of 'joint enterprise' prosecution likewise rested upon an a priori racist assumptions of gang involvement, intent and, therefore, shared culpability (Squires, 2016; Williams & Clarke, 2020).

Demonstrating the essentially discriminatory purpose underpinning the proposed *Prevention of Crime* legislation Mr. Harford Hyde MP, raised a question regarding the *purpose* for which an item, capable of serving as a weapon, was carried, and who was doing the carrying. He cited a case apparently familiar to many MPs.

There is a question about the use of a weapon which may be intended by the person carrying it to be for an offensive object but nevertheless for the purposes of self-protection. I can recall an example of what I mean. There is a lady who is actually employed within the precincts of this honourable House who has to cross a heath or common on her way home. Because attacks have been taking place there, she armed herself with a knitting needle as a means of protection. A month or so ago on her way home she was attacked by a youth who tried to snatch her handbag from her, and she promptly jabbed him on a tender part of his body and the result was he made off. Is it to be regarded as an offence to carry a knitting needle or other object for the purpose of self-defence? (Hansard, 1953: vol. 511 cc 2375)

Only three years after the introduction of the new legislation, a case arose which starkly exposed the wide discretion afforded police and prosecution in determining the potential culpability of suspects. During his summing up, in a 1957 murder case, the judge directed angry comments at the failure of parliament to specifically outlaw certain specific types of knife while lamenting the growth in crimes of violence involving young people. According to a court report in *The Times*, Mr. Justice Streatfield, commented, 'What an invention of the devil is the "flick knife" which unhappily so often features in crimes of violence in this country, often committed by young people'.

He continued,

> Personally I do not agree that there is any room for thankfulness or self-congratulation or complacency in that these articles are manufactured abroad. The fact is they are used over here far too frequently…. One would have thought it was high time that parliament considered either making the sale of these articles in this country entirely illegal or, at any rate that they should be controlled by strict licence, like firearms or other dangerous weapons. (*The Times*, November 15, 1957)

His lordship acknowledged that the charge facing the defendant was no longer regarded as capital murder. The accused had said, in his defence, that he had no intention of knifing Gibson. But he had panicked when chased by a gang after a dance and so drew out his knife to frighten them off. Gibson had charged straight into him. When the jury had returned their verdict, the foreman said: 'the jury respectfully request to bring to the notice of the authorities concerned their unanimous opinion that the sale of these offensive weapons shall be banned' (ibid.). These calls, by both judge and jury, were acceded to in January 1959 when Mr. Barnett Janner M.P., proposed a new Bill in the House of Commons to prohibit the sale and possession of 'flick knives' and other dangerous and offensive weapons. His argument rested upon the 'increasing number of murders and stabbings with flick knives and similar weapons [which] have taken place … I have frequently endeavoured to rouse the Home Office out of its complacency, unfortunately, so far without success', and he cited the support of 'judges, magistrates, social workers and others' in his cause (Hansard, HC Deb 21 January 1959 vol. 598 cc202-5).

He drew comparison with a time when, he said, use of knives in crime would have been regarded both as quite alien and unmanly, a time 'when the use of cold steel at an argument was regarded with contempt and described as being un-English, but unfortunately', he noted, 'as time has gone on, we can no longer point the finger of scorn and contempt upon certain foreign races of whom we used to think [such violence] was very typical. It is now the unhappy fact that very often it is our countrymen who use them.' He went on to cite the words of another judge who had claimed that 'the flick knife now appears to be regarded by teenagers as a "badge of manhood"' (Hansard, HC Deb 21 January 1959 vol. 598 cc. 202–3). Anticipating themes arising in more contemporary debates about knives, Janner quoted young people who claimed that they carried knives 'for protection from other gangs' and police officers and authority figures, who claimed that knives were carried for a combination of fashion and bravado. As a police sergeant said: 'It's the fashion. A certain class of youngster thinks it's big to be able to flash a knife' (ibid.).

The new legislation and the issues arising during its passage were particularly timely. In 1959, however it was white British 'teddy boys' committing the violence, a rash of racially motivated stabbings were taking place in London. Kelso Cochrane (originally from Antigua) was fatally stabbed in Notting Hill by a single thrust with a stiletto knife and the police, erroneously dismissing a racial motive for the murder and, following an investigation lacking rigour and urgency, failed to apprehend the suspect (Olden, 2011). The parallels with the Stephen Lawrence case, 34 years later, are all too apparent. The same month a twenty-five-year-old man was executed for fatally stabbing a police officer who was trying to break up a fight outside a dance hall involving rival groups of 'teddy boys' armed with a meat cleaver, axes, several knives, knuckle dusters and broken bottles. The murder weapon was a sharp-pointed diver's knife which penetrated five layers of clothing and produced a single, fatal, four-inch wound (Gruner, 2009; Police Roll of Honour). While the killing of a police officer was a cause of much concern, it was the execution, one of the first 'capital murder' cases prosecuted under the provisions of the 1957 Homicide Act,[14] which excited most attention and prompting 150 MPs to demand a reprieve. The deterrent impact of the legislation might be judged by the fact that, only a month after the execution, Terrence Cooney (aged 19) stabbed Allan Johnson at a dance hall in Barking during a gang fight between the 'Dagenham Boys' and the 'Canning Town Boys'. In this case Cooney received a life sentence.

The Restriction of Offensive Weapons Act, was finally passed in 1959. It was, to some extent, modelled upon an American law of 1958, the 'Switchblade Act' and laws passed in New York, prohibiting flick knives or 'switch-blades' and similar weapons.[15] Despite this burst of legislative attention, endorsed by many passionate and well-intentioned voices, as we can see from Figs. 1.4 and 1.5, the new laws apparently did little to halt the increase in woundings and violence occasioned 'through stabbing with "flick knives" and the like, in the hands of irresponsible youths and certain foreigners, when alone, and more often in gangs' (Hansard, HC Deb 21 January 1959 vol. 598 cc202-5). All told, alongside an arguably futile search for supply-side solutions, the concerns of the 1950s seem to have done more to reinforce an association between knife violence and young people, especially the violence of 'foreigners' and gangs, as opposed to offering sustainable solutions to problems of weapon-involved violence. In this regard, the debates of the 1950s have a great deal in common with those arising during our more recent 'knife crime' crisis, which is the chief focus of this book. This vindicates our intention to 'rethink' contemporary conceptions of knife crime, to offer a different understanding of the issue and, accordingly, different solutions.

---

[14] The Homicide Act 1957 restricted the use of capital punishment to certain types of murder, but retained it for the murder of a police officer on duty.

[15] In fact the federal US legislation to prohibit switchblades only affected knives produced or advertised for 'interstate commerce', it was left to individual states to legislate for knife possession, so knife laws vary considerably state by state in a confusing patchwork. In the UK, subsequent legislation, in particular the 1988 Criminal Justice Act now prohibits the carrying of any knife with a locking blade or a cutting edge longer than 3 inches, in a public place.

Discussion topic 4: Historical Concerns About Knife Violence

What were the major issues and concerns expressed by politicians and other commentators concerning knife violence and offensive weapons in the 1950s. To what extent have these same kinds of concerns continued to surface in more recent discussions of knife violence?

The last few pages have sought to unearth some of the pre-history of the modern knife crime crisis, the issues emerging even anticipate the important analysis in Hall et al.'s *Policing the Crisis*, revealing the still deeper origins of the nexus of race and class which animates many contemporary concerns regarding crime and violence. Today's debates about knives and gang crime continue to resonate with what Nijjar (2018) describes as 'overlapping conceptions of race and collective criminality that were a central modality of British colonial control, punishment, and exploitation' (2018: 150). For, in a post '*Policing the Crisis*' world, the emergence of 'knife crime' as a particularly racially coded category of crime is a significant moment. And it draws upon entrenched British historical and imperial practices and experiences, or colonial myths 'defining colonized subjects as naturally lawless, having yet to fulfil their historical potential for law and order' (Nijjar, 2018: 150). Through the culmination of various establishment criminologies, the public and political response to youth violence since the 2000s has produced a highly compelling, though increasingly selective, narrative of 'knife crime' as a young, Black, male, pathology. For Gilroy, the construction of this black criminalised identity represented a particular kind of cultural closure, 'black law breaking [came] gradually to be seen as proof of the incompatibility of blacks with Britishness. [While...] ideologies of legality and of blacks as a high crime group are also identified as constitutive of the new racism' (1987: 13). This has been an important achievement for the state and the law and order society. Just as the historic 'construction of Black communities as networks of criminality [provided] the corresponding legitimization of racism as a strategy for policing and punishing groups of racial subjects' (Nijjar, 2018: 150), the racialisation of knife crime has allowed, yet again, for increasingly authoritarian policing strategies to be rolled out with substantial public consent and apparent moral authority.

So, despite our repeated question, the deep historical roots attaching to youthful urban violence and the racialised framing to which they were often subject, when explaining increasing rates of wounding from the middle years of the twentieth century, caution against any simple point at which knife crime 'began'. Even though the many factors in play and the gradual but steepening rate of climb in woundings throughout the final decades of the century suggest that the selection of any given point in time would be quite arbitrary. This tends to confirm that the key to understanding the emergence of 'knife crime' has far more to do with the social reactions to it, the arrangement of law enforcement resources around it, the creation of new offences, tougher sentences and the increasingly proactive efforts to police knife carrying offenders. The definition and social construction of knife crime was a process involving connections between many elements and the cooperation of many agencies. It was only completed when agencies had fabricated a new offence, drafted laws in its name and produced credible statistics of its frequency, all the while (and with the aid of the media) discovering new perpetrators, chilling examples of the weapons they used and, of course, victims. With these elements in place the knife crime story could run and run—as indeed it has.

Once labelled and established, 'knife crime' forcefully engages the concerns of everyday people, their demand for 'something to be done' providing a platform to gain public support through a proactive, realist, political response. 'Knife crime' also uniquely provides a physical justification for proactive 'realist' policing. It has, in a very material sense, given law enforcement something to look for and especially in press releases and public events where police seek public support for their tactics by displaying knives 'recovered'. Critics of stop and search find it hard to argue with tables laden with knives, albeit most frequently kitchen knives rather than exotic 'zombie killers' or samurai swords, confiscated through extensive search operations. Such displays are accompanied by solemn mathematically realist claims from police commissioners reinforcing the idea that 'It is incumbent on us to recognise that every one of these knives recovered represents a tragedy averted and a life saved' (Glendinning, 2008).

Towards a Different Understanding

It should now be clear that, in this book we are pursuing a different kind of answer for the knife crime question. Despite the dominant positivist approach in established criminology, even as reformulated as 'left realism' in the latter decades of the twentieth century, we intend to show that a social construction perspective provides a firmer grasp upon contemporary manifestations of knife crime. By contrast, positivism devoted itself to the search of 'cause-effect' relations in crime. Positivism began with the argument that crime resulted from a number of biological, physiological causes and, subsequently, psychological predispositions—ideas which still resurface, but which we now tend to criticise as blinkered and racist and denying of human agency. Positivism later adapted to the rising influence of sociology, and sought explanations of crime in disrupted families, broken homes, fractured communities, frustrated opportunities and divided societies, coalescing around an essentially social or cultural pathology that saw crime, violence and phenomena such as gang formation as an adaptation—indeed, one of Downes' (ill-advised) 'delinquent solutions' (1966)—to the deprived and often oppressive circumstances in which young people grew up. Peer group influences assert themselves, alternative and resistant value systems arise, partly as defensive, partly in justification, as young people negotiate the strains and contradictions between what their discriminatory society promised and what it has delivered. Addressing these 'unfortunate', prejudicial or deprived, circumstances is still an established and recognised preoccupation in the field of juvenile anti-social behaviour and violence for example, where research is focused on identifying causes, establishing methods of prevention and evaluating the effectiveness of these interventions (Muncie, 2009; Silvestri et al., 2009; WHO, 2010). However, the positivist tradition in criminology is widely criticised for its 'failure to look beyond the official statistics of recorded crime or beyond legal definitions of crime' (Muncie, 2009: 114). We have already seen how feminist academics have sought to unpack different spatialised aetiologies of knife-involved violence (Cook & Walklate, 2020) Here, by contrast, we are engaging with the more prevalent representation of 'knife crime' treated as an established fact of deprived urban masculinity.

The positivist identification of violence causation is often equated to the measurement of 'risk factors' present in a young person's life that increase the potential of violent behaviours; 'Findings suggest that there are problem areas, known as "risk factors", which can predict the likelihood of future violent criminal behaviour among young people' (Silvestri et al., 2009: 15). The influences identified as correlating with knife-related offences can be subcategorised into individual, relationship, community or societal factors (WHO, 2010) in order to coordinate and target preventative responses to specific aspects of a young person's life. One of the earliest research projects in the UK to adopt such an approach to 'knife crime' was published in 2004 and became an influential reference for many that followed. Written by Lemos and Crane (2009) with the title 'Fear and Fashion', the report used hospital admission data, MORI survey results and anecdotal evidence from youth practitioners to reach several conclusions about risk factors for knife offences. Young people carry knives in school, youth clubs and on the street. Boys are more likely to carry knives than girls, although a Canadian study found that knives were the most frequently carried weapon by samples of 'at risk' young women in Toronto, Montreal, Philadelphia and Amsterdam (Erickson et al., 2006). Young people who had been excluded from school were the most likely to carry, and use, knives and other weapons, as well as commit other offences. Fear was the most common reason given by young people themselves for carrying knives, a claim frequently endorsed by youth workers and teachers. Referring to a perceived 'security gap' in the lives of many young people, Traynor (2016) has argued that knife carrying could be seen as a misguided 'proxy for resilience' by many under-protected young people. A 2019 OFSTED report from London confirmed that young people who carried knives were around twice as likely to be injured in assaults, a finding which might reflect that their sense of the risks they ran was fairly accurate but their means of avoiding them rather less so. On the other hand, evidence of more benign intentions behind knife carrying might come from McVie's study in Scotland: 'when young people carry knives they are used sparingly and, when used, this may often be with the aim of warning off or threatening others rather than to attack them aggressively' (McVie, 2010: 34). Peer group influences, group identity and fashion also appeared to play a part in encouraging young people to carry knives (Lemos & Crane, 2009: 27), a practice with a substantial historical pedigree (Macaraeg, 2007). Risk factors here appeared to centre upon gender, school exclusion, fear of violence and peer pressure. In turn, these issues became central to the development of preventative projects with young people (Kinsella, 2011).

There are also influences in a young person's life that are widely considered by positivist criminology to *decrease* the likelihood of violence and offending behaviours. These are referred to as 'protective factors'. Protective factors include positive relationships with parents, high academic achievement, positive friendships with non-delinquent peers, extracurricular school activities, belonging to smaller (in terms of numbers of children) families, good problem solving skills and empathetic skills (Silvestri et al., 2009: 17). Many young people who are exposed to a variety of risk factors do not manifest violent or criminal behaviours, and it is sometimes suggested that this is because these young people have access to protective factors that reduce or mitigate the impact of their risks. This is often referred to as 'resilience' (ibid.) whereby young people develop or acquire coping strategies or the ability to resist peer group influences tending towards anti-social or violent behaviour. Resilience programmes or individual therapies have been developed from such understandings, but sometimes face the criticisms that they are premised upon bolstering internal or individual coping strategies rather than addressing more structural causes: in effect, teaching individuals to swim rather than preventing them from falling in the water.

Research attempting to identify protective factors fostering a resilience specifically to 'knife crime' has offered several suggestions. 'Deterring [young people] from carrying knives requires decreasing their fear of crime, and giving them alternative strategies to build self-esteem...' (Gliga, 2009: 20). Quantifying and reducing 'the fear of crime' is a rather abstract variable to attempt to influence. Yet it is sometimes suggested that news media reporting may have *increased* the fear of crime thus contributing to the risks perceived by young people: 'The way crime is covered by the media could be a source of disinformation and in consequence, create excessive fear of "knife crime"… it is desirable that media presentation of news be more factual and less sensationalist' (Gliga, 2009: 21). This view was reiterated by other researchers who advised that the 'possible role of media amplification in reinforcing a sense of fear seems an area worth exploring, especially in relation to the carrying of knives' (Silvestri et al., 2009: 68). Other recommendations have included calls for targeted and earlier intervention. This might include violence awareness education in schools about the dangers of knife carrying (Kinsella, 2011; Lemos & Crane, 2009). The 'Tackling Knife Crime Together' review states 'knife crime is now such a big issue, embedded in their culture… if all schools had some kind of knife crime programme, just as they all have sexual health and drug awareness programmes, this would help overcome the problem' (Kinsella, 2011: 23). Other recommendations include targeted programmes for those calculated to be 'at risk' of knife offences (Kinsella, 2011: 28), 'gang reduction projects' (Lemos & Crane, 2009: 23) and public awareness advertising campaigns to demonstrate the health and legal implications of knife carrying (Lemos & Crane, 2009: 28). Unfortunately, there are some obvious contradictions between risk factors and prevention strategies that demonstrate the limitations of positivist approaches. Increasing the visibility of 'knife crime' through school assemblies and billboard posters might also increase the fear of 'knife crime', an identified risk factor for violence.[16] It is also rather problematic that the recommended 'widening of the net' to facilitate early intervention actually brings more young people in contact with the criminal justice system, encounters that are themselves identified as risk factors for violence in a young person's life (Schur, 1973; Silvestri et al., 2009: 69). A more nuanced understanding of 'risk and protection'

---

[16] A Metropolitan Police schools initiative from 2010, *Joint Enterprise: Knife Crime* comprised a DVD to be shown in targeted schools in order to warn young people of the potential consequences of knife carrying and gang involvement. As a strategy it both risked increasing the fear of crime as well as implying that young people might face joint enterprise murder charges for offences committed by their associates, thereby suggesting that young people had plenty to be concerned about as regards the police. As Brennan (2019) has shown a lack of confidence in the police is one of three key factors prompting increase resort to weapons by young people.

and of the choices open to young people is offered by Irwin-Rogers and Harding (2018), they point to the opportunities that some young people are able to take, transitioning away from 'gang identities' when in school. The point is important, reinforcing the sense of school as a potential lifeline, but one that might be suddenly ripped away if a pupil is excluded or 'off-rolled'.

In spite of such dilemmas the pursuit of proactive prevention remains a core feature of positivism and continues to hold high regard in mainstream criminology. Its central commitment to answering the 'why' questions may appear to address the urgent demand for answers that concern over 'knife crime' incites, but the conflation of cause and correlation often creates confusion. Furthermore the relative neglect of human agency—young people's choices are more than just the outcome of a given distribution of risk and protection factors—has been accused by some commentators of fundamentally restricting the criminological imagination for over a century (Brown, 2005). Likewise its ability to deliver a 'knife crime' strategy has been disappointing. As we have seen, academic literature has drawn attention to the lack of reliable data (Eades et al., 2007; Squires, 2009a) and the harm of sensationalist constructions of 'knife crime' in the media (Gliga, 2009). All told, the commitment to identifying risk and protective factors in 'knife crime' research serves mainly to preserve the validity of the label and its assumed parameters for preventative action. Common phrases such as 'becoming involved in knife crime' or 'a culture of knife crime' (Lemos & Crane, 2009: 4) reinforce an idea of 'knife crime' as a distinct form of criminality; an autonomous 'new thing' that exists independent of the actions, strategies and policies of the police and enforcement authorities and existing outside of the actions of young people, but having its influence on each of them. Through this uncritical approach, positivist criminology reproduces a particular understanding of 'knife crime' as if it were a universal criminological 'truth'. These observations become especially important when we move to consider some of the more social, cultural and subjective influences coming to bear upon young people and their resort to weapons.

Studies around the world have acknowledged both fear, vulnerability and attraction factors—alongside a number of context specific issues—as contributing to young people's weapon choices. Studies have shown that the fear of violence coupled with peer influences were the most prominent risk factors for carrying or using knives (Bartels, 2011; Gliga, 2009; Kinsella, 2011; Silvestri et al., 2009; WHO, 2010). This has been described in a psychological contribution to the field as an emerging 'youth knife culture' in which 'young people carry knives because they want to protect themselves, or because they want to be respected by peers' (Gliga, 2009: 20). The World Health Organisation (WHO) identified the same risks as 'fear of violence in the community' and 'associating with peers who are violent' (WHO, 2010: 42). While a report by the Children's Commissioner for England (2019) estimated that while only 27,000 children identified themselves as involved in gang activity, over 300,000 were at risk because they knew gang members, 34,000 of who had already been victims of gang violence.

Another common risk measurement for 'knife crime' was affiliation with 'gangs', seen as a risk factor for knife carrying and group violence (Bannister et al., 2010; Kinsella, 2011; Lemos & Crane, 2009; Silvestri et al., 2009). In the identification of risk factors associated with knife offending, Silvestri et al. (2009) noted that, statistically, Black and minority ethnic young people appeared to have a higher likelihood of involvement in 'knife crime'. ONS data from 2019, for example, shows that a disproportionate 25% of knife crime victims are black (ONS, 2019), although the clear corollary is that 75%, an overwhelming majority, are white. It has also been acknowledged that when the ethnic dimension of offending is considered in isolation it can lead to dangerously misleading simplifications, given that 'race, social exclusion and community deprivation are correlated and compound each other' (Silvestri et al., 2009: 69). Furthermore, racial discrimination combined with inequality produces a 'toxic mix of deprivation and social exclusion' which is often exacerbated by police enforcement practices (Squires, 2011: 161) and contributing to an over-representation of young Black people as both victims and perpetrators of interpersonal violence.

While individual and relationship risk factors such as gender, ethnicity and the family context are frequently identified, until recently environmental or societal influences have been less common in the 'knife crime' literature. Although it is acknowledged that there are strong connections between social and economic inequality and violence amongst young people (WHO, 2010), there is 'difficulty in demonstrating that a deprived neighbourhood "causes" those living in it to commit crime; it is extremely difficult to isolate the various elements that, combined together, constitute environmental facilitators to offending' (Silvestri et al., 2009: 27). Thus the strong correlation between social and economic deprivation, and particularly high rates of unemployment, is a risk factor rarely targeted for intervention and mostly acknowledged only by critical researchers in the field (Eades et al., 2007; Silvestri et al., 2009; Squires, 2011). Clement (2010) draws on the sociological work of Norbert Elias (1978) and Loic Wacquant (2004) to produce a critical interpretation combining a variety of risk factors. This included the neoliberal social and economic policies which contributed to a decivilising, poor and opportunity bereft, environment for youth. Resisting the positivist isolation of individual and social factors in cause and effect relationships, Clement (2010) suggests that knife violence represents an inevitable outcome of the decivilising conditions of neoliberal late capitalism, and this 'tendency should… be understood as a structural property of social systems where social polarization and inequality are present or deepening and not as a property of pathological individuals' (Rodger, 2008: 129). Clement (2010) argues that apparent increases in the severity of interpersonal violence, such as in the case of 'knife crime', signal that inequality and its decivilising effects have extended and worsened. Considering the realities of the contemporary conditions in which marginalised teenagers must survive, Clement (2010) concludes that our surprise should not be that a number of young people commit knife offences, but that so many of them do not—despite the increasing brutality of their daily lives. This contribution to the debate stands out in its focus on structural antecedents as a predictable aspect of neoliberal social and economic policy and its emphatic rebuttal of 'knife crime' as youth pathology.

Other research has emphasised a 'London effect' in the distribution of serious violence, compounded by often highly localised strings of violent attacks and retaliations (Allen & Kirk-Wade, 2020; Massey et al., 2019; Wood, 2010). Such work, to some extent, reinforces Loftin's culturally informed 'assaultive contagion' argument which emphasised how 'serious assaultive violence is sub-cultural and therefore analogous to disease… [having] the potential to spread explosively in a vulnerable population' and thereby best viewed epidemiologically (Loftin, 1985). We will return to these issues later, when considering 'knife crime' prevention strategies. First, however, a few comments are in order regarding more recent attempts to explore this phenomenon.

Recent approaches to gang violence have lately come to focus upon sub-cultural, contextual, subjective and interactionist accounts to understandings of youth violence. In some senses they can still be seen within a 'modified positivist' perspective in the sense that new identities, cultural contexts, relationships and perceptions influence young people's decision-making and violence choices. While such accounts are all different, they share a certain *psycho-social* focus pointing to the influence of external factors and conditions upon internal thought and decision processes and external actions. In a wide-ranging literature review of the performance of aggressive and violent behaviour and weapon carrying, Brennan and Moore (2009) attempted to produce a simple model of the cognitive and social processes and choices involved in 'instrumental' or 'expressive' weapon use.

Drawing upon a range of such approaches we might mention explanations centred upon 'respect', hierarchy and identity, the projection of 'hardness' and a refusal to back down or be seen as an 'easy mark' (Hallsworth, 2005). A number of such studies also drew upon Anderson's idea of being 'streetwise' or his 'code of the street' (1999). Based upon his ethnographic research in Philadelphia, Anderson argued that keeping safe on the streets required the learning and internalisation of certain street behaviour rules (where you could be at certain times, where to avoid, who to defer to and who to resist). Following the rules, it was argued, could help to keep you safe. Despite a certain intuitive sense to these ideas, other researchers also pointed out that following the street codes could also get you into trouble—sometimes you had to fight, other times you had to break the rules (Mullins, 2008; Stewart et al., 2006). Fagan and Wilkinson (1998, 2000) draw attention to these issues in their 'ecological' study of violent encounters between young gang members in New York. Here an 'anticipatory' mode of 'violent alertness' was deemed essential to staying safe on the dangerous streets even, as Winlow and Hall (2009) implied, anticipating the need to 'retaliate' first. In turn, the 'ecological' approach developed by Fagan and Wilkinson, in which adopted forms of behaviour or 'dispositions' arose out of given environments (see also Fraser, 2013), drawing upon Bourdieu's work on 'habitus' (Bourdieu, 1977). Similarly, Bourdieu's notion of personal capital (or capacities) has also been adopted by gang researchers who have developed a notion of 'street capital' (Sandberg, 2008) which might roughly equate to a notion of 'respect' or reputation and designating that someone might be a power on the street and not to be messed with (Palasinski, 2013; Squires, 2009b). While some commentators (Bourgois, 2003; Short, 1997) have suggested that the intense focus upon 'respect' in deprived black communities is related to the relative shortage of other markers of success or value, other researchers have reiterated longstanding associations between black masculinity and 'hardness' and white racism (Sandberg, 2008). Drawing upon similar constructions of tough racialised masculinity (Messerschmidt, 2000), Harding has argued how 'weapon-carrying facilitates construction of a hypermasculinty: widely seen as advantageous in navigating street life' (Harding, 2020). In such accounts, analytic attention is paid to behaviour as *performance*, designed perhaps to impress, intimidate or befriend (Garot, 2010) and where everyone present knows the scripts, or codes, of the street (Holligan et al., 2017). Such interpretations here draw close to 'Actor/Network' theories (Holligan, 2014; Latour, 2005) whereby violent street behaviours represent a playing out of mutual assumptions and expectations.

The purpose of this brief review of more *psycho-socially* inspired theories of youthful violence is to re-centre individuals (and their assumptions, beliefs and perceptions) into their youthful decision-making in order to acknowledge the importance of social relationships in youthful violence. This is certainly not to suggest that young people are necessarily making free and independent choices (an argument which often precedes a case for more punitive responses), still less that they are making the most rational, wise or well-informed decisions. For it is clear that, in each of the various accounts addressed above, the choices made and the behaviours adopted—the decision, for instance to carry a knife or not—can only be understood in the fullness of its context and on the basis of an individual's own predispositions as mediated by what his friends might think, what his girlfriend might say, the dangers he perceived locally and, perhaps, his assessment of the likelihood of being stopped and searched by the police. While positivist accounts of youth violence took account of socio-economic disadvantages, oppressive environments and discriminatory relationships—and leant themselves to preventive social strategies by which these inequities might be addressed, they did so often at the cost of reproducing a counterproductive stigma of exclusion, overlooking important relationships between young people living in challenging environments.[17] On the other hand, where interventions centred largely upon individual risk and protection factors, such as depicted in the UK Government Gang Strategy (UK Govt, 2011), then they fell close to the problematic 'child saving' or 'rescue' paradigm (Platt, 1977) of social intervention which depended for its success on young people both rejecting *and escaping from* their social origins. An unlikely strategy for widespread adoption.

We have noted earlier how strategies to tackle an 'epidemic' of violence cannot be expected to succeed one weapon at a time (especially when knives are so prevalent). In like fashion, former Prime Minister Theresa May acknowledged that the UK could not expect the police to 'arrest our way out of a knife crime crisis'—one arrest at a time (Heffer, 2019). Although her comment was made in the midst of a dispute with police commentators regarding the extent to which cuts in police numbers had any bearing upon rates of youth violence, it does seem an appropriate endorsement of the need for effective multi-agency intervention. And finally, as we have just noted, it seems equally unlikely that the prevention of youth violence can succeed one young person at a time. By mid-2020 two new voices had entered the fray over the knife crime moral

---

[17] Media reports sometimes express surprise when high achieving young people are caught up in knife/gang crime, but reports often acknowledge the difficulty of avoiding violence risks where they may live (Gayle & Marsh, 2019; OFSTED, 2019; Scheerhout & Osuh, 2019).

panic, these were the 'Youth Select Committee' which published a report in 2019 (British Youth Council, 2019) and the Youth Violence Commission (YVC) which published its final report in July 2020 (Irwin-Rogers et al., 2020). Both reports brought more critical voices—especially the experiences of young people and the kinds of committed, professional youth workers as are represented in our Chapter 7. Similarly, both reports endorsed the kind of 'public health' strategic approach to serious youth violence, which we discuss in Chapter 8, even though the jury may still be out regarding whether the governments newly established 'violence reduction units' will have the resources or the strategic capability to take necessary initiatives forwards. As the YVC report noted:

> Regional VRUs have been given insufficient, short-term funding. Furthermore … too many of the regional VRUs have already been pressured to spend money in haste, resulting in short-sighted attempts to achieve immediate (yet inevitably elusive) results. This is antithetical to an evidence-informed, public health approach to reducing violence and sets the VRUs up to fail… adopting a relatively narrow vision of their potential role, acting primarily as commissioning bodies for local level violence reduction initiatives. (Irwin-Rogers et al., 2020: 12)

These are issues we will return to later in the book.

Learning Exercise 5: End of Chapter Activity, Alternative Accounts of Knife Violence

We have itemised below many of the contrasting criminological theories which have arisen offering different explanations for rising crime and violence in the twentieth century. We are certainly not suggesting that we would subscribe to all of these, indeed, three of them strike us as *explicitly* racist, but each has nevertheless surfaced at various times and places in the ongoing debate on the causes of (knife) crime. It might be a useful exercise to undertake, to assess each of these differing theories, decide which of them you find most persuasive (you can select more than one) and find occasions when commentators have expressed thoughts similar to these theories. What kinds of evidence might different theories use to argue their case?

Theory/Perspective[18]	Issues
Neo-Classicism	A failure of social control: enforcement deficits, lack of appropriate laws or deterrent impact
Racism 1: Biological determinism/socio-biological theories	'Natural' physicality, inherited characteristics, violent disposition, under-socialised persons
Racism 2: Black culture/pathology	Racial and cultural practices promoting violence, norms and values, legacies of impoverishment and abuse
Racism 3: Family Dysfunction	Absent parental role models (father figures), neglect, lack of discipline, social pathology
Social Marginality	'Tough at the bottom'—living on the streets, making ends meet informal/illegal economies
Peer Group Pressure/resistance	*Fear & Fashion*, Safety in numbers, 'protection', self-defence
Control Theories	Soft controls of family, community supervision, mentoring. Young people as, perhaps, 'over-controlled', and/or 'under-protected'
'Respect'—Masculinity, identity	Social or 'Street' Capital, Street Rules—'walking the walk', cultivating 'hardness', male honour
Right and Left Criminological Realism	Morality, responsibility, order, 'just deserts' Communities and victims, harm, vulnerability
Social Ecology	'Turf' and territoriality, Post-Codes and 'Endz', 'anticipatory violence' on dangerous streets
Street Scripts	Actor Network theory, 'Codes' of the street
Recreation and/or Instrumentality	Performance, 'buzz', drugs ... or money
Signal Crime Theory	Meanings and interpretations: 'them', 'us', society, risks

(continued)

---

[18] Perhaps it goes without saying but we will be critically unpacking such accounts, and we certainly don't subscribe to all of them but they frame a great deal of what is and what has been said about knife crime.

(continued)

Theory/Perspective	Issues
Labelling and Moral Panic theory Deviancy Amplification	The 'Usual suspects', and use of knife crime by policy entrepreneurs The harder the police look, stop and search, the more they find
Social Construction	How the phenomenon known as *knife crime* is reproduced and sustained
Strain Theories	Poverty and inequality, relative deprivation, blocked opportunities, unemployment
Critical and conflict theories: Marxism, Radical deviancy theory	Growing inequality and social division/exclusion, racism. Strain theory, Materialism/consumerism

References

Allen, G., & Audickas, L. (2018). *Knife crime in England and Wales*. House of Commons Briefing Paper, Number SN4304, November 9th.

Allen, G., & Kirk-Wade, E. (2020). *Knife crime in England and Wales* (2nd ed.), House of Commons Briefing Paper, Number SN4304, October 6th.

Amnesty International. (2018). Trapped in the Matrix: Secrecy, stigma, and bias in the Met's Gangs Database. www.amnesty.org.uk/gangs.

Anderson, E. (1999). *Code of the street*. W. W. Norton.

Arkwright, A. (2019). A prevent style plan will not reduce serious violence. *The Chartist*, May 30th.

Athwal, H. (2002). Black deaths in custody. Institute for Race Relations [online]. 573. http://www.irr.org.uk/news/black-deaths-in-custody/.

Bailey, V. (1987). *Delinquency and citizenship: Reclaiming the young offender: 1914–1948*. Oxford University Press.

Bannister, J., Pickering, J., Batchelor, S., Burman, M., Kintrea, K., & McVie, S. (2010). *Troublesome Youth Groups, Gangs and Knife Carrying in Scotland*. Scottish Centre for Crime and Justice Research. Report No. 24.

Bartels, L. (2011). *Knife crime in Australia: Incidence, aetiology and responses*. Australian Institute of Criminology, Technical and Background Paper 45.

Blackall, M. (2020). Police officer stabbed in Glasgow says his colleagues saved lives. *The Guardian*, June 27th.

Bourdieu, P. (1977). *Outline of a theory of practice*. Cambridge University Press.

Bourgois, P. (2003). *In search of respect: Selling Crack in El Barrio* (2nd ed.). Cambridge University Press.

Bourke, J. (2000). *An intimate history of killing: Face-to-face killing In twentieth-century warfare*. Granta.

Bowling, B., & Phillips, C. (2002). *Racism, crime and justice*. Harlow, Pearson.

Bradley, G. M. (2019). A prevent-style plan for knife crime is not just misguided, it's dangerous. *The Guardian*, April 2nd.

Brennan, I. (2019). Weapon-carrying and the reduction of violent harm. *The British Journal of Criminology, 59*(3), 571–593.

Brennan, I., & Moore, S. C. (2009). Weapons and violence: A review of theory and research. *Aggression and Violent Behaviour, 14*, 215–225.

Brewer, J., & Styles (ed.). (1980). *An ungovernable people: The English and their Law in the 17th and 18th centuries*. Hutchinson University Press.

British Youth Council. (2019). *Our generation's epidemic: Knife crime*. Youth Select Committee Report, British Youth Council.

Brogden, A. (1981). "Sus" is dead but what about "Sas"? *New Community, 9*(1, Summer).

Brookman, F. (2005). *Understanding Homicide*. London: Sage.

Brown, S. E. (2005). *Criminology: Explaining crime and its context*. Lexis-Nexis/Anderson Pub.

Clarke, R., Chadwick, K., & Williams, P. (2017). Critical social research as a 'Site of Resistance': Reflections on relationships, power and positionality. *Justice, Power and Resistance, 1*(2), 261–282.

Clement, M. (2010). Teenagers under the knife: A decivilising process. *Journal of Youth Studies, 13*(4), 439–451.

Cohen, S. (1972). *Folk devils and moral panics*. Paladin: St Albans.

Collier, I. (2020). Mayfair robbery: Three men hunted after man stabbed for £115,000 watch. *Sky News Online*, February 6th.

Cook, E. A., & Walklate, S. (2020). Gendered objects and gendered spaces: The invisibilities of 'knife' crime. *Current Sociology [Online]*, June 27th: 1–16.

Cruse, E. (2020). Teen jailed for stabbing to death participant on knife awareness course in west London. *The Standard*, October 12th.

Dearden, L. (2017). Police five times more likely to use force against black people than white people in England and Wales. *The Independent*, December 17th.

Delice, M., & Yasar, M. (2013). Examination of knife crimes against women. *European Scientific Journal, 9*(34), 370–390.

Demuth, C. (1978). *'Sus': A report on the Vagrancy Act*. Runnymede Trust.

Dodd, V. (2020). NHS worker stabbed to death by gang 'wearing medical masks'. *The Guardian*, April 28th.

Downes, D. (1966). *The delinquent solution*. London: Routledge.

Eades, C. (2006). The year of the knife. *Criminal Justice Matters*, No. 66 Winter 2006/07. London, CCJS, pp. 10–12.

Eades, C., Grimshaw, R., Silvestri, A., & Solomon, E. (2007). *'Knife crime' a review of evidence and policy* (2nd ed.). Centre for Crime and Justice Studies. Available at: http://www.crimeandjustice.org.uk/opus439/ccjs_knife_report.pdf.

Edwards, J. (1953). Prevention of crime act 1953. *Modern Law Review, 16*, 482–484.

Edwards, R., Farmer, B., & Allen, N. (2008). Met declares war on knife crime gangs. *Daily Telegraph*, May 13th.

Elias, N. (1978). On the transformation of aggressiveness. *Theory and Society, 5*(2), 229–242.

Elliott-Cooper, A. (2021a). *Black resistance to British policing*. Manchester University Press.

Elliott-Cooper, A. (2021b). 'Knife crime': Prevention and order. In G. Bhattacharyya et al. (eds.), *Empire's endgame: Racism and the British state*. Pluto Press.

Erickson, P. G., Butters, J. E., Cousineau, M.-M., Harrison, L., & Korf, D. (2006). Girls and weapons: An international study of the perpetration of violence. *Journal of Urban Health, 83*(5), 788–801.

Fagan, J., & Wilkinson, D. (1998). Guns, youth violence and social identity in inner cities. *Youth Violence, 24*, 108–188.

Fagan, J., & Wilkinson, D. (2000). *Situational contexts of gun use by young males in inner cities*. US Department of Justice, National Criminal Justice Reference Service.

Farrall, S., & Hay, C. (2010). Not so tough on crime?: Why weren't the thatcher governments more radical in reforming the criminal justice system? *British Journal of Criminology, 50*(3), 550–569.

Farrall, S., Jennings, W., Gray, E., & Hay, C. (2017). Thatcherism, crime and the legacy of the social and economic 'storms' of the 1980s. *The Howard Journal of Criminal Justice, 56*(2), 220–243.

Finch, J. (2019). Government proposal that nurses must report knife crime could undermine confidentiality. *British Journal of Community*

Nursing, 24(5), 244–247. Available at: https://doi.org/10.12968/bjcn.2019. 24.5.244.

Fraser, A. (2013). Street habitus: Gangs, territorialism and social change in Glasgow. *Journal of Youth Studies, 16*(8), 970–985.

Garot, R. (2010). *Who you claim: Performing gang identity in school and on the street*. New York University Press.

Gayle, D. (2019). Half of children shot by Tasers are from BAME groups. *The Guardian*, March 12th.

Gayle, D., & Marsh, S. (2019). Knife crime victims: The Teenagers killed in 2019. *The Guardian*, March 4th.

Gilroy, P. (1982). *'The myth of black criminality', socialist register*. Merlin.

Gilroy, P. (1987). *There Ain't no Black in the Union Jack*. Hutchinson University Press.

Gliga, T. (2009). *The 'knife crime' phenomenon—A psychological perspective on youth knife culture*. Parliamentary Office: British Psychological Society.

Glendinning, L. (2008). Knife crime: Police seize 200 weapons in stop and search blitz. *The Guardian*, May 29th.

Gramsci, A. (2005). *Selections from the prison notebooks*. Lawrence & Wishart.

Gruner, P. (2009). Policeman whose murder led to end of the death penalty. *Islington Tribune*, Jan 2nd.

Grunhut, M., et al. (1948). *Lawless youth: A challenge to the new Europe*. London, Allen & Unwin.

Hall, S. (1980). *Drifting into a 'law and order' society*. Cobden Trust Lecture.

Hall, S. (1985). Authoritarian populism: A reply. *New Left Review*, No. 151, May/June.

Hall, S., Roberts, B., Clarke, J., Jefferson, T., & Critcher, C. (1978). *Policing the crisis: Mugging, the state, and law and order*. Macmillan.

Hallsworth, S. (2005). *Street crime*. Willan Publishing.

Hansard (British Parliamentary Debates). (1953). *Hansard parliamentary record*.

Harding, S. (2020). Getting to the point? Reframing narratives on knife crime. *Youth Justice, 20*(1–2), 31–49.

Harper, T. (2017). Eleven serious stabbings a day. *The Times*, February 19th.

Hebenton, W., Shaw, D., & Pease, K. (2010). Sentencing guidance on knife possession. *Criminal Law and Justice Weekly, 174*(43), 662–666.

Heffer, S. (2019). We can't arrest our way out of this epidemic: As knife crime reaches crisis point. *Daily Telegraph*, March 17th.

Holligan, C. (2014). Disenfranchised violent young offenders in Scotland: Using actor-network theory to explore an aetiology of knife crime. *Sociology, 49*(1), 123–138.

Holligan, C., McLean, R., & Deuchar, R. (2017). Weapon-carrying among young men in Glasgow: Street scripts and signals in uncertain social spaces. *Critical Criminology, 25,* 137–151.

Home Affairs Committee. (1980). *Race Relations and the 'SUS' Law: Report and Proceedings,* HC559 Session 1979–80. HMSO.

Home Affairs Select Committee (HASC). (2009). *Knife crime: Seventh report of session 2008–09,* HC 112, 2 June 2009. The Stationery Office.

Innes, M. (2004). Signal crimes and signal disorders: Notes on deviance as communicative action. *British Journal of Sociology, 55,* 335.

Irwin-Rogers, K., & Harding, S. (2018). Challenging the orthodoxy on pupil gang involvement: When two social fields collide. *British Educational Research Journal, 44*(3), 463–479.

Irwin-Rogers, K., Muthoo, A., & Billingham, L. (2020). *Youth violence commission, final report.* YVC, July.

Joseph, I., & Gunter, A. (2011). *Gangs revisited: What's a gang and what's race got to do with It?* Runnymede Trust.

Kelbie, P. (2011). The streets of Scotland: Britain's knife capital. *The Independent,* October 23rd.

Kinsella, B. (2011). *Tackling knife crime together: A review of local anti-knife crime projects.* February, London, Home Office.

Lemos, G., & Crane. (2009). *The fear and fashion evaluation, a summary report.* London: Clear Plan.

Lanham, D. (2005). Offensive weapons and self defence. *Criminal Law Review,* February, pp. 85–97.

Latour, B. (2005). *Reassembling the social: An introduction to actor-network theory.* Oxford University Press.

Lincoln et al. (2006). Inmate made weapons in prison facilities: Assessing the injury risk. *Injury Prevention, 12*(3), 195–198.

Loftin, C. (1985). Assaultive violence as a contagious social process. *Bulletin of the New York Academy of Medicine, 62*(5), 550–555.

Long, L. (2018). *Perpetual suspects: A critical race theory of black and mixed-race experiences of policing.* Palgrave Macmillan.

Long, J., et al. (2020). *Femicide census 2009–2018.* Femicide Census.org.

Macaraeg, R. A. (2007). Dressed to kill: Toward a theory of fashion in arms and armour. *Fashion Theory, 11*(1), 41–64.

Malcolm, J. L. (2002). *Guns and violence: The English experience.* Harvard University Press.

Marfleet, N. (2008). *Why carry a weapon?: A study of knife crime amongst 15–17 year old males in London.* London: Howard League for Penal Reform.

Marx, K. (1937). *The 18th Brumaire of Louis Bonaparte (first published 1852).* Lawrence & Wishart.

Massey, J., Sherman, L., & Coupe, T. (2019). Forecasting knife homicide risk from prior knife assaults in 4835 local areas of London, 2016–2018. *Cambridge Journal of Evidence-Based Policing, 3,* 1–20.

Maxwell, R., Trotter, C., Verne, J., Brown, P., & Gunnell, D. (2007). Trends in admissions to hospital involving an assault using a knife or other sharp Instrument, England, 1997–2005. *Journal of Public Health, 29*(2), 186–190.

McAra, L., & McVie, S. (2005). The usual suspects?: Street-life, young people and the police. *Criminology and Criminal Justice, 5*(1), 5–36.

McCandless, R., Feist, A., Allan, J., & Morgan, N. (2016). *Do initiatives involving substantial increases in stop and search reduce crime? Assessing the impact of operation BLUNT 2.* Published March 2016, Home Office.

McLaughlin, E. (2005). From reel to ideal: The Blue Lamp and the popular cultural construction of the English 'bobby'. *Crime Media, Culture, 1*(1).

McKenzie, L. (2017). The class politics of prejudice: Brexit and the land of no-hope and glory. *British Journal of Sociology, 68*(S1), 5265–5280.

McVie, S. (2010). *Gang membership and knife carrying: Findings from the Edinburgh study of youth transitions and crime.* The Scottish Centre for Crime and Justice Research.

Medina Ariza, J. J. (2014). Police-initiated contacts: Young people, ethnicity, and the 'usual suspects'. *Policing and Society, Volume, 24*(2), 208–223.

Messerschmidt, J. W. (2000). *Nine lives: Adolescent masculinities, the body and violence.* Westview Press.

Ministry of Justice: Knife and offensive weapon sentencing statistics 10th Sept 2020: Table 2A. https://www.gov.uk/government/statistics/knife-and-offens ive-weapon-sentencing-statistics-year-ending-march-2020.

Morris, K. (2009). UK Doctors begin reporting gun and knife crime. *The Lancet.* Available at: http://www.thelancet.com/pdfs/journals/lancet/PII S0140-6736(09)62138-3.pdf.

Mullins, C. W. (2008). *Holding your square: Masculinities, streetlife and violence.* Willan Publishing.

Muncie, J. (2009). *Youth and crime* (3rd ed.). Sage.

Murdie, A. (2003). Fifty years of offensive weapons. *Justice of the peace issue, 17*(April), 308–315.

Murray, K. (2018). The modern making of stop and search: The rise of preventative sensibilities in post-war Britain. *The British Journal of Criminology, 58*(3), 588–605.

Newsinger, J. (2013). *The blood never dried: A people's history of the British empire* (2nd ed.), Bookmarks.

Nijjar, J. (2018). Echoes of empire: Excavating the colonial roots of Britain's "war on gangs". *Social Justice* (San Francisco, Calif.), *45*, 147–161.

Noor, P. (2018). Met use tasers and restraints more often against black people. *The Guardian*, December 5th.

Office for National Statistics. (2019). *Homicide in England and Wales: Year ending March 2018*. ONS.

Ofsted. (2019). *Safeguarding children and young people in education from knife crime: Lessons from London*. Ofsted, Crown Copyright.

Olden, M. (2011). *Murder in notting hill*. Zero Books.

Palasinski, M. (2013). Security, respect and culture in British Teenagers' discourses of knife carrying. *Safer Communities, 12*(2), 71–78.

Palasinski, M., & Riggs, D. (2012). Young white British men and knife-carrying in public: Discourses of masculinity, protection and vulnerability. *Critical Criminology, 20*(4), 463–476.

Pantazis, C., & Pemberton, S. (2009). From the "old" to the "new" suspect community: Examining the impacts of recent UK counter-terrorist legislation. *British Journal of Criminology, 49*, 646–666.

Platt, A. (1977). *The child savers: The invention of delinquency* (2nd ed.). University of Chicago Press.

Radzinowicz, L., & King, J. (1977). *The growth in crime*. Basic Books.

Roberts, S. (2021). *Solutions to knife crime: A path through the Red Sea?* Vernon Press.

Rodger, J. (2008). *Criminalising social policy: Anti-social behaviour and welfare in a de-civilised society*. Willan Publishing.

Sandberg, S. (2008). Street capital: Ethnicity and violence on the streets of Oslo. *Theoretical Criminology, 12*(2), 153–171.

Scheerhout, J., & Osuh, C. (2019). The dark fascination with knives that ended the promising life of Manchester Grammar School pupil Yousef Makki. *Manchester Evening News*, July 13th.

Schur, E. (1973). *Radical non-intervention: Rethinking the delinquency problem*. Prentice-Hall.

Seenan, G. (2005). Scotland has second highest murder rate in Europe. *The Guardian*, September 26th.

Sethi, D., Hughes, K., Bellis, M., Mitis, F., & Racioppi, F. (eds.). (2010). *European report on preventing violence and knife crime among young people.* WHO.

Sharpe, J. A. (2016). *A Fiery and Furious People: A history of violence in England.* Random House.

Shaw, D. (2019). Ten charts on the rise of knife crime in England and Wales. *BBC News Website,* July 18th.

Shaw, D., Pease, K., & Hebenton, B. (2011). Possession of a knife and Private defence: Dilemmas in the pursuit of personal security in England and Wales. *International Journal of Law Crime and Justice, 39*(4), 266–279.

Short, J. R. F. (1997). *Poverty, ethnicity and violent crime.* Westview Press.

Siddique, H. (2018). Black people more likely to have force used against them by police. *The Guardian,* December 13th.

Silvestri, A., Oldfield Squires, P., & Grimshaw, R. (2009). *Young people, knives and guns: A comprehensive review, analysis and critique of gun and knife crime strategies.* Centre for Crime and Justice Studies.

Solomos, J., & Back, L. (1996). *Racism and society.* Palgrave Macmillan.

Squires, P. (2009a). The knife crime 'epidemic' and British politics. *British Politics, 4*(1), 127–157.

Squires, P. (2009b). 'You lookin' and me?: Discourses of respect and disrespect, identity and violence. In A. Millie (Ed.), *Securing respect: Behavioural expectations and anti-social behaviour in the UK.* Policy Press.

Squires, P. (2011). Young people and 'weaponisation'. In B. Goldson (Ed.), *Youth in crisis ? gangs 'territoriality and violence.* Routledge.

Squires, P. (2014). *Gun crime in global contexts.* London: Routledge.

Squires, P. (2016). Voodoo liability: Joint enterprise prosecution as an aspect of intensified criminalisation. *Oñati Socio-legal Series, 6*(4), 937–956. https://ssrn.com/abstract=2871266.

Squires, P., & with Solomon, E., & Grimshaw, R. (2008). *'Gun crime': A review of evidence and policy.* Centre for Crime and Justice Studies.

Squires, P., et al. (2008). *The street weapons commission evidence: Guns, knives and street violence.* London: CCJS, Kings College.

Stewart, E. A., Schreck, C. J., & Simons, R. L. (2006). 'I ain't gonna let no-one disrespect me': Does the code of the street reduce or increase violent victimisation among African American adolescents? *Journal of Research in Crime and Delinquency, 43*(4), 427–458.

Storer, R. (2020). Birmingham stabbings: Footage released as police hunt suspect. *The Guardian,* September 6th.

Tiratelli, M., Quinton, P., & Bradford, B. (2018). Does stop and search deter crime? Evidence from ten years of London-wide data. *The British Journal of Criminology, 58*(5), 1212–1231.

Traynor, P. R. (2016). *Closing the security gap: Young people, street life and knife crime.* Ph.D. Thesis, University of Leeds.

Vegh-Weis, V. (2017). *Marxism and criminology: A history of criminal selectivity.* Haymarket Books.

Wacquant, L. (2004). De-civilizing and demonizing in the dark ghetto. In S. Loyal & S. Quilley (Eds.), *The sociology of Norbert Elias.* Cambridge University Press.

Wacquant, L. (2016). A concise genealogy and anatomy of habitus. *The Sociological Review, 64,* 64–72.

Walby, S., et al. (2015). Is violent crime increasing or decreasing? A new methodology to measure repeat attacks making visible the significance of gender and domestic relations. *British Journal of Criminology, 56*(6), 1203–1234.

Williams, P. (2015). Criminalising the other: Challenging the race-gang nexus. *Race & Class, 56*(3), 18–35.

Williams, P., & Clarke, R. (2018). The black criminal other as an object of social control. *Social Sciences, 7*(11), 234–234.

Williams, P., & Clarke, R. (2020). (Re)producing guilt in suspect communities: The centrality of racialisation in joint enterprise prosecutions. *International Journal for Crime, Justice and Social Democracy, 9*(3), 116–129.

Winlow, S., & Hall, S. (2009). *Violent night: Urban leisure and contemporary culture.* Oxford: Berg.

Winlow, S., Hall, S., & Treadwell, J. (2017). *The rise of the right: English nationalism and the transformation of working-class politics.* Policy Press.

Wood, R. (2010). UK: The reality behind the 'knife crime' debate. *Race & Class, 52*(2), 97–103.

World Health Organisation (WHO). (2002). *World report on violence and health.* WHO.

World Health Organisation. (2010). *European report on preventing violence and knife crime among young people.* WHO.

Young, J. (1999). *The exclusive society.* Sage.

Young, J. (2011). *The criminological imagination.* Polity Press.

Younge, G. (2017). Beyond the blade: The knife crime crisis is national. The solutions must be local. *The Guardian,* May 1st.

Younge, G., & Barr, C. (2017). How Scotland reduced knife deaths among young people. *The Guardian,* December 3rd.

2

Knives and Violence in History and Culture: A Global History of Stabbing

Is this a dagger which I see before me, the handle
towards my hand? Come, let me clutch thee.
Macbeth: Act 2, Scene 1.

In this chapter we aim to complement and extend our analysis of the British 'knife crime crisis'. Ambitious as it might seem, the purpose of the chapter is to add a wider global context and a longer historical perspective to the British 'knife crime' story. We intend to address three themes, for the relevant literatures on knives seem to cluster into three main strands.

A first strand drawing upon history, archaeology and anthropology, explores the evolution and cultural significance of knife design, symbolism and use, referring to what Vollman (2005) has referred to as the 'aesthetics of weapons'. Closely related to this is a field of what we might call 'knife advocacy' or knife collection and publishing, extolling the virtues of particular knives in a variety of cultures or celebrating their characteristics, production and craftsmanship and their use in a variety of

© The Author(s), under exclusive license to Springer Nature
Switzerland AG 2021
E. Williams and P. Squires, *Rethinking Knife Crime*,
https://doi.org/10.1007/978-3-030-83742-6_2

applications (hunting, survival, self-defence and the military). Commentaries in this vein impinge directly on aesthetic and commercial issues; what is it that makes a knife valuable, interesting, desirable or collectible?

Secondly, there is a rather smaller literature, typically centred upon historical criminology, and histories of violence, which has depicted the distinct 'knife fighting' cultures of particular times and places. This strand of analysis also blends into particular notions of 'warrior masculinity', anthropologies of honour and heroism and the identification of certain national or regional cultures and values.

A third and final strand in the global knife crime literature, one that we would argue is still rather underdeveloped, but which brings us back to the core criminological concerns of the book, involves when, where and how knives manifest themselves as a *crime* problem. As we have briefly noted stabbings occur in all societies and at varying rates and frequencies but few, indeed, hardly any, have declared an equivalent 'war on knife crime' and few appear so animatedly preoccupied by it. It is important to consider the wider influences which might predict and go on to shape such reactions. As we do so it is also clear that aesthetics, culture, history, knife advocacy, production and availability all play their parts.

Knives in History and Culture

Knives have played many roles in culture, history and society. They are loaded with enormous cultural, practical, economic and symbolic significance, and often ceremonial significance that, at times, seems even to surpass their status as one of humanity's oldest weapons. In the Bible (Genesis, 22: 9–12) Abraham was poised, knife in hand, to sacrifice his son, as a demonstration of his devout religious faith, until an angel interrupted him. In a more secular reading, historians have claimed that the knife represents 'the most reliable useful and important tool in human history', with six of the top 20 tools essential to the development of civilisation—the chisel, axe, lathe, scythe, saw and sword—being simply specialised variants on the knife (Ewalt, 2005).[1] The first knives were made of sharpened flint or animal horn; the oldest blades, dating back some half a million years were discovered in several sites in the region of modern Kenya (Gibbons, 2009). Fired stone knives are thought to be amongst the first real innovations to the 'stone age' tool kit (Callaway, 2009) credited with kick-starting the process we have called human civilisation. It is intriguing—but not historically unique—that the vital catalyst for the process we call 'civilisation' should be the refinement of a weapon technology (Brown et al., 2009).

Around ten thousand years ago metals, first copper, followed some 5000 years later by bronze and, later still, iron and steel, began to make their appearance in knife and blade manufacture. A great deal of the cultural significance deriving from knives rested upon the knife's status as a weapon, whereby masculine honour and warrior-like qualities attached themselves to those who would carry or display knives. Knives (and swords) have often signified honour and power. Even the surgeon's blade, the scalpel, cements the cutter's status at the head of medicine's esteemed pyramid. Similarly, Todd (1938) lyrically extols the potent relationship between Roman legionary and his sword, 'his broadsword was more than his weapon, it was the soul of his tactics and the symbol of his sturdy psychology' (1938: 139). Because real swords were expensive to produce and acquire, they also marked out wealth and status (Ager, 2011), whereas the weapons of the poor were often refashioned agricultural tools, wooden spears or much smaller knives. Hoefle (2006) describes the conflict still occurring between commercial and landowning interests and the Amerindian peasants in Amazonian Brazil. The former armed with firearms and the latter with knives, machetes and axes, this was—and still is—an unequal contest of peoples and a profound mismatch of weapons.

Writing in the journal of African Arts, McNaughten describes the particular evolution of throwing knives in central Africa. Designed either for fighting or hunting, the knives were thrown spinning towards the legs of their target, to bring down an opponent or animal, 'a properly thrown knife could sever a leg at twenty metres' (McNaughton, 1970: 55; Thomas, 1925). Distribution of the knives, from as early as 400

---

[1] Ewalt, D. The Knife. *Forbes Magazine*, 31st August.

BC, can help trace the development of patterns of settlement and related metalworking skills, as differing styles of knife were favoured by different peoples. The knives afforded a psychological advantage to their users both in the whine they produced when thrown and the flashing when they caught the sunlight, McNaughten suggests that the knife throwers were known as 'the people of the lightning', their fearsome reputation proceeding before them augmenting their power and influence. Yet while 'the throwing knife's importance as a weapon can only be guessed at... we may conclude that the knives were very important' (ibid., 55). In this way, something so ordinary as a knife might profoundly represent a culture especially where they symbolised power and virility within the social hierarchy of a people. Knives represented 'power symbols', invested with secular authority and magical power they were used in court rituals and circumcisions in Darfur, and on ceremonial occasions or dances they became invested with a similar phallic symbolism and were 'carried by young men to impress women' (ibid.). So fundamental, representational and multi-functional a simple knife becomes. During the nineteenth century the throwing knife began to decline in both prac-tical and symbolic power, eclipsed largely by the firearms flooding into Africa from the Europe (Satia, 2018).

Archaeological, anthropological, military and historical research has revealed many forms of knife culture in a great many historical soci-eties, taking in Mayan civilisation, and Egyptian culture, while central European Bronze Age culture had its '*sica*' dagger, a tool for assassins and for self-defence. Archaeological discoveries have revealed elaborately engraved '*sica*' knives suggesting either the bearer to be a member of some notable armed brotherhood or a figure of noble status. Greek and Persian military cultures had their '*xiphos*' and '*kopis*' weapons, each of them heavy, short bladed swords, which influenced the design of many other fighting weapons of the Mediterranean and Middle-East regions (not to mention the fighting tactics and organisation), including the Iberian '*falcata*' and the Roman military '*gladius*', or short sword (source of the 'gladiator' cult). In India the Sikh '*kirpan*' knife, was said to have embodied the virtues of the 'saint-soldier' or compassion, courage and honour, not unlike the infamous Nepalese kukri, both resembling aspects of Japanese Samurai culture. In the Philippines and Malaysia, the 'bolo knife' (similar to the widely distributed machete, weapon of peasant uprisings: Braid, 1999; Verwimp, 2006) reigned, both as a tool for cutting vegetation (and other generic agricultural tasks) and also featuring in martial arts (Bethge, 2007). In contrast, the Greek '*machaira*, a longer curved bladed weapon designed for mounted fighting employing a cutting, rather than stabbing, action found itself reflected in the Turkish/Ottoman scimitar' (now represented on the flags of Saudi Arabia, Yemen and, not to overlook contemporary Jihadist banners as well as, rather contrastingly, the US 7th Cavalry, of Little Big Horn infamy, which later became an attack helicopter unit). Similar in style to the Russian '*shaska*' favoured by Cossack warriors, these curved swords evolved to become the sabres of the massed cavalry units of the European empires and beyond, until the First World War and industrial scale killing technologies finally terminated the military role of cavalry. Of course, in the *Star Wars* film franchise these iconic blades—colour coded to reflect the character and prowess of their owners—were to experience a slight return as 'light sabres'.

An important (British) quasi-mythological example might be *Excalibur* (the sword in the stone), drawn, according to the legend, by a young Arthur; the man who would be king. Drawing the sword, as if by divine permission, Arthur miraculously acquired the vital characteristics associated with chivalric power: honour, integrity and authority. The weapon in effect, 'made the man', although this was far from the only or last occasion upon which this would be claimed. In Japanese Samurai culture, the sword was similarly thought to be inseparable from the man, the warrior who embodied the core virtues of military skill, discipline, loyalty and selfless service. Commentators have explained contemporary Japan's comparatively high suicide rates, rising dramatically during Japan's economic downturn in the 1990s, roughly twice the international average (WHO, 2021) to the samurai legacy, where an individual atoned for his failings via an honourable 'suicide of resolve' (Russell et al., 2017).

Similar attachments between blades and wider cultures have been unearthed rather closer to home. The recent discovery, near Chichester, West Sussex, of the 2000 year-old tomb of a 'Saxon Warrior', buried alongside his sword to ensure his safe passage to the afterlife, points to the inseparability of man and weapon and the spiritual resonance of this most personal weapon-companion. During the Crusades the sword, its crossguard a reflection of the Christian cross, also embodied spiritual power and influence (reminding Christian soldiers of the righteous character of their cause), not unlike *Gram*, the magical sword of Sigmund in Norse mythology. Reflecting many of the characteristics of *Excalibur*, *Gram* was drawn from a tree by Sigmund into which the god, Odin, had thrust it as a test for men. Passing through many hands, in Nordic and Germanic mythology, not overlooking Wagner's *Ring des Nibelungen* opera cycle; it was used to slay dragons in a strong echo of the fable of St. George (Orchard, 1997). Swords embodied chivalric codes of values and spoke for the character of the knights who carried them (Oakeshott, 2018), more recently reflected in the sword of retribution grasped in the hand of 'justice', the figure standing today on top of the Central Criminal Court, The 'Old Bailey'. And when the Queen confers a 'knighthood', this is achieved by a simple tap on the shoulder with a sword. Continuing the theme, many contemporary video games avatars and cartoon superheroes carry highly anachronistic swords as their principle combat weapons. As a recent industry review of video games reported, 'Swords rank among the most common weapons in all of gaming' for while they 'typically lack the destructive power of firearms, … they are seen as more honourable and noble weapons since they allow their users to get up close and personal with each other' (Blockfort, n.d.). Many of these swords, like those of mythology, are invested with special powers, sometimes even a will of their own. Only heroes can truly own and use these weapons— effectively becoming one with the blade—following a profound personal and spiritual transformation, as in the case of the Marvel superhero *Blade* played by Wesley Snipes in a series of films from the late 1990s. In other words, to understand knives and knife culture, we need to pay attention to their meanings and grasp the symbolic significances they often embody. Writing the definitive guide to the medieval sword, Oakeshott (1991) readily admits to the 'glamour and romance' intimately wrapped up in his subject matter.

Referring to a different time and place, Frank Dobie (1931: 351) celebrates another culturally significant blade, the Bowie knife, while telling of 'the glory of the "knife men" wearing proudly their ivory handled Bowies in embroidered sheaths in … traditional tales of the frontier…

and heard all over the South West'. The knife takes its name from Colonel Jim Bowie, one of the supposed 'heroic' American defenders of the Alamo in 1836 who certainly popularised it, although it appears far less likely that he, in any sense, 'invented' the knife (Ericson & Shulman, 1937). Edgar (1949), links these South-western frontier knife men with the knife culture of Scandinavian immigrants to the USA, the Finnish 'knife men' who became the hunters, trappers and lumberjacks of Northern Minnesota, bringing their material culture, songs, ballads and knives with them. One knife in particular, the *puukko*, with a birch handle and a long curved blade, resembled the Bowie knife in appearance and function. The knives would hang in a scabbard from the belt, being used in hunting and trapping, 'and the old bullies of the ballads used it as a fighting weapon' (Edgar, 1949: 53). Dobie suggests that the Bowie knife 'has become nothing less than the American counterpart of King Arthur's *Excalibur*, or of Sigmund's great sword *Gram*, and its origin is wrapped in multiplied legends as conflicting and fantastic as those that glorify the master weapons of the Old World'. Testifying to the power of the knife, perhaps even before the USA became a fully fledged 'gun culture' (Haag, 2016), Dobie continues, 'on the bloody grounds of Kentucky, in the mountains of Tennessee, and all down the Mississippi Valley the frontiersman's knife was used to deadly effect' (Dobie, 1931: 351), always symbolising the ruggedly individual virtues of a noble and independent frontier masculinity.

Connecting these disparate times, a time of frontiers and the supposed age of chivalry, and tracing another line of descent towards knives of impressive cultural symbolism, the knights of the middle ages carried stiletto knives (of Italian origin) as 'back up weapons' to slip between the armoured plates, or into the visors, of their metal-clad opponents. Later the stiletto was said to have become the weapon of choice of Mediterranean assassins, before eventually evolving into the American V-42 'military stealth knife' (rather similar to that as depicted in the emblems of the SAS, US 'Special Forces' or Royal Marine Commandos). As Todd (writing in 1938) acknowledged, the dagger 'became the emblem of a distinct cult of individual combat and physical prowess which has continued to this day and forms a definite part of the ideology of fascist states' (1938: 139). A troubling symbol for a tainted democracy, perhaps.

Equally controversially, on the mean streets of the modern city (before public opinion began to move against it in the 1950s, and prohibition followed), it became the 'flick-knife' or 'switch-blade' as fatally depicted in *West Side Story* (1961). Exempt from such regulation, the ceremonial Scottish dirk, an object of concern for MPs in 1953, steeped in history and cultural significance, also offered physical testimony to ferocious fighting skills and a man's loyalty, honour and integrity, their blades often inscribed with manly virtues (Milne, 2010).

Just as the implied characteristics of swords and knives transferred themselves to the men who carry them, the Bowie knife or the assassin's stiletto prominent amongst them, so, in 'knife advocacy' or 'knife enthusiast' and collector publishing we find similar anthropomorphic claims about the nature of forged steel. Advertisements for 'Zero Tolerance' knives in the USA, for instance, promise a 'bold and robust', hardworking and 'professional', blade, a 'reliable' knife which 'exudes trust' (ZT knives website).[2] Just to emphasise the point, soldiers, police and fire-fighters are referenced, endorsing the qualities of these apparently so versatile blades. The same company's 'survival knife' is similarly strong and 'able to take a punch'. A number of glossy knife magazines, many originating in the USA—with extensive archives and online presence— help sustain a specialist knife market, current titles include *Knife World* (becoming *Knife Magazine* in 2015), *Knives Illustrated*, and *Blade*. Magazine reviews wax lyrical about the virtues and characteristics of a near infinite variety of favoured knives honed by decades of experience, the craftsmanship poured into their production, their 'classic styling', 'heritage value' and timeless reliability: 'I take comfort in knowing how useful my knives have been. We have a history together… A knife is like a dependable old friend who has shared many experiences with you and has been at your side through good times and bad' (Barlow, 2020). Articles describe knives for every occasion: working, hunting, all round utility, survival, combat and self-defence, their sharpened,

---

[2] The ZT knives sales pitch spoke volumes as to its intended market. Its advertisement featured an image of a young woman, concerned but confident and prepared, a double-handed grip on her semi-automatic pistol, looking out from the darkness. 'Shoot straight and go bold' urged the headline, 'your choice of EDC (every-day carry) knife should be as precise as your choice of firearm'.

pointed steel suggesting something basic and elemental to the human condition, an essential prerequisite of modern living—both 'last resort' and 'first responder'. As Thakur (2019) writes in the *Knives Illustrated* 'tactical buyer's guide' for 2020: 'Emergencies come in many forms. From being locked in an overturned vehicle, to a family trapped in a burning building, to facing a crazed attacker, a tactical knife fills the position of "first responder" for numerous and varied crises'.

At just one remove from such knife advocacy publications, we find another sub genre of publications devoted to instruction in the 'arts' of knife fighting. Some such manuals lean more towards a cultural and martial arts take upon fighting with a knife,[3] such as *Sevillian Steel: The Traditional Knife-Fighting Arts of Spain* (Loriega, 1999), or *Sicilian Blade: The Art of Sicilian Stiletto Fighting* (Quattrocchi, 1992) whereas others aim more at the practical self-defence or 'survivalist' markets with books such as *The Complete Book of Knife Fighting* (Cassidy, 1997) or *Master of the Blade* (Ryan, 1999). Some such publications drew upon 'frontier heritage values' such as *American Bowie Knife Fighting Techniques from the 1880s* (Lawrence, 2020) or McLemore's *Bowie and Big Knife Fighting System* (McLemore, 2017) which he followed up, a year later, with *Advanced Bowie Techniques: The Finer Points of Fighting with a Large Knife* (McLemore, 2018). Amongst a number of military knife fighting guides and histories, and technical manuals for particular weapons perhaps the most unusual is Pentecost's *Put 'em Down, Take 'em Out: Knife Fighting Techniques from Folsom Prison* (Pentecost, 2016). Described as a book written by someone who has 'been there and back', Pentecost challenges 'theoretical approaches' to knife fighting, insisting from the start that, your only motivation for engaging in a knife fight should be to 'survive ... by killing your enemy as quickly as possible... Never giving an opponent time to defend, think or run. Be quick and brutal' (Pentecost, 2016: 3). A truly 'deadly symbiosis' as Wacquant (2001) might have put it, as fighting principles from one of California's

---

[3] Many such books were published by Paladin Press, launched in 1970, and specialising in military, survival and martial arts publications. The company, once described as 'the most dangerous publisher in the world', faced legal difficulties when its books were implicated in a number of homicide cases and eventual ceased trading in 2018.

more infamous prisons script wider decivilising behavioural norms. No wonder there are concerns.

As in the case of concealed carry gun ownership, Anglo-American cultural differences emerge amidst such belligerent knife advocacy. Suggestions about the inappropriateness of knife carrying 'for protection' seem unlikely to achieve much purchase here.[4] Taken together, the US knife magazines (not unlike American gun industry publishing—Squires, 2018) speaks to a broad American demographic with deeply ingrained values, stoicism and independence and an uncanny facility for righteous, redemptive violence. There have been suggestions that this rugged frontier, masculine-centred culture may be waning in late modernity (Carlson, 2015; Gibson, 1994; Pridemore & Freilich, 2005), but not, it has to be said, in the pages of the knife publishing industry.

Recently, a rather more exotic brand of knife and sword marketing has emerged offering historic swords, such as samurai swords, machetes or 'collectable weapons' often franchised by Films or TV programmes, such as *Rambo*, *Game of Thrones* or the *Walking Dead*. Such shows were partly the inspiration for the marketing of so-called 'zombie-killer knives', weapons which were prohibited in the UK in 2016 by an amendment to the Criminal Justice Act (Offensive Weapons) Order 1988, although, three years later, such knives were still being advertised in online marketing websites.[5]

---

[4] Taking up this very point, Shackleford, writing in *Blade Magazine* (describing itself as 'the world's number one knife publication'), took up the cause of 'Knife Rights' an organisation campaigning against knife prohibitions and discriminatory enforcement of knife laws in New York City. Shackleford referred to British knife laws citing the case of a Scottish man prosecuted for carrying a potato peeler. He also quoted London Mayor, Sadiq Khan who had announced, 'No excuses: there is never a reason to carry a knife. Anyone who does will be caught, and they will feel the full force of the law'. American libertarian David Kopel, more usually an advocate for gun rights, knives should be covered by the US 2nd Amendment: Kopel et al. (2013).

[5] The so-called 'Zombie knife' was defined as: a weapon sometimes known as a 'zombie killer knife' or 'zombie slayer knife', being a blade with—(i) a cutting edge; (ii) a serrated edge; and (iii) images or words (whether on the blade or handle) that suggest that it is to be used for the purpose of violence.

And yet, even as knives extolled a heroic element in man, especially for those men accustomed to living, literally, on a knife edge (or imagining they did), they also came to occupy a more prosaic place in human society, as cutlery. According to Elias's account of the 'civilising process' (Elias, 1983) the distinct evolution of cutlery, and in this regard, the partial 'taming of the knife' in civilised society, occurred prior to the seventeenth and eighteenth centuries. It involved one of the most decisive civilising transitions, as Elias puts it, 'from warriors to courtiers' (1983: 259). Hitherto it had been customary for travellers to carry their own 'cutlery'—a multi-functional knife—around with them. This knife was used to cut food and its sharp point might be used to spear chunks of meat for the mouth (in place of the hand). Considerations of hygiene and social etiquette came to dictate that the knife as outdoor tool or weapon had no place at the dinner table; good manners dictated a whole new approach to eating, involving a fork to transfer food to the mouth and a smaller more discreet knife to politely slice food into bite-size portions, rather than hacking away at a central carcass. Etiquette books spelled out the new conventions of civilised dining: everyone was to have their own cutlery, knives were not shared. 'At table you should not keep the knife always in your hand, it is sufficient to pick it up when you wished to use it… it was impolite to transfer food to the mouth with a knife… it was most improper to lick a knife if it became greasy' or 'wipe them on the tablecloth'. A man should 'take care not to put his knife into his mouth… a mark of the peasant'. Diners were likewise discouraged from picking their teeth with knives (quoted in Elias, 1983: 92–98). In 1689 Louis XIV is reputed to have decreed that all knives carried in public or used at dinner should have their points ground down to reduce the spontaneously lethal violence that could be occasioned when quick tempers coincided with lethal implements (Hern et al., 2005: 1222). Yet whilst civilised society was presumed to have advanced with a careful differentiation between the knife as tool or weapon—separating cutlery from weaponry, eating from fighting and violence from the domestic sphere—only a rather less successful separation was ever achieved. The evidence suggests that a substantial proportion of knife-enabled violence is inflicted not by specific *fighting* knives but rather by more mundane blades designed for cooking and kitchen use (Home Affairs Select Committee, 2009: para. 55; Hughes et al., 2012; Malik et al., 2020) and this has given rise to experimental testing of a variety of knives in order to factor more safety features into knife design (Hainsworth et al., 2008) notwithstanding the fact that the cutlery drawer has already been open for quite a whilst. The fact that a significant proportion of knife violence occurs in the home rather than in the streets, might suggest a double-edged shift. For whilst the migration of knives from the kitchen to the street became a cause for popular concern (wrong implement, wrong place, wrong purpose), the resurgence of violence in the apparently 'safe haven' of the home has tended not to arouse similar concerns (Cook & Walklate, 2020). For as Cook and Walklate argue, 'the knife, as a relatively mundane and freely accessible household object, [challenges] a whole range of assumptions about who requires protection, from whom, and where this is needed' (ibid., 2020: 9). In simple terms, the knife unsettles a number of the boundaries of our civilised modern social order for danger is never far away, even as we try to overlook it.

Learning Exercise 6: Discussion Activity: The Many Uses of Knives

From cutlery to surgical instruments, survival tool and badges of honour, knives have embodied many diverse social values for human societies—how many can you identify?

Intriguing evidence of this 'denial' surfaced in 2008, roughly coincident with the upscaling of the 'war on knife crime' we have already described. The AQA (the Assessment and Qualifications Alliance) a secondary school examinations agency, announced it was withdrawing an anthology of poetry, part of the GCSE literature syllabus, containing a poem, *Education for Leisure*, written by Carol Ann Duffy (then tipped to be the next Poet Laureate). The poem, originally written in the mid-1980s (that is, some *20 years earlier*), was intended as a reflection upon educational disadvantage, alienation and wasted lives. It features a depressed young man contemplating, somewhat ahead of his time, the 'dark celebrity' of killing (Drageset, 2013). The poem begins: 'Today I am going to kill something. Anything. I have had enough of being ignored'. It ends as the protagonist takes a bread knife out into the street. The AQA pulled the poem from the syllabus and instructed schools to destroy the books, acknowledging that it had done so following a number of complaints and that 'the decision had been made in the context of the current spate of knife-related murders' (Curtis, 2008). Duffy's agent condemned the decision, 'It's a pro-education, anti-violence poem written in the mid-1980s when Thatcher was in power and there were rising social problems and crime. It was written as a plea for education… You can't say that it celebrates knife crime. What it does is the opposite'. Michael Rosen, the children's laureate, agreed, commenting that, following the same logic, we should also be banning Shakespeare's *Romeo and Juliet*, a story 'about a group of sexually attractive males strutting round the streets, getting off with girls and stabbing each other'. Rather than 'censorship and blanket condemnation', he continued, 'we want children to be talking about knife crime and poems like these are a terrific way of helping that happen' (quoted in Curtis, 2008).[6] Duffy retaliated by publishing another poem, *Mrs. Schofield's GCSE*, targeting the school examinations officer who, in misunderstanding the original poem, had helped prompt the complaints that led to the AQA censorship. The poem comprised extracts of Shakespearean dialogue anticipating brutal knife violence but laid out as if an English comprehension examination question. The point is well made that global culture is literally saturated with references to knives and blades, they have been central to so many of the rhythms of life: eating, working, fighting, artistry and healing. Perceptions may have changed but the knives cannot be hidden indefinitely from young people. Duffy's later poem pointedly demonstrated the futility of ignorance and denial. Indeed, 'nothing will come of nothing'.

---

[6] Trauma surgeons have likewise undertaken 'simulation' exercises in order to encourage 'groups of young people vulnerable to knife crime' to engage with and discuss knife-enabled violence and its consequences. Tribe et al. (2018) describe some success in using such simulation exercises 'for engaging young people about the issues surrounding criminal knife behaviour in a safe and cooperative environment', suggesting that such workshop could be used as an educational tool [to] facilitate behavioural change.

> **Learning Exercise 7: Knife Crime Poems and Reflect Upon What They Might Mean**
> Carol Ann Duffy—Education For Leisure | Genius
> Carol Ann Duffy—Mrs. Schofield's GCSE | Genius
> When Duffy writes: 'Explain how poetry pursues the human like the smitten moon above the weeping, laughing earth' What is she getting at? How does this help us think the question of 'knife crime'?

Just as they have embodied characteristics of heroic (even savage) masculinity, incorporated the values of symbolic authority, justice and political order, and—as cutlery—featured importantly in the story of civilisation, at the same time knives have been instruments of the most bloody, visceral and even *intimate* killing. These have been played out, as we have seen, all the way from Shakespearean tragedy ('*et tu, Brute?*') to Victorian serial killing and, more recently, in contemporary 'slasher' movies (such as the *Scream* franchise (1996–2011), *Nightmare on Elm Street* (2010) and *Child's Play* (2019)). Generals and military tacticians have debated the importance of knives and bayonets amidst our most defining national conflicts, trench warfare on the Western Front in 1916, just as other blades have animated theatrical performances, saved lives in surgical procedures or featured in artistic and literary productions, and virtual reality fantasy gaming. Knives have even found their place in domestic tragedies in the most ephemeral of cultures—pop music ('*I felt the knife in my hand and she laughed no more*').[7] As we have suggested, multiple tensions and contradictions settle upon the edge of the knife, reflecting both historic and distinctly modern sensibilities. Knives also entertain; many a circus or variety show has featured a 'knife throwing' act, invariably involving a woman spread-eagled on a spinning backboard and a blindfolded artist throwing knives within inches of her. The husband and wife team '*Deadly Games*' appearing on *America's Got Talent* in 2016 teased the audience, before their performance, with the line 'we love to live dangerously', although it was hard to avoid the conclusion that one of the pairing was living rather more dangerously than the other.

---

[7] *Delilah* sung by Tom Jones was a major hit for the singer, reaching number 2 in the UK pop-charts, the sixth best-selling single that year.

Knife Fighting Cultures

As we saw in relation to depictions of the 'Bowie men', the tough frontiersmen of the American South West, and their prowess with a large hunting knife could, to some extent, define and shape a culture. Just as the knife could *represent* a range of values, so the man who carried the knife could also embody many of its steely virtues. These relationships between blades and men and social contexts arise a number of times in received histories of violence but despite their sometimes powerful legacies for contemporary crime and violence they are seldom drawn together for an assessment of their significance. One attempt to provide some broad historical context for the role of weapons in fatal violence can be found in Eisner's paper tellingly titled 'from swords to words' (Eisner, 2014: 13). He collates data from a range of indicative studies undertaken in England (London, Northampton and Kent) from 1300 to the twenty-first century. In the following diagram we have converted Eisner's numbers into a simple linear graph representing fatal murder weapon proportions (Fig. 2.1).

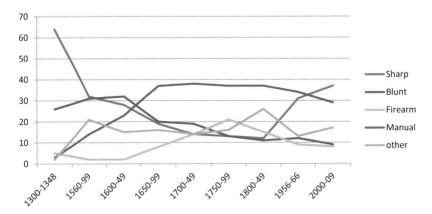

Fig. 2.1 Method of killing/weapons (percentages) from the fourteenth to twenty-first centuries (*Source* Eisner, 2014)[8]

---

[8] Care should be taken interpreting the graph, the data is intended as simply indicative, the time periods are not uniform and the data collated from differing studies relates to differing geographical locations.

Most obvious in the graph is the long decline in sharp/bladed fatal violence until the mid-nineteenth century. Stabbings/Cutting and blunt instrument killings closely track one another (this is slightly less true for shootings and other means of killing except between 1700 and 1850) until stabbings pull away into the twentieth century. Throughout the second half of the twentieth century, as we saw in Chapter 1 (Figs. 1.5 and 1.6) woundings rise significantly. The trend which bucks the pattern (manual killings, hitting and strangulation), likely including a greater proportion of domestic and intimate murders, persist at a higher level throughout the eighteenth and nineteenth centuries, overtaken by knife killings in the late twentieth century.

A more qualitative attempt to make such historical connections, Judith Flanders' *The Invention of Murder* (2011) draws attention to the apparent Victorian penchant for grisly tales of brutal killing. Her book begins and ends with tales of despicable violence: blades drawn, throats cut, bodies disfigured and copious amounts of blood spilled. The gruesome accounts of such killings, preserved especially by the newly established popular press, 'penny dreadfuls' and scandal sheets catering to an increasingly literate public which delighted in the spectacle and sensation of violent death, established an enthusiasm for homicide, crime and detective fiction which continues to this day. Not unlike the popular fascination which turned a series of murders in London's Whitechapel district in the late 1880s into a major publishing sensation (Curtis, 2001), Flanders describes the ways in which the mundane details of killing were embellished and milked for a publishing (and sometimes theatrical) profit by prurient entrepreneurs quick to exploit any opportunity to turn murder into money. Contemporary cultural criminologists have frequently drawn attention to the many vicarious satisfactions of murder as selectively represented in 'crime drama' and the 'true crime' genres (Durham et al., 1995; Wiltenburg, 2004), and the ways in which these have tended to bolster various forms of moral order or social distinctions between 'respectable, law abiding majorities' and 'dangerous others' (Biressi, 2001). Flanders likewise demonstrates how a new, nineteenth century, murder publishing industry constructed a modern template and a language for comprehending, accounting for and responding to violent death that is still influential today. In a later chapter we account for the ways in which a contemporary 'knife crime industry' has established and recycled many similarly selective misunderstandings of knife crime.

It follows that, in reproducing accounts of earlier knife fighting cultures and contexts we have to be wary of imposing upon the violences of the past the kind of misunderstandings sometimes imposed upon recent knife-enabled violence, its perpetrators, their contexts and motives and their unfortunate victims. Spierenburg (2008) pursuing a different line to that offered by Flanders' 'invention' of murder thesis, provides an important clue to its contemporary interpretation by reference to the long-term decline of homicide in Europe between 1450 and 1750 (2008: 4). The increasing rarity of killing and the civilising constraints imposed upon the practice of impulsive violence (rather less than the deterrence to be found in the due process of law) and the gradual refinement of masculine honour (1994; 1998; 2008: 9–10), marked in part by the decline of duelling (Kiernan, 1988), made the exceptional even more notorious and symbolic. Although, even as Wiener (2004) shows, whilst public violence was beginning to 'decline markedly', domestic or intimate violence in private, failed to show the same civilising progression. Nevertheless, as the final section of this chapter will show, this development, the increasing scarcity of murderous violence, also provides us with an important key to understanding the contemporary significance of knife crime.

Discussing the evolution of the means of killing throughout the late Middle Ages and early modern period, Spierenburg notes how the choice of murder weapons 'reflected medieval life and technology'. In the thirteenth century, he suggests 'thirty per cent of murder victims died of knife wounds' although by the following century it had risen to 42% (Spierenburg, 2008: 35). Violence was primarily driven by feuds and alcohol and across continental Europe, from Paris and Zurich to Krakow, sharp and bladed weapons, routinely carried by many men for their simple versatility or retained by disbanded soldiers (the tools of their trade) predominated. Spierenburg (1998) presents evidence that the authorities in certain towns in Holland enforced regulations restricting the size, width or length of blades, whereas, Bologna, amongst other fifteenth century Italian cities, prohibited the carriage of bladed weapons, even though such ordinances were typically rather ineffectively enforced (Dean, 1994). Reviewing criminal cases recorded, Dean notes some indications that violence of an honourable kind was treated more favourably than that implying dishonour (stabbings in the back or buttocks) suggestive of unfair fights or attacks from behind (1994: 18). Spierenburg likewise cites evidence of magistrates in Germany and Switzerland turning a tolerant eye upon so-called 'honorific fights' where men were apparently required to defend their reputations (2008: 38; Weiner, 2004: 28, 42) or facing unreasonable provocations. Distinctions of this sort might be detected in the 1604 *Stabbing Act* which criminalised stabbings where the perpetrator attacked another person who did not have his weapon drawn or who had not otherwise provoked the assailant (Smith, 1999). According to Polk (1994) arguments about provocation continue to feature in cases of male confrontational homicide and regarding the role of provocation as a partial defence to homicide charges (Wells, 2000). These traces of much older attitudes to 'righteous violence' tend to bear out Spierenburg's observation that 'popular attitudes to lethal but honest violence were slow… to change' (2008: 42). Such attitudes also reflect a tradition of elite duelling that persisted well into the early nineteenth century when gentlemen generally ceased to carry 'street weapons' (Wiener, 2004: 5, 28) even though various die-hard pockets of clannish, lower class knife fighting and vendetta violence clung on in a variety of European cities and regions. Increasingly, however, in Britain from the mid-nineteenth century, fighting with weapons, especially knives, although never eliminated entirely, came to be seen as 'unmanly' and 'foreign', and where death resulted incurred 'outrage and serious prosecution' (Wiener, 2004: 51). Weiner references a case involving a fist fight in 1875 which had resulted in the death of one of the participants. The judge took a lenient view as to sentencing because neither fighter had resorted to weapons other than his fists. An opinion column in *The Times* supported the judge's stance regarding the 'alien nature' of knives, noting that it was 'a redeeming point in even the violence of Englishmen, that they have retained the spirit of fair play and have refrained from gratifying their revenge, as in some other countries, by the … cowardly use of the knife or dagger' (in Wiener, 2004: 53, 57–58).

Spierenburg (1994, 1998, 2008) substantially develops a wider argument concerning the gradual civilising, disciplining and criminalisation of male violence although noting that this was a process fragmented by status distinctions, local cultures and more traditional conceptions of male honour. Drawing examples from Dutch records, he shows how the duel itself marked a refining of elite male combat, 'stylized and highly regulated' and fought with gentleman's weapons, a rapier, foil or épée, swords requiring skill and dexterity. Honour could be satisfied by achieving a first cut, for example marking the face of an opponent (the original meaning of 'losing face'), killing was not essential (2008: 87).[9] Frevert (1998) remarks that, in later duelling, real honour resided in taking up the challenge, testing one's courage, rather than by winning the fight (see also Gallant, 2000: 371). By contrast, the 'knife culture' of the rougher classes, even as it was underpinned by traditional conceptions of masculine honour, responded more spontaneously to threats and insults, conflicts over women and debts (2008: 66–67). Even here, however, 'knife fights resembled duels in several respects', they were 'fought within a peer group' (2008: 76, 82) 'located within a particular social mileu' (2008: 90). As today, knife fighting was associated with youth, but not early adolescence, most Amsterdam knife homicide defendants were in their twenties. Furthermore street rules were reflected in legal interventions, attacks from behind and other 'unfair' fights were discouraged, likewise, injuries to bystanders and third parties. Conflicts which began indoors 'in line with an implicit code against fighting indoors' (2008: 82) were taken outside, where fighting began by mutual consent and akin to more formal duelling, could be ended by a facial cut, which both restored the necessary respect and could avoid criminal proceedings.

In Britain, such developments were also reflected a number of legislative shifts, in the turbulent early decades of the nineteenth century the British parliament became sufficiently concerned about robbery and interpersonal violence, exacerbated following the troop demobilisation towards the conclusion of the wars with France, which gave rise to

---

[9] Fencing manuals of the early nineteenth century depicted diagrams of the face showing areas where slashing strikes might be made (Mele, 2018. Sette Colpi: Understanding the Seven Blows of the Sword in Armizare).

violence, begging and vagrancy scares, to pass a series of Acts tightening up the definition and sentencing for personal violence. The first, in 1803, the *Malicious Shooting and Stabbing Act* (also known as Ellenborough's Act) strengthened the penalties for the malicious commission of potentially fatal acts of violence committed with weapons. This was followed by the 1828 *Offences Against the Person Act* which widened the range of grievously violent acts punishable by death, and the 1837 *Offences Against the Person Act* which, although it set aside some of the Capital penalties introduced nine years earlier, firmed up the meaning of 'wounding' as arising from an assault which we used, in Chapter 1, as a proxy for knife violence (Wiener, 2004: 23–24). By mid-nineteenth century therefore enlightened opinion, popular attitudes, the press and legislative change had effected important shifts in the perception of knife violence. Knives had become cowardly and un-British weapons, the tools of untrustworthy foreigners and the use of a knife whilst fighting had increasingly come to imply a malicious *intention* to kill.

From 1750, Spierenburg reports, public knife fighting was in marked, if uneven, decline across most of Europe, the result of many pressures and changes. Cultural shifts, economic advancement, civilised condemnation and increasing social (and self-) discipline, more efficient law enforcement and stronger penalties but also, the more widespread availability of firearms, all played their parts, including changing conceptions of masculine identity which no longer rested so heavily upon a capacity for violence (2008: 108–112; Shoemaker, 2001, 2002; Wiener, 2004). Social class differences continued to play a role in the generation of and reactions to violence, civilised attitudes 'trickled down' and knife fighting, alongside street brawling became relegated to the lowest classes and 'foreigners'. Even so, Frevert (1998) finds evidence of duelling persisting in German elite military cultures until WW1, Hughes (1998) shows that whilst the Italian authorities prohibited duels between its officers during the war, an apparent backlog of disputes, led to a resurgence of fights up until the 1930s, whilst Nye concludes that, in France, 'the duel was still in robust health in 1914' but declined thereafter, 'perishing in the bloody trenches of the Western Front' (1998: 83).

As regards knives, Gallant (2000) describes how knife fighting was common-place amongst men in nineteenth century Greece, 48% of the assaults he sampled in the Ionian Islands between 1817 and 1864, involved knives, but 89% of assaults with a deadly weapon. Conflicts followed a precise format, 'once certain words were uttered in specific contexts ... there was no turning back. A man had to rise to the challenge or lose status. Once the knives were drawn, the men followed a known script. They aimed not to kill but to maim, not to slay but to scar ...cutting the face of their opponents' (2000: 363). Boschi (1998) likewise shows how a culture of lower class knife fighting persisted in Italy into the twentieth century, wrapped in a cultural and artistic aesthetic of male honour. No self-respecting women, it was said, could contemplate 'marrying a man who had never shown his bravery in a knife fight' (1998: 129). More enlightened opinion, however, condemned the practice for suggesting Italy to be 'uncivilised' with one of the highest homicide rates in Europe. Murders in Rome were dominated by knives, between 1845 and 1906; knives were responsible for 74% of killings in the city (Boschi, 1998: 140). Anticipating more recent gang research on the motivations of gang fighters (Fagan & Wilkinson, 2000; Wolfgang, 1958: 188–189), Boschi's evidence suggests that fatal conflicts frequently resulted from often fairly trivial causes, insults and disrespectful behaviour, disputes over women, money or property (1998: 141). E. M. Forster's novel, *A Room with a View* (published in 1908) offers an interesting contrast between British and Italian, male and female, attitudes to such violence. Walking in Florence, a refined young woman witnesses a knife fight which resulted in a bloody killing; she is appalled and overcome by the violence and its dreadful conclusion.

Even so, Britain certainly had its own knife fighting subcultures; Davies (1998) introduces us to the 'Scuttler' fighting gangs of Manchester and Salford, active towards the end of the nineteenth century. They performed hard masculinity earning great respect for displays of violent bravado and the casual endurance of pain. They were renowned for their willingness to use weapons, 'by the late 1880s knives were increasingly used in affrays to inflict wounds, usually to the body which required hospital treatment' (Davies, 1998: 355; 1999), although their customary weapon was a thick leather belt, wrapped around the wrist so that the heavy brass buckle might be used to strike an opponent. Davies' research uncovered only five fatalities resulting from their violence in the period

1870–1900, 'but reports of severe woundings are commonplace' (1999: 75). Despite their frequent resort to weapons they also retained a notion of the 'fair fight', which we have encountered before, man against man, fists only (1998: 357). In Birmingham there were the 'slogging gangs' inhabiting a prohibited underworld of rough sports, fighting, gambling and hard drinking (Gooderson, 2013). The 'sloggers' were replaced by the 'Peaky Blinders' (of television notoriety) after about 1890, so named because of the razor blades supposedly sewn into their peaked caps, ready to be slashed in the face of opponents (Chinn, 2019). Whilst in London, the figure of the youthful 'Hooligan' addressed a generic middle class fear of urban crime and disorder (Pearson, 1983). Although, in common with the knife fighting gangs on the European mainland, most such 'gang subcultures' apparently disappeared from view during the First World War, notwithstanding that the TV series *Peaky Blinders* (set in the early 1920s) was contextualised by reference to its male protagonists damaged by the desensitising violence of trench warfare (Larke-Walsh, 2019). Ireland had its own culture of recreational fighting (Conley, 1999) with as many as 41% of homicides attributed to 'recreational violence'. O'Donnell (2002, 2005) agrees, suggesting that the 'civilising impulse' we have considered in respect of other European societies, pulling down homicide rates, was rather delayed in its appearance in Ireland.

In Scotland, finally, long traditions of knife carrying (McKeganey & Norrie, 2000) and sectarian divisions overlapping later with football allegiances (Holligan & Deuchar, 2009) led to the establishment of an entrenched gang fighting subculture—knife fighting and razor gangs— that (unlike elsewhere) were still prominent in the 1930s (Davies, 2007, 2008). As Davies has noted, however, whilst the Glasgow/Strathclyde region's reputation for gang-involved crime and violence earned the city comparison with Chicago (Davies, 2007), until recently, the gangs themselves have been relatively little studied. According to Bartie (2010) and Fraser (2013, 2015), however, Glasgow experienced a 'new wave' of gang violence and hooliganism in the 1960s with an annually rising number of stabbing injuries between 1962 and 1965 (Batey & McBain, 1967). A Glasgow youth gang provided the case study for one of the earliest British studies of 'the gang' (Patrick, 1973) whilst the city earned an unwanted reputation as the 'murder capital of Europe' (Fracassini, 2005;

McLaughlin, 2019) and home of the infamous 'Glasgow Smile' (Conway et al., 2010; Mills, 2008).[10] Hospitals in Glasgow treated a serious facial injury every six hours, whilst the number of knife-related facial trauma injuries is said to exceed 10,000 per year (Carnochan & McCluskey, 2010: 401).

Data reviewed by Squires et al., in 2008 indicated that, 'The rate of murder committed with a knife in Scotland is 3.5 times higher than that in England and Wales.... [while] levels of violent crime, in particular knife crime, have remained relatively constant for the last 40 years... High levels of knife carrying, gang violence and feuds between rival criminal gangs are common features, often fuelled by alcohol' (2008: 73; Forsyth et al., 2010). A substantial body of clinical research identified the Glasgow and Strathclyde regions of Scotland as notorious for gang violence involving knives reaching back to 1980 and earlier (Bleetman et al., 1997; Fraser et al., 2010; Leyland, 2006; Leyland & Dundas, 2010), long before these issues generated equivalent concern in England and Wales and launched the 'war against knife crime'. By the same token, as 'knife crime' has come under the glare of a national spotlight, the Strathclyde experiences have been drawn back into the public and political framing of the problem and the intervention strategies to address it (Fraser, 2015: 209). The region has also pioneered an often cited, apparently successful, collaborative public health intervention to tackle knife-related violence (Carnochan & McCluskey, 2010; Rainey et al., 2015; Williams et al., 2014). An evaluation of the initiative in 2014 reported that 'young men who engaged with CIRV greatly reduced their carriage of weapons (principally knives)… while gang-related youth reduced their rate of physical violence after engagement with [the project]'. In addition, 'there is evidence of an effect that lasting beyond the initial year … such evidence … goes some way to indicating the strength of association between the intervention and reduced offending' (Williams et al., 2014: 688).

Subsequently, the idea of a 'public health' approach has achieved something of a 'holy grail' status in efforts to tackle knife crime south of

---

[10] The Glasgow 'smile injury' occurred when the face was cut or slashed across both or either cheek, giving the appearance of widening the mouth, or smiling.

the border, even though the idea has been much more talked about than delivered and attempts to replicate the model have faltered (HASC, 2019, paras. 50–55). These are issues we will be exploring further in the final chapter of the book.

Yet despite increasing condemnation and legal prohibition, knife violence never went away entirely and, confined especially to less civilised contexts and cultures, it began to resurface in certain occupational or regional, criminal and gang cultures in the twentieth century. Rather paradoxically, whilst Gorn's (1985) study of lower class fighting practices in the American South adds support to a, frequently cited, under-lying 'honour code' motivating much bitter personal conflict it does so notwithstanding the sheer visceral brutality of the violence entailed—gouging eyes, tearing hair by the roots, biting and ripping away of facial features. Later in the 1950s and 60s, sociologists began to char-acterise new and emerging US gang cultures as reflecting an *inversion* of mainstream middle-class values (Cohen, 1955; Miller, 1958), although seldom was the cultural inversion so marked. Just as we noted the steep increase in woundings in England and Wales from the mid-1950s, in Chapter 1, as gang culture began to mark its reappearance in the USA, rates of knife violence appeared to increase.

Even though many commentators (Brown, 1975) had begun to acknowledge the enduring role of violence in American culture, the knife problem was frequently portrayed as a minority or immigrant culture issue—whites tended to use firearms (Lane, 1979), not least because discriminatory enforcement of gun laws restricted firearms to African Americans and immigrants (Johnson, 2014). At the same time, certain ethnic groups were deemed to have a particular affinity for knives, for example, Moreno's ethnographic study of Mexican-American gangs in the Pacific North West reports interviewees who, in earlier decades had observed knife fights between gang members. Rival gangs would 'jump' one another deploying street weapons such as knives, bicycle chains and clubs—'gunfire was rare'. One interviewee, a young girl in the 1950s, witnessed a knife fight between two men she knew to be 'Pachucos' (Mexican gang members), 'they could manipulate those blades like nobody's business' she remarked (Moreno, 2006: 132). And by the 1950s, as we have seen, public reaction against knife culture was beginning to mobilise against 'switch blades' and 'gravity knives' in a number of cities in the USA (Ben-Dan, 2018).[11] Rising public concern about knife violence in the USA coincided with two important films from the 1950s (and the original Broadway production of *West Side Story*, in 1957). Each featured knife violence. The first film was *Rebel without a Cause* (1955) in which Dean's character is goaded into a switchblade fight by the local gang leader, and *Twelve Angry Men* (1957) a jury room crime drama which features a 'widely available and easily purchased' switchblade as the murder weapon employed by the Hispanic defendant.

Since the passage of the 1958 knife prohibitions in New York, the laws have been subjected to aggressive but selective racist enforcement. Ben-Dan shows that 84% of those prosecuted for knife possession were of African-American or Latino ethnic origin, 'Blacks and Latinos are disproportionately arrested and prosecuted for gravity knife offenses because Blacks and Latinos are disproportionately stopped and frisked by police' (2018: 198). Compounding the discriminatory impact of the knife laws are provisions within the New York Penal Code allowing prosecutors to convert the misdemeanour offence to a felony where the knife is in the possession of someone with a previous conviction for any crime. Commentators from 'knife advocacy' publishing have also spoken out against the laws, a headline in *Blade Magazine* declared 'Ridiculous, Racist knife bans reinforce Inequality' (Shackleford, 2018), referencing to a long established perception that knife fighting was still largely the preserve of disreputable lower class, typically minority, delinquents. The title of Leney's, 2018 article comparing police enforcement of 'spring assisted knife laws' in Massachusetts and New York, speaks volumes: 'I thought only punks fought with knives' (Leney, 2018).

---

[11] These were not the first knife restriction laws in the USA, 1909 legislation in New York State had prohibited a defined range of weapons amidst concerns about immigrants, crime and disorder. Two years later similar concerns resulted in the 'Sullivan law', restricting the possession of small concealable handguns ('Saturday Night Specials'). In 1930 a number of knife types 'possessed with unlawful intent' were prohibited and in 1954 spring-activated switchblades ('flick-knives') were added to the prohibited list. By the late 1950s, following campaigning by the 'Committee to ban Teen-age Weapons' supported by the police, the state legislature was forced to act. Switchblades and gravity knives were prohibited irrespective of the purposes for which they were purchased or used. A Federal law followed shortly.

Knives and the Military

Despite such a dismissive modern judgement, knife fighting had made a brief and apparently honourable return for a whilst in the twentieth century. Military tacticians in both the First and Second World wars debated at length the role of the knife, and the bayonet, attached or unattached, in close quarters fighting. Senior officers discovered soldiers equipping themselves with knives for trench fighting. Todd, writing in 1938 explains how knife fighting, which had substantially diminished with the massed infantry battle tactics of the nineteenth century, found a new role in the gritty hand-to-hand fighting of trench warfare. 'The knife and the club are very ancient weapons... as old as man', he asserts, 'infinite in their form and utility... and their comparative simplicity, whether designed for cutting or thrusting, has made [the knife] the most democratic of weapons' (Todd, 1938: 139). And yet, despite the awesome power of modern weapons, during the First World War, combat conditions, placed a renewed emphasis upon 'individual initiative in combat... and the need for a tangible agency from which a bewildered enemy could run' leading to a greater emphasis upon 'actual physical shock - even hand to hand fighting' (ibid.) than had been seen in military encounters for many years. The trench knife and the bayonet were the principle tools of this tactical rethink. By World War Two American military training had also incorporated knife fighting and the Philippine 'Bolo Knife' that we encountered earlier became part of hand-to-hand combat training for troops facing jungle deployment.

When attached to the end of an infantryman's musket, the dagger became a *bayonette* (Akerman, 2012), the overall weapon now resembling the medieval pike (or long-bladed spear), a weapon for thrusting.

The bayonet, and new tactics of battle-fighting, were said to have proved their ruthless worth against the Jacobites at Culloden in 1746 (Prebble, 2002). The earliest bayonets were of a 'plug' type, slotted *inside* a rifle barrel, thereby preventing the rifle being fired (Stone, 2012). Something of this practice remained, centuries later, on the battlefields of WW1. Prior to launching themselves into no-man's-land, attacking troops might be ordered to *unload* their rifles for a bayonet charge. Such an apparently perverse instruction entailed two related aspects of military tactics and doctrine, connecting directly with the anthropomorphic connection between man and blade that we have encountered in earlier knife fighting cultures and contexts. In the first place it reflected a projection of the paralysing terror presumed to be experienced by defending troops confronted by the waves of cold steel bearing down upon them and, secondly, it underlined the discipline and resolve (bravery) required to advance to within arm's length of an opponent's position, there to engage in visceral hand-to-hand fighting, with such enemy as remained (Monteath, 2019). The main purpose, therefore, of bayonet drill, was less its *direct* value as a battlefield tactic and rather more for its disciplinary capacity to instil the attitudes of absolute obedience and 'intimate brutality', individually and collectively, within a body of troops. Even as the reality and the battlefield injury statistics showed that many soldiers appeared to avoid bayoneting the enemy (Bourke, 2000; Grossman, 1995), military training redoubled its efforts to turn conscripts into killers, demanding a 'screaming war face' as the trainee acquired the appropriate moral convictions enabling them to repeatedly thrust bayonets into dummies. As suggested by Lee (1985),[12] 'the fixing of bayonets is more than the fixing of steel to a rifle, it puts iron into the soul of the soldier' (quoted in Stone, 2012). Whilst this reiterates the symbolic connections between manly virtues and weapons, this 'conditioned aggression' gives us a further clue to the uncomfortable contemporary reactions to 'knife violence' arising in our civilised modernity. The morality, intent and resolve required to thrust a blade

---

[12] Lee, R. G. 1985. *Introduction to Battlefield Weapons Systems and Technology*, 2nd Edition. London: Brassey's.

into the torso of a fellow human being speaks to an alien and dehuman-
ising 'will to violence' in the supposedly distorted value systems of street
gangs.[13] Yet if we treat knife crime, in its entirety, as a kind of signal
crime or disorder (Innes, 2004), this is undoubtedly a part of what is
being signalled.

If this image of brutal bladed violence has troubled British culture,
we have managed to cover it up uncomfortably well. Cy Endfield's
epic war film *Zulu* (1964) which told the bloody imperial story of the
defence of Rourke's Drift in which an outnumbered force of British
troops fought off an overwhelming force of Zulu warriors in January
1879. Bayonets are much in evidence, stabbing black bodies. Apparently
more Victoria Crosses were awarded for this bout of colonial violence
than for any other engagement fought by the British Army. Only four
years later, British television broadcast the first episodes of *Dad's Army*,
a sit-com based upon the antics of the Home Guard during World War
Two. One central character was the doddery Corporal Jones, himself a
veteran of the Sudanese wars (of the 1890s). Jones was a firm advocate
of the bayonet, coining a catch-phrase telling how the Sudanese warriors
(referred to as 'Fuzzy-Wuzzies'—Kipling, 1892) 'didn't like it up them'.
Stabbing as racist humour had never garnered so many laughs. Another
twist in our complex relationship with blades and racism.[14]

A Global Criminology of Knife Violence?

As we have learned a great deal from a cultural history of knives and
blades and the values entailed within knife fighting cultures, both of
which throw more light upon the problematisation of 'knife crime'
we still have a way to go in our wider contextualisation of the issue.
Following an international review of violent and weapon-related youth

---

[13] Not that all 'knife violence' does involve attempted killing, the practice of simply 'marking'
victims, often with facial scars, also needs understanding.

[14] A further irony of the 'fuzzy-wuzzy' story is that, although Kipling's poem recycled a patronising form of racism, it painted the Sudanese warriors as brave adversaries—'the finest of the
lot', who broke the British lines. Whereas in Corporal Jones' catchphrase, these warriors were
no match for British valour or British steel.

crime intervention programmes, Silvestri concluded, 'the UK stands out, among English-speaking and European countries, for the media and political attention it devotes to knife-related violence. Yet, despite the wealth of anti-knife crime initiatives (e.g. enforcement strategies, campaigns and awareness programmes) in this country, there is very little research carried out' either to understand the underlying causes of knife violence or to assess the effectiveness of social prevention programmes (Silvestri, 2009: 49). When and where, for instance, is knife crime a problem, and what makes it so? International context helps give us some of the answers.

There exists a contemporary, but rather uneven, international criminology of knife violence. It is uneven because only certain cultures problematise knife violence in quite the way of the UK. As the recent global homicide survey by the United Nations Office for Drugs and Crime (UNODC, 2019) has acknowledged, 'Countries where sharp objects are the main mechanism of killing tend to have low homicide rates' (UNODC, 2019: 19–20). This, allied with Shepherd and Brennan's observation that knife injuries reported to hospital A&E departments after 2000, 'may have become more serious' (2008: 187) may give us some clues towards understanding the nature of the reaction to knife violence in civilised modern cultures, Britain especially. A BBC report of 2009 (BBC, 2008) which compared knife crime rates in London, Paris, Moscow, New York, Copenhagen, Tokyo and Madrid found increasing rates of youth violence in some of these cities, although this was not always matched by significantly rising concerns, nor even by common explanations proffered, although gang cultures were mentioned by several commentators, racism by others and a diminishing confidence in authority.

The UNODC *Global Homicide Report* (2019), referred to earlier, comparing the Americas and Europe, identified 8 societies where 'sharp objects' account for the largest number of homicides: Poland, Hungary, Slovenia, Guyana and Cuba, where 'sharp objects' account for a *majority* of killings, and Sweden, Canada and Austria, where they are the *most frequently employed* murder weapon, although not accounting for a majority of homicides. In England and Wales, the proportion of recorded violence involving knives hovered around 7% in the decade after 2000, roughly the same proportion as in the USA (6.3%), although in the USA, this was exceeded by firearm violence (at 8.8% of all recorded violence) (US DOJ, 2008: Table 66). The *International Criminal Victimization Survey* of 2007 reported on knife violence rates for a list of 'contact crimes' (robbery, sexual offences and assaults) for a range of 30 developed countries. Knife-enabled offending in England and Wales and/or the UK as a whole exceeded the average rate in each type of offence, with only Spain, Portugal, Switzerland, Mexico and Iceland revealing higher rates of knife crime (ICVS, 2007: 284). Repeating the same exercise for major cities, the ICVS found that for the three contact crimes reported on, proportions of knife crime were as follows (Fig. 2.2).

Only in respect of assaults and threats does the proportion of knife-enabled contact crimes exceed the average of the cities studied, although four other cities exceed the London rate. As regards sex offences committed with the aid of a knife, London falls precisely on the cities average, only exceeded by Madrid, whereas eight other European cities have higher proportions of knife-enabled robbery. An apparent 'London effect' regarding race and violent crime in England and Wales later has been noted before (EHRC, 2010; Elliott-Cooper, 2021; Squires et al, 2008), but there may be something about the way that rates of knife-enabled assaultive violence are recorded and reported in the

City	robbery	Sex offences against women	Assaults and threats
Average	**18.6**	**9**	**9.4**
London	18	9	16
Madrid	36	12	25
Istanbul	41	9	29
Amsterdam	22	7	11
Lisbon	28	3	19
Paris	23	0	10
Rome	26	3	9
Vienna	24	0	7
Zurich	22	0	20

Fig. 2.2 Proportions of knife-enabled contact crimes: rates reported in the 2007 ICVS (*Source* ICVS, 2007, Appendix 9, page 285)

London-centric media that goes some way to account for British reactions to knife crime.[15] As Chakelian's fact-check for the *New Statesman* reported in 2018 'London is the safest *global* city and one of the safest cities in the world'. This claim was endorsed by the global *Safe Cities Index*, which put London as the 20th safest out of sixty examined (and rising to 14th overall by 2019: SCI, 2019) and *Safearound* which put London as 46th safest out of 148 world cities.

Further clarification comparing the British reaction to knife crime to recorded knife victimisation rates in European countries can be derived from the WHO European knife crime survey (WHO, 2010: 90). The following graph depicts age-standardised mortality rates per 100,000 males aged between 10 and 29, from all causes of homicide and from knives and sharp instruments.

At first sight, the comparative distribution depicted in Fig. 2.3 might not suggest the UK as the country most likely to be experiencing a 'knife crime' crisis. Indeed with only four out of the 35 European states reporting a lower overall homicide rate, and only four with an appreciably lower rate of *knife-enabled* homicide, the UK might not be the first place to start exploring this phenomenon. Except, of course, for the fact that what matters as regards the problematisation of crime is not so much the underlying rate of such incidents but, as we have said, the way these are perceived, understood and responded to. As we suggested in Chapter 1, societies with low homicide rates and which proclaim significant law and order traditions are likely to react more animatedly to each homicide than societies where murder is commonplace; stabbings and acute interpersonal violence resulting in fatalities, especially when perpetrated by young people, and resulting in the deaths of young people, are considered especially alarming. We have referred to these events as 'signal crimes' (Innes, 2004) and signal crime *trends*. What they appear to signal are decivilising processes closely tracking our unequal, divided and discriminatory culture: the brutalisation of youth social relationships and the establishment of gang cultures where life is cheap. And although young people are by no means the majority perpetrators of

---

[15] This 'London effect' is also reflected in the fact that some 50% of police stop and search interventions are undertaken by the Metropolitan police, as we discuss later, in Chapter 4.

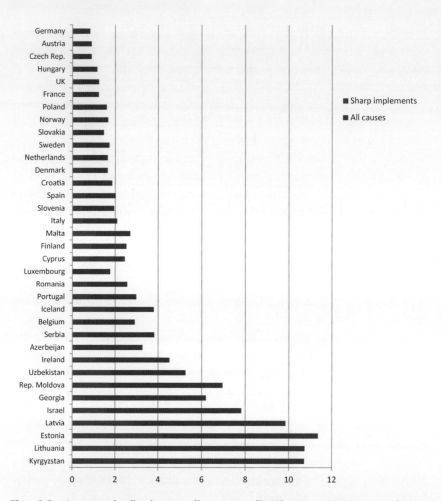

Fig. 2.3 Age-standardised mortality rates (SMR) per 100,000 population amongst males aged 10–29 years from <u>all causes of homicide</u> and from sharp implements in selected countries in the WHO European Region 2004-206 (*Source* WHO and European Mortality Database)

knife violence, their lives are rendered cheap because many young people have become seemingly expendable (Squires & Goldsmith, 2017). It matters not that these conditions are the result of established social and economic processes—even explicit *policy* decisions—for young people are simply, albeit violently, asserting their sense of self and identity, or defending themselves, in brutalising and impoverishing environments. We want them to stop, there are better ways; in the meantime we want to *stop them*, for each death is a sign of a wider social and cultural crisis *confronting us* and *condemning our society* in roughly equal measure. Knife crime is both a symptom of our crisis and yet, in other respects, for some, a *solution* to it. It represents a crisis for those who care about inequality, racism and youthful violence but at the same time it is a solution in that it appears to confirm that the issue lies firmly at the feet of 'other people', a problem of 'them', even if they are victims of inequality and exclusion and have been made to be like this. The entanglement of these contrasting perspectives, and the ideological and political assumptions underpinning each, define to a large degree, our current predicament with 'knife crime'.

In societies where the homicide rate has fallen significantly, in Japan, for instance, as the homicide rate has fallen, so the proportion of killings attributable to 'sharp objects' has increased to some 25% of total homicides (UNODC data, 2014). And despite having one of the lowest international homicide rates, Japan has recorded the most numerous mass killing with knives. Whilst the rest of the world has become preoccupied by the mass shooting phenomenon, a former care worker with declared Nazi-sympathies, attacked residents at a care home near Tokyo, killing 19 and seriously injuring 26. In Australia, by 2011, where a less pronounced overall homicide decline is evident, 'sharp objects' had come to represent the most common means of killing (some 41% of homicides). In England and Wales, the 285 fatal stabbings in 2018, representing 39% of recorded homicides, were the highest knife homicide figures since WW2. Even so, this was still very close to a European average as the WHO report noted: 'overall, about 40% of homicides in the European Region are due to knives and sharp implements' (WHO, 2010: v), although the range stretched from over 60% of homicides (victims aged between 10 and 29) in Sweden and Estonia, to less than 20% in Luxembourg, Georgia and Azerbaijan (WHO, 2010: 92).

What may have been an average for Europe, however, signalled a powerfully decivilising trend in Britain. For instance, of the countries identified in Fig. 2.3, only Finland, Ireland and the UK responded affirmatively to a WHO survey acknowledging that 'knife crime' was a big problem and a major social and political priority in their respective countries and for which a range of national policy interventions were in place (WHO, 2010: 76, 92). Lithuania, Israel, Belgium and Italy, also acknowledged that knife crime was a *growing* problem but had no specific policy interventions in place. Clearly the available recorded evidence regarding the scale of youthful knife violence did not translate directly into a public or political priority to tackle it. Societal reactions clearly differed.

In the UK, this most visceral form of interpersonal violence seemed to confront a progressive trend hitherto apparently assured by a declining homicide rate; in Carter-Wood's terms it represented the 'shadow' on our progress (Carter-Wood, 2015). It was a form of brutality perceived (though not always accurately) to be the especial preserve of the young, marking a significant generational disconnect nurtured and exacerbated in Britain during the decade and a half preoccupied by the perceived 'anti-social' tendencies of youth (Haydon & Scraton, 2000; Squires, 2008; Squires & Stephen, 2005). Like mugging in the 1970s, knife crime had also acquired a misleadingly racialised aspect, pointing to continuing racial tensions, reflected in heavy-handed street policing encounters, especially stop and search, disproportionately endured by young black men (Long, 2018). Just as, in the wake of austerity, economic inequalities and social divisions were increasingly manifesting themselves across a range of stalled indicators of well-being, social mobility and social inclusion (the marginalised, the NEET generation, the disconnected, 'feral' youth, the 'left behind') so the young denizens of 'broken Britain' appeared to exhibit a deeply anachronistic facility for knife violence.

Across the English-speaking world, only Canada, Australia and the UK appear to have devoted much explicitly *criminological* attention to knife crime. In Canada, three out of ten homicides involved a knife and roughly 50% of perpetrators were aged under 25, but crucially, knife violence rates were stable (Dauvergne, 2008). A number of research initiatives in Australia drew attention to the demographic profile and social circumstances associated with knife carriage. Some of this work was collated by the Australian Institute of Criminology (AIC) in 2011 (Bartels, 2011) which noted a 'dramatic increase' in knife-involved homicides and attempted homicides. The research report went onto describe differing patterns of knife carriage and use in different offender cohorts whilst reviewing the often contrasting state by state responses (education, prevention, enforcement and sentencing) being adopted. The AIC closed by quoting from a UK report by the CCJS which itself had noted, the whole question of 'knife crime':

> Still suffers from a lack of useful, specific, reliable, longitudinal research on the nature, extent, cause, motivation, frequency and possible growth of knife carrying. Without such research, designing and implementing programmes to reduce the incidence of knife carrying will be difficult. (Eades et al., 2007: 14)

In an effort to address this suggested research deficit, a wide range of studies have sought to bring greater understanding to the problem of 'knife crime'. The best of this work often involves qualitative work with young people themselves and, perhaps inevitably, much of this work overlaps with wider research on youth violence and gangs, much of the latter often already loaded with its own conceptual baggage and assumptions (Alexander, 2008; Hallsworth & Young, 2004, 2008). As Bartels noted, knife crime research was 'at times contested' (2011: ix) whilst too many knife crime 'interventions', though popular, lacked reliable research support, for as Eades noted back in 2006: 'without such research, constructing responses that might achieve even small decreases in illegal knife use will amount to fumbling around in the dark' (Eades, 2006). Our argument is that despite a welter of committees and enquiries, government strategies, reviews, policy papers and think tank reports, seminars and knowledge exchanges (APPG, 2019; Frater & Gamman, 2020; Golding & McClory, 2009; Kinsella, 2011; MOPAC, 2017; Royal Armouries, 2007; Ward et al., 2011; Youth Violence Commission, 2018) and the creation of a virtual 'knife crime' industry (see Chapter 6), things are little better a decade and a half further on. Too many 'knife crime strategies' remain based upon too many unexamined assumptions about the 'usual suspects' and familiar policies. These include high profile police enforcement and tougher penalties, although risk-led education, public health diversion and prevention interventions also feature, sometimes fronted by celebrities and sports stars or reformed former gang members. Later in the book we will outline some of the key interpretations of 'knife crime' surfacing in British debates and reflecting upon the intervention strategies deriving from them, drawing conclusions from the best available recent research, research which points towards rather more holistic, grounded, evidentially validated and long-term strategies for addressing 'knife crime' as an aspect of youth violence, although this is certainly not to concede that 'youth' has any kind of monopoly on knife violence.

In the following chapter we will explore what we have described as the first phase of explicit mobilisation constructing the phenomenon of 'knife crime' in the British context. This includes a mass media preoccupied by 'bad news', a sceptical public seeking reassurance, a law and order lobby keen to re-establish its credentials and above all an overstretched police force facing profound operational, legal, legitimacy and resourcing challenges. At this point, 'knife crime'—like mugging in the 1970s—offered a timely opportunity to reassert both purpose and response.

Learning Exercise 9: Analysis Exercise

The societies with the highest levels of knife crime do not appear to be the most alarmed by this phenomenon.
Why might this be? What social characteristics of certain societies appear to be associated with a high level of sensitivity to knife crime?

References

Ager, B. (2011, March 29). Viking weapons and warfare. *BBC History*.

Akerman, J. Y. (2012). Notes on the origin and history of the bayonet. *Archaeologia, 38*(2), 422–430.

Alexander, C. (2008, June). *(Re)thinking gangs*. The Runnymede Trust.

APPG (All Party Parliamentary Group). (2019). *All party parliamentary group on knife crime*. Barnado's/RedThread.

Barlow, S. P. (2020, December 1). Why case knives aren't just for collectors. *Knives Illustrated*.

Bartels, L. (2011). *Knife crime in Australia: Incidence, aetiology and responses.* Australian Institute of Criminology, Technical and Background Paper 45.

Bartie, A. (2010). Moral panics and Glasgow gangs: Exploring 'the new wave of Glasgow Hooliganism', 1965–1970. *Contemporary British History, 24*(3), 385–408.

Batey, N. R., & McBain, G. C. (1967). Injury by stabbing. *Scottish Medical Journal, 12*(7), 251.

BBC News. (2008, July 16). *Knife crime cuts a global trail.* BBC NEWS | World | Europe.

Ben-Dan, Z. (2018). Law and or law and order without justice: A case study of gravity knife legislation in New York City. *City University of New York Law Review, 21*(2), 177–224.

Bethge, W. (2007). The Bolo knife – An indispensable utensil in the Philippine household. *Insights-Philippines*.

Biressi, A. (2001). *Crime, fear and the law in true crime stories.* Palgrave Macmillan.

Bleetman, A., Perry, C. H., Crawford, R., & Swann, I. J. (1997). Effect of Strathclyde police initiative 'operation blade' on accident and emergency attendances due to assault. *Journal of Accident and Emergency Medicine, 14*, 153–156.

Blockfort. (n.d.). Live by the sword. In *Top 10 video game swords* (block-fort.com).

Boschi, D. (1998). Homicide and knife fighting in Rome, 1845–1914. In P. Spierenburg (Ed.), *Men and violence: Gender; honour; and rituals in modern Europe and America.* Ohio State University Press.

Bourke, J. (2000). *An intimate history of killing: Face-to-face killing in twentieth-century warfare.* Granta.

Braid, M. (1999, March 3). The jungle massacre: African rebels who revel in their Machete genocide. *The Independent*.

Brown, K. S., et al. (2009). Fire as an engineering tool of early modern humans. *Science, 325*(5942), 859–862.

Brown, R. M. (1975). *Strain of violence: Historical studies of American violence and vigilantism.* Oxford University Press.

Callaway, E. (2009, August 13). Earliest fired knives improved stone age toolkit. *New Scientist*.

Carlson, J. (2015). *Citizen-protectors: The everyday politics of guns in an age of decline.* Oxford University Press.

Carnochan, J., & McCluskey, K. (2010). Violence, culture and policing in Scotland. In D. Donnelly & K. Scott (Eds.), *Policing Scotland*. Routledge.

Carter-Wood, J. (2015). *Violence and crime in nineteenth century England: The shadow of our refinement*. Routledge.

Cassidy, W. L. (1997). *The complete book of knife fighting*. Paladin Press.

Chakelian, A. (2018, April 3). The truth about violent crime in London: Busting myths about the 'lawless' capital. *The New Statesman*.

Chinn, C. (2019). *Peaky blinders: The real story of Birmingham's most notorious gangs*. John Blake Publishing.

Cohen, A. K. (1955). *Delinquent boys: The culture of the gang*. Free Press.

Conley, C. (1999). The agreeable recreation of fighting. *Journal of Social History, 33*(1, Fall), 57–72.

Conway, D. I., McMahon, A. D., & Goodall, C. (2010). The scar on the face of Scotland: Deprivation and facial injuries in Scotland. *Journal of Trauma, 68*(3), 644–649.

Cook, E. A., & Walklate, S. (2020, June 27). Gendered objects and gendered spaces: The invisibilities of 'knife' crime. *Current Sociology [Online]*, 1–16.

Curtis, L. P. (2001). *Jack the ripper and the London Press*. Yale University Press.

Curtis, P. (2008, September 4). Top exam board asks schools to destroy book containing knife poem. *The Guardian*.

Dauvergne, M. (2008). *Knives and violent crime in Canada*. Statistics Canada. statcan.gc.ca.

Davies, A. (1998). Youth gangs, masculinity and violence in late Victorian Manchester and Salford. *Journal of Social History, 32*(2), 349–369.

Davies, A. (1999, January). These viragoes are no less cruel than the lads': Young women, gangs and violence in late Victorian late Manchester and Salford. *The British Journal of Criminology, 39*(1), 72–89.

Davies, A. (2007). The Scottish Chicago: From hooligans to gangsters in inter-war Glasgow. *Cultural and Social History, 4*(2), 511–527.

Davies, A. (2008). *The gangs of Manchester*. Milo Books.

Dean, T. (1994). Criminal justice in 15th century Bologna. In T. Dean & K. J. P. Lowe (Eds.), *Crime, society and the law in renaissance Italy*. Cambridge University Press.

Dobie, F. (1931, April). Bowie and the bowie knife. *Southwest Review, 16*(3), 351–368.

Drageset, D. (2013). Constructing 'dark' celebrity: The case of Anders Breivik. *Pacific Journalism Review, 19*(2), 70–85.

Durham, A. M., Elrod, H. P., & Kinkade, P. T. (1995). Images of crime and justice: Murder and the 'true crime' genre. *Journal of Criminal Justice, 23*(2), 143–152.

Eades, C. (2006). The year of the knife. In *Criminal justice matters* (pp. 10–12), No. 66 Winter 2006/07. CCJS.

Eades, C., Grimshaw, R., Silvestri, A., & Solomon, E. (2007). *'Knife crime' a review of evidence and policy* (2nd ed.). Centre for Crime and Justice Studies. Available at: http://www.crimeandjustice.org.uk/opus439/ccjs_knife_report. pdf.

Edgar, M. (1949). Ballads of the knife-men. *Western Folklore, 8*(1), 53–57.

Eisner, M. (2014). From swords to words: Does macro-level change in self-control predict long-term variation in levels of homicide? *Crime and Justice, 43*(1), 65–134.

Elias, N. (1983). *The civilising process.* Blackwell [Original publication, 1939].

Elliott-Cooper, A. (2021). *Black resistance to British policing.* Manchester University Press.

Equality and Human Rights Commission. (2010). *Stop and think: A critical review of the use of stop and search powers in England and Wales.* EHRC.

Ericson, E. E., & Shulman, D. (1937). Bowie knife. *American Speech, 12*(1), 77–79.

Ewalt, D. (2005, August 31). The knife. *Forbes Magazine.*

Fagan, J., & Wilkinson, D. (2000). *Situational contexts of gun use by young males in inner cities.* US Department of Justice, National Criminal Justice Reference Service.

Flanders, J. (2011). *The invention of murder.* Harper Press.

Forsyth, A., Khan, F., & McKinlay, W. (2010). Is there a 'booze n' blades culture' in Scotland? Evidence from young offenders. *Scottish Journal of Criminal Justice Studies, 16*, 32–46.

Fracassini, C. (2005, September 25). Scotland second in Europe for murder. *Sunday Times.*

Fraser, A. (2013). Street habitus: Gangs, territorialism and social change in Glasgow. *Journal of Youth Studies, 16*(8), 970–985.

Fraser, A. (2015). *Urban legends: Gang identity in the post-industrial city.* Oxford University Press.

Fraser, A., Burman, M., Batchelor, S., & McVie, S. (2010). *Youth violence in Scotland: Literature review.* Scottish Centre for Crime and Justice Research.

Frater, A., & Gamman, L. (2020). *Beyond knife crime: Towards a design-led approach to reducing youth violence.* University of the Arts London's Strategic Priorities Initiative.

Frevert, U. (1998). The taming of the Nobel Ruffian: Male violence and duelling in early modern Germany. In P. Spierenburg (Ed.), *Men and violence: Gender; honour; and rituals in modern Europe and America*. Ohio State University Press.

Gallant, T. W. (2000, April). Honor, masculinity, and ritual knife fighting in nineteenth-century Greece. *The American Historical Review, 105*(2), 359–382.

Gibbons, A. (2009, April 2). Oldest stone blades uncovered. *Science Magazine*, AAAS.

Gibson, W. (1994). *Warrior dreams: Violence and manhood in post-Vietnam America*. Wang & Hill.

Golding, R., & McClory, J. (2009). *Getting to the point: Reducing gun and knife crime in Britain: Lessons from abroad*. Policy Exchange.

Gooderson, P. (2013). Noisy and dangerous boys: The slogging gang phenomenon in late nineteenth century Birmingham. *Midland History, 38*(1), 58–79.

Gorn, E. J. (1985). "Gouge and bite, pull hair and scratch": The social significance of fighting in the Southern Backcountry. *American Historical Review, 90*(1), 18–43.

Grossman, D. (1995). *On killing: The psychological cost of learning to kill in war and society*. Back Bay Books.

Haag, P. (2016). *The gunning of America*. Basic Books.

Hainsworth, S. V., Delaney, R. J., & Rutty, G. N. (2008). How sharp is sharp? Towards quantification of the sharpness and penetration ability of kitchen knives used in stabbings. *International Journal of Legal Medicine, 122*, 281–291.

Hallsworth, S., & Young, T. (2004). Getting real about gangs. *Criminal Justice Matters*. London/CCJS, p. 55.

Hallsworth, S., & Young, T. (2008). Gang talk and gang talkers: A Critique. *Crime, Media, Culture, 4*(2), 175–195.

Haydon, D., & Scraton, P. (2000, September). 'Condemn a little more, understand a little less': The political context and rights' implications of the domestic and European rulings in the Venables-Thompson case. *Journal of Law and Society, 27*(3), 416–448.

Hern, E., Glazebrook, W., & Beckett, M. (2005). Reducing knife crime. *British Medical Journal, 330*(7502), 1221–1222.

Hoefle, S. W. (2006). Twisting the knife: Frontier violence in the central Amazon. *The Journal of Peasant Studies, 33*(3), 445–478.

Holligan, C. P., & Deuchar, R. (2009). Territorialities in Scotland: Perceptions of young people in Glasgow. *Journal of Youth Studies, 12*(6), 731–746.

Home Affairs Select Committee (HASC). (2009, June 2). *Knife crime: Seventh report of session 2008–09*, HC 112. The Stationery Office.

Home Affairs Select Committee (HASC). (2019). *Report: Serious youth violence.* 16th Report of Session 2017–19. HC 1016. House of Commons.

Hughes, N. S., McCauley, A. M., & Crichton, J. M. H. (2012). Kitchen knives and homicide by mentally disordered offenders: A systematic analysis of homicide inquiries in England 1994–2010. *The Journal of Forensic Psychiatry and Psychology, 23*(5–6), 559–570.

Hughes, S. (1998). Men of steel: Dueling, honor and politics in liberal Italy. In P. Spierenburg (Ed.), *Men and violence: Gender, honour, and rituals in modern Europe and America.* Ohio State University Press.

ICVS. (2007). *International criminal victimization survey of 2007 United Nations UNICRI.*

Innes, M. (2004). Signal crimes and signal disorders: Notes on deviance as communicative action. *British Journal of Sociology, 55*, 355.

Johnson, N. (2014). *Negroes and the gun: The black tradition of arms.* New York: Prometheus Books.

Kiernan, V. G. (1988). *The duel in European history: Honour and the reign of the aristocracy.* Oxford University Press.

Kinsella, B. (2011, February). *Tackling knife crime together: A review of local anti-knife crime projects.* Home Office.

Kipling, R. (1892 [1941]). Fuzzy-wuzzy (Soudan expeditionary force). In T. S. Eliot (Ed.), *A choice of Kipling's verse.* Faber and Faber.

Kopel, D., Cramer, C., & Olson, J. E. (2013). Knives and the second amendment. *University of Michigan Journal of Law Reform, 47*(1), 167–215.

Lane, R. (1979). *Violent death in the city: Suicide, accident and murder in 19th century Philadelphia.* Harvard University Press.

Larke-Walsh, G. S. (2019). The king's shilling': How peaky blinders uses the experience of war to justify and celebrate toxic masculinity. *The Journal of Popular Television, 7*(1), 39–56.

Lawrence, M. J. (2020). *American bowie knife fighting techniques from the 1880s.* Independently Published.

Lee, R. G. (1985). *Introduction to battlefield weapons systems and technology* (2nd ed.). Brassey's.

Leney, K. J. (2018). 'I thought only punks fought with knives': Comparing criminal enforcement of carrying spring-assisted knives in Massachusetts with New York. *Suffolk University Law Review, 51*, 479.

Leyland, A. H. (2006). Homicides involving knives and other sharp objects in Scotland, 1981–2003. *Journal of Public Health, 28*(2), 145–147.

Leyland, A. H., & Dundas, R. (2010). The social patterning of deaths due to assault in Scotland, 1980–2005: Population based study. *Journal of Epidemiology and Community Health, 64*(5), 432–439.

Long, L. (2018). *Perpetual suspects: A critical race theory of black and mixed-race experiences of policing.* Palgrave Macmillan.

Loriega, J. (1999). *Sevillian steel: The traditional knife-fighting arts of Spain.* Paladin Press.

Malik, N. S., Munoz, B., de Courcey, C., Imran, R., Lee, K. C., & Chernbumroong, S. (2020, March 1). Violence related knife injuries in a UK City; epidemiology and impact on secondary care resources. *The Lancet/EClinical Medicine, 20,* 100296.

McKeganey, N., & Norrie, J. (2000). Association between illegal drugs and weapon-carrying in young people in Scotland: Schools' survey. *British Medical Journal, 320*(7240), 982–984.

McLaughlin, M. (2019, June 5). Glasgow shed 'murder capital' reputation as youth crime falls dramatically. *The Times.*

McLemore, D. C. (2017). *Bowie and big knife fighting system.* McLemore, Independent Publication.

McLemore, D. C. (2018). *Advanced bowie techniques: The finer points of fighting with a large knife.* CreateSpace Independent Publishing Platform.

McNaughton, P. R. (1970). The throwing knife in African history. *African Arts, 3*(2), 54–89.

Mele, G. (2018, September 10). *Sette Colpi: Understanding the seven blows of the sword in Armizare—International Armizare Society.*

Miller, W. (1958). Lower class culture as a generating milieu of gang delinquency. *Journal of Social Issues, 14,* 5–20.

Mills, R. (2008, October 27). Surgeon says hospitals treat a knife victim every six hours. *The Daily Express.*

Milne, N. C. (2010). *Scottish culture and traditions during the late 17th and early 18th centuries.* Paragon Publishing.

Monteath, P. (2019, November 7). A short, sharp history of the bayonet. *The Conversation.*

MOPAC. (2017). *The London knife crime strategy.* Greater London Authority.

Moreno, M. (2006). Mexican American street gangs, migration, and violence in the Yakima valley. *The Pacific Northwest Quarterly, 97*(3), 131–141.

Nye, R. (1998). The end of the modern French duel. In P. Spierenburg (Ed.), *Men and violence: Gender; honour; and rituals in modern Europe and America.* Ohio State University Press.

Oakeshott, E. (1991). *Records of the medieval sword.* Boydell Press.

Oakeshott, E. (2018). *The sword in the age of chivalry.* Boydell Press.

O'Donnell, I. (2002). Unlawful killing past and present (New Series). *Irish Jurist, 37,* 56–90.

O'Donnell, I. (2005). Lethal violence in Ireland, 1841 to 2003: Famine, celibacy and parental pacification. *The British Journal of Criminology, 45*(5), 671–695.

Orchard, A. (1997). *Dictionary of Norse Myth and legend.* Cassell.

Patrick, J. (1973). *A Glasgow gang observed.* Neil Wilson Publishing.

Pearson, G. (1983). *Hooligan: A history of respectable fears.* Macmillan.

Pentecost, D. (2016). *Put 'em down, Take 'em out!: Knife fighting techniques from Folsom Prison.* Paladin Press.

Polk, K. (1994). *When men kill: Scenarios of masculine violence.* Cambridge University Press.

Prebble, J. H. (2002). *Culloden.* Pimlico Books.

Pridemore, W. A., & Freilich, J. D. (2005). Gender equity, traditional masculine culture, and female homicide victimization. *Journal of Criminal Justice, 33*(3), 213–223.

Quattrocchi, V. (1992). *Sicilian blade: The art of Sicilian stiletto fighting.* Desert Publications.

Rainey, S. R., Simpson, J., & Page, S. (2015). The impact of violence reduction initiatives on emergency department attendance. *Scottish Medical Journal, 60*(2), 90–94.

Royal Armouries. (2007). *Tackling knife crime: A review of literature on knife crime in the UK.* A report for the Royal Armouries Museum. Leicester, Perpetuity Research & Consultancy International (PRCI) Ltd.

Russell, R., Metraux, D., & Tohen, M. (2017). Cultural influences on suicide in Japan. *Psychiatry and Clinical Neuroscience Frontier Review, 71,* 2–5.

Ryan, R. (1999). *Master of the blade: Secrets of the deadly art of knife fighting.* Paladin Press.

Safe Cities Index. (2019). Urban security and resilience in an interconnected world. *The Economist,* Intelligence Unit.

Satia, P. (2018). *Empire of guns: The violent making of the industrial revolution.* Duckworth.

Shackleford, S. (2018, July 24). Ridiculous, racist knife bans reinforce inequality. *Blade Magazine.*

Shepherd, J., & Brennan, I. (2008, July 26). Tackling knife violence: Emergency departments should contribute to local crime reduction partnerships. *British Medical Journal*: Editorial, *337*, 187–188.

Shoemaker, R. B. (2001). Male honour and the decline of public violence in eighteenth-century London. *Social History, 26*, 190–208.

Shoemaker, R. B. (2002). The taming of the duel: Masculinity, honour and ritual violence in London, 1660–1800. *The Historical Journal, 45*(3), 525–545.

Silvestri, A. (2009). Young people, 'knife' and 'gun' crime: Policy in an evidence vacuum. *Criminal Justice Matters*, No. 76. London, Centre for Crime and Justice Studies.

Smith, G. T. (1999). *The state and the culture of violence in London: 1769–1840*. Ph.D. Thesis, University of Toronto.

Spierenburg, P. (1994). Faces of violence: Homicide trends and cultural meanings: Amsterdam, 1431–1816. *Journal of Social History, 27*(4), 701–716.

Spierenburg, P. (1998). Knife fighting and popular codes of honour in early modern Amsterdam. In P. Spierenburg (Ed.), *Men and violence: Gender, honour; and rituals in modern Europe and America*. Ohio State University Press.

Spierenberg, P. (2008). *A history of murder: Personal violence in Europe from the middle-ages to the present*. The Polity Press.

Squires, P. (Ed.). (2008). *ASBO nation: The criminalisation of nuisance*. The Policy Press.

Squires, P. (2018). Semi-automatics for the people: The marketing of a new kind of man. In J. Carlson, K. A. Goss, & H. Shapira (Eds.), *Gun studies: Interdisciplinary approaches*. Routledge.

Squires, P., & Goldsmith, C. (2017). Broken society, anti-social contracts, failing state? Rethinking youth marginality. In S. Blackman & R. Rogers (Eds.), *Youth marginality in Britain: Contemporary studies of austerity*. The Policy Press.

Squires, P., Silvestri, A., Grimshaw, R., & Solomon, E. (2008). *Street weapons commission evidence: Guns, knives and street violence*. CCJS, Kings College.

Squires, P., & Stephen, D. (2005). *Rougher justice: Anti-social behaviour and young people*. Willan.

Stone, J. (2012). The point of the bayonet. *Technology and Culture, 53*(4), 885–908.

Thakur, D. (2019). Tactical buyers guide for 2020. *Knives Illustrated Magazine*. https://www.knivesillustrated.com/knives-illustrated-tactical-buyers-guide-2020.

Thomas, E. S. (1925, January–June). The African throwing knife. *The Journal of the Royal Anthropological Institute of Great Britain and Ireland, 55*, 129–145.

Todd, F. P. (1938). The knife and club in trench warfare. *The Journal of the American Military History Foundation, 2*(3, Fall), 139–153.

Tribe, H. C., Harris, A., & Kneebone, R. (2018). Life on a knife edge: Using simulation to engage young people in issues surrounding knife crime. *Advances in Simulation, 3*, Article 20.

UNODC (United Nations Office of Drugs and Crime). (2014). *Global study on homicide*. Vienna: United Nations.

UNODC (United Nations Office of Drugs and Crime). (2019). *Global study on homicide*. United Nations.

US DOJ. (2008). *Criminal victimisation in the United States*. Table 66. Washington, DC, May 2011, NCJ 231173.

Verwimp, P. (2006). Machetes and firearms: The organisation of massacres in Rwanda. *Journal of Peace Research, 43*(1), 5–22.

Vollman, W. T. (2005). *Rising up and rising down: Some thoughts on violence, freedom and urgent means*. Ecco/HarperCollins.

Wacquant, L. (2001). Deadly symbiosis: When ghetto and prison meet and mesh. *Punishment and Society, 3*(1), 95–134.

Ward, L., Nicholas, S., & Willoughby, M. (2011). *An assessment of the tackling knives and serious youth violence action programme (TKAP)—Phase II*. Home Office, Research Report 53.

Wells, C. K. (2000). Provocation—The case for abolition. In A. Ashworth (Ed.), *Re-thinking English homicide law*. Oxford University Press.

WHO. (2016). *Suicide worldwide in 2019: Global health estimates*. World Health Organisation.

WHO. (2021). *Suicide worldwide in 2019: Global health estimates*. Geneva: World Health Organisation.

Wiener, M. J. (2004). *Men of blood: Violence, manliness and criminal justice in Victorian England*. Cambridge University Press.

Williams, D., Currie, D., Linden, W., & Donnelly, P. (2014). Addressing gang-related violence in Glasgow: A preliminary pragmatic quasi-experimental evaluation of the community initiative to reduce violence (CIRV). *Aggression and Violent Behavior, 19*(6), 686–691.

Wiltenburg, J. (2004). True crime: The origins of modern sensationalism. *The American Historical Review, 109*(5), 1377–1404.

Wolfgang, M. (1958). *Patterns in criminal homicide*. University of Pennsylvania Press.

World Health Organisation. (2010). *European report on preventing violence and knife crime among young people*. WHO.
Youth Violence Commission. (2018). *Interim report*. YVC.

3

A Prelude to 'Knife Crime': Gangs, Weapons and the 'Macpherson Effect'

Introduction

The two previous chapters have explored something of the 'pre-history' of knife violence in the UK, and have particularly questioned the sense we can make of rising violence or the significance of certain weapons in the performance of serious violence. At the same time we have traced many of the broader social and cultural values wrapped up in the idea of knife violence, revealing both the broad significance of knives in history and culture and the civilised sensibilities which can combine to make knife violence appear so especially heinous. In this chapter, by contrast, we focus upon three strands of ideas (and the policies and practices arising from them) that went much of the way towards crystallising our contemporary, although misleading, conception of 'knife crime'. We have called these: (i) the politics of youth crime; (ii) police force and reassurance; and (iii) police legitimacy. Of course, these three strands were thoroughly intertwined and lacing through each of them was a theme of race discrimination and racialisation. We will briefly introduce the inter-connectedness of these 'strands' before exploring each in more detail.

© The Author(s), under exclusive license to Springer Nature
Switzerland AG 2021
E. Williams and P. Squires, *Rethinking Knife Crime*,
https://doi.org/10.1007/978-3-030-83742-6_3

Reflecting the kind of 'pre-public' mobilisation around the phenomenon of 'mugging' described by Hall et al., in *Policing the Crisis* (1978), this crucial stage in the history of 'knife crime' explores the cultural context within which an institutional mobilisation towards this new category of crime was achieved. A number of important political shifts and cultural events at the end of the twentieth century—not least the category of mugging itself, a 20th century, post-colonial, example of an explicitly racist crime category—were the catalyst for a further racialisation in youth crime management, in turn, the contemporary label 'knife crime' can itself be seen as a direct product of these particular interactions.

As we have suggested, a number of elements come together to bring 'knife crime' into especially sharp focus at this time. These includes a particular focus upon violent and 'anti-social' youth, a preoccupation that began in the wake of the Bulger murder in 1993 and gathered pace with new Labour's '*No More Excuses*' White Paper and its embrace of the realist 'Broken Windows' agenda (Wilson & Kelling, 1982). Both the delinquent and the merely anti-social became subject to a process of early intervention net-widening and deviancy amplification that funnelled more and more young people into an expanded, even 'hyperactive' (Goldson, 2010) youth justice system. Tackling youth crime acquired a deeply populist aspect, recycling popular fears (Brown, 1998; Pearson, 1983) that young people were enabled to offend ever greater impunity (Campbell, 2002), an idea reinforced by what Prime Minister Blair described as his personal 'crusade' against youth delinquency (Squires, 2008a; Squires & Stephen, 2005). Even as more and more young offenders found their way into secure custody, American criminologist Michael Tonry, drawing upon US parallels, concluded that the net-widening resulting from ASB enforcement in the UK represented a profound political and criminological error, 'making a small problem larger' (Tonry, 2004: 57) creating the impression that youthful social problems were amenable to *enforcement solutions* (Squires, 2006). The emphasis upon 'pre-criminal enforcement', early intervention, net-widening, simplified due process, and police performance targets can be read as an injunction to police managers to become more assertive and proactive in tackling youth crime. The simple numbers came to tell their own story. In the fifteen years from 1993 to 2008 the number of young people in youth custody doubled but then, in 2007–2008, coinciding with the banking crisis and the 'credit crunch' something very unusual began to happen. The total number of youthful arrests began to fall dramatically, from a high of around 350,000 arrests per year, to just over 60,000 in 2020 (Ministry of Justice/YJB, 2021). These dramatic reductions were reflected in similarly significant falls in the numbers of under 18s cautioned or prosecuted; there was an 84% reduction in the number of first time entrants to the youth justice system since 2010, and a 68% reduction in the number of young people in custody. However, there was no correspondingly large reduction in serious violence; knife and other weapon offences were down by only 5% across the decade and custody lengths for more serious offences (especially including violence) grew by over a third. Most concerning of all, however, was that the proportion of youth arrests comprising black and minority ethnic young people had risen from 20% to 33% in the decade to 2020 whilst the custody population of young people had risen from around 25% BAME to 45% since 2007, a period during which the youth justice system had otherwise been shrinking significantly (Squires, 2021: 363).

Such trends interacted with a number of related developments, the first of which involved a shift towards a more confrontational style of urban policing addressing new kinds of criminal threats. In the late 1980s and early 1990s a debate had already been engaged between academics regarding the alleged 'militarisation' of the police (Ingleton, 1997; Jefferson, 1990, 1993; Waddington, 1987, 1991; Waddington & Hamilton, 1997). There was genuine disagreement and debate; it was often less a question of simple facts (the deployment of new force technologies including firearms, new powers, new police tactics and specialist operational units) but rather how these developments needed to be understood especially in relation to the crime, both organised and disorganised, domestic militancy and the global and international threats the police were having to face. At times, however, the debate seemingly bogged down in competing definitions of 'paramilitarism' and what this meant in the context of a policing culture that had hitherto celebrated (rightly or wrongly) both the 'minimal use of force' and policing by consent (Hills, 1995). From the late 1980s, however, it had become obvious that the police in London and some of the Britain's major conurbations were facing a qualitatively new domestic crime problem involving criminal gangs, drugs and the criminal use of firearms (Silverman, 1994). While 'gun enabled crime' only represented a small fraction of recorded crime in the UK (approximately 0.3% of annual recorded crime) it was regarded as an especially new—an 'alien' and threatening type of criminality (Squires, 2000, 2008b). Furthermore it had undergone a fourfold increase between the mid-1980s and the mid-1990s (Squires, 2014).

The terrible school shooting at Dunblane in 1996 led to legislation prohibiting the private possession of handguns, and stiffening a broad based cultural shift against firearms in British society. Senior Conservative MP, David Mellor, caught the national mood when describing his own personal response to Britain's second mass shooting: 'If we import the American way of life, we must expect the American way of death' (cited in Squires, 2000). But it was a burst of sub-machine gun fire in a Birmingham street, in the early hours of 2 January 2003, which left two young women dead, the innocent victims of a drive-by gang shooting, which really catapulted gun crime and gangs to the top of the political agenda. New mandatory penalties for handgun possession were introduced (five years imprisonment), the police were given new powers and new criminal orders to deploy and given the green light, alongside Customs, Immigration and subsequently the Borders Agency to prioritise the control of the illegal firearm supply. The criminal charge of 'joint enterprise murder' was dusted off and brought back into use following a joint initiative of ACPO and the Crown Prosecution Service (Squires, 2016; Williams & Clarke, 2020) while the Prime Minister launched the first of three national 'Connected Communities' conferences looking for a broad based, joined-up, response to gun crime, keen to secure buy-in from the urban communities most affected by the problem (Squires, 2014). Yet with gun crime continuing to rise, ACPO invested in a new national ballistic intelligence management system (NABIS) to collate all ballistic trace information and coordinate the tracking of criminal firearms. The vastly improved investigative potential resulting, close monitoring of known and prominent gang members, along with two further developments: the 2003 Anti-Social Behaviour Act (Sects. 37–38) which effectively took public possession of

lower-powered 'air weapons' out of gun crime recording, and the 2006
Violent Crime Reduction Act which further tightened up possession of
air weapons and prohibited the sale and possession of 'realistic imitation' firearms, eventually began to suppress rates of gun crime in England
and Wales.[1] From 2004 and throughout the following decade recorded
gun crime fell by about a half. Notwithstanding the fact that much
of this reduction had been achieved by an administrative and statistical recalculation, it was clear that 'hard core' gang involved gun crime
was less prevalent than once thought, that gun supply and availability
were more restricted and the close surveillance of known gang offenders,
coupled with what were referred to as 'robust' stop and search policies
and tough sentencing for simple firearm possession offences, appeared to
have discouraged somewhat the routine criminal carrying of firearms.[2]
    It is entirely plausible that the enforcement efforts directed at illegal
firearms (with consequences for their supply and availability) the close
surveillance of gangs, tougher penalties, and even a degree of community discouragement of gun ownership, may be, in part, responsible for
the emergence of 'knife crime', a case of weapon displacement from 'gun
crime', as an offence label. After all, knife crime was unaffected by any
similar supply issues and the penalties for being caught in possession
were nowhere so severe. However, a number of caveats need entering.
In the first place, knife-enabled violence never went away, as we saw
in Chapter 1 it had continued on a rising trajectory throughout the
late twentieth century and beyond. This knife-enabled violence affected
most groups in society, a significant proportion of it arising as 'intimate'
or 'domestic violence' (Cook & Walklate, 2020; Wood, 2010). Furthermore, as we saw in Chapter 1, the key to understanding the way the issue

---

[1] A fuller account of these changes can be found in Squires (2014: Chapters 2 and 3). By the
early 2000s it had become clear that recorded gun crime figures were substantially inflated by
'air weapon' offences and offences committed in possession of imitation firearms and 'BB guns'.
As much as 50% of British gun crime might be attributed to such weapons. The police became
better able to identify and distinguish between 'junk guns' and real, factory quality dangerous
firearms and concentrated their efforts accordingly on a numerically smaller but nonetheless
serious problem.

[2] The close surveillance of gang elders led to some suggestions, although mostly anecdotal,
that older gang members were passing weapons (and other contraband) to younger boys or
girlfriends in order to evade search and detection.

surfaced lay in the existing media narratives about urban youth gangs and violence and the social reaction to the series of high profile, youth-involved, stabbings in the years after 1993. Both perpetrators and victims were often black, and a moral panic about race, crime and violence was quickly rolled into another one about race and knife crime (Squires, 2009). As had been the case on many previous occasions, the state of youth became a barometer for the state of the nation (Bottoms, 1974). It was not that all such notions were wrong, it was simply that, as we showed in Chapter 1, until very late in the day there was little in the way of clear empirical evidence about the actual scale of youth involved knife crime. Accordingly, in the absence of clear evidence, the 'knife brandishing young thug' (the tabloids seldom pulled their punches here), often, if only by implication, black or minority ethnic, was conscripted to represent the face of the new crime wave (Wood, 2010).[3] A good head-line usually trumps pages of statistics, and as Lugo-Ocando and Brandao (2016) have noted in their study of knife crime news-making, statistical evidence was usually selectively resorted to by news journalists in order to *reinforce* a storyline arising from some given event, such as a recent stabbing. Often, although there was very little consistent or reliable data, A&E medics and surgeons stepped up to detail their reactions to the 'appalling rise in serious knife injuries amongst young people' (Konig

---

[3] In a detailed analysis of youth homicide evidence, Wood (2010) reveals how the picture of youth violence differed markedly inside and outside of Greater London: 'Forty-three teenagers died in violent circumstances outside the Greater London area in 2008. The majority of these teenagers were killed by adults, with a large number killed in instances of domestic violence or in late-night drunken fights. Only seven teenagers (of the cases successfully prosecuted) were killed by other teenagers carrying knives. All of these teenagers were White and were killed by other White teenagers, and only one of these was possibly linked to gangs' (2008: 99). A different picture arose *within* Greater London: 'There were more teen deaths, many at the hands of other teenagers (most of whom were Black or Asian), a very high number of knife deaths and a large number of newly arrived migrants or refugees who were caught up in the violence... The use of knives in Greater London was significant. There were more teenagers stabbed to death in London by other teenagers than in the whole of the rest of Britain... There was also a disproportionately high number of knife attacks in Greater London: twenty-two deaths compared to twenty-one in the rest of Britain. The large majority of victims were Black or Asian, as were their attackers. (90 per cent of victims were Black or Asian, compared to 20 per cent outside Greater London).' Furthermore, while two-thirds of the London teenage homicides were thought to have 'some association' with gangs, this was only proven in three cases that were successfully prosecuted. Finally, 'a third of those killed in Greater London were either refugees or newly arrived migrants' (Wood, 2010: 99–100).

et al., 2006) and the senior police spokesman on this issue, the 'Knife Czar', outlined the elements of a specific broad based initiative to 'tackle teenage knife crime' (Hitchcock, 2009).

Contemporary gang crime, much like mugging before it, was always perceived as a profoundly racialised label in the UK (Gilroy, 1982). Once again, just like mugging, the 'gang' label carried considerable ideological baggage with it from the USA (Hallsworth & Young, 2008) coming to signify black urban crime, drug dealing and violence. Gang crime became the catalyst for the establishment of specialist gang squads in major cities, Operation Trident in London, the Met Police's specialist 'Black on Black' homicide unit (McLagan, 2005) followed by Operation Xcalibre in Greater Manchester and similar units in other cities. Gang units combined extensive surveillance, intensified street policing and a hard hitting armed raid capability (Squires & Kennison, 2010). Amongst other research exposing the highly racialised picture of gang crime in greater Manchester (Aldridge et al., 2011; Bullock & Tilley, 2002), a survey of Greater Manchester Police officers affiliated with the gang crime programme revealed their perception that 'gang crime' in the city was almost entirely perceived as a black and minority ethnic phenomenon (Squires, Magnet Project). This was confirmed in 2007 with the launch of the Tackling Gangs Action Programme (TGAP) in the four British cities deemed to have the more significant gang problems. Offenders were targeted to the extent that they were reported to have 'gang affiliations' and of the 774 individuals identified, fully 75% had a Black/Caribbean background (Squires et al., 2008: 100–103). Essentially the same racialised targeting became apparent with the transformation of the Trident Unit, becoming the Trident Gang Crime Command in 2012 and the establishment, in the wake of the 2011 riots, of the Metropolitan Police Gang Matrix database which collated information on supposedly 'gang involved' young people in London (Amnesty International, 2018). Researchers consistently criticised the Matrix database for its disproportionate profiling of young black Londoners as 'gang involved' offenders—fully 78% of those included in the database were black (Shiner et al., 2018; Williams, 2015; Williams & Clarke, 2018). During 2020, London Mayor Sadiq Khan ordered a review of the database leading to the finding that 38%

of the people named on the database 'posed no risk' and, in due course, over a thousand names were removed. Critics have complained however that eight out of ten of those still on the Matrix database are from an African-Caribbean background (Dodd, 2021).

Complementing the new 'politics of youth crime' and the marked ramping up of police enforcement practices regarding gang violence, our third element, concerns the precarious state of police legitimacy, in the wake of profound criticisms regarding the challenge of institutional racism and discriminatory policing practices. This strand of issues both ties together many of the foregoing issues and certainly animates the whole debate with a much broader political tension. It too begins with a stabbing, the racially motivated murder of Stephen Lawrence in April 1993. The wider story of the death of Steven Lawrence and the subsequent Macpherson public inquiry is sufficiently well known and recorded not to require repeating here (Bowling & Phillips, 2002; Hall et al., 2009; Rowe, 2004). While police may have initially construed their own Lawrence murder investigation as 'incompetent' rather than racist (Foster, 2008) a broad consensus eventually settled upon the need for a more fundamental rethink around the Macpherson Report's (1999) critical diagnosis that 'institutional racism' influenced the Metropolitan Police strategy and practice for policing London. The report had enormous ramifications for whole areas of police policy and practice, and not just in London. These involved police recruitment, retention and the career development of Black officers, training, surveillance and profiling, and, most controversially from our current perspective, 'stop and search', use of force, and deaths following (or during) police contact. The conclusion that institutional racism fundamentally underpinned policing culture, policies and practice signalled a major crisis of credibility and legitimacy for the organisation at a time when policing at large was seeking to rearticulate its role as a 'service' (supporting communities and victims and tackling youthful anti-social behaviour) or as a 'force' (confronting gangs, terrorism and serious urban violence) (Holdaway, 1996; Stephens, 1994). Yet without legitimacy, policing risked being unable to deliver either strategy effectively and, straining around competing imperatives centred upon race, justice and order, policing priorities seemed to pull in different directions.

This 'perfect storm' for law and order had the phenomenon that came to be labelled as 'knife crime' at its centre. For the public it reflected the sense that our anti-social youth, especially the denizens of the disadvantaged inner cities and sink estates, were becoming increasingly decivilised, amoral and violent, echoing a media narrative, 'if it bleeds it leads', endlessly recycling the news of yet another 'mindless' stabbing on the front pages of the tabloids and the hourly news bulletins. For the broad social care and health sector, including charities, NGOs, left of centre think tanks and research institutes still wedded to a 'Left Realist' criminological paradigm, it pointed to the growing social division, disadvantage, poverty and racism that still fundamentally structured our crime trends. For the police, however, gangs and 'knife crime' offered a route back to legitimacy, a serious crime trend with an assumedly distinct perpetrator against which robust, proactive, enforcement could, it appeared, be popularly applied. Each strand of this context was thoroughly and unmistakably racialised.

The processes of racialisation unleashed by the publishing of the Macpherson Report (1999) will be discussed here, coinciding with the first official uses of the phrase 'knife crime' in the aftermath of the report and its criticisms of disproportionate police use of stop and search. These first representations of 'knife crime' as a category of crime in England and Wales highlight the label's powerful interaction with stop and search and the controversies surrounding proactive policing. Yet before outlining the strange policing dialectic which followed publication of the Macpherson Report, the initial policy critique followed by the attritional police response to it, it is necessary to acknowledge, as Gilroy has shown, the very same process which played out in the wake of the Scarman Report (1981) after 1981. This occurred on two fronts, in the first place, under the Newman policing strategy, it heralded a strategic assault upon so-called 'criminal areas' where a common denominator of black criminality was held responsible for urban crisis, social disorder and moral decay and required confronting at street level. In the second place it entailed an ideological response to the symbolic challenges posed by black and 'alien' cultures to English ideals of order and authority. If the first was a job specifically for the police, the latter represented a broader social and political injunction that has continued to sustain a strand of

English xenophobia (Gilroy, 1987: 108–110). The gradual erosion of the liberal insights and understandings of race and crime and policing developed by Scarman were a potent indication of what would follow Macpherson's own report almost two decades later. The first capitulation to racism might represent a tragedy, the second surely a farce, as Marx might have commented.[4]

In Chapter 1, we briefly considered the historic construction of 'Black criminality' in the UK in relation to *Policing the Crisis* (Hall et al., 1978). However, to understand the pre-public mobilisation towards a racially defined conception of 'knife crime' it is important to recognise the particular forms of racialisation that were active and popular when this distinct crime category emerged. Accordingly, we turn first to an analysis of the ideology of New Labour's 'democratic and authoritarian conception of 'community' which underpinned much of its criminal justice policy-making (Hughes, 1998) and the impact of its inherent contradictions on ideas of race, crime and 'race relations'.

The Two Sides of New Labour; Youth Offending and Racialisation in the Third Way

Racialisation has been defined as 'the processes by which racial meanings are attached to particular issues - often treated as social problems – and with the manner in which race appears to be a, or often the, key factor in the ways they are defined and understood' (Murji & Solomos, 2005: 3). In the case of 'knife crime' this is concerned with the processes that came to understand violence between young people as racialised and how race became the key factor in the way interpersonal violence with knives was defined and understood.

The focus on processes of racialisation recognises that these processes are not static; they involve 'change and ongoing practices that attach racial meanings to people' (Gonzalez-Sobrino & Goss, 2019: 507). Within this approach it is acknowledged that the interactions that defined 'mugging' as a 'Black crime' in the 1970s (Hall et al., 1978) were

---

[4] Karl Marx, paraphrasing Hegel in *The 18th Brumaire of Louis Bonaparte* (first published 1852).

specific to their particular conjuncture and the processes of re-making 'race' must adapt and evolve to continue the work of racialisation in new ideological terrains. To understand how 'knife crime' became so proficient at this task, the distinct dualism of New Labour ideologies that define the era of the label's inception need to be closely considered.

From the landslide New Labour victory in 1997, through to the re-election of Tony Blair and the start of the new millennium, this is a particularly difficult conjuncture to politically 'pin down'. The political shift referred to by New Labour as 'the third way' defined a new centre ground in British politics from 1997 onwards, merging policies from both the left and the right. Crucially there was renewed commitment to Thatcher's neoliberal project, but now it was repackaged as a 'revolutionary', socially democratic modernisation (Hall, 2005). The tension in this contradiction would be formative, not only in the inventive methods of spin required, but also in the reproduction of popular consent.

New Labour introduced a political strategy that Hall (2005) described as the double shuffle: 'it combines economic neo-liberalism with a commitment to "active government"… New Labour is a hybrid regime, composed of two strands. However, one strand – the neo-liberal – is in the dominant position. The other strand – the social democratic – is subordinate' (Hall, 2005: 19). Yet the subaltern programme makes the dominant project possible, not just by securing votes during elections, but also by constantly translating the needs of corporate capital as common sense societal 'reforms' that were to the benefit of all. Thus the relationship between the two sides of New Labour is in constant flux, adapting to both the needs of the neoliberal economy and public sensibilities—a double shuffle.

During this time spin is not just surface level gloss rather it performed a much deeper function of 'rhetorical sleight of hand' (Hall, 2005: 23), able to represent the interests of global, corporate capital in ways that maintained popular consent and the support of the less-well-off (ibid.). This was a hegemonic shift towards a managerial authoritarianism; a marketisation ideology that transformed clients into consumers under the spin of modernisation, whilst simultaneously opening all doors to private investment in the public sector (Hall, 2005). Key policies during this time enabled processes of devolution, passing responsibility to local authorities and onto communities themselves. This worked to distance government from the social consequences of neoliberalism. Under New Labour the economic responsibility was 'delegated', 'increasingly offloaded on to individuals, communities, cities or regions... 'individuals' become new objects within regimes of governmentality' (Back et al., 2002: 448). Within this framework, the visibility of localised responsibility—or 'responsibilisation'—was reinforced by increased language of 'civilised' behaviour (Back et al., 2002).

These 'two faces' of New Labour are also prominent in their contradictory race and immigration policies during this period. On the one hand there is a celebration of 'multiculturalism' and tolerance of difference as a signifier of globalisation and modernity; 'Race relations' became a new British concern and exposing and combating institutionalised racism was on the agenda for the first time (Back et al., 2002). On the other hand, there was a renewed commitment to a nationalistic identity based on a protected notion of 'Britishness', characterised by immigration control and assimilation rhetoric: 'At the heart of what has become the New Labour project lies an uncertainty about the challenge contemporary multiculturalism poses to the very constitution of the nation... ambivalence around the melancholic desire for an imperial past sits alongside the contradictions that surface in both liberal models of social inclusion and the attempt to define a social democratic model of national economic growth in a globalised economy' (Back et al., 2002: 447). In time, such insular nostalgia would grow to underpin the dream of lost empire/lost sovereignty that, many argued, sustained the appeal of Brexit. New Labour wanted it both ways, oscillating between multicultural democracy and imperialist nationalism. Within this tension racialisation took on some innovative forms; simultaneously evoking a nostalgic past and a progressive future in the construction of racial difference and the processing of social issues through a discourse on race out of which the label 'knife crime' emerged. The particular alignment of interests that led to the making of the label are discussed below with particular attention to policing and enforcement as key initiators of an ideological mobilisation towards a particular focus upon 'knife-enabled offences'. At the beginning of the 2000s a series of policing reforms and a more proactive and confrontational enforcement agenda in UK policing suggested new problems and concerns (as we have seen) comprising the creation of the public discourse on crime. These are discussed below in relation to the key reforms in youth justice policy which ran parallel to an increasing authoritarianism (Goldson, 2010; Muncie, 2002; Muncie & Goldson, 2006; Haydon & Scraton, 2000).

Institutionalisation of Youth Deviance

Replicating the successes of Clinton's Democratic Party in the 1993 US election, '*Tough on crime, tough on the causes of crime*' was one of New Labour's key 'law and order' sound bites in 1997. Once elected New Labour published the '*No More Excuses*' White Paper (Home Office, 1997), policy reform that epitomised the party's dual ethos of individual responsibility and government intervention. In this reform the government detailed a complete youth crime policy and policing overhaul; radical and systemic changes to the youth justice system and policing all with the core aim of 'tackling youth violence' with tough measures. In a preface to the White Paper the then Home Secretary Jack Straw described how, 'Today's young offenders can too easily become tomorrow's hardened criminals' and promised to 'break the link between juvenile crime and disorder and the serial burglar of the future … nipping offending in the bud, to prevent crime from becoming a way of life for so many young people (Home Office, 1997).

The mobilisation towards youth surveillance and control, from the Crime and Disorder Act (1998) through to the Police Reform Act (2002), extended the capacity of the state to intervene and increased the range of behaviours considered criminal during this period. New Labour's reinvigorated law and order policies directly impacted on the daily realities of young people. Legislative changes in The Crime and Disorder Act (1998), The Youth Justice and Criminal Evidence Act (1999) and The Powers of the Criminal Courts (sentencing) Act (2000), extended the powers of surveillance and early intervention. The principle of *Doli Incapax* was removed in 1998, effectively lowering the age of criminal responsibility from 14 to 10. Electronic monitoring and pre-emptive tracking through 'tagging' of young people was introduced, along with an extended referral order for 'pre-criminal' acts established as a result of the introduction of 'Anti-social Behaviour Orders' (ASBOs) and Acceptable Behaviour Contracts (ABCs) (Squires & Stephen, 2005).

The emphasis on 'pre-criminal' behaviour and the increasing proliferation of ASBOs during this period shifted the direction of policing, the justice system and youth services towards a younger and broader sample of children. In addition to this, the devolution of power to local authorities, youth offending services and housing associations increased the number of institutions involved in the management of youth behaviours and movement. The introduction of Local Strategic Partnerships (LSPs) in 2000 and the annual National Policing Plan in 2002 linked youth services, youth justice, community monitoring and policing into a multi-agency network with cross-institutional strategies to 'deal with' young people. A caution for delinquent behaviour was no longer a transient event during maturity. It now initiated a more coordinated system of response that would integrate a child into the institutional mechanisms of intervention.

Referral orders with compulsory attendance drastically increased the contact time between children and the corrective institutions. With minimum orders of two years for an ASBO such interactions with state institutions could dominate a teenager's formative years. To put this in perspective, the number of ASBOs issued in England and Wales increased from 104 in 1999 up to 4122 in 2005 (Berman, 2009). A total of 24,324 ASBOs were issued between 2000 and 2013. Around 58% of these ASBOs were breached at least once and of those breaches 53% received immediate custodial sentence (Home Office, 2014). That is, 7503 custodial sentences (an average of five months in length) for behaviours that prior to 1997 may have fallen below the level that required police or criminal justice invention. The suggestion had been that 'something had to be done' to sever the connection between youthful anti-social behaviour and crime, but in reality New Labour's hyperactive early intervention policies were expanding and institutionalising these connections (Squires & Stephen, 2005: 33). This intensification of youth crime policy can be seen to reconcile the contradictions of New Labour's dual strategy. On the one hand the hardening of the state response to disorder in the streets both appealed to and reflected a colonial nationalism of the past; an imperialist imagination of 'Britishness' as a civilising force (Elliott-Cooper, 2021). On the other, it appealed to the ideology of modernisation; a youth justice reform that increased efficiency and coordinated services in a more productive way. Beyond this, the devolution of youth justice to local authorities and YOTs acted to distance government from social and economic accountability whilst increasing the capacity for 'joined-up' early interventions (Pitts, 2001; Smith, 2003).

These reforms represented a significant shift in crime prevention in England and Wales. New Labour boasted a new regime of early intervention based on risk, assessment and scrutiny and 'streamlined' process rather than formal proof of guilt, pre-empting crime by targeting the potential 'persistent and prolific' offender of tomorrow. In turn, highly preoccupied by these 'criminals to come' crime prevention became increasingly concerned with intelligence and surveillance, followed by intense and robust deterrent interventions. The power of the police to intervene proactively and forcefully was also extended throughout this period, justified by reference to the emerging threats posed by gangs and the criminal use of firearms (Bullock & Tilley, 2002; Hales et al., 2006).

Gangs, Guns and 'Total Policing'

The years that preceded the emergence of the 'knife crime' label witness a creeping shift towards an increasingly proactive and confrontational model of policing. The gradual extension of police powers in the 1990's accompanied a rise in the use of covert operations, surveillance and robust intervention in the policing of new 'suspect communities' (Pantazis & Pemberton, 2009). 'Total policing' (Fekete, 2013; Innes, 2012) combined 'pre-emptive policing ' with 'enforcement-led' operations, and in this the creeping authoritarianism of UK policing increasingly came to resemble aspects of the US model of policing, incorporating 'zero tolerance' and 'escalating force' and new tactics.

Unlike the majority of police forces globally, the UK police are traditionally routinely *unarmed* (Squires & Kennison, 2010: 16). Arguments in favour of more routinely arming British police have gradually increased in recent decades, reflecting related concerns about police officer safety, the numbers of police killed while on duty and the pressures of armed crime and terrorism (Squires & Kennison, 2010: 97). However, the 1990s saw a rising advocacy for the use of firearms by police particularly in inner cities (Squires & Kennison, 2010: 107, 108). Within these discussions arguments can be seen to draw heavily on rhetoric of violence as culture, linking weaponisation and gangs with race in the urban context. In 1993 and 1994 neighbourhoods in South London, Manchester and Liverpool began to gain a media propelled reputation for drug and gang related gun crime (Silverman, 1994; Squires & Kennison, 2010: 108). Accompanied by a racialised discourse centred upon supposedly 'wild inner-city areas' and 'yardie-style gangsterism'. Rising concern about the criminal use of firearms increasingly underpinned arguments favouring use of armed police units and specialist operations and tactics against gangs (McLagan, 2005; Squires & Kennison, 2010: 107, 108).

Anxieties over an emergent 'gun culture' became particularly significant during this 'pre-knife crime' moment. The perceived weaponisation of criminality alongside 'cultural' explanations of violence has many similarities in the case of both knives and guns. The ill-defined notion that the UK had acquired a new and rapidly deteriorating 'gun culture' in the 1990s has, 'been used to convey a wide array of presumptions, preoccupations and prejudices... often drawing upon so-called 'lifestyle choices' rather than the socio-economic and 'environmental' influences more familiar to traditional criminology' (Squires & Kennison, 2010: 122). Furthermore, the arguments surrounding 'gun culture' centred especially on the significance of race and the symbolic value of weapons as supposed 'fashion accessories' (BBC News, 2007; Hales et al., 2006; Lemos, 2004), and a racialised discourse on music genres and urban style still reflected in discussions of contemporary 'knife culture' (Day & Gibson, 2006; Fatsis, 2019; UKPOL, 2007; Weathers, 2005).

Whilst criminal gangs have been a feature of criminological concern in urban sociology since the early twentieth century (Thrasher, 1926), in the years leading up the emergence of 'knife crime' there is a distinct re-imagination of the notion of a UK 'gang' that becomes influential in policy-making at this time (Alexander, 2008). Researchers continues to contest the definition of a 'gang' in the UK context (Hallsworth & Young, 2004; Nijjar, 2018; Pitts, 2008; Smithson et al., 2012; Williams, 2015) with particular attention to the use of 'gang' labels as a mythologizing rhetoric importing vivid representations of criminality from America (Alexander, 2008). The racialisation of 'gangs' as a discursive tool in the explanation of violence and justification of proactive policing is a process that has been well documented in academic research (Alexander, 2000, 2008; Fekete, 2013; Williams, 2015; Williams & Clarke, 2018). As we have seen, the 'gang' label has been likened to the earlier mugging moral panic with particular concern attaching to the extension of policing powers which followed (Hallsworth & Young, 2008; Williams, 2015). One key development in the authorisation of policing powers occurring in the years preceding the 'knife crime' label was the launch of Operation Trident in 1996.

Originally a specialist police intelligence unit in response to rising gun violence in London in the 1990s, Trident re-launched in July 2000 tasked specifically with reducing so-called 'Black on Black' gun crime in London (Squires & Kennison, 2010: 118). Along with community consultancy, partnership work and public advertising campaigns, a key feature of specialist gang units has been the development of gang-databases and the growing capacity of intelligence building and its use to inform policing and enforcement activity (Williams, 2015: 28). The application of the 'gang' label introduces high risk and this 'intensifies levels of surveillance and justifies more stringent forms of intervention and monitoring' (Smithson et al., 2012).

Alongside this extension and intensification of policing powers, the attention to 'gangs' has increased the racialisation in targeted interventions. A recent report by Amnesty International (2018) into the use of the 'Gangs Matrix', a database system for measuring and collating gang association used by the Met Police and its partner agencies since 2012, described it as form of digital profiling:

> Many of the indicators used by the Metropolitan Police to identify 'gang members' simply reflect elements of urban youth culture and identity that have nothing to do with serious crime. This conflation of elements

of urban youth culture with violent offending is heavily racialised. The result is that the matrix has taken on the form of digital profiling; 78 per cent of individuals on the Gangs Matrix are black, a number which is disproportionate both to the black population of London (13 per cent of the whole) and the percentage of black people among those identified by the police as responsible for serious youth violence in London (27 per cent). (Amnesty International, 2018: 3)

Accordingly, in the years preceding the emergence of 'knife crime' the policing climate in the UK was adopting a more robust, proactive and confrontational style of operation. Specialist units were already mobilising around notions of a gun and gang culture, with rhetoric and administration that appeared both implicitly and explicitly racialised. Official justifications drew attention to the heightened threats—gun crime and suicide terrorism—with which officers had to contend but there was also a sense that the police's 'event driven' agenda might become a slippery path towards a more routinely armed policing culture. A TV documentary broadcast in the wake of the mistaken shooting of Jean Charles de Menezes and ostensibly intended to 'reassure' Londoners that the police could maintain safe streets showed scenes of young black Londoners being 'kicked to the floor' or dragged bodily through the windows of vehicles. Despite the fact that such action was justified by an operational protocol—overwhelming force to ensure instant compliance—one can only imagine what it might feel like to be on the receiving end of such treatment. It is worth recalling that the Brixton Riots of 1981 were prompted by a perceived excessive use of 'stop and search'.

Of particular concern to many commentators (Punch, 2011) was the fact that the police resort to arms and increasingly aggressive tactics was not subject to any public or parliamentary accountability but involved a policy entirely developed by police chiefs (ACPO) themselves. In turn, a series of, arguably avoidable, fatal shooting incidents between 1998 and 2011 caused serious controversy, casting a shadow over police armed response. Officer tactics were considered too confrontational, often poorly planned, reliant upon dubious intelligence while officers were thought too quick to pull the trigger (Squires & Kennison, 2010: 165–185). The most notorious of these was undoubtedly the mistaken shooting of innocent Jean Charles de Menezes, at Stockwell underground station in 2005, employing a controversial anti-terrorism protocol designed to instantaneously incapacitate a suspected terrorist by repeated shots to the head. In due course, in this case, the Metropolitan Police were found guilty of corporate manslaughter with 15 explicit operational failings cited in the armed operation resulting in Mr. Menezes' death.

Ironically, however, it was another police shooting incident earlier the same year, which raised a broader question about police armed response in London. Azelle Rodney, a suspected gang member believed to be en route to rob some drug dealers, was shot and killed following a police 'hard vehicle stop' outside a pub in Barnet, North London. The instant the vehicle carrying Rodney and the engaging police vehicles had come to a halt, one of the police officers fired eight shots at virtual point-blank range, hitting Rodney in the face, head, neck and chest. The first shot was fired a mere 0.06 after the vehicles came to a stop, all eight rounds being discharged in 2.04 seconds (Holland, 2013: 58–59, 86–87). One concern arising from the incident was that armed response officers were using a firearm engagement protocol intended for use against suicide bombers against criminal gang offenders. The officer who fired the shots insisted he thought Rodney was about to shoot, although no one saw him holding a gun, let alone a machine gun believed (mistakenly) to be in the vehicle. An inquest into the death was indefinitely suspended when police refused to describe their armed response tactics in open court and it was a full five years later that Sir Christopher Holland was instructed to conduct an independent public inquiry into the incident. The IPCC had concluded its investigations, the CPS had decided there was insufficient evidence to prosecute and senior police officers defended the police marksman as having 'no choice'. However the Holland Inquiry described a host of errors and failings: the police operation was deeply flawed, the intelligence upon which it was based was not accurate, the decision-making poor, the tactics adopted dangerous and the shooting itself an unnecessary, disproportionate and unreasonable use of force for which there was no lawful justification (Holland, 2013: 87–88). Three years later, and fully ten years after the incident itself, the police officer who had fired the fatal shots was found not guilty of murder at the Old Bailey.

However, just three years before that, in 2011, an almost identical 'hard stop' had seen Mark Duggan killed (Squires, 2014), an incident that went on to trigger the 2011 English riots leading to an even greater focus upon the assumed role of race and gangs in Britain's urban disorders.

This increasingly militarised response to a perceived 'gang weapons culture' reflected a form of racialisation continuing throughout the mobilisation towards the focus upon 'knife crime' in the new millennium. However, a vitally significant event in 1999 caused a significant disruption to the processes of 'race making' and the robust authority attaching to proactive total policing at this time.

The publication of the long awaited Macpherson Report (Macpherson, 1999) into the murder of Stephen Lawrence (in 1993) brought racial disproportionality in policing under public scrutiny as never before, becoming the first official acknowledgement of 'institutional racism' in the Met Police. The findings of this report and its political aftermath suggest the early articulation of a 'knife crime' problem in the early 2000s was for the police a timely and constructive development. The analysis of the interaction of these narratives: the loss of trust and confidence amongst key sections of the community, the seeming de-legitimisation of police actions vis-à-vis black people and the first representations of a racialised 'knife crime' in the printed press will now be explored.

"Institutionally Racist": Questioning Police Legitimacy

Four years after Stephen Lawrence was murdered by a group of White extremists in South London, the newly elected Labour government responded to the demands for a full-scale inquiry and set about commissioning Sir William Macpherson a retired High Court judge to lead the inquiry. In 1999 the inquiry report that would change the racial politics of British policing forever was published. The report is presented in two parts. The first part comprised a meticulous and detailed scrutiny of the events of the night, the actions of first responders and the debacle of the police investigation that followed. The second part consisted of consultations around the country, in Manchester, Bradford, Bristol, and Birmingham as well as London aiming 'to gather information and opinions from a broad cross-section of people to inform the recommendations which we would ultimately make, and to "take the temperature" of the community and of the Police and other agencies' (Macpherson, 1999: para 45.5). It was this part of the inquiry that performed the crucial task of linking up the Lawrence case with the shared experiences of police racism and the failures of the justice system across the UK. It was this that enabled the report to draw his critical conclusions.

Macpherson concluded unequivocally that the original murder investigation 'was marred by a combination of professional incompetence, institutional racism and a failure of leadership by senior officers' (Macpherson, 1999: para 46.1). The phrase 'institutionally racist' would become synonymous with the Macpherson report in the years to follow. The inquiry defined the term as:

> [T]he collective failure of an organisation to provide an appropriate and professional service to people because of their colour, culture, or ethnic origin. It can be seen or detected in processes, attitudes and behaviour which amount to discrimination through unwitting prejudice, ignorance, thoughtlessness and racist stereotyping which disadvantage minority ethnic people. (Macpherson, 1999: para 6.34)

Secondly, the consultation around the country highlighted the consistency of a form of racism experienced in significantly disproportionate rates of police stops and searches. The Inquiry and its findings helped launch a significant outpouring of new research on stop and search and community reactions (Bland et al., 2000; MVA & Miller, 2000; Quinton et al., 2000), a body of work that has continued to this day, drawing often problematic conclusions for the police about the impact of stop and search (Bowling & Philips, 2007; Bradford, 2017). In the conclusion to his report, Macpherson made a specific recommendation; 'It is essential to obtain a true picture of the interactions between the police and minority ethnic communities ... All "stops" need to be recorded, and related self-defined "ethnic data" compiled' (Macpherson, 1999: para 46.31).

The report's criticism of stop and search, combined with the evidence of institutional racism within the police service, marks a significant cultural moment. The recommendations of the Macpherson report were material realities, but beyond this was a strong sense of symbolic retribution; the police had been charged with racism and were found culpable. The report 'represented the Establishment's symbolic recognition that widespread racism in the organization existed' (Henry & Smith, 2007: 80). The verdict validated the experiences which had been articulated by Black people in the UK for decades. The Report's findings were a historic recognition of racism in British society, 'not only with racism's violent and hateful face but also its more genteel institutional quality' (Back, 2010: 457). Politically this exposure of inequality was consistent with New Labour's self image as a radical modernising government. Racism was now unfashionable and the coverage of the inquiry, along with New Labour's promotion of multiculturalism, would demonstrate that personal acts of overt racism were no longer publicly acceptable (Sayeed, 2017: 108).

Beneath the optimistic political spin however, New Labour's hybrid politics and especially its neoliberal economic project simultaneously reinforced the inequality and social exclusion of which institutional racism was a principal, even constitutive feature. On the one hand 'it seemed that the country had moved into a bright and shining era of liberal tolerance, and [and yet] this obscured the survival of deep institutional racism. Britain was still racist, but in a modern way' (Sayeed, 2017: 114). Nevertheless, it would still be several years before this racist politics harnessed the full combination of little-England xenophobia and post-colonial forgetfulness that was wrapped up in Brexit, notions sovereignty and secure borders and hostile attitudes towards migrants (Virdee & McGeever, 2018). In a post-Macpherson Britain such contradictions represented a significant challenge for the law and order society; how can authoritarianism be maintained whilst condemning institutional racism? In time however, the reaction to the report from critics and the events following its publication revealed how its findings and prescriptions became gradually mitigated and the authority and legitimacy of proactive and disproportionate policing eventually restored.

Criticism of the Report; the 'Macpherson Effect'

In the aftermath of the inquiry the government promised judicial reforms and the report findings were celebrated as sign of political progress towards a fair modern society. However, the acknowledgement of institutional racism stopped short of proposing any structural change, and the concept was met with resistance from particular factions—including the police (Foster, 2008). The war of attrition against Macpherson continued with the Institute for the Study of Civil Society (known as the think tank *Civitas*) which published a paper titled '*Racist Murder and Pressure Group Politics*' (Dennis et al., 2000) in which the validity of Macpherson's definition of 'institutional racism' was contested. It stated:

> The Macpherson inquiry, unable to find evidence of racism, produced a definition of racism that at first glance absolved it from producing any... It switched attention, in the other direction, away from observable conduct, words or gestures and towards the police officer's 'unwitting' thoughts and conduct. But how could the Macpherson inquiry know what was in an officer's unconscious mind—except through the failure of the police to be effective in the investigation of a racist crime? This definition puts charges of racism outside the boundaries of proof or rebuttal. (Dennis et al., 2000: xix–xx)

Dissecting the events of the inquiry the authors claimed Macpherson's conclusions were the harmful consequence of 'the fateful meeting of the stricken Lawrences, an unworldly High Court judge, a feckless social-affairs intelligentsia, and what is currently fashionable in political militancy' (Dennis et al., 2000: 148). In particular, they claimed that the 'unscientific' conclusions of the inquiry caused 'real harm' by putting restrictive measures on police work. They called this; 'The Macpherson effect'.

The Macpherson Effect developed as a term used by critics of the inquiry to refer to the increase in recorded crime in 1999 which they believe to be a direct consequence of labelling the police 'institution-ally racist', criticising stop and search, weakening police authority on the streets and 'undermining their morale':

> In August 1998, while the inquiry was going on, there were 27,300 searches by the MPS. In August 1999, six months after Macpherson reported, the figure was down to 13,600... The only group for which both recorded searches and arrests fell consistently across the MPS area over the year was the black group.

They continued,

> The graph of crime trends in the MPS area shows a sharp upturn of 'street crimes' from the time of the publication of the Macpherson report, from 2,800 a month to over 3,500 a month... nationally the number of crimes had increased 2.2 per cent to 5.2 million in the year October 1998 to September 1999. That increase, the first in six years, was largely due to increases in two police areas, London and the West Midlands, the areas with the highest concentrations of ethnic minorities. (Dennis et al., 2000: 29)

Using such data to link the reduced disproportionality of stops experienced by Black people to an increase in crime in areas where ethnic minorities live was, in itself, a form of institutional racism. There is often an assumption that 'street crime' denotes 'Black crime', although there was no follow up analysis of the impact on arrest rates when fewer Black people are stopped and searched, and no mention of how the Crime and Disorder Act (1998) itself may have impacted underlying crime trends. As we have seen, this legislation had explicitly encouraged the police to detect and record more crime and youthful anti-social behaviour; it was itself already part of a deviancy amplification process. The coining of the phrase 'the Macpherson Effect' was simultaneously a rejection of the legitimacy of the label 'institutional racism' and a warning of the perils of restricting police work and the street-level discretion and authority of officers. The retreat from stop and search in 1999 was a spontaneous policing response to the Macpherson report and not a response to any official policy change; in due course it would come to be used as evidence in a reoccurring warning about the consequences of questioning police tactics.

This elective reduction in rates of stop and search could be read as an act of resistance by the police; a refusal to bridge the contradicting ideologies of the Government. In any event, it was clear that the proactive policing strategies that had dominated previous decades were now encountering resistance. From the stop and search data now available, however, we know this retreat was short lived. Just as the years after the Scarman Report witnessed a renewal of robust proactive policing on the streets of London (Gilroy, 1987) so the frequency of racially disproportionate stops increased dramatically from 2001 onwards (a mere two years after the publication of the Macpherson Report), and peaking in 2008/2009 with over 1.5 million searches in England and Wales. During this time Black people in some parts of the UK were up to 28 times more likely to be stopped (Dodd, 2012). Despite the political and social impact of the Macpherson report, the decade or so following its publication saw a vast expansion of the use of police stop and search powers. This reversal was, at least in part, enabled through the emergence of a new crime label, 'knife crime'.

A Knife Code for a New Millennium

At no point in the Crime and Disorder Act (1998), The Macpherson Inquiry (1999), the 'Blueprint for Reform' White Paper (2001), the first National Policing Plan (2002), The Policing Reform Act (2002) or in any of the other official policy discourse of this period does the phrase "knife crime" appear. But behind the scenes there were early signs of a growing orientation towards knife-enabled crime. A first indication here may have been the 1997 Knives Act, a piece of legislation that outlawed the marketing of knives 'for combat' or for use as a weapon and which authorised the use of s.60 stop and search powers 'in anticipation of' knife-enabled violence. But perhaps the most significant change occurred in 2001 when a new policing 'feature code' was introduced to the crime recording system of the Metropolitan Police to specifically register 'knife-enabled offences' (KEO) on computerised crime records. It was this subtle change in the way crimes involving knives were recorded, quantified and grouped together that brought 'knife crime' into being. Without this shift in approach, the statistical reports regarding 'knife crime' in London that define the category as a precise and bounded criminality would never have been possible. It is unclear from available evidence if the police or the Home Office decided on this new direction of measurement. Whilst the Police Act (1996) gave powers to the Home Secretary to specify the form in which crimes are recorded (HMICFRS, 2017) the localised use of the new code in London rather than nationally suggests it was an innovation specific to the Metropolitan police.

The process of recording a crime is subjective. How an incident is recorded often relies on the discretion of the responding police officer, but it is worth noting that the Home Office Counting Rules (HOCR) seek to 'promote a victim-oriented approach to crime recording' (ibid.) in which the way that the victim describes or believes a crime has occurred is, in most cases, the basis for its recording as a crime. Along with details of the incident and the individuals involved, officers are required to provide an 'opening code':

> When recording an incident, staff allocate an "opening code" to the incident log. Opening codes indicate the nature of the incident, for example whether it relates to a road traffic accident or a burglary. Opening codes are important because they allow supervisors to see immediately what types of incidents are currently open and prioritise resources accordingly. (ibid.)

Prior to the feature code of 'knife-enabled offence' being added, crimes that had included or intimated the use of a knife would have been recorded and prioritised based upon the intent referenced in the 'opening code'. For example; Burglary, theft, sexual assault, drugs or criminal damage would be the defining category of the offence. But after the feature code of KEO is added data analysts and police supervisors were able to extract crime figures from across different opening codes to prioritise those with a feature code for 'knife enabled'. For the first time it became possible to analyse crime data based on whether a 'knife' was present, used or involved during various different crime contexts. As we have already noted in Chapter 1, before the advent of the new 'knife code' any attempt to compare knife-enabled crimes year on year would likely have be highly flawed, selective and unreliable.

A report by the Metropolitan Police Authority in 2005 described their analytical use of knife-enabled feature code in this way:

> Knife enabled crime is defined as any offence within the categories violence against the person, sexual offence, robbery or burglary that has been recorded on the Metropolitan Police Service's (MPS) crime recording system with a feature code that shows specifically that a knife was used during the commission of the offence... Knife enabled crime has been selected as the MPS measure of knife crime as it closely aligns with the PPAF (Policing Performance Assessment Framework) definition of gun enabled crime. This approach enables the MPS to monitor the impact of the use of weapons, particularly guns and knives, in a consistent way. (Commissioner MPA, 2005)

This explanation reveals several points. Firstly that data was drawn from different categories of criminal activity (violence, sexual offence, robbery or burglary) to collectively group knife-enabled crime by the weapon used. Secondly, that there was a direct relation to the PPAF monitoring agenda in the decision to include 'knife-enabled' as an extension of 'gun enabled' crimes. Thirdly, in common with gun enabled crime, the code did not include simple illegal possession of a knife in a public place as legislated for in 1953 and 1959 (see Chapter 1).[5] And finally, the knife-enabled code was selected by the MPS as a measure of 'knife crime' before any mention of 'knife crime' in official legislation or strategic partnership documents. In other words, the mobilisation towards the category precedes a public definition of the label, just as with the notion of 'mugging' in the 1970s (Hall et al., 1978).

In common with the emergence of 'mugging' (Hall et al., 1978) there is considerable likelihood of an amplification of crime rates occurring

---

[5] By 2005, handguns having been prohibited in 1998, illegal possession of a firearm was a much clearer matter. The difficulty with knives, as MPs discussed at length in 1953, was that there were numerous legitimate reasons for possessing a knife, implying that enforcement of knife possession laws might quickly become highly arbitrary and discretionary law enforcement based upon police officers' subjective inferences about a suspect's motive for carrying the knife.

when new recording practices and categories are introduced (Cohen, 1972). There is a marked chance of 'knife-enabled' being increasingly selected as a feature code by police officers during the crime recording process, especially as the 'knife crime' category, in a circular and self-fulfilling sense, attracts growing public attention. In turn, the public themselves were increasingly likely to report a knife being present and/or report 'knife-enabled' offending as the label gathered its own momentum.

Despite such potentially confounding influences, the data collected from the new crime code was used immediately as a reliable representation of a new crime category. As early as 2002 we began to see the data collated through the feature code used to report on specific knife crime concerns and on a few occasions the term 'knife crime' appears in police statements or press releases (Alleyne, 2002; Bamber, 2002). How the problem was framed in these first 'knife crime' reports was indicative of what followed during the succeeding decade, revealing the constitutive interaction of the concept with the political events of this moment. But before considering what was included it is also important to note what is absent.

Whilst the 'Macpherson effect' became central to early discussions of 'knife crime', the murder of Stephen Lawrence itself did not—despite arguably being the most famous knife homicide of this entire period. A suggestion of why this might be is revealed within the *Civitas* critique of the Macpherson inquiry. The authors argue that the knife featured in Stephen Lawrence's murder is significant; that this particular choice of weapon represents a foreign or primitive method of assault and that our questioning should focus on the preservation of English civility rather than the identification of institutional racism. They argued, erroneously but not unlike their predecessors in the 1950s and earlier, condemning the supposed foreign-ness of knife violence:

> Not long ago the use of knives in private quarrels or obsessions was as a matter of fact very unusual. As a matter of culture it was defined as something men from some countries might resort to in certain circumstances, but not English men in English civilian life… English culture had for long succeeded in inculcating an abhorrence of any violent use of knives.

> The murderous use of knives in private life, and above all the murderous use of knives on a complete stranger, a kind of running amok, was for centuries almost unknown... therefore, how had English society come to produce the young men who had killed him...? (Dennis et al., 2000: 4, 5)

This construction of violence with knives as something 'un-English' drew heavily upon colonial ideas of 'English civility', a pervasive image arising throughout the emergence of 'knife crime'. And, whilst the brutality of the stabbing in the Lawrence case might have suggested this murder would be central to early discussions of 'knife crime', it becomes apparent, as concern about the new offence type gathered pace, that the death of Stephen Lawrence did not fit the emerging criteria defining knife crime.

By 2002 there were only two prominent news articles published in England and Wales employing the exact phrase 'knife crime', the earliest media representations of the new crime category. The content of these formative mentions poignantly demonstrated the exclusion of Stephen Lawrence as a victim within the 'knife crime' category and yet, simultaneously, emphasised the centrality of race and policing in their comprehension of knife related violence. The article in the *Daily Telegraph* reported selectively on the first 'knife crime' data produced through the new crime code, suggesting several causes for a perceived rise in knife offences:

> Senior officers blame the huge increase in knife-carrying partly on the result of the Macpherson Report, following the murder of Stephen Lawrence, which curbed officers' use of stop and search on the streets... Crack-cocaine dealing by so-called Yardie gangs in the inner cities has also fuelled the carrying of knives. Many of the drug pushers come from Jamaica and openly carry knives there. (Bamber, 2002)

This remarkable claim attributed to senior police officers, a mere three years after the publication of the inquiry report, demonstrated the dexterity and power of the 'knife crime' label even in its earliest public use. Attributing apparently rising rates of violence involving knives to the impact the Macpherson report on stop and search rates, *and*

Caribbean migrants, whilst ignoring Stephen Lawrence's own victim status in this story, entails a quite disingenuous sleight of hand. However, set within the newly constituted parameters of the 'knife crime' category (discussed in greater detail in the next chapter) these incongruities became increasingly naturalised assumptions as the label itself gathered strength.

It is likely the knife code was introduced primarily as a performance-monitoring tool, under the guidelines of the PPAF and in response to government pressure to produce evidenced work outcomes and increased efficiency. However, the introduction of the knife-enabled crime code and its subsequent reporting revealed three core aspects of the label; Firstly, defining 'knife crime' as a separate category to that of the criminal intention of the act (theft, sexual assault, robbery etc.) begins with this code; Secondly, this happened before there was any public definition or explicit concern over a perceived 'knife crime' category (or crisis); and thirdly, the data produced by this code was used immediately to support and defend stop and search by police in the press, even referencing the Macpherson 'effect' as a cause of increased knife violence along with migration. From its inception then, collectively grouping crimes with different criminal intentions as 'knife crime' was a practice subsumed by the racialisation of crime, both manufacturing consent and defending authoritarian policing at a moment of increased police scrutiny and performance pressure.

Conclusion

Following the intellectual approach of *Policing the Crisis* (Hall et al., 1978) this chapter has considered the context in which a mobilisation towards 'knife crime' occurred, before the label was publicly defined. The analysis of events and interactions during the years leading up to the introduction of the 'knife crime' label present three core points for noting by way conclusion.

Firstly, the New Labour government from 1997 onwards introduced an adapted neoliberal strategy, reworking the authoritarianism of the exceptional state to appear socially democratic, 'multicultural' and progressive. The result of this ideological shift was a growing reliance on political 'spin' to navigate the contradictions of competing priorities. The re-articulation of the law and order society focuses heavily on 'youth crime' and extending the powers of the state to intervene in 'pre-criminal' anti-social behaviours.

Secondly, it is clear that in the years preceding the moral panic centred upon 'knife crime', that 'gun' and 'gang' speak had already begun a process of weaponised racialisation that justified intensive surveillance, increased militarisation and the use of 'hard stop' and robust proactive police tactics. Specialist mobilisations such as 'Trident Gang Command' and the 'gangs matrix' demonstrate how the rhetoric of 'crime as culture' acted as a broader racialising narrative of criminality at this time—and into which, at a key moment, 'knife crime' emerged.

This timely mobilisation towards 'knife crime' relates to the third aspect of the pre-public history of the crime label discussed in this chapter; the publication of the Macpherson report and the official recognition of institutional racism within the Metropolitan Police. This significant cultural moment interrupted the widespread use of stop and search in 1999 and was a challenge to the legitimacy of policing. The assertion of a 'Macpherson effect' on crime rates, as discussed in this chapter, are formative in the early definitions of 'knife crime'; linking the restriction of police racial profiling to increases in knife incidents.

In summary, the end of the twentieth century is marked by uncertainty and political dualism. New labour's social democratic authoritarianism presented new challenges for the legitimization of force within neoliberalism. Existing racialised discourse of 'gun culture' and 'gang culture' provided justifications for militarization and robustness in policing, along with extensive surveillance and early state intervention. It is on this foundation, following the cultural event of the Macpherson report, that a mobilisation towards 'knife crime' was built. Although there is no mention of 'knife crime' in any official documents at the turn of the twenty-first century, there is evidence of a shifting focus towards knives in crime recording practices. The introduction of the 'knife-enabled' feature code in 2001 fundamentally changed the way crimes were categorised and reported, ultimately leading to a public definition of 'knife crime' through police crime data that will be discussed in detail in the following chapter.

Learning Exercise 10: Recap and Reflection:

What factors appear to have paved the way towards the emergence of the knife crime problem in the early 2000s.

References

Aldridge, J., Ralphs, R., & Medina, J. (2011). Collateral damage: Territory and policing in an English gang city. In B. Goldson (Ed.), *Youth in crisis*. Routledge.

Alexander, C. (2000). *The Asian gang: Ethnicity, identity, masculinity*. Berg.

Alexander, C. (2008, June). *(Re)Thinking gangs*. The Runnymede Trust.

Alleyne, R. (2002, August 22). Met's baton rounds to fight knife crime. *The Telegraph*.

Amnesty International. (2018). *Trapped in the matrix: Secrecy, stigma, and bias in the Met's gangs database*. www.amnesty.org.uk/gangs.

Back, L. (2010). Whiteness in the dramaturgy of racism. In P. H. Collins & J. Solomos (Eds.), *Handbook of race and ethnic studies*. Sage: London.

Back, L., Keith, M., Khan, A., Shukra, K., & Solomos, J. (2002). The return of assimilationism: Race, multiculturalism and new labour. *Sociological Research Online, 7*(2), 96–105.

Bamber, D. (2002, March 10). Rising knife crime deals further blow to blunkett. *The Sunday Telegraph*. UK.

BBC News. (2007, January 10). D&G criticised over knife adverts. *BBC News Website*.

Berman, G. (2009). Anti-social behaviour order statistics. Social and General Statistics Section. House of Commons Library.

Bland, N., Miller, J., & Quinton, P. (2000). *Upping the PACE? An evaluation of the recommendations of the Stephen Lawrence Inquiry on stops and searches*. Police Research Series Paper 128. Home Office.

Bottoms, A. E. (1974). On the decriminalisation of English Juvenile Courts. In R. Hood (Ed.), *Essays in Honour of Sir Leon Radzinowicz*. Heinemann.

Bowling, B., & Phillips, C. (2002). *Racism, crime and justice*. Pearson.

Bowling, B., & Philips, C. (2007). Disproportionate and discriminatory: Reviewing the evidence on police stop and search. *Modern Law Review, 70*(6), 936–961.

Bradford, B. (2017). *Stop and search and police legitimacy*. Routledge.

Brown, S. (1998). *Understanding youth and crime: Listening to youth*. Open University Press.

Bullock, K., & Tilley, N. (2002). *Gangs, shootings and violent incidents in Manchester: Developing a crime reduction strategy*. Home Office Crime Reduction Series, Paper 13. The Home Office

Campbell, S. (2002). *A review of anti-social behaviour orders*. Home Office Research Study 236. Home Offices Research and Statistics Directorate.

Cohen, S. (1972). *Folk devils and moral panics: The creation of the Mods and Rockers*. Routledge.

Commissioner MPA. (2005). Knife enabled crime. Report 10 of the 19 January 2005 meeting of the planning, performance & review committee. MPA: Committees: Planning, performance and review reports—19 Jan 05 (10) (policeauthority.org).

Cook, E. A., & Walklate, S. (2020, June 27). Gendered objects and gendered spaces: The invisibilities of 'knife' crime. *Current Sociology* [Online], 1–16.

Day, J., & Gibson, O. (2006, June 8). Cameron raps Radio 1 DJ for violent lyrics. *The Guardian.*

Dennis, N., Erdos, G., & Al-Shahi, A. (2000). *Racist murder and pressure group politics*. Institute for the study of civil society.

Dodd, V. (2012, June 12). Police up to 28 times more likely to stop and search black people. *The Guardian.*

Dodd, V. (2021, February 3). A thousand young, black men removed from Met gang violence prediction database. *The Guardian.*

Elliott-Cooper, A. (2021). *Black resistance to British policing*. Manchester University Press.

Fatsis, L. (2019). Policing the beats: The criminalisation of UK drill and grime music by the London Metropolitan Police. *Sociological Review, 67*(6), 1300–1316.

Fekete, L. (2013). Total policing: Reflections from the frontline. *Race & Class, 54*(3), 65–76.

Foster, J. (2008). 'It might have been incompetent, but it wasn't racist': Murder detectives' perceptions of the Lawrence Inquiry and its impact on homicide investigation in London. *Policing and Society, 18*(2), 89–112.

Gilroy, P. (1982). *The myth of black criminality. Socialist Register*. Merlin.

Gilroy, P. (1987). *There ain't no black in the Union Jack*. Hutchinson University Press.

Goldson, B. (2010). The sleep of (criminological) reason: Knowledge-policy rupture and New Labour's youth justice legacy. *Criminology and Criminal Justice, 10*(2), 155–178.

Gonzalez-Sobrino, B., & Goss, D. R. (2019). Exploring the mechanisms of racialization beyond the black–white binary. *Ethnic and Racial Studies, 42*(4), 505–510.

Hales, G., Lewis, C., & Silverstone, D. (2006). *Gun crime: The market in and use of illegal firearms*. Home Office Research Study 298: Home Office.

Hall, N., Grieve, J., & Savage, S. P. (Eds.). (2009). *Policing and the legacy of Lawrence*. Cullompton.

Hall, S. (2005). New labour's double-shuffle. *Review of Education, Pedagogy, and Cultural Studies, 27*(4), 319–335.

Hall, S., Roberts, B., Clarke, J., Jefferson, T., & Critcher, C. (1978). *Policing the crisis: Mugging, the state, and law and order*. Macmillan.

Hallsworth, S., & Young, T. (2004). Getting real about gangs. *Criminal Justice Matters, 55*, 12–13.

Hallsworth, S., & Young, T. (2008). Gang talk and gang talkers: A critique. *Crime Media Culture, 4*, 175–195.

Haydon, D., & Scraton, P. (2000, September). 'Condemn a little more, understand a little less': The political context and rights' implications of the domestic and European rulings in the Venables-Thompson case. *Journal of Law and Society, 27*(3), 416–448.

Henry, A., & Smith, D. (2007). *Transformations of policing*. Law and Society Series. Edinburgh/Glasgow, Routledge 'not only with racism's violent and hateful face but also its more genteel institutional quality' (Back 2010: 457).

Hills, A. (1995). Militant tendencies: Paramilitarism in the British Police. *British Journal of Criminology, 35*(3), 450.

Hitchcock, A. (2009). Tackling teenage knife crime. *Policing, 4*(2), 149–151.

HMICFRS. (2017). *Crime recording process*. Available at: https://www.justicein spectorates.gov.uk/hmicfrs/our-work/article/crime-data-integrity/crime-rec ording-process/.

Holland, C. (2013). *The report of the Azelle Rodney Inquiry*. HC 552. The Stationery Office.

Home Office. (1997). '*No more excuses': A new approach to tackling youth crime in England and Wales*. Home Office.

Home Office/Ministry of Justice. (2014). *Anti-social behavior order statistics: England and Wales—2013 key findings*. London: Home Office.

Holdaway, S. (1996). *The racialisation of British policing*. Macmillan.

Hughes, G. (1998/2003). *Understanding crime prevention: Social control, risk, and late modernity*. Open University Press Hall.

Ingleton, R. (1997). *Arming the British police; the great debate*. Frank Cass & Co Ltd.

Innes, M. (2012, January 18). 'Total policing' requires doing less, not more. *The Guardian*.

Jefferson, T. (1990). *The case against paramilitary policing*. Open University Press.

Jefferson, T. (1993, Summer). Pondering paramilitarism: A question of standpoints. *The British Journal of Criminology, 33*(3): 374–381

Konig, T., Knowles, C. H., West, A., Wilson, A., & Cross, F. (2006, September 23). Stabbing: Data support public perception. *British Medical Journal, 333*(7569), 652.

Lemos, G. (2004). *Fear and fashion: The use of knives and other weapons by young people*. London: Lemos and Crane.

Lemos, G., & Crane, P. (2009). *The fear and fashion evaluation: A summary report*. Clear Plan.

Lugo-Ocando, J., & Faria Brandao, R. (2016). Stabbing news: Articulating crime statistics in the newsroom. *Journalism Practice, 10*(6), 715–729.

MacPherson, W. (1999). *The Stephen Lawrence inquiry. Report of an Inquiry*. The Stationery Office.

McLagan, G. (2005). *Guns and gangs: Inside black gun crime*. London: Allison & Busby.

Ministry of Justice/YJB. (2021). *Youth justice statistics, 2021*. Youth justice statistics—GOV.UK (www.gov.uk).

Muncie, J. (2002). A new deal for youth? Early intervention and correctionalism. In G. Hughes, E. McLaughlin, & J. Muncie (Eds.), *Crime prevention and community safety: New directions*. Sage.

Muncie, J., & Goldson, B. (2006). The new Correctionalism. In J. Muncie and B. Goldson (Eds.), *Comparative youth justice*. Sage.

Murji, K., & Solomos, J. (2005). Racialization in theory and practice. In K. Murji & J. Solomos (Eds.), *Racialization: Studies in theory and practice*. Oxford University Press.

MVA & Miller, J. (2000). *Profiling populations available for stops and searches.* Police Research Series Paper 131. Home Office

Nijjar, J. (2018). Echoes of empire: Excavating the colonial roots of Britain's "War on Gangs." *Social Justice, 45,* 147–161.

Pantazis, C., & Pemberton, S. (2009). From the "old" to the "new" suspect community: Examining the impacts of recent UK counter-terrorist legislation. *British Journal of Criminology, 49,* 646–666.

Pearson, G. (1983). *Hooligan: A history of respectable fears.* MacMillan.

Pitts, J. (2001). Korrectional karaoke: New Labour and the zombification of youth justice. *Youth Justice, 1*(2), 3–16.

Pitts, J. (2008). *Reluctant gangsters: The changing face of youth crime.* Willan.

Punch, M. (2011). *Shoot to kill: Police accountability, firearms and fatal force.* Policy Press.

Quinton, P., Bland, N., & Miller, J. (2000). *Police stops, decision-making and Practice.* Police Research Series. Home Office, Policing and Reducing Crime Unit.

Rowe, M. (Ed.). (2004). *Policing beyond Macpherson: Issues in policing, race and society.* Willan.

Sayeed, R. (2017). *1997: The future that never happened.* Zed Books.

Scarman, L. S. (1981). *The Brixton disorders 10–12 April 1981: Report of an inquiry.* H.M.S.O.

Shiner, M., Carre, Z., Delsol, R., & Eastwood, N. (2018). *The colour of injustice: Race, drugs and law enforcement in England and Wales.* Stopwatch & Release.

Silverman, J. (1994). *Crack of doom.* London: Hodder.

Smith, R. (2003). *Youth justice: Ideas, policies, practice.* Willan.

Smithson, H., Ralphs, R., & Williams, P. (2012). Used and abused: The problematic usage of gang terminology in the United Kingdom and its implications for ethnic minority youth. *British Journal of Criminology, 53,* 113–128. https://doi.org/10.1093/bjc/azs046

Squires, P. (2000). *Gun culture or gun control? Firearms, violence and society.* Routledge.

Squires, P. (2006). Anti-social behaviour and New Labour. *Critical Social Policy, 26*(1), 144–168.

Squires, P. (2007). *Police perceptions of gang and gun related offending: A key informant Q49 survey, magnet project, greater Manchester police.* https://www.york.ac.uk/management/magnet/.

Squires, P. (2009). The knife crime 'epidemic' and British politics. *British Politics, 4*(1), 127–157.

Squires, P. (Ed.). (2008a). *ASBO nation: The criminalisation of nuisance.* Policy Press.

Squires, P. (2008b). *'Gun crime': A review of evidence and policy, centre for crime and justice studies.* Kings College.

Squires, P. (2014). *Gun crime in global contexts.* Routledge.

Squires, P. (2016). Voodoo liability: Joint enterprise prosecution as an aspect of intensified criminalisation. *Oñati Socio-Legal Series, 6*(4), 937–956.

Squires, P. (2021). Youth justice: Changing institutions, changing contexts. In H. Bochel & G. Daly (Eds.), *Social Policy* (4th ed., pp. 261–379). Routledge.

Squires, P., & Kennison, P. (2010). *Shooting to kill: Policing, firearms and armed response* (p. 2014). Wiley/Blackwell Home Office.

Squires, P., & Stephen, D. E. (2005). *Rougher justice: Young people and anti-social behaviour.* Willan Publishing.

Squires, P., Silvestri, A., Grimshaw, R., & Solomon, E. (2008). *Street weapons commission evidence: Guns, knives and street violence.* London: CCJS, Kings College.

Stephens, M. (1994). *Police force, police service: Care and control in Britain.* Palgrave.

Thrasher, F. (1926). The gang as a symptom of community disorganization. *Journal of Applied Sociology, 1*(1), 3–27.

Tonry, M. (2004). *Punishment and politics: Evidence and emulation in the making of English crime control policy.* Willan.

UKPOL. (2007). *Tony Blair—2007 Callaghan Memorial Speech.* UKPOL (online). Available at: http://www.ukpol.co.uk/tony-blair-2007-callaghan-memorial-speech/.

Virdee, S., & McGeever, B. (2018). Racism, crisis, brexit. *Ethnic and Racial Studies, 41*(10), 1802–1819.

Waddington, P. A. J. (1987). Towards paramilitarism? Dilemmas in the policing of public order. *British Journal of Criminology, 27*(1), 37–46.

Waddington, P. A. J. (1991). *The strong arm of the law: Armed and public order policing.* Clarendon Press.

Waddington, P., & Hamilton, M. (1997). The impotence of the powerful: Recent police weapons policy. *Sociology, 31*(1), 91–109.

Weathers, H. (2005, April 26). A knife to our hearts. *Daily Mail.*

Williams, P. (2015). Criminalising the other: Challenging the race-gang nexus. *Race & Class, 56*(3), 18–35.

Williams, P., & Clarke, R. (2018). The black criminal other as an object of social control. *Social Sciences, 7*(11), 234–234.

Williams, P., & Clarke, R. (2020). (Re)Producing guilt in suspect communities: The centrality of racialisation in joint enterprise prosecutions. *International Journal for Crime, Justice and Social Democracy, 9*(3), 116–129.

Wilson, J. Q., & Kelling, G. L. (1982, March 29–38). Broken Windows. *The Atlantic Monthly.*

Wood, R. (2010). UK: The reality behind the 'knife crime' debate. *Race & Class, 52*(2), 97–103.

4

A Public Definition: The Making of the 'Knife Crime' Label

Introduction

In the previous chapter we explored the ways in which three important discourses in policing and law and order—a politics of youth, race and nation (often signified by the 'gang problem'), the police use of force, and growing challenges to the legitimacy of the police—discourses that, in the decade after 2000, came to settle around the 'signal crime' of knife-enabled violence. Knife-enabled violence came to embrace and distil both the connected threats represented by anti-social youth and racial otherness and the challenge to which robust 'total policing' represented a response. At the same time policing was held in partial check by a discourse on police legitimacy emanating from the Macpherson Report. In this chapter we turn to explore the ways in which the label 'knife crime' came to establish and reinforce itself across the media and in public and political consciousness, a consensus building ideological resource facilitating the re-establishment of social and political order and resurrecting, in particular, the authority of enforcement-led policing. We described the previous chapter as involving a phase of pre-public mobilisation around 'knife crime' whereas this chapter, a second stage, is defined by the earliest public definitions and use of the term in news reports and the first interpretations of data collected through the new police 'knife-enabled' crime code. This chapter comprises a close analysis of the events that constituted 'knife crime' in broad popular usage whilst showing how meaning was constructed around this label in conjunction with existing news values and shifting public concerns.

This chapter examines how the reporting of high profile cases defined as 'knife crimes' became instrumental in the development of the label's narrative; firstly through age and location, and later by social class and ethnicity. Producing an analysis of 'knife crime' news throughout this period, we discuss the combined use of images, language and data in the making of 'knife crime', leading to a new understanding of the 'knife crime' label as a particular response to crime and violence. Retracing the increasing press attention from 2002 onwards, the analysis of news stories reveals the processes that transformed a relatively innocuous collective noun, and the largely tolerated practice of knife possession,[1] into an insidious adjective, newly synonymous with a dangerous urban youth culture in need of proactive policing.

The previous chapter detailed the dualism of Blair's New Labour Britain and the inherent contradictions of a law and order neo-liberalism combined with a social democratic ideology of community safety. In this context, the emergence of the new crime category is understood here in conjunction with the wider tensions thrown up by youth, race, violent disorder and policing. Our account of events will demonstrate the important constitutive relationship between 'knife crime' and robust police enforcement and proactive stop and search strategies—arguing that the effective mobilisation of police as an occupying and hostile force in the urban environment suburbs seeks justification through the label 'knife crime'. Our analysis of this period will suggest that rather than stop and

---

[1] Despite periodic concerns with knife-involved violence and, not least, the legislative changes described in Chapter 1, one of us can certainly remember a time when knives, blades being one of the most regularly deployed hand tools (in gardening, fishing, woodworking, arts and crafts, camping) were broadly accepted and commonly carried. Boy-scouts will doubtless recall a time when possession of a multi-tool Swiss Army knife was part and parcel of 'being prepared' although the practice certainly extended far beyond scouting. Grayston (2017), for instance describes a *Victorinox* penknife endorsed by the Duke of Edinburgh's award scheme, for additional safety it had a rounded blade end.

search returning in response to 'knife crime', rather 'knife crime' is established as a public concern in response to an already increasing stop and search agenda. Drawing parallels with the case of 'mugging' in the 1970s, this chapter will explore how the racialisation of 'knife crime' responded to specific sociologies of the city—equipping an occupying force in the former Black enclaves of the suburbs. To begin with however, a clear distinction will be made between the emerging category 'knife crime' in England and Wales at this time and the label previously limited to defining crimes located in Scotland.

When 'Knife Crime' Was a Scottish Problem

We have earlier discussed the historical reputation of Glasgow gangs for knife fighting. Perhaps because of this, British news articles appearing during 2002 using the phrase 'knife crime' were almost entirely concerned with Scotland. Scottish publications of the *Daily Mail* refer to 'knife thugs' long before this kind of language is common south of the border (Mega & Grant, 2004). We have already discussed the distinct tradition of knife fighting encountered in Scotland. Much existing research sets Scotland apart from England and Wales as having its own highly specific history of crime labelling and response to knives and bladed weapons. This is undoubtedly also true of the more recent phase of public concern about knife crime arising north of the border.

On the one hand, the Scottish 'knife crime' label included specific sharp instruments and bladed weapons that have their own localised social histories; such as the 'razor gangs' of the 1920s divided along religious and sectarian lines (Davies, 2013). On the other, entering the twenty-first century, it is clear that age and ethnicity are not defining features of Scottish 'knife crime' in the way they are in the English version of the label. Whilst there is some concern in Scottish 'knife crime' reports about the age of victims and perpetrators ('At the Sharp End', 2003; 'McConnell pledge', 2003), none of the articles analysed during this period mention ethnicity as a defining feature of Scottish 'knife crime'. This is a crucial distinction that will come to fundamentally separate the term and its functionality in the two contexts. Scotland's political separation is also significant. Since May 1999 Scotland has had its own parliament bringing many aspects of governance under national control. Policing, courts, housing, social work and education were all under Scotland's own jurisdiction during this time, meaning that the Scottish response to 'knife crime' has been notably different from that of England and Wales.

When The Scottish Police undertook a series of knife targeted weapon searches and home raids in the late 1990s as part of 'Operation Spotlight', for example, it did so from within its own political context. For instance, critics have argued that Operation Spotlight was one element of a 'revanchist or vengeful approach to urban policy in Glasgow… in which attempts to improve the economic fortunes of the city involved the targeting of vulnerable groups like the homeless and prostitutes, who were viewed as detracting from attempts to revitalise the city centre' (Donnelly & Scott, 2005: 116). Accordingly, any resulting 'knife crime' data trends arising from this proactive approach to urban social problems would need to be contextualised in a specifically 'Scottish moment'. A distinction between Scotland and England is also evident in the way English news often 'looks to' Scotland; as an area of exceptional violence in 2003 (Kelbie, 2003), and then for advice on violence reduction in 2017 (Younge & Barr, 2017). Scotland also set itself apart from the rest of the UK having adopted a highly regarded and apparently successful public health approach to 'knife crime' in 2005 (Carnochan & McCluskey, 2010). This shift away from a criminal justice approach in Scotland at a time when England and Wales were intensifying a policing and criminal justice response to 'knife crime' further reinforces a distinction between different aspects of the label's significance and use on either side of the border.

Acknowledging the above, it would be inaccurate to conflate the 'knife crime' of Scotland in 2002 and the 'knife crime' that later became a moral panic in England and Wales. The labels were defined separately, operating in different ways, and the responses to each had distinct histories, significances and consequences. Whilst Scottish 'knife crime' was at peak concern in 2002, use of the concept in relation to crime in England and Wales was still very rare. Other than a few uses as a collective noun, such as to announce that baton rounds that will be used to fight knife crime and riots ('Met's Baton Rounds...', 2002), and in reference to 'the Macpherson effect' as discussed earlier (Bamber, 2002), there was a notable absence of 'knife crime' news concerning England and Wales in 2002. This is not to say that there were not occasional articles about knives, violence and young people but simply that these were not yet captured within the symbolic discourse of 'knife crime', the concept was neither fully formed or mobilised the way it would be within a few years.

Towards the end of 2003, however, a series of violent events began to align discourse and public concern around a distinctive 'knife crime' narrative reflecting a seemingly new form of violent criminality in England and Wales. Three related factors are influential in this development. In the first place, the rural school setting of a teenage murder in November 2003 sparked national interest, invigorating coverage of knife-related crimes within particular contexts. Secondly, high news value is sustained and cultivated for this emerging new crime category by the focus on younger children and a broad range of authorised spokespeople ('primary definers': police, politicians, childhood experts, victims' advocates) in turn, endorse the new reality. Thirdly, the narrative linking crime to knives insinuates (or in some cases openly condemns) aspects of a new criminogenic 'knife culture' amongst young people which, in turn, rapidly becomes an urgent argument for more proactive interventions.

The Case of Luke Walmsley

On 4th November 2003, the murder of 14-year-old Luke Walmsley in a school corridor in rural Lincolnshire became the catalyst for a coordinated response to a perceived violent youthful knife crime culture that was supposedly emerging throughout the country. The following day the case was given high news status in both national and regional papers. Headlines included:

BOY, 14, KILLED IN SCHOOL ATTACK: He ran .. then he fell ; PUPILS FLEE IN TERROR AS LUKE KNIFED ON HIS WAY TO LESSON. (McComish et al., 2003) in *The Daily Mirror*

A scuffle, then panic grips children and staff at village school; Chief constable pledges support for community in shock. (Laville, 2003) in *The Daily Telegraph*
Youngsters Caught in Tide of Horror. (Barker, 2003) in *The Sun*

The tabloid language used to describe the incident, 'terror', 'panic' and 'horror', are journalistic embellishments that significantly sensationalised the coverage. Early reporting focused heavily on school safety, seeking teacher's opinions on pupil violence and their powers to prevent another event like this. In an effort to include the 'teachers perspective' and still with no official statement from Luke Walmsley's school, the press coverage the day after the murder widely quoted a comment by David Hart, General Secretary of the National Association of Head Teachers. The full comment stated:

> My reaction is one of utter horror. To think a youngster can be stabbed to death in a school in a relatively quiet part of the country will send shock-waves through the school system. It does demonstrate very clearly the fact that although this level of violence is very rare, there are an incredible number of youngsters who are willing to sign up to the knife culture and bring an offensive weapon into school. (David Hart quoted in 'Classmates See...', 2003)

As the only official statement available, this immediate anecdotal connection made by Hart between the isolated incident of Luke Walmsley and a 'knife culture' with 'incredible numbers' or young people willingly 'signing up', instigated a public debate on what the national response to Luke's death should be. Within two days of Luke's murder the conversation shifted from a specific incident at a school in Lincolnshire to include knives and schools in general. On the 6th of November, The Guardian reported 'Unions call for review of security' with representatives of teachers split on what the course of action should be.[2]

---

[2] Somewhat underscoring the very selectivity of the dominant interpretation placed upon Luke Walmsley's death, an article in *The Independent* (10.10.2011) gave a very different account: 'The descent of a quiet boy who never got over the death of his mother'. It described how Walmsley's killer was an introverted and withdrawn young man who had never overcome the tragedy of his mother's death when he was aged six. He was said to be very defensive regarding

The National Association of Schoolmasters Union of Women Teachers (NASUWT) warned that crime involving weapons was 'spilling over from the streets into schools' and that a working party on school security should be assembled. Parent-teacher associations were equally proactive, suggesting the installation of metal detectors in schools to stop students 'attempting to smuggle in knives and guns'. Police demonstrated their position with action, deploying 100 extra officers to 'patrol the playgrounds of British schools identified as breeding grounds for young offenders' (Goodchild, 2003). The evocative and metaphoric language used by apparently reliable spokespeople at this time was widely reported. It was indicative of a developing narrative—In which the knife was seen as an alien threat, based in the street, but 'spilling into' or being 'smuggled' in to the otherwise safe spaces of schools. The police went on to describe schools as 'breeding grounds' for criminality, an early indication that the perceived threat of contagious influence spreading from one young person to others would be formative in shaping the response to a phenomenon that would come to defined as 'knife crime'.

Other public reactions voiced disagreement with the proactive measures taken and feared that the frequency of violence in schools was being exaggerated in the hastiness of the response. The then Schools Minister, David Miliband, was reported as cautioning against 'knee-jerk reactions' to the school-time incident, stating; 'the death of Luke Walmsley at his Lincolnshire school was not evidence of rising violence throughout the education system' ('Call for Caution...', 2003). The general secretary of the National Union of Teachers concurred, saying 'This is an absolutely tragic incident, but there are 7.5 million children in

---

his mother's reputation, and already, at age sixteen, was demonstrating a range of alcohol and anger management issues. He also collected knives. In his sixteenth year he was also beginning to come to police attention for violent outbursts and bullying, and even earlier on the day of the stabbing had brandished his knife at a fellow pupil in the schoolyard. The incident was not reported. The stabbing itself seems to have been verbally provoked, a dispute over a girlfriend and an alleged insult directed at his mother. The incident back-story, in other words, exposed a whole world of human drama: family trauma, hurt, social problems and psychological suffering, isolation and pent-up aggression, missed clues and opportunities to intervene, insult and provocation, and a young immature masculinity more inclined to lash out than back down. So much youthful turmoil, so many different angles but all reduced to a flat descriptor—'knife crime'—how and why this particular interpretation became the overwhelmingly dominant one is amongst our key concerns.

our schools 190 days a year and our surveys show the number of weapons being brought into our schools is absolutely minuscule' (ibid.). The chairman of the Youth Justice Board warned that over-reacting could exacerbate the issue saying; 'it's a great tragedy when you start making schools into fortresses. It creates a fear culture and this can beget even more problems' (Goodchild, 2003).

What was significantly absent in these early debates on the urgency of the problem was any reliable supporting data. Although plenty of anecdotal evidence was offered, the early reports lack any statistics demonstrating that knives represented a significant problem either for 'young people' or 'schools'. There was a concerted effort, however, by journalists across the country to produce valid evidence of the scale of the knife problem whilst public concern was still running high. Birmingham City Council announced their investigation into whether violence was increasing in schools ('Call for Caution…', 2003). The *Sunday Mirror* ran its own surveys in Bristol, Cardiff, Birmingham, Newcastle and Liverpool, sending children to attempt to purchase knives at high-street shops and publishing the results (Ellam, 2003). The BBC online published an article 'Is knife crime really getting worse' (2003) attempting to collate available data. Meanwhile, *The Observer* conducted its own investigation and published its findings November 23rd 2003 (Townsend & Barnett, 2003). This was the *first* news article reporting on Luke Walmsley that used the phrase 'knife crime'.

Opting for the sensationalist headline: 'Scandal of pupils aged five carrying knives' the findings of *The Observer* investigation consolidated the idea that Luke was not the victim of an isolated attack, but the latest casualty in a national 'epidemic' in which 'nowhere is safe' (Townsend & Barnett, 2003). Amongst other shocking statistics the Observer listed four other young people involved in knife-related news since Luke's death, two stabbings, one in-school knife possession incident and one court case currently at trial. The specific circumstances of these incidents were not described; the cases were not viewed in isolation but as one collective crime: 'knife crime'.

Violence and Children: The Gold Standard of Newsworthiness

In the chain of events from Luke Walmsley's death to the collective grouping of incidents as 'knife crime', what was especially striking was the constitutive power of the collective noun 'youth' in the making of the 'knife crime' label. It was the school setting and the notion of a specific threat to children that provided the initial momentum that would eventually link crimes together by virtue of the age of the perpetrators and victims and the type of weapon used. Rather than acts of 'knife crime' representing a phenomenon exclusive to youths, it suggested a type of incident only defined as phenomenal when connected to children and the exceptionality bestowed by their age. Were it not for the news value of childhood violence, 'Knife crime' as a tangible form of criminal behaviour would be inconceivable.

Exploring this aspect further, research in media studies suggests that that violence continues to hold a dominant (although perhaps diminishing) news value:

> The news value which is arguably most common to all media is that of 'violence' because it fulfils the media's desire to present dramatic events in the most graphic possible fashion... However, violence has become so ubiquitous that – although still considered newsworthy it is frequently reported in a routine, mundane manner with little follow-up or analysis. Unless a story involving violence conforms to several other news values or provides a suitable threshold to keep alive an existing set of stories, even the most serious acts of violence may be used as 'fillers' consigned to the inside pages of a newspaper. (Jewkes, 2015: 63–64)

Many instances of non-fatal stabbings, threats made with knives, knife carrying and knife homicides were not considered to have a great deal of news value before the emergence of the 'knife crime' label. But in the early stages of the social reaction cycle, the very youth of both victims and perpetrators became ever more significant. As those involved became younger and younger the range of incidents considered newsworthy increased, age itself became a central dynamic of newsworthiness.

Luke Walmsley was 14 and this, in itself, was an alarming fact, but by the end of the same month headlines were connecting the case with 5 year olds carrying knives (Townsend & Barnett, 2003). This pursuit of youth in the making of 'knife crime' reflects the evolving priorities, sensitivities and interests of media audiences and news reporting techniques as much as it does any underlying changes in the scale or seriousness of youth crime (Muncie & Goldson, 2006). It was this process of attaching children to the violence of knives, beginning with Luke Walmsley, which pushed the media headlines towards increasing hysteria. In the days following the stabbing the news headlines from a range of national newspapers focused especially upon on 'kids', 'children' and 'school' as they extrapolated from one case to a national crisis. Within one week the headlines included:

Kids carry knives and hammers: they have to look after themselves. (Johnson, 2003a)

Is your kid taking a knife to school? (Johnson, 2003b)

Shops, stalls and web illegally sell knives to children. (Woolcock, 2003)

SOLD.. TO A 12-YR-OLD; Shop charges £25 for this 12in blade. Boy of 14 is stabbed to death but stores still flout law on children buying knives. (Ellam, 2003).

Not even your school is safe. ('Not Even…', 2003)

The particular value of the symbolic innocence and victim status of youth has been identified as a means of sustaining news value which has become significantly more intense over recent decades:

[W]riting in 1978, Stuart Hall and his colleagues argued that any crime can be lifted into news visibility if violence becomes associated with it, but three decades later it might be said that any crime can be lifted into new visibility if children are associated with it… The focus on children means that deviant behaviour automatically crosses a higher threshold of victimization than would have been possible if adults alone had been involved... children who commit crimes have arguably become especially newsworthy. (Jewkes, 2015: 66, 67)

Yet whilst age was certainly a formative element of the 'knife crime' category, it was not the only criterion. In the same month Luke Walmsley was killed, 18-year-old Ronald Pattinson was given a life sentence for stabbing 12-year-old Natalie Ruddick 25 times, murdering her in her home after a domestic dispute ('Teenager Guilty...', 2003). At no point during the emerging media focus upon 'knife culture' concern during the latter part of 2003 was this case referred to. Similarly, there was no mention of Pattinson's connection with the knife he used, or any sense that a developing 'knife crime culture' might be a contributing factor to the tragedy. Despite the youth of the victim and the brutality of the violence, as we have noted previously, the domestic location of this murder appeared to exclude it from the 'knife crime' news reports at this time. For 'knife crime' has always been about the actions of particular groups in particular (public) settings and this, perhaps inconsistent, or selectively constructed preoccupation with knife crime became increasingly focused as the label's distinct character developed. The parameters of the perceived problem certainly evolves over time but in 2003 public concern was very much focused on knives in schools, the availability of knives to school aged children and what could be done to address the dangers facing school aged children.

Learning Exercise 11: Examining Knife Crime Reporting

Find two or three news articles that report on a recent knife-enabled crime or violent knife offence using the phrase 'knife crime'. Read these through carefully, critically analysing the chosen content and inferred meaning. As prompts for your analysis try to answer the following questions:

- Does the event being reported on involve young people in inner-city settings? Is their ethnicity included in the story?
- Does the article link this event to broader changes in 'knife crime' rates or data trends in knife offences? If so, is it clear if this data is youth-specific or adult inclusive?

- Does the article include any images? If so, what do these show, and is it clear how they are connected to the incident? What do the images add or communicate?
- Are there any 'spokespeople' chosen to comment on the event—if so who are they and why have they been chosen? Are they invested in knife crime for professional or personal reasons?

Reflection
Thinking about the harmful narratives constructed through selective and often manipulated crime news, who do you think has greater responsibility; the news media who make irresponsible editorial decisions to grab and sustain the attention of their audiences? Or the audiences themselves, for continuing to buy and click on news stories that sensationalise child on child violence?

Reporting the Knife Crime Report

On 1 June 2004 the Met Police published their first 'Knife Crime Report' containing a comprehensive breakdown of the statistics collated since the introduction of the 'knife-enabled code' in 2001—itself a significant shift in police crime recording as we have shown. The content of this report was especially meaningful as the data would not only be used to evidence the scale of the supposed violence 'epidemic' for an eager press, but it also provided the justification for the targeted police mobilisation against young people announced later that same month: Operation Blunt. In the following paragraphs we will examine the content of this document followed by a close scrutiny of how the report and the data and issues it addressed was reported in the press immediately following its release.

Considering the heightened media concern and growing public panic over knife offences in 2003, it was anticipated that the report would reveal rather shocking figures, but the evidence itself was rather more underwhelming. A data table of knife-enabled offences (but excluding simple knife possession offences) covering the three years from June 2001 to March 2004 showed a rather fluctuating pattern, *overall* the trend was downwards across the three years (by 5.2%), but followed by an

Offences involving a knife for FY 04 are up 9.3% on FY 03.

Offence table

	Jun 01 to Mar 02	Jun 02 to Mar 03	Jun 03 to Mar 04	% change Jun 03-Mar 04 V Jun 01-Mar 02	% change Jun 03-Mar 04 V Jun 02-Mar 03
Knife Offences	14881	12454	14110	-5.2%	13.3%

Knife crime as a percentage of TNO was 1.6% in Jun 03-Mar 04, a slight increase from last year but is down against two years ago when knife crime represented 1.7% of TNO.

Fig. 4.1   Knife crime offence trends June 2001–March 2004 (TPHQ, 2004: 3)

increase of 13.3% during the final year of the sequence. However the Metropolitan Police chose to highlight the latest year on year increase rather than the overall decline and even though 'Knife crime' as a percentage of the Total Number of Offences (TNO) had remained relatively constant at around 1.6–1.7% (Fig. 4.1).

Reflecting public interest and media priorities, special attention was paid to comparing data by the age, sex and ethnicity of both offenders and victims. The highest victim group was reported to be white males between the ages of 14 and 21. The data showed a consistent peak victim age of 15–18 over the three years, but the breakdown of knife offences by offence type showed that once 'robbery' offences were removed as an offence motive the victim levels stayed consistently in the 15–35 range. Further analysis revealed that robbery had much lower rates of injury than Violence against the Person, suggesting that although knife offences disproportionately affected younger age categories, these were indicative of the less serious types of offences—and certainly far less often fatal than those committed by their adult counterparts (Figs. 4.2 and 4.3).

Along with a borough-by-borough breakdown the report examined at the location codes relating to knife offences. One of the biggest percentage increases in the report was related to domestic violence; 'Domestic Knife crime has seen a 22% increase against both last year and a 23% increase against two years ago' (TPHQ, 2004: 9). The category of knife offences with the highest likelihood of serious or fatal injury

If we take just the victims for Jun 03 to Mar 04 and split it into crime categories we
see that it is victims of robbery that caused the large peak for 15-16 year olds.
Violence Against the Person is at a fairly steady rate between the ages 15 to 35 this
then steadily decreases

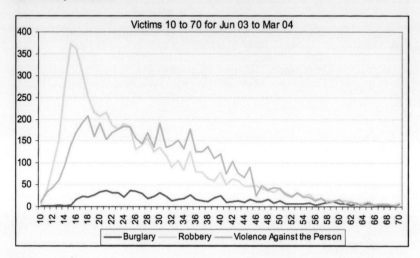

Fig. 4.2   Victims of knife-enabled crime June 2003–March 2004: By age (TPHQ,
2004)

Injury Degree	Total	Violence Against the Person	Robbery
Fatal	0%	1%	0%
Serious	7%	16%	2%
Moderate	11%	22%	5%
Minor	20%	26%	20%
No Injury	48%	25%	56%
Threats Only	13%	11%	17%

Fig. 4.3   Knife crime Injuries June 2003–March 2004: By offence and seriousness
(TPHQ, 2004: 11, 12)

was 'Violence against a Person'. Fully 53% of incidents within this category occurred within the home whilst 'nearly 80% of domestic knife
crime was violence against the person' (ibid.). Much as we have noted
already (Cook & Walklate, 2020), despite this significant increase in the

knife crime offence category with the highest likelihood of serious harm, domestic violence was entirely overlooked in the media reporting of this released data.

The police report acknowledged the complexities of 'knife crime' data. It was careful about making assumptions and urged caution about drawing too many conclusions when aggregating different types of offences (Violence against a Person, Robbery, Burglary and Domestic Violence) merely by reference to the fact that a widely available weapon type was employed in each case and arbitrarily collated together as 'knife crime' data. However, no such subtleties of interpretation were apparent when the report was covered in the press, when a priori considerations of newsworthiness, established narratives about youth and violence, sensationalism, and a highly selective use of the data painted a very different picture of this apparently emerging new crime trend. For example The *Evening Standard* under the misleading headline '*Increase in Knife Crime Led by Young*' (Davenport, 2004) summarized the Knife Crime Report thus:

> The scale of London's growing knife culture is revealed today. Figures show a crime involving a knife is committed once every 25 minutes in the capital.

> An internal study carried out by the Metropolitan Police shows a total of 14,110 knife offences occurred between June 2003 and March - a rise of 13 per cent over the same period the previous year.

> The figure excludes the offence of simply possessing a knife. The Met report also shows that 39 per cent of offenders are aged between 14 and 21.

> The findings are revealed as the Met announced tough new measures to clamp down on knife crime under Operation Blunt. For the first time police are to routinely deploy a scanner which can see through people's clothes to detect hidden weapons...

Commander Simon Foy, head of the Met's anti-knife crime campaign, said: "The most worrying aspect of this report is that this is almost exclusively a young people's phenomenon." (Davenport, 2004)

Analysing the specific ways in which the knife crime report was translated in this article revealed how the 'knife crime' narrative began to be scripted through a distortion of data for the benefit of increased news value. The Evening Standard began with a high impact headline that simultaneously; (a) assumed a 'knife crime' category as predefined; (b) selectively claimed 'it' has increased and, (c) misleadingly attributed the increase to the violence of young people. As we have already acknowledged, however, it is no surprise to see the media producing and endlessly recycling such highly popular stories about youth and delinquency, the well-established narrative plays to a particular kind of audience, forever rekindling a familiar series of values and concerns (Brown, 1998; Pearson, 1983).

The second sentence of the news article, 'Figures show a crime involving a knife is committed once every 25 minutes in the capital' (Davenport, 2004), represented a common example of a very familiar technique employed to report knife-related data with maximum effect. By transforming a static, abstract and aggregated quantity into an experiential and temporal relation the emotional impact is greatly increased. In this case the number 14,110 without context is anonymous and hard to conceptualise and therefore carries little meaning. But when represented as yet another knife crime *every twenty-five minutes* this is, as Appadurai has argued in the *Fear of Small Numbers* (2006) experienced as an urgent direct and personalised threat. Add to this the common yet erroneous assumption that every knife offence involved a violent assault upon a young victim and this became a particularly alarming claim. The selective dramatisation of the reported knife-enabled offence figures, pointing only to years in which knife-related offence trends were increasing and the implication that these offences represented a much wider culture of youthful knife carrying, whilst overlooking the fact the not every knife offence involved an injury were just some of the ways in which a distorting impression of knife crime in London was created. For instance, none of the media reporting referred to the fact that fully

61% of all victims in the latest year of data were 'threat only' or offences involving 'no injury' (TPHQ, 2004: 12). There was no mention of this in the *Evening Standard*'s summary. Finally, much was made of the evidence that 39% of all offences were committed by young people in the 14–21 age range, reinforcing a direct connection between the narrative of extreme violence and youth culture, even though there was evidence in the MPS report which firmly contradicted this media narrative, in particular evidence that: (a) that the age of accused knife offenders was increasing (TPHQ, 2004: 15); (b) that this same 14–21 age bracket had made up 47% of offences two years earlier (ibid.) and; (c) that younger offenders made up a much larger proportion of the least violent offences (TPHQ, 2004: 11, 12).

With the narrative of an increasingly violent youth laid out, the rationale Operation Blunt was introduced, as a 'tough new measure to clamp down on knife crime' (Davenport, 2004). The article closed with a final seal of approval from Police Commander Simon Foy, who, despite all the evidence to the contrary detailed throughout the police report, remarkably claimed that the most worrying aspect of contemporary 'knife crime' was it's 'exclusively' youthful character. Yet with Foy's stamp of approval, the selective and decidedly fabricated *misrepresentation* of knife-enabled crime data had definitively replaced the actual data as the inspiration for strategies to tackle 'knife crime'.

Operation Blunt, expanding from a three borough pilot project in 2004 to a London wide mobilisation in 2005, was targeted at young people in the city. Perhaps the most immediate impact of the operation as a proactive police intervention strategy based upon stop and search was to amplify the rates of knife possession amongst the targeted group. It was subsequently acknowledged that a significant part of the rise in detected knife crime was itself a result of Operation Blunt (McCandless et al., 2016). Operation Blunt also included educational projects visiting many of London's secondary schools, talking about 'knife crime' and showing images of knives. Later, the force produced an educational video *Joint Enterprise: Knife Crime* to support this school-based work warning young people of the dangers of socialising in 'gangs' and carrying weapons. Ironically, one of the dangers the film warned against was the possibility of being charged as an accessory under the joint enterprise gang prosecution strategy lately adopted by the CPS and facing a life sentence for murder (Squires, 2016). In time, the increasing presence of knife imagery in campaigns, operations and reports became a defining feature in the making of 'knife crime'. For many young people the images constructed an increasingly serious and all-pervasive threat, exacerbating the dangers they faced on the urban streets, it is little surprise that, as the knife crime drama grew, survey after survey reported young people admitting that they carried knives 'for protection' (Marfleet, 2008; Palasinski & Riggs, 2012; Sethi and World Health Organization, 2007). The heightened visibility of knives and of 'knife crime' formed a kind of vicious circle increasing both fear and the resort to self-protective behaviours (behaviours which could include both carrying weapons and socialising in groups: Eades et al., 2007; Marshall et al., 2005; Measor & Squires, 2000) as the 'knife crime' label gained more and more attention.

Making 'Knife Crime' News

The distortion and 'tabloidization' of 'knife crime' from its very inception, caused both public concern and knife crime visibility to gather momentum as the pressures of sustaining newsworthiness grew. Shaped by the willing spectatorship of news consumers these influence manifested themselves in particular representational techniques adopted by journalists and editors. Recognising the imagery that journalists wanted police press officers have been quick to oblige. Publishing images of confiscated knives and bladed weapons is a technique frequently used to represent both the scale and viciousness of the knife crime phenomenon.[3] Following a knife amnesty or police stop and search operation there is often a tendency to include an image of a table displaying

---

[3] The same has been true of pictures of collections of firearms confiscated from offenders, although when firearms are displayed they already tend to have an element of 'exceptionality' about them. Knives are clearly more available and many of them quite mundane, kitchen knives, in appearance. So when knives are displayed it is often the case that the biggest and most brutal in appearance take centre stage, even though these weapons are not necessarily representative of the knives employed in most stabbings or violent incidents. Undoubtedly, however, they certainly *look* dangerous and, as regards the representation of knife crime, that is certainly what matters.

the range and quantity of weapons found or confiscated. Occasionally there are also speculative examples of fascinating weapons that *could* be on the streets—images of concealed blades were displayed in one article that informed the reader that knives 'can be concealed in belt buckles' (Omaar, 2004) or 'hidden in combs' (ibid.) although often without any direct empirical evidence of such weapons.

The analysis of images accompanying 'knife crime' news throughout this defining period in the history of the making of the knife crime label revealed a reoccurring misalignment between the news content and the image displayed. In several articles reporting on recent police search operations an image accompanying the news item showed an array of weapons displayed even though the written text reported only one or two knives found ('College gets...', 2006; 'Rail Police...', 2006). Exploring this representational device further we closely analysed the reoccurring use of one particularly powerful image of a collection of blades that seemed to accompany a wide range of 'knife crime' stories over a substantial period of time. The particular framing of this popular image is also of interest. The photograph does not allow perspective or even include the edges of the table so one can only assume this image is one section of a larger sample of confiscated weapons (Fig. 4.4).

Fig. 4.4 News media image of weapons said to be confiscated by the police in 2003

A wide variety of blades are on display in this one image but the machete is dominant and central. Along with a few kitchen knives, the display comprises a variety of bladed weapons; a dagger, a hunting knife, two bayonets (one alongside its sheath) and a flick knife are amongst the collection. The first occasion on which we encountered this image it was attached to a BBC news article published in November 2003. The title of the piece was '*Warning over More Weapons in Schools*' ('Warning of…', 2003) and the caption beneath the image read; 'Debate about whether there are more weapons in schools' (ibid.). However, the *earliest* use of this photo unearthed during our research, just like the term 'knife crime' itself, was found in Scotland in 1999 where the accompanying article makes no specific reference to young people or schools at all. On the contrary, the image accompanies an article reporting on Strathclyde's policing operation 'Spotlight' with police stating that 'in the last five weeks of the force's latest Operation Spotlightcrackdown, 500 offensive weapons had been seized' ('Knife Culture…', 1999) (Fig. 4.5).

Operation Spotlight took place during a particularly heightened period of proactive policing in Scotland that included widespread stop and search along with home raids targeting drug dealers. Without more information it is impossible to know whether the knives and bladed

Fig. 4.5 News media image accompanying article on a knife crime crackdown in Strathclyde (1999) (Image copied from 'Knife Culture…', 1999)

weapons in this photo were found carried in the street or discovered during raids inside people's homes, but certainly adults were significant amongst the owners and all resided within the Strathclyde region (Fig. 4.6). In 2000 the photo was used twice again to refer to knife carrying in Scotland and Scottish murder rates, both uses apply indirect generalised captions and neither contain any youth-specific concern (see below).

The same image resurfaced south of the border in 2003 and was first encountered when it was used in reference to knives in English schools in the period of heightened focus immediately following the death of Luke Walmsley. At a time when knife violence and school safety was high on the public agenda an image of a table of offensive-looking weapons seized during a Scottish police operation which had targeted adults and homes in 1999 was attached to an article stating 'There is a growing problem of children bringing weapons to school' ('Warning of…', 2003), without any reference to its actual source. Misleading and arguably quite irresponsible in its placement, the image had been thoroughly disconnected from the context it had originally claimed to represent.

In 2004, in an even further distanced misrepresentation, the photo appeared on a children's news website under the headline 'Knife crime

Image copied from 'Police Target Knife…(2000) and from 'Scotland Tops…' (2000)

Fig. 4.6   Further uses of the 'knife array' in Scottish news reporting (Image copied from 'Police Target Knife …', 2000, and 'Scotland Tops …', 2000)

getting worse in UK' ('Knife crime getting...', 2004) with specific reference to 'young people' under the image. The Lemos and Crane Report (2009) originally published in 2004 had recognised that a fear of knife violence was itself one of the most significant contributing factors to youthful knife carrying. And yet, despite this, a five-year-old image likely to stimulate precisely such concerns was reproduced on a children's news website even though it was entirely unrelated to the story in question (Fig. 4.7).

Used yet again in reference to knives in schools, the photo reappeared in an article about schools being given new powers to search students in 2004. With the caption 'schools could get new search rights' the presumed inference was that *these* were the kinds of weapons that would, or indeed had, been already found on students. Knowing the history of this photo, as we do, its selection for this article suggested a clear editorial bias. This was not primarily an ideological bias about police powers and searching versus children's rights and school safety, but rather

Fig. 4.7 The 'knife array' photograph on a children's TV News website, 2003 (Image copied from 'Knife Crime Getting ...', 2004)

a more pointed confirmation bias, that 'knife crime' was real, that these weapon risks existed—there they were, pictured on the table—and had to be taken seriously. The story confirmed existing dominant news narratives regarding young people, knives and violence and did so by blatantly juxtaposing this unrelated array of dangerous-looking knives with an expressed need to keep such weapons out of schools. Undoubtedly any readers, reasonably but inaccurately, assuming that such weapons had been confiscated from school children would be much more likely to support increased powers to search students (Fig. 4.8).

Likewise the same photograph was used to similar effect, two years later, in 2006, when it was reported that 'Rail police mount knife crackdown' ('Rail Police Mount...', 2006) in London. Despite the fact that the news article had stated that only two knives had been found during the knife arch operation (the size or type of knives confiscated was not reported) the photograph accompanying the piece was the familiar table of lethal blades photographed seven years earlier in Scotland. As before, the image clearly exaggerated the scale and nature of the problem of knife possession, implicitly reinforcing the need to take the issue seriously and

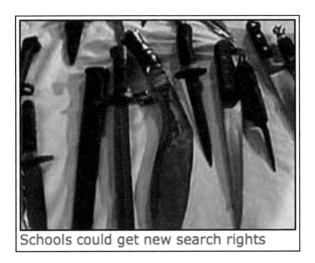

Schools could get new search rights

Fig. 4.8 The 'knife array' photograph utilised in support of new school search powers (Image copied from 'Knife fears could...', 2004)

to confront the illegal knife possession, seemingly a growing problem, by all means necessary (Fig. 4.9).

Finally, and somewhat ironically, the most recent use of this image we have detected was in 2008, nine years since its first appearance. On this occasion, however, the image was used to illustrate an article questioning whether the realities of 'knife crime' may have been distorted through sensationalised reporting (Warren, 2008). Again, however, the photograph was reproduced without any reference to its origin. In any event, despite the critical tone of the article, questioning whether *knife crime reporting* was too alarmist, the piece also reiterated the 'no smoke without fire' subtext: knife crime was real, the pictured array of knives was real, and a strapline beneath the picture spoke of four people 'stabbed on same day', even if the reporting was occasionally a little over the top (Fig. 4.10).

The suggestion that news photographs may be selected in order to influence readers, shaping and accenting the written word, may be both revealing and troubling. Especially so, in light of Jewkes suggestion that 'it is the incorporation of images that most directly communicates the

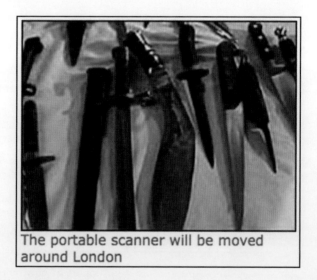

The portable scanner will be moved around London

Fig. 4.9 The 'knife array' photograph utilised in justify the use of knife arch scanners at stations (Image copied from *'Rail police mount …'*, 2006)

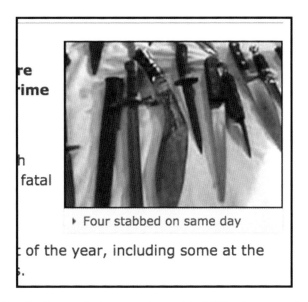

Fig. 4.10 The 'knife array' photograph used in 2008 when questioning 'knife crime' reporting (Image copied from Warren, 2008, *Is Knife Crime Really Increasing?*)

intended message' of news reports (Jewkes, 2015: 280). Visual cues in newspaper articles are often the elements which engage our emotions, excite further interest, triggering our world views whilst drawing us in. As Jewkes continues,

> Looking at and judging the lives of others… harnesses a 'peculiar energy' bound up in the enduring human fixation on the traumatic and grotesque. In a similar way to passing the scene of an accident and feeling compelled to look, shocking images are a defining feature of spectatorship. (Jewkes, 2015: 280)

The graphic images and carefully fashioned visual imagery of 'knife crime' news, either in print or online, played upon popular values and judgements. They helped reproduce an enduring and often conservatively accented narrative about social change, society and social values articulated through its contrived uncertainties about contemporary youth. Audiences for 'knife crime' were simultaneously shocked, yet also fascinated, always keen to *see* the weapons and yet still be disturbed by them. It was this dilemma of condemnation and entertainment, a familiar characteristic of populist media reporting (Ditton & Duffy, 1983; Williams & Dickinson, 1993) which even now sustains the knife crime story. An enthusiasm for the lurid is cultivated by the press, willing (as we have seen) to persistently reuse a powerful image of knives over a nine-year period even though the image had no direct relevance to the news content it was presumed to illustrate.

The knife-enabled police recording code may have underpinned the aggregation of 'knife crime' *data*, clustering different offences under a single label, but it was news media *spectatorship* which really established 'knife crime' as we understand it today. Potent images, along with evocative language, constructed an enthralling moral panic for audiences, forever building the 'knife crime' drama (in later accounts a variety of exotic, even 'photogenic' blades, such as 'zombie knives',[4] also joined the story). These mediated responses delivered quite contrary messages at one and the same time: 'stop the knife crime—show us more knife crime'. And within this developing contradiction, the combination of 'knife crime' rhetoric and imagery allowed audiences to moralistically condemn violence even whilst being simultaneously enthralled by the spectacle and eager to consume more.

Making Knife Crime a 'Black Crime'

The case of Luke Walmsley in 2003 triggered a media response that brought authorized spokespeople (such as high ranking police officers, public health advocates, representatives of teaching associations and politicians) together to fashion a public definition of 'knife crime'. As we have seen, the media helped sustain the news value attaching to 'knife crime' and keep the story alive by using graphic photographic imagery and the latest available crime data, generated by proactive policing operations. At this stage in the history of the knife crime label it was

---

[4] Although such knives were banned in the UK from August 2016.

predominantly the youth and the public setting that defined the parameters of the category, but this began to change significantly over the
following years. By 2019, Trevor Phillips, former head of the Equality
and Human Rights Commission, openly urged Government ministers
and policy-makers to take seriously the racial impact of knife violence
(Sharples, 2019). There was a subtle but significant difference, however,
in the way that Phillips described the black community as sitting at the
centre of a series of factors which directly resulted in heightened rates
of crime and violence and the spin given this story in the *Daily Mail*,
suggesting that black communities were themselves *responsible* for the
violence.

It was not until 2006, however, that 'knife crime' began to be
openly and regularly defined through ethnicity, eventually coming to be
perceived as a distinctively 'Black crime'. Earlier mentions of race in the
reporting of knife violence incidents tended only to indirectly reference
a racial dynamic to their stories. Such accounts might allude to 'gang'
affiliations for instance or, in other later cases, stories might describe
a victim as a 'Somali boy' whilst failing to mention the nationality or
ethnicity of others involved (Davenport et al., 2018; France et al., 2019),
or when referring to a youth anti-violence project specializing in working
with Black adolescents (Lane & Wheeler, 2003), or criticizing Black
music genres for promoting 'gangster' culture and glamorizing knives
and violence (Gibbons, 2003; Weathers, 2005). By the end of 2006 there
were increasing references to 'knife crime' in relation to 'Black communities' and, partly as a consequence, rising support for the reinstatement
of police stop and search to its pre-Macpherson proportions.

Although the connection between gang culture and knife crime had
been developing following the fatal stabbing of ten-year-old Damilola
Taylor in 2000, a particular catalyst for the accelerating racialised narrative shift was a growing social anxiety amongst suburban middle classes.
The increasing concern was vividly illustrated in the reaction to the
murder Tom Rhys Pryce, a wealthy White lawyer killed by two working
class Black teenagers near his home in north London. The disproportionate level of coverage given to this case was marked by the fact that the
new, recently appointed, Metropolitan Police commissioner Sir Ian Blair,
evoking the language of the Macpherson inquiry, accused the media press

of 'institutional racism'. He compared the extensive coverage of Pryce's death to the routine, almost anonymous, reporting of several BAME murder victims killed on the same day (Gibson & Dodd, 2006).

The headlines given to the Tom Rhys Pryce case could easily be confused with the sensationalist 'mugging' reports Hall et al. analysed in 1978. The police described the suspects as 'two black males' to the press in an appeal witnesses following the incident. Below are the 'mugging' headlines that were published within 24 hours followed by how the article included the ethnicity of the suspects.

The Evening Standard 13 January 2006:
'CITY LAWYER IS MURDERED BY MUGGERS; Call to fiancée, then attack on way home'…

Police said members of the public witnessed the struggle between two black men and the victim. ('City lawyer…', 2006)

Birmingham Post 14 January 2006:
'Muggers Brutally Murder Lawyer…'.

Detectives believe he had been trying to defend himself when the two young black men launched their "ferocious" assault. They stabbed him in the head, torso and hands and left him dying on the pavement. (Dean & Marsden, 2006)

The Daily Mail 14th January 2006:
NO MERCY; Highflying young lawyer knifed to death outside his flat AFTER handing everything to muggers…

Police said the lawyer was ambushed by two black men as he walked home from a local station after attending a social event with colleagues on Thursday night. (Wright & Koster, 2006)

The Daily Mail 14th January 2006:

HIS LIFE; He gave muggers all his possessions but they wanted more…' Officers were yesterday retrieving CCTV footage from several cameras in the area in a bid to trace the killers - two black men thought to be in their 20s. (Edwards & Parry, 2006)

The Sun 14th January 2006:
'Mugged… and then stabbed to death…

Smartly-dressed Tom had been stabbed in the head, body and hands. He had been robbed of his wallet by two young black men as he walked to his home in Kensal Green, North West London, from the local Tube station. Police say the killing was unprovoked. (Sullivan, 2006)

Only one of the newspaper articles referenced the ethnicity of the perpetrators in connection with the police investigation to find the killers (Edwards & Parry, 2006). The others used 'Black' as part of the description of the incident—and none of them mentioned the ethnicity of the victim, his whiteness was assumed. Unlike the death of Luke Walmsley, where news value was increased by the youth of the victim and school setting, Tom Rhys Pryce was exceptional and especially newsworthy because of the contrast between his social class and the setting of his death. It is more shocking (and therefore more newsworthy) for a 'smartly-dressed', 'highflying', 'city lawyer' to die in an outbreak of street violence given that the privileges of his gender, class and area of residence would generally be assumed to offer enough protection from such violence (Gekowski et al., 2012). But the middle classes in London were increasingly beginning to find themselves confronted by disadvantage and disorder on their doorsteps. In this sense, the Pryce murder resonated with a number of rising anxieties and social dilemmas at this time, even though it was little surprise to the black community that affluent parents, a nice address and the right school uniform might not guarantee a sufficient umbrella of safety for their children (Firmin et al., 2007; Hirsch, 2019; Johnson, 2003a).[5]

---

[5] Johnson (2003b) writes: "The school sits in leafy streets still blazing with the late autumn colours - north London Victorian terraces where houses fetch upwards of £400,000. Far from being a stereotype secondary "sink" school, it's high-achieving - as the exam results show … So why does it need a policeman permanently stationed on the site? Jane and her friends (their names have all been changed) are as normal as you would hope children of their age to be. They are confident and happy in school and all intend to go to university. Their parents

Political decisions and hard socio-economic processes profoundly framed these developments. Along with developing the 'right to buy' initiative, New Labour 'regeneration' housing policies had extended the work that the Conservatives had started in the late 1980s of transferring housing stock to private sector management. Known as state-led 'third-wave gentrification' this process was 'characterised by state encouragement of gentrification within previously hard-to-reach, deprived urban neighbourhoods including public housing estates' (Watt, 2009). A combination of financial and legal pressures conspired to force London local authorities to sell or transfer housing stock they could often scarcely afford to maintain in areas that, throughout the post-war era, had largely been protected from competitive market forces (ibid.). Urban areas in conditions of 'managed decline' (Beaumont, 2006), typified by 'intense and extensive deprivation of various kinds, run-down housing, a poor image and a general air of neglect' (Watt, 2009), were also areas with 'large black African/Caribbean populations' (ibid.). Once locations were targeted for regeneration the number of council owned properties rapidly decreased. Between 1981 and 2001 census the number of households in council owned properties in the Borough of Tower Hamlets reduced from 82 to 37.4%, whilst Lambeth dropped from 43.2 to 28.5% (Thapar, 2021: 136–162; Watt, 2009).

The murder of Tom Rhys Pryce took place in Kensal Green within the Borough of Brent, a district selected for state-led gentrification in 1999 under the New Deal for Communities (NDC) funded development scheme. Along with performance indicators centred upon house price increases (Batty et al., 2010: 24) the NDC measured its success through crime rate reduction (ibid.). The privately and publicly funded project boasted 'an enhanced police service and neighbourhood warden

---

are architects, teachers, housewives or technicians. They only live five minutes away from the school and walk there and back. But while Luke Walmsley's death upset them, it didn't shock them. They spoke of daily exposure to drugs, alcohol and violence - it was so familiar to them as to be unremarkable… "Kids carry knives and hammers," says Jane. "One of my friends got threatened with a hammer." Michael adds: "There are rival gangs and they carry knives and go off at lunchtime to have a fight. They bring knives to school because people know who they are, and they could be attacked on the way. They carry knives to look after themselves." They are ordinary knives, just kitchen knives say the children.

scheme' (Batty et al., 2010: 15) in its districts. Implementing a partnership with local police the NDC 'supplemented mainstream police
budgets in order to fund more police and police community support
officers, and to provide a flexible additional resource through which the
police can respond to trouble "hotspots"' (ibid.).

Two articles In the *Evening Standard* on 16 January 2006 appeared to
recognise the gentrification context of Kensal Green murder but both to
different effect. The first, employing language that appeared to conjure
up images of a gentrification process driven by brave new settlers forging
domestic peace on London's uncivilised frontiers, Gilligan wrote:

> As the middle classes have pressed ever westward, the onward march
> into new territory has brought prosperous, professional London hard
> up against the toughest areas in the capital. For all the political flannel
> about inclusiveness and multiculturalism, London has some of Europe's
> most savage inequalities of status and wealth. Sandwiched between North
> Kensington and Harlesden, Kensal Green puts those inequalities side by
> side. (Gilligan, 2006)

Gilligan went on to point out that the area had always had violent stabbings, but without the 'men in suits [they] did not attract the attention
of the media' (ibid.). By contrast Paul Barker, writing in the same paper,
suggests the presence of men in suits increases the frequency of jealous
violent crime:

> Some social changes make confrontations more likely. Entire swathes of
> London - where once you'd have to scour around to find a single middle-
> class achiever - are busily being gentrified. This puts the well-off bang
> next door to the envious poor or the wholly criminal. (Barker, 2006)

However, as Gilligan pointed out violent confrontations were not 'more
likely', only *more likely* to involve the middle classes—and therefore more
likely to be reported; both to the police and in the press. Barker went
further in his article, proposing that the best solution for suppressing the
criminal poor and discouraging them from attacking the wealthy was to
'Step up stop-and-search'. He added that 'after the stabbing by muggers

of lawyer Tom Rhys Pryce, we shouldn't be afraid to extend controversial police powers on our streets' (Barker, 2006). Such arguments found many receptive ears as the process of gentrification gained momentum during that latter part of 2006, regularly endorsed and reinforced by private housing developers investing in these rapidly changing residential areas.

Undoubtedly, this was a significantly different moment in London's social history than that which Hall and his colleagues described of Handsworth, Birmingham in *Policing the Crisis* (1978), and yet nevertheless the connections between 'mugging' and 'knife crime' are readily apparent. The same inner-urban residential communities are in contestation. These are the previously 'sub-standard and decaying' areas, the only spaces made available to the newly arrived Caribbean workforce invited to rebuild post-war Britain in the 1950s and 1960s (Hall et al., 1978: 342). Often treated often with hostility and overt racism by the resident English communities[6] these areas were gradually transformed into enclosed safe spaces for black families and communities. As Hall et al. acknowledged, 'for a *'West Indian Culture' to take root and survive in Britain, it required a solid framework and a material base: the construction of a* West Indian enclave community – the birth of colony society' (Hall et al., 1978: 344). This 'colonisation' of streets, neighbourhoods, markets and cafes in the 1960s suburbs were features of a community, on the one hand, forced upon itself by an excluding racism that (amongst other channels) reproduced through employment, urban and residential processes whilst simultaneously defending itself from that external public racism, on the other.

In the 1970s narrative of 'mugging' this collective capacity for a Black social and cultural existence was considered by the British conservative elite to be a dangerous consolidation of class and race, geographically

---

[6] As Verma (2018) has described, it was common to see, posted in lodging house windows or in the Small Ads sections of newspapers advertising flats and bedsits, signs declaring 'Room (or flat) to let. No Blacks, No Dogs, No Irish'. Living in a privately rented flat in Putney in the early 1980s, one of us once cleared out an old chest of drawers provided by the landlady. Lining the bottoms of the drawers were old copies of the local paper, the *Wandsworth Borough News*. Flats were for rent, dozens of them: but 'No Blacks, No Dogs, No Irish'.

facilitated by 'colony life' into a seemingly vengeful 'militant consciousness' (Hall et al., 1978: 326).[7] These were the anxieties for which the
label 'mugging' became a powerful means of justification, providing
police with a reason to enter, supervise, disrupt and punish [the seemingly unattached] young Black people in these communities (Hall et al.,
1978: 351). Over the years, the social order of black communities have
persistently reflected such rhythms of disruption, repression, violence
and resistance (Briggs, 2010; Gunter, 2010, 2017; Palmer, 2012; Pryce,
1979; Sharp & Atherton, 2007) culminating in the reinforcement, in
many urban centres, of what Hallsworth and Silverstone (2009) have
described as 'on-road' marginal street cultures, contraband economies
of the socially excluded and semi-criminal entrepreneurs, characterised
by frequent contacts with the police and, just as frequent, territorial
(or 'postcode') conflicts with competitors. Sociologists have come to
refer to these locations as 'liminal space' (Heale, 2008) where violence,
weapons and masculine respect could bring 'a fleeting sense of empowerment' (Hallsworth & Silverstone, 2009: 365) but where the police,
could just as quickly take it away again. In once declining inner cities
and sprawling post-war housing estates scarred by protracted reces-
sion, under-investment and permanent unemployment, the apparently
'surplus' former 'immigrant' populations, marginalised and excluded,
have borne the brunt of a destructive globalised modernisation from
above and the *self-destructive* 'reproduction from below' (2009: 372).
In this hostile domestic environment, the new frontiers of the late
modern city, relatively small numbers have responded angrily and
self-destructively. For instance a GLA report examining the correlation between poverty, disadvantage and violence revealed that whilst
young black people were disproportionately the victims of 'serious youth
violence' in London, less than one per cent of them were involved in it
(GLA, 2019). Unfortunately, the angry reactions of a few have shaped
the labelling of the many; 'gang culture' became its own explanation
(Smithson et al., 2012; Williams, 2015) and the pretext for heavy police

---

[7] In many respects, the emergence of this new black consciousness paralleled developments
earlier—in the decade in the USA, for instance the Black Power movement, the development
of which, an often overlooked issue, had its roots in black community self defence initiatives
such as the 'Deacons for Defense' (Wendt, 2007).

intervention (Williams & Clarke, 2018). As Hallsworth and Silverstone continued, 'the internalized anger and rage among depoliticized and deeply alienated young men finds violent expression… [But] the rage and anger they feel is not directed outwards the world that marginalizes them. Instead it is directed inward and against each other. Guns [and knives] have become a part of this logic of self-destruction as young men pointlessly die at each other's hands' (2009: 373). Making matters worse, a number of these young black men came to die at the hands of the police, whilst many more endured the indignities of disproportionate rates of taser use (Dymond, 2020; Gayle, 2019; Noor, 2018), or stop and search and arrest, all of which still bearing the hallmarks of institutional racism.

Thirty years later similar culturally rich urban areas, with their colourful markets and lively high-streets, began to become attractive to the modern commuter-class property market seeking large family homes within a short train ride from the city centre. Under cover of the potent new label 'knife crime', police began to re-enter these former black communities on behalf of the new white settlers, facilitating the recent gentrified occupation through surveillance, interruption and physical confrontation with young Black men in the street, searching their bodies in symbolic and practical reassertion of street control, always an underlying purpose of 'SUS' (Demuth, 1978) and its more modern counterpart. Coleman (2004) describes similar processes at work in the disciplined reclamation of Liverpool city centre. To some extent crime and disorder in the streets, and its most acute modern form—'knife crime'—has always represented an anxiety about the control of public spaces (Pearson, 1983), but the resurgence of stop and search in *these* areas at *this* time was a clear reminder of who was welcome and who not, who was a citizen and who was '*Other*'.

The reporting of the case of Tom Rhys Pryce was a pivotal moment in the social history of 'knife crime', whereby the ethnicity of the assailant became formative in the understanding of the crime. We argue that it was this crucial shift towards 'knife crime' as a racialised crime category that increased its persuasive utility as a deviance label. Not only did it divert the discussion from class to culture in the crime and disorder dilemmas of the city, but it also produced a common sense rhetoric on stop and search that would help nullify the findings of the Macpherson report and its restraints on policing.

Stop and Search—"For Their Own Good"

Once ethnicity was established as a defining feature of 'knife crime', discriminatory police practices became justified once more and worthy of public support. Over the course of 2006 the growing demand for stop and search hinged on the idea that, whilst the findings of the Macpherson report were correct, if 'knife crime' was a 'Black crime' then it would young be Black people who stood to gain the most from the return of stop and search. This argument was reinforced through the increased visibility given to so called 'Black on Black' murders at this time (McLagan, 2005). The separate cases of 15-year-olds Kiyan Prince and Alex Kamondo, killed within one month of each other in 2006, represent a particular example of how ethnicity became amplified in crime news reporting at this time.

When news broke of Kiyan Prince's death in May 2006 the papers immediately focused upon the ethnicity of both victim and the perpetrators. The *Guardian* reported; 'Kiyan Prince, who was 15 and a member of Queens Park Rangers' youth team, was attacked after an argument with another black teenager outside a block of flats' (Jones, 2006). The assumption reflected in the statement was that the ethnicity of those involved was an important detail in both the dynamics of the incident and our understanding of it. In a report of the same incident *The Daily Mail* made a much more laboured connection to 'ethnic minorities' and 'Somalian youth'. In the absence of any direct empirical evidence they relied upon local hearsay—unattributed and anecdotal evidence—from anonymous local residents:

> Residents said there had been a series of fights between local youths, many from ethnic minorities, 'trying to establish their territory', as one put it. Graffiti and 'tag names' are sprayed on several walls. One tenant said she saw a Somalian youth brandishing a machete last month. (Harris, 2006)

A month later in June 2006 Alex Kamondo lost his life in Lambeth. When asked about the motive for his murder the police were reported as replying; 'Other than to say it was a fight between two groups of black youths, we don't know' (Vasagar, 2006). Prefacing their comment with 'other than to say' implied that the ethnicity of those involved in the fight was itself part of an obvious and largely self-contained explanation of a motive. The *Daily Telegraph* reported the same police statement as; 'Police have described [the incident] simply as a "fight between two groups of black youths"' (Condron, 2006). In each case race was positioned as a predictable and largely self-explanatory component of either incident, an 'open and shut' descriptor comprising and conveying all we needed to know about these violent events.

In addition to centring the ethnicity of victims and perpetrators in crime news, the representation of 'knife crime' as rooted in black culture was enacted in more direct ways. In criticism of police knife amnesties an ironic article, aspiring to humour, was published in the *Evening Standard* with the title, '*Hand Over his Knife? No Rude Boy Will do That?* ('Hand In…', 2006). The article contained a mocking phonetic impression, using a self-described 'Jamaican-inflected cockney accent', of a young person's response to an Knife Amnesty proposal: 'Yeah man, *I gotta go down the cop shop and ditch me shank, innit. Gotta do the right fing an' that*' (ibid.). The piece was later justified by its author in the following terms:

> I don't think it's divisive to associate Afro-Caribbean youths with knife crime… Just as with gun crime, black lads are disproportionately responsible for knife crimes - and disproportionately its tragic victims. Furthermore, the type of the "rude boy" is what all of London's malcontents black, white or brown - aspire to. ('Hand in…', 2006)

This idea that 'knife crime' was a fashion expression, made 'cool' through its associations with Black culture became a pervasive idea (Lemos & Crane, 2009). Yet looking back at the response to Luke Walmsley's death in 2003 there was an immediate conception of an outside threat from the streets that was spreading, weapons being smuggled and violence spilling into schools, but there was no explicit language describing what that dangerous culture was. Only three years later it was confidently and relentlessly asserted—black knife crime was a scourge of the streets—with stop and search repositioned as in the best interest of Black children. One article in the *Daily Telegraph*, having explained how knife carrying was no longer an exception but 'the norm' amongst urban black youth went on to insist how objections 'that the stop and search policy was racist [were] misguided. On the contrary he claimed, 'young black people would be the biggest beneficiaries of proactive policing, 'because they are the people who are most likely to be attacked' (Bailey, 2006). Even on its own terms the article made little sense, if knife carrying was, as was claimed, 'normalised' amongst young black people, they would find themselves increasingly criminalised by police interventions, hardly the 'beneficiaries' of stop and search at all. However, the 'evidence' alluded to in the article was not borne out by the facts, the 2004 Metropolitan Police Knife Crime Report found young *white* men to make up the largest part of the knife carrying fraternity (TPHQ, 2004). Nevertheless the racialised language employed and the selective visibility of 'knife crime' in 2006 meant that such social construction of 'black knife crime' had become increasingly taken for granted.

Seemingly oblivious to historic anti-racist campaigns against stop and search, the *Evening Standard* suggested that ethnic minority parents had just two options; either they should accept that their sons will be racially profiled or they should simply allow them to become victims of 'knife crime':

> Some in the black community have complained in the past that they are unfairly targeted, and that has rightly been a point of concern. Yet today many ethnic minority parents may prefer their law-abiding sons to be stopped occasionally by police than see them fall victim to knife crime. Both the police and the courts must now respond more decisively to this exceptionally dangerous street trend. ('Knife Crackdown…', 2006)

Whilst much of the press in 2006 began demanding a *return* to police stop and search, even with the overtly racialised justification, evidence from the Home Office demonstrated that stop and search had *already* been increasing significantly since 2002—refer to Fig. 4.11 (EHRC,

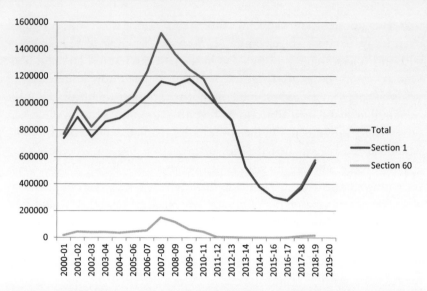

Fig. 4.11 Police stops and searches in England and Wales 2000–2019. Total searches and those under Section 1 (PACE) and Section 60 (CJPO)—excluding S.44

2010; MPA, 2004). It is generally recognised that roughly half of such stops occur in London, and fully eighty per cent of stops of black people (Miller, 2010: 956). These shifting trends in police action have been variously justified and explained, and in many areas directly funded by a new Street Crimes Initiative launched in 2002, and the private–public redevelopment schemes of the NDC. Some element of the increase in police stops can be attributed to the growing surveillance of young Asians in the UK in the wake of the US 9/11 terrorist attack (Dodd, 2005), but it is hard to avoid the conclusion that the gathering media storm over black youth and knife violence was having a major impact. The increasing use of 'blanket', area-based, s.60 searches in particular,[8]

---

[8] Section 60 of the *Criminal Justice and Public Order Act 1994* empowered a senior police officer to designate a defined area as a s.60 search area based upon recent or anticipated violence, or a belief that offensive weapons were being carried in the area in question. Such a designation empowered police officers to initiate searches 'without suspicion' in order to search for offensive weapons. The power existed for a 24 hour period, but could be rolled over for further periods at the discretion of a senior police officer.

prompted by concerns about violence or 'anticipated' violence, pointed directly to the mobilising power of the knife crime label (including under Operation Blunt). Searches under s.60 demonstrate almost twice the rate of racial disproportionality compared with s.1 searches, but yield rather limited 'positive' results. Between 2000–2001 and 2009–2010, s.60 searches produced an average of just over two weapons per 100 stops, this is close to the ratio of weapon seizures during Operation Blunt in 2007–2009 (Ward & Diamond, 2009: 5) and arrests during Operation Blunt II (McCandless et al., 2016: 19) but higher than the overall ratio of knife seizures reported by Operation Blunt II (0.6 knives per 100 searches: MPA, 2009). Along with Asian youths, Black young people were becoming increasingly over policed during this period: 'between 1998–1999 and 2001–2002, the use of Sect. 60 search powers nearly tripled, with black people 28 times and Asians 18 times more likely to be stopped than white people' (Jefferson, 2013: 391).

There are doubtless many complications to undertaking research on stop and search, although this is not the place to discuss them at length. As is already clear, police stop and search can be undertaken using a range of different powers, depending on the type of search (person or vehicle) or the items searched for.[9] For our purposes s.1 and s.60 have been the most important, a further search power, under s.44 of the Terrorism Act was discontinued following an ECHR ruling in 2009. However, not all stops and searches are formally recorded by the police, when a member of the public *consents* to be searched, this is considered a 'consensual' search and is not generally recorded. A search is only recorded when the police officer invokes a police power to *insist* upon the search, although practice here is highly subject to police discretion and therefore very variable—and especially where, as in the case of stop and search, there was, as Savage and others have noted, 'institutional resistance' to the monitoring of searches (McLaughlin, 2007a, 2007b; Savage, 2003: 171; Shiner, 2015). A second range of issues have concerned the controversy over disproportionality and stop and search. In 2009, according

---

[9] For example, section 23(2) of the Misuse of Drugs Act 1971 allows police to stop and search a person in a public place where they reasonably suspect the person is in possession of a controlled substance.

to Fig. 4.12, virtually the highest point in rates of recorded stop and search the relative rates of stop and search were as follows:

White people were stopped and searched at a rate of 19 per thousand; Asian people were stopped and searched at a rate of 40 per thousand; But Black people were stopped and searched at a rate of 120 per thousand.

Throughout the following decade, even as rates of stop and search fell away markedly to 2019, considerable disproportionality persisted. As Fig. 4.12 shows, the reduction in the frequency of stop and search fell for all ethnic groups, but far more dramatically in respect of black people.

Yet what do such variations mean and how might they constitute 'disproportionality'. Early research on disproportionality simply compared police rates of stop and search with the composition of the local population. Where the rate of stops exceeded respective proportions in the population resident locally, disproportionality was suggested. A number of researchers criticised this method of calculation, pointing out that stop and search was not random, but targeted, furthermore the

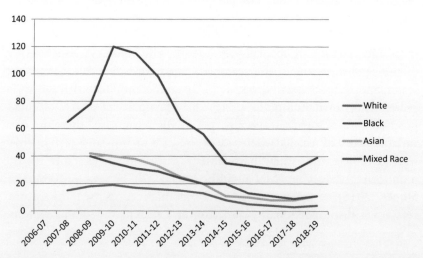

Fig. 4.12 Apparent disproportionality in stop and search: 2009–2019. Stops per 1000 people

police could only stop and search people who were out in public, *available* to be stopped (MVA & Miller, 2000; Waddington et al., 2004). The police generally stepped up their stop and search activities in the evening and night-time effectively ruling out significant sections of the population (older households, families) and focusing instead on street-socialising young people, thereby building in forms of disproportionality. Stop and search became the subject of a great deal of academic and policy research (Bradford, 2017), some of this was originally undertaken in support of the work of the Steven Lawrence Inquiry, later the central question settled upon whether stop and search was an effective police strategy contributing overall to crime reduction.[10] On the other side, stop and search was criticised where it appeared to undermine community confidence in the police—especially the confidence of those sections of the community it was supposed to reassure—and when the practice seemed to be informed by racialised suspicion or institutional racism (Bowling & Philips, 2007; Miller, 2010). This very dilemma at the heart of stop and search was spelled out in a report on Operation Blunt 2 (OB2) to the Strategic and Operational Policing Committee of the Metropolitan Police Authority in June 2009.

> **Learning Exercise 12: Assessing the Evidence About Stop and Search**
>
> Explore the arguments for and against police stop and search activity. What does the evidence say?
> What are the arguments for it and why do the police consider it an important power to use?
> What are the arguments against stop and search?
> Using the MET Police Stop and search dashboard:
> https://www.met.police.uk/sd/stats-and-data/met/stop-and-search-dashboard/
> Choose a particular borough of interest and consider the following points of interest;

---

[10] That stop and search 'contributed overall' to crime reduction represented the ultimate case for it, but it could achieve this by virtue of stop and search assisting police intelligence gathering, supporting crime investigation, communicating deterrence by street presence or simply by asserting 'street authority' (Bradford & Loader, 2016). The contribution to crime reduction however seemed to represent a researchable, measurable and defensibly *objective* outcome.

- Have the search rates fluctuated significantly in the past year? If there were peaks can you investigate from news sources what this was in response to?
- What are the disproportionality rates for ethnicity, age and gender per 1000 of population? Did you expect this? Why?
- What are the most come reasons for a search and what are the most common offence recorded?
- What percentage of searches successfully retrieve bladed weapons?

Discussion

If you were tasked with using stop and search to prevent 'knife crime' what intelligence or indicators would you use to decide who to stop and what areas to target? If stop and search lacks evidence of successfully reducing violence why do you think it remains such a popular response to knife crime?

In what ways might stop and search be reformed?

To begin with, the MPA Report acknowledged that Operation Blunt 2 (OB2) represented 'a significant enhancement of enforcement tactics in response to concerns regarding public place violence in London, notably that affecting young people and involving the use of knives' (MPA, 2009: 1). The strategic intention of the operation was described as an 'intelligence-led focus upon *dangerous places* and *dangerous people*… To stop the killing of young people on the streets of London; to reduce serious violence involving young people as victims and offenders; to reduce the carrying of weapons by young people on the streets of London; and to maintain the support of communities and young people for police action to reduce youth violence (paras. 4–5). To that end the report acknowledged the need to base the operation upon a 'sustained and intelligence-led enforcement response with close community engagement [and…] ensuring that tactics recognise and respond to the concerns and expectations of the community, *including young people*' (para. 5). However, the operational objective was to be delivered by a stop and search strategy which would create and maintain 'an environment that is hostile to the routine acquisition, carriage and use of lethal weapons in public space' (para. 5). Supporting the enforcement strategy was a community impact assessment which monitored daily and weekly 'tension indicators' claiming a 'broad and consistent' level of support for enhanced stop and search tactics including from BME communities and young people 'who appreciate the requirement to remove lethal weapons from the few for the safety of the many'. Caution was expressed towards the end of the report, however, regarding 'a perception amongst BME groups that police officers are sometimes unprofessional when exercising [stop and search] powers' and reiterating 'the continuing need for courtesy and information on search grounds (including S60) when conducting large numbers of searches involving a similar target group' (para. 29). The fact that such concerns were acknowledged, points to their continuing significance as issues in relation to stop and search, although the report went on to recommend a future strategy of supposedly 'intelligence-led' stop and search, later endorsed by the NPIA (Chainey & MacDonald, 2012).

The extent to which this 'new' stop and search assuaged the concerns articulated by the black community whilst striking an appropriate balance between 'creating a hostile environment for those carrying knives' and reassuring the rest of the black community (including young people) is an open question. As we will see in the next chapter, the signs were not so good. The particular timeline of events at this time was highly important and essential to chart accurately. In 2006 whilst the news media were demanding that stop and search be brought back, in fact it was already returning with a vengeance, it had even been described by Black Londoners as 'terrorising' and 'harassing', and 'SUS by the backdoor'. In this light, the police mobilisation against Black youth in London actually predated the intensified racialisation of 'knife crime' in the news. This rather inverted both our understanding of events and the entire rationale behind the policing strategy: stop and search was not responding to 'knife crime', instead 'knife crime' was responding to stop and search. In the manner of deviancy amplification's self-fulfilling character, however, in so doing so it provided a growing justification for the increasingly robust policing of 'dangerous' young Black people in the 'dangerous' spaces of the city targeted for regeneration.

Conclusion

In the previous chapter it was argued that the change in police crime codes and a mobilisation towards knife-enabled violence at the turn of the twenty-first century brought a particular focus to a disparate range of violent behaviours involving knives, reifying some rather incomplete and eclectic knife-involved data-sets yet underpinning the construction of the 'knife crime' label. In this chapter a close analysis of early public uses of the phrase 'knife crime' have demonstrated the central role of news media in the production and amplification of a 'crime wave'. It was, above all, the news media so dramatically shaping this issue, reinforcing a sense of increasing seriousness by reference to a strain of intimate and visceral violence involving children, race and knives.

Dictated by the demands of its consumers, news producers considered violence that involved children and knives in public spaces—by all accounts an exceptional crime in the UK[11]—to have an incredibly high news value. But the news analysis in this chapter has suggested that, in order to maintain and refresh the interest of 'knife crime' consumers, the label had to constantly evolve, moving through several stages of narrative development. First the children in 'knife crime' headlines became younger and then the focus shifted to the erstwhile 'safe spaces' such as schools[12]; language, images and data were deployed to maintain a developing shock value for audiences. Eventually the full significance of 'knife crime' came to rest on its most impactful and yet most predictable representation, the dangerous threat of the 'criminal other', young black males in the 'dangerous' inner London suburbs.

When The Met Police's Commander Foy told the press in 2004 that 'knife crime is almost exclusively a young people's phenomenon', he was in some respects correct. Without the news value of youth, employed to redefine knife data through selective reporting, there would be no

---

[11] Refer to the third section of Chapter 2, for our discussion of international comparative rates of knife involved crime and violence.

[12] A good deal of American research has drawn particular attention to the nature of public reactions to school violence, not least the spate of school shootings experienced in the USA, arguing that such reactions are in part driven by the assumptions that schools are—and indeed should be—especially safe spaces for young people (Newman, 2006).

knife crime phenomenon of which to speak. The exclusion of domestic violence from the discussion of 'knife crime', despite the high incidence of injury and the statistical contribution such offences made to the overall totals also demonstrated the inherent subjectivity in the construction of the 'knife crime' label. The label can be seen to respond to demands of spectatorship; 'knife crime' came to represent what audiences expected. If there is a 'knife culture' in Britain it is surely most powerfully manifest in news reports, fabricated through the practice of selective reporting that revelled in images of bladed weapons (the more exotic the better), lurid and gory details, moral tales of good and evil, black and white, safety, danger, irresponsibility and 'just deserts', and the ultimate spectacle of violence. The vast majority of the public will only experience violence with knives through marketed crime news, as an audience simultaneously entertained and disgusted, consuming and condemning. In turn such moralistic judgement leads to proactive responses; 'no excuses', enhanced and 'mandatory' sentences, intensive surveillance, robust policing and, inevitably, stop and search.

As ethnicity became a defining feature of the label in news reporting, the construct of 'youth knife crime' became increasingly racialised. The findings of this chapter suggest that during a time of state-led gentrification of the suburbs, anxiety over 'knife crime' justified policing powers to re-occupy the contested spaces of the city. Stop and search expanded to exceed its pre-Macpherson (1999) levels, justified by 'knife crime'. The analysis of defining events during this period has presented a new understanding of 'knife crime' as a specific response to particular crimes, reflecting the anxieties of mainstream society and the pragmatic priorities of press reporting and proactive policing at this time.

References

Appadurai. (2006). *Fear of small numbers: An essay on the geography of anger*. Duke University Press.
'At the Sharp End' (2003, November 9). *The Scotsman*. Scotland.

Bailey, S. (2006, June 1). Carrying a knife is no longer the exception—It's the rule. *The Daily Telegraph*. London, UK.

Bamber, D. (2002, March 10). Rising knife crime deals further blow to Blunkett. *The Sunday Telegraph*. UK.

Barker, W. (2003, November 5). Youngsters caught in tide of horror. *The Sun*. UK.

Barker, W. (2006). Step up stop-and-search; After the stabbing by muggers of lawyer Tom Rhys Pryce, we shouldn't be afraid to extend controversial police powers on our streets. *The Sun*. UK.

Batty, E., Beatty, C., Foden, M., Lawless, P., Pearson, S. & Wilson, I. (2010, March). *The new deal for communities experience: A final assessment The New Deal for Communities Evaluation: Final report—Volume 7*. Centre for Regional Economic and Social Research. Sheffield Hallam University. Department for Communities and Local Government.

Beaumont, J. (2006). London: Deprivation, social isolation and regeneration. In S. Musterd, A. Murie, & C. Kesteloot (Eds.), *Neighbourhoods of poverty*. Palgrave Macmillan.

Bowling, B., & Philips, C. (2007). Disproportionate and discriminatory: Reviewing the evidence on police stop and search. *Modern Law Review, 70*(6), 936–961.

Bradford, B. (2017). *Stop and search and police legitimacy*. Routledge.

Bradford, B., & Loader, I. (2016). Police, crime and order: The case of stop and search. In Bradford et al. (Ed.), *The SAGE Handbook of Global Policing*. London: Sage.

Briggs, D. (2010). True stories from bare times on road: Developing empowerment, identity and social capital among urban minority ethnic young people in London, U.K. *Ethnic and Racial Studies, 33*(5), 851–871

Brown, S. (1998). *Understanding youth and crime: Listening to youth*. Open University Press.

'Call for caution over stabbing' (2003, November 7). *The Birmingham Post*. Birmingham, UK.

Carnochan, J., & McCluskey, K. (2010). Violence, culture and policing in Scotland. In D. Donnelly, D., & K. Scott (Ed.), *Policing Scotland*. Routledge.

Chainey, S., & Macdonald I. (2012). *Stop and search, the use of intelligence and geographic targeting findings from case study research*. NPIA.

'City Lawyer is murdered by muggers; Call to fiancée, then attack on way home'. (2006, January 13). *The Evening Standard*. UK

'Classmates See Boy of 14 Stabbed to Death at School' (2003, November 5). *The Yorkshire Post*, Leeds, UK.

Coleman, R. (2004). *Reclaiming the streets: Surveillance, social control and the city.* Cullompton, Willan.

'College Gets Anti-Knife Scanners' (2006, May 17). *BBC News Online.*

Condron, S. (2006, June 10). Boy, 15, is stabbed to death in street fight. *The Daily Telegraph.* UK.

Cook, E. A., & Walklate, S. (2020, June 27). Gendered objects and gendered spaces: The invisibilities of 'knife' crime. *Current Sociology* [Online]: 1–16.

Davies, A. (2013). *City of gangs: Glasgow and the rise of the British gangster* Hodder and Stoughton.

Davenport, J. (2004, September 30). Increase in knife crime led by young. *Evening Standard.* UK.

Davenport, J., Frodsham, I., & Dunne, J. (2018, February 21). Camden stabbing victim pictured: Teen, 17 murdered along with another victim, 20 as detectives probe gang links. *Evening Standard.*

Dean & Marsden. (2006, January 14). Muggers brutally murder lawyer... *Birmingham Post.*

Demuth, C. (1978). *'Sus': A Report on the Vagrancy Act* (Runnymede Trust).

Ditton, J., & Duffy, J. (1983). Bias in the reporting of crime news. *British Journal of Criminology, 23*(2), 159–165.

Dodd, V. (2005, August 17). Asian men targeted in stop and search: Huge rise in number questioned under anti-terror laws. *The Guardian.*

Donnelly, D., & Scott, K. (2005). *Policing Scotland.* Routledge.

Dymond, A. (2020). Taser, taser'! Exploring factors associated with police use of taser in England and Wales. *Policing and Society, 30*(4), 396–411.

Eades, C., Grimshaw, R., Silvestri, A., & Solomon, E. (2007). *'Knife crime' a review of evidence and policy* (2nd ed.). Centre for Crime and Justice Studies.

Edwards & Parry. (2006, January). HIS LIFE; He gave muggers all his possessions but they wanted more... *The Daily Mirror.* UK.

Ellam, D. (2003, November 9). Sold.. to a 12-yr-old; Shop charges pounds 25 for this 12in blade Boy of 14 is stabbed to death but stores still flout law on children buying knives. *Sunday Mirror.* London, UK.

Equality and Human Rights Commission. (2010). *Stop and think: A CRITICAL REVIEW of the use of stop and search powers in England and Wales.* EHRC.

Firmin, C., Turner, R., & Gavriliedes, T. (2007). *Empowering young people through human rights values: Fighting the knife culture.* Building Bridges Project, London, Race on the Agenda.

France, A., Coleman, L., & Dunne, J. (2019, June 27). Shepherd's Bush stabbing: Teenager knifed 'after showing attackers he wasn't armed' in London's eighth murder in 12 days. *Evening Standard*.

Gayle, D. (201, March 12). Half of children shot by police stun guns are from BAME groups—Report. *The Guardian*.

Gekowski, A., Gray, J., & Adler, J. (2012). What makes a homicide newsworthy? UK national tabloid newspaper journalists tell all. *The British Journal of Criminology, 52*(6), 1212–1232.

Gibbons, F. (2003, January 6). Minister labelled racist after attack on 'black idiots' *The Guardian*.

Gibson, O., & Dodd, V. (2006, January 27). Met chief labels media institutionally racist. *The Guardian*. UK

Gilligan, A. (2006, January 16).Violent menace that stalks neighbourhood; Now locals walk the streets in pairs, gripped by fear of the gangs who rob at knifepoint. *Evening Standard*. London, UK.

Greater London Authority (GLA). (2019). *A public health approach to serious youth violence: Supporting evidence*. GLA.

Goodchild, S. (2003, November 9). Is your kid taking a knife to school? *The Independent on Sunday*. London, UK.

Grayston, G. (2017, May 27). *Pen knives and kids* [On-line]. Pen Knives—The Law, Best for Kids, and Top 5 Swiss Army Knives. getoutwiththekids.co.uk.

Gunter, A. (2010). *Growing up bad? Black youth, 'road' culture and badness in an East London neighbourhood*. Tufnell Press.

Gunter, A. (2017). *Race, gangs and youth violence: Policy*. Bristol, Policy Press.

Hall, S., Roberts, B., Clarke, J., Jefferson, T., & Critcher, C. (1978). *Policing the crisis: Mugging, the state, and law and order*. Macmillan.

Hallsworth, S., & Silverstone, D. (2009). "That's life innit": A British perspective on guns, crime and social order. *Criminology and Criminal Justice, 9*, 359–377.

'Hand in his Knife? No Rude Boy Will do That' (2006, May 25). *Evening Standard*. London, UK.

Harris, P. (2006, May 20). Find the boy called killer; Streets where the knife is king. *Daily Mail*. UK.

Heale, J. (2008). *One blood: Inside Britain's new street gangs*. London: Simon & Schuster.

Hirsch, A. (2019, January 15). Rod Liddle is wrong about the causes of black teenage deaths. *The Guardian*.

Jewkes, Y. (2015). *Media and crime* (3rd ed.). Sage.

Johnson, U. (2003a, November 9). Kids carry knives and hammers: they have to look after themselves. *The Independent on Sunday.* UK

Johnson, U. (2003b). Is your kid taking a knife to school? *News of the World.* London, UK.

Jones, S. (2006, May 19). Pupil, 15, stabbed to death in argument after school. *The Guardian.*

Kelbie, P. (2003, November 29). Glasgow is Britain's murder capital as knife crime spirals. *Independent.*

'Knife Culture Under the Spotlight' (1999, August 17). *BBC News Online.*

'Knife Crackdown' (2006, February 6). *Evening Standard.* London, UK.

'Knife crime getting worse in UK' (2004, October 18). *BBC Newsround.* Available at http://news.bbc.co.uk/cbbcnews/hi/uk/newsid_3753000/375 3722.stm

Knife Fears Could Prompt New Law' (2004, December 12). *BBC News.*

Lane, M., & Wheeler, B. (2003, November 7). Is knife crime really getting worse. *BBC News Online.* UK

Laville, S. (2003, November 5). A scuffle, then panic grips children and staff at village school. *The Daily Telegraph.* London, UK.

Lemos, G., & Crane. (2009). *The fear and fashion evaluation, a summary report.* Clear Plan.

Marfleet, N. (2008). *Why carry a weapon? A study of knife crime amongst 15–17 year old males in London.* Howard League for Penal Reform.

Marshall, B., Webb, B., & Tilley, N. (2005). *Rationalisation of current research on guns, gangs and other weapons.* Phase 1. UCL, Jill Dando Institute of Crime Science.

McCandless, R., Feist, A., Allan, J., & Morgan, N. (2016). *Do initiatives involving substantial increases in stop and search reduce crime? Assessing the impact of operation BLUNT 2.* Published March 2016, Home Office.

McComish, S., Armstrong, J. Bryne, P., & Disley, J. (2003, November 5). BOY, 14, KILLED IN SCHOOL ATTACK: He ran .. then he fell. *The Daily Mirror.* London, UK.

'McConnell pledge to cut knife crime' (2003, March 3). *The Daily Mail.* Scotland.

McLagan, G. (2005). *Guns and gangs: Inside black gun crime.* Allison & Busby.

McLaughlin, E. (2007a). *The new policing.* Sage.

McLaughlin, E. (2007b). Diversity or anarchy? The post-Macpherson Blues. In M. Rowe (Ed.), *Policing beyond Macpherson: Issues in policing, race and society.* Willan.

Measor, L., & Squires, P. (2000). *Young people and community safety: Inclusion tolerance and disorder*. Ashgate Publishers.

Mega, M., & Grant, G. (2004, May 28). Zero tolerance for knife thugs. *Daily Mail*. London, UK.

Metropolitan Police Autrhority. (MPA). (2004). *Report of the MPA scrutiny on MPS stop and search*. Metropolitan Police Authority, UK.

Metropolitan Police Authority (MPA). (2009, June 8). Report of: Strategic and Operational Policing Committee: Operation Blunt 2. Agenda Item 20.

Met's Baton Rounds to fight knife crime' (2002, August 22). *The Telegraph*.

Miller, J. (2010). Stop and search in England: A reformed tactic or business as usual? *British Journal of Criminology, 50*(5), 954–974.

Muncie, J., & Goldson, B. (2006). The new Correctionalism. In J. Muncie & B. Goldson (Ed.), *Comparative youth justice*. Sage.

MVA & Miller, J. (2000). *Profiling populations available for stops and searches* (Police Research Series Paper 131). London: Home Office.

Newman, K. S. (2006). *Rampage: The social roots of school shootings*. New York Basic Books.

Noor, P. (2018, December 5). Met use tasers and restraints more often against black people. *The Guardian*.

'Not Even Your School is Safe' (2003, November 6). *The Sun*. London, UK.

Omaar, R. (2004, October17). Knives: The teenage war zone. *BBC News Online*.

Palasinski, M., & Riggs, D. (2012). Young white British men and knife-carrying in public: Discourses of masculinity, protection and vulnerability. *Critical Criminology, 20*(4), 463–476.

Palmer, S. (2012). Dutty Babylon: policing Black communities and the politics of resistance. *Criminal Justice Matters*, No. 87. London, CCJS.

Pearson, G. (1983). *Hooligan: A history of respectable fears*. Macmillan Press.

'Police Target Knife Carriers' (2000, February 5). *BBC News Online*.

Pryce, K. (1979). *Endless pressure: A study of West Indian life-styles in Bristol*. Penguin.

'Rail Police Mount Knife Crackdown' (2006, February 7). BBC News Online.

Savage, S. (2003). Tackling tradition: Reform and modernization of the British police. *Contemporary Politics, 9*(2), 171–184.

'Scotland Tops Murder League' (2000, March 3). *BBC News Online*.

Sethi, S., & World Health Organization (Eds.). (2007). *European report on preventing violence and knife crime among young people*. Copenhagen, Denmark: World Health Organization.

Sharp, D., & Atherton, S. (2007). To serve and protect: The experiences of policing in the community of young people from black and other ethnic minority groups. *British Journal of Criminology, 47*, 746–763.

Sharples, E. (2019, March 1). Admit gang knife crime is a black issue, says former Equality Commission chief Trevor Phillips *Daily Mail*.

Shiner, M. (2010). Post-Lawrence policing In England and Wales: Guilt, innocence and the defence of organizational ego. *British Journal of Criminology, 50*, 935–953.

Shiner, M. (2015). Regulation and reform. In R. Delsol & M. Shiner (Eds.), *Stop and search: The anatomy of a police power*. Palgrave MacMillan.

Smithson, H., Ralphs, R., & Williams, P. (2012). Used and abused: The problematic usage of gang terminology in the United Kingdom and its implications for ethnic minority youth. *British Journal of Criminology, 53*, 113–128.

Squires, P. (2016). Voodoo liability: Joint enterprise prosecution as an aspect of intensified criminalisation. *Oñati Socio-legal Series, 6*(4), 937–956. https://ssrn.com/abstract=2871266

Sullivan, A. (2006, January14). Mugged… and then stabbed to death… *The Sun*. UK.

Thapar, C. (2021). *Cut short: Youth violence, loss and hope in the city*. Viking, Random House.

'Teenager Guilty of Murdering Girl' (2003, October 31). *BBC News Online*.

Townsend, M., & Barnett, A. (2003, November 23). Scandal of pupils aged five carrying knives. *The Observer*.

TPHQ (2004, June). *Knife crime report*. TP Strategic Analysis Unit.

Vasagar, J. (2006, June 10). Police hunt teenage gang after boy, 15, is stabbed to death in street. *The Guardian*.

Verma, R. (2018, November 29). It was standard to see signs saying, 'No Blacks, No Dogs, No Irish. *Each-Other*.

Waddington, P. A. J., Stenson, K., & Don, D. (2004). In proportion: Race, and police stop and search. *British Journal of Criminology, 44*(6), 889–914.

Ward, L., & Diamond, A. (2009). *Tackling Knives Action Programme (TKAP) Phase 1: Overview of key trends from a monitoring programme*. Home Office Research and Statistics Directorate, Research Report 18.

Warren, T. (2008, July 11). Is knife crime really increasing? *BBC News*.

'Warning of More Weapons in Schools' (2003, November 5). *BBC News Online*.

Watt, P. (2009). Housing stock transfers, regeneration and state-led gentrification in London. *Urban Policy and Research, 27*(3), 229–242.

Weathers, H. (2005, April 26). A knife to Our Hearts. *Daily Mail*. London, UK.

Wendt, S. (2007). *The spirit and the shotgun: Armed resistance and the struggle for civil rights*. University Press of Florida.

Williams, P. (2015). Criminalising the other: Challenging the race-gang nexus. *Race & Class, 56*(3), 18–35.

Williams, P., & Clarke, R. (2018). The black criminal other as an object of social control. *Social Sciences., 7*(11), 234–234.

Williams, P., & Dickinson, J. (1993). Fear of crime: Read all about it? The relationship between newspaper crime reporting and fear of crime. *The British Journal of Criminology, 33*(1), 33–56.

Woolcock, N. (2003, November 6). Shops, stalls and web illegally sell knives to children. *The Daily Telegraph*.

Wright and Koster. (2006, January 14). NO MERCY; Highflying young lawyer knifed to death outside his flat AFTER handing everything to muggers. *Daily Mail*.

Younge, G., & Barr, C. (2017, December 3). How Scotland reduced knife deaths among young people. *The Guardian*.

5

A Moral Panic: The 'War on Knife Crime'

Introduction

In Chapter 3 we showed that the vital early mobilisation towards today's conception of 'knife-enabled crime' took place at an especially significant moment in the transformation of policing (Jones & Newburn, 2002) and the evolving context of New Labour's hybrid law and order politics. During this time, Labour's mantra 'tough on crime, and tough on the causes of crime' resolved itself into a precise targeting of the 'usual suspects' by robust enforcement-led policing. Following that, chapter four retraced the increasingly specific character of the public definition of 'knife crime', constructing a criminality primarily located geographically and ethnically amongst inner city Black youths. In this chapter we continue our chronological retelling of the emergence of 'knife crime' into a third and 'established' phase (refer to our first *knife crime timeline*, Fig. 1.4), beginning around 2008, and reflecting the emergence of a substantial moral panic which set the scene for a significant expansion of police powers and related enforcement activity, a renewed commitment to stop and search, a major roll-out of Tasers to frontline police, new legislation, new offences, enhanced sentencing, and new criminal orders.

© The Author(s), under exclusive license to Springer Nature
Switzerland AG 2021
E. Williams and P. Squires, *Rethinking Knife Crime*,
https://doi.org/10.1007/978-3-030-83742-6_5

All of this effectively framed the dominant response to knife crime within a policing and enforcement paradigm which, until challenged by recent advocacy for a 'public health approach', persists to this day. And as we showed in chapter four, broad popular support for discriminatory and selectively targeted policing strategies remained strong. In Fig. 5.1, however, we have refined the original timeline in order to focus more closely upon just the last ten years. Here we have included new legislation and police powers, including the Offensive Weapons Act, and the new Knife Crime Prevention Order and Serious Violence Prevention Order, and 'Operation Sceptre'. We have also added indicative trend lines (not drawn to scale) for rates of police-recorded knife crime (rising), the knife homicide trend (rising), and the custodial sentence trend for knife-enabled offences (also rising). By contrast, the police knife crime sanction detection trend is clearly falling. Whatever else the data tells us, these trends do not suggest that strategies to tackle knife crime are succeeding, quite the opposite.

As we have already suggested the persistent criminalisation and 'Othering' of Black youth very much mirrors the response to 'mugging' in the 1970s. Just as, three decades earlier, a politics of law and order

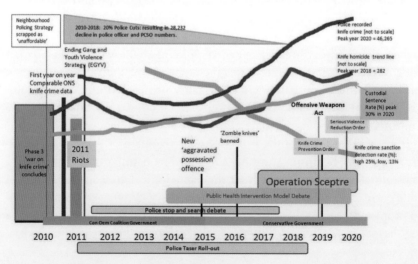

Fig. 5.1 The knife crime timeline 2010–2020

helped re-establish political authority in the midst of the then British economic crisis, so the uncertainties following the global banking crisis and, not least, the contrived politics of austerity which followed, established the foundations for a more authoritarian and disciplinary public policy regime, from the delivery of health and welfare to policing and criminal justice (Rodger, 2008). Accordingly this chapter situates the political focus on 'knife crime' at this moment as one amongst a number of important political shifts during a temporary rupture in the maintenance of political authority. Put another way, 'knife crime' provided an opportunity to re-authorise and legitimate a model of robust crime control driven policing which had suffered a few setbacks in recent years.

Three decades separate the mobilisation that defined 'mugging' and the emergence of the concept of 'knife crime'. In that time neo-liberalism had strengthened its grip, social divisions had deepened the financial crisis and austerity had taken its toll shrouding inequality and social exclusion, or 'advanced marginality' (Wacquant, 2004) with a series of extended ideological rationalisations: the undeserving poor, 'shirkers' versus 'strivers', violent 'chavs', feral youth, the 'gang involved' and supposedly 'feckless' teenage mothers (Hayward & Yar, 2006; Jeffs & Smith, 1996; Kehily, 2017; Tyler, 2013; Wacquant, 2009; Yardley, 2008). New cultural expressions for the criminal, deviant and excluded clearly emerged although whilst the 'knife crime' context certainly bears comparison with the 1970s 'mugging panic' we will also be concerned with how they differed. Overall, this chapter explores how both depictions of and explanations for 'knife crime' were formed by and distinctly suited to this historical moment and thereby contributed to restricting both criticism and resistance. Subsequently this chapter follows the 'knife crime' chronology and narrative up to the present, including its return to the headlines around 2015, finally drawing attention to the interaction between the extension of police powers and the political uncertainty during and after Britain's Brexit referendum and the Covid 'lockdowns' which soon followed. It may be too soon to draw major conclusions, but the unprecedented Covid pandemic brought tremendous social pressures and cultural adjustments. In particular, it was widely anticipated that the various lockdowns would generate increasing pressures towards violence even as the strategy of 'governing through public health' might suggest wider applications in tackling urban violence.

A Spike in 'Knife Crime'?

It is widely acknowledged that 2007 and 2008 witnessed unusually high levels of violence involving young people which came to represent a 'spike' on graphs of knife homicides in London (Wood, 2010). There were twenty-six teenage deaths in 2007 compared to a relatively stable average of seventeen a year since 2000 (Wood, 2010: 97). This figure increased to thirty teenage deaths in the capital in 2008, twenty-four of whom were killed by knives (Barr, 2017), before dropping to the lower level of thirteen in 2009 (Wood, 2010). The available data does not specify the precise ages of the perpetrators or victims, or the precise contexts of the teen deaths at this time, but news reports from the time indicate a variety of settings; such as fights in a nightclubs/pubs, domestic violence cases, although one stalker and a racially aggravated murder of a 17 year old by a 31 year old man, are included in the figures. Obviously caution should apply when discussing short-term fluctuations in offence rates ('spikes'), especially when the underlying numbers are relatively low, a few unusual events can appear dramatic at this scale. On the flip side low numbers of incidents tends to mean that each one is front page news, although there are aspects of the statistical representation of knife crime that causes valid concern. Teen-on-teen homicides made up a larger proportion of youth deaths in London in 2008 as compared with the rest of the country; half of the young people killed in the capital were killed by other teenagers compared with a third of youth homicides outside of the city (Wood, 2010: 99). Youth work practitioners interviewed in London also described the increasing intensity of violence between young people at the time, an issue that we will return to in greater detail in Chapter 6.

However, at such an important stage in the history of the 'knife crime' label, when a newly defined crime category transitions into a full societal moral panic, it is important that the reality of violence between children and its devastating consequences at this time is not simply denied.

Just as Cohen (1972) and Hall et al. (1978) were clear, the depiction and analysis of a moral panic does not deny the reality of the acts—the violence—but rather, draws attention to the 'particular character of the social reaction' occurring (Squires, 2009: 129). Recognising the escalating rates of teenage homicides in 2007 and 2008 this research strongly endorses the need for increased visibility and public attention to the harms associated with interpersonal violence between teens. However, our critical approach to the particular forms that the media, police and government, responses took at this time will show that the expression of this violence through the loaded category 'knife crime' had profound and detrimental consequences for young people themselves. Not only did the established parameters and discourse of the label dictate what was included in the reporting of cases, it also established what was left out. Previous chapters have detailed the processes through which 'knife crime' came to be understood as a criminal youth culture that was largely racially defined. By attaching the label 'knife crime' almost exclusively to Black victims of violence at this time any disproportionate representation of this demographic is considered in isolation from wider socio-economic factors (deprivation, social exclusion, educational under-achievement, lack of employment opportunity), in favour of broadly cultural explanations (race and ethnicity, even gang involvements).

Clearly economic forces and social influences provide a compelling explanation for the disproportionate representation of Black children in violent crime at this time. Housing statistics for England show that 8.7% of the white population live in the most deprived 10% of neighbourhoods, compared to 19.6% of the black population (Gov.uk, 2018b). In London in 2007, 40% of people from Black or minority ethnic backgrounds lived in low-income households, compared to 20% of the white population (MacInnes & Kenway, 2009: 61). Living in deprived areas significantly increases the probability of encountering everyday violence (Bellis et al., 2011)—with knives a particular risk in these conditions; 'members of those communities are more likely to experience violent crime, and muggings in particular, which involve a high proportion of knife usage' (Eades, 2007: 24). It is also recognised that death by sharp instrument is twice as common a method of homicide in poor areas compared to wealthy parts of Britain (Eades, 2007) whilst London has the highest rates of child poverty compared to other regions (Wood, 2010). Yet despite the clear connections between homicide methods, poverty, and the disproportionate representation of Black and minority ethnic groups living in deprived neighbourhoods, the proximate context of profound social and economic inequality is entirely overlooked during the frenetic reporting which followed the fatal stabbing of three Black teenagers in February 2007.

Suggesting culture as cause and punitive action as the solution, Tony Blair's comments on youth homicides in early 2007 characterised a reaction that would continue to dominate the following years. Speaking at an event in Cardiff in April 2007 he was reported as saying: 'In respect of knife and gun gangs, the laws need to be significantly toughened. There needs to be an intensive police focus, on these groups. The ring-leaders need to be identified and taken out of circulation; if very young, as some are, put in secure accommodation. The black community—the vast majority of whom in these communities are decent, law-abiding people horrified at what is happening—need to be mobilised in denunciation of this gang culture that is killing innocent young black kids. But we won't stop this by pretending it isn't young black kids doing it' (Hall, 2007; Tony Blair cited in UKPOL, 2007). The explicit abstraction of 'Black kids' and the 'Black community' in the framing of these deaths has been a process of articulation that has been gradually building over the preceding years. McMahon and Roberts (2011), following Gilroy (1982) have described this as the black crime myth. Whilst New Labour's 'tough on crime' rhetoric in the late 1990s had not been overtly racialised the development of a distinct and 'new' criminality understood as 'knife crime' in the 2000's increasingly normalised a discourse that centred race and culture in both the identification of cause and the proposed robust enforcement solutions. As Tendler and Ford (2007) put it in an article in *The Times*, 'Armed police [were to be] sent out in force on a mission to reclaim the badlands'. Important shifts in the discourse on race and criminality will be followed closely in this chapter, as we show how these new forms of racism became vital to the coordination of exceptional force and hegemonic governance in law and order.

'Knife Crime' as Culture; Slippery Racism

In chapter three the social and political implications of the MacPherson report were discussed in detail, along with the particular ideologies of 'multiculturalism' and 'race relations' that defined the language of social policy and politics at that time. Whilst overt racism and discrimination were no longer publicly acceptable, a decade later expressions of racism can be seen to have shifted and taken on discrete new forms, enabling the continued communication of racist ideas in the new political context. Miller (2008) describes the same phenomenon in the USA, with certain words, 'street crime', 'gangs' or 'urban violence' operating as code words for black criminality, much as 'mugging' had served in the 1970s. According to Gilroy, 'Casual talk of "black youth" had been replaced by superficially anodyne, technical disquisitions of "antisocial behaviour" and the quantifiable perils of ungovernable gang culture' (Gilroy, 2013: n.p.). The notion of inherent racial difference was preserved through a shift to socially acceptable forms of 'cultural racism' (Gilroy, 1987), or what Barker had earlier termed the 'new racism' (Barker, 1981). Within this new paradigm difference was attributed to culture rather than biology but the same racially defined hierarchy remained (Grosfoguel, 1999).

> This ability of racist ideologies of white supremacy to produce new socially acceptable forms was reliant on the adaptability of its concepts, remaining fluid in expression but consistent in meaning: '[W]hat is really interesting about racism as a set of ideas and political practices is that it is able to provide images of the 'other' which are simple and unchanging and at the same time to adapt to the changing social and political environment. Thus contemporary racist ideas are able to maintain a link with the mystical values of classical racism and to adopt and use cultural and political symbols that are part of contemporary society'. (Solomos & Back, 1996: 210)

The racism communicated through 'knife crime' was certainly not new, but the articulation of racism through this label gave it new symbolic forms, epitomising what has been called 'the slippery nature of contemporary racisms' (Solomos & Back, 1996: 213). The accumulating rhetoric of 'knife crime' as a 'trend' or 'dangerous culture' was accompanied by an assortment of racist stereotypes including 'gangsters' (Weathers, 2005), 'absent Black fathers' (Wintour et al., 2008), 'dysfunctional families' (Weathers, 2005) and hip-hop music ('Cameron Attacks …', 2008) all surreptitiously make their appearance. Subsequently 'drill music' in police minds became the essential signifier of a lethal ethnicity (Elliott-Cooper, 2021: 156–158; Fatsis, 2019, 2020). Yet whether race was explicitly mentioned or not, the construction of the label ensured that the phrase 'knife crime' came to stand for a criminality that is distinctly 'other'—a threat stemming from outside of English civility, the same in 2008 as it was in 1953.[1]

Racism like a 'scavenger ideology' (Solomos & Back, 1996: 213) is constantly adapting to fit the changing politics of each moment. Analysis of this period concludes that 'knife crime' is a particularly effective synthesis for our time, embodying both the old imagination of a violent, primitive and under-civilised 'other' and the new language of crime as 'culture'. A report by the Runnymede Trust published in 2008 showed that the deployment of 'culture' as a discursive device in the media coverage of crime related to 'gangs', guns and knives is a largely contemporary phenomenon (Sveinsson, 2008). Plotting the frequency with which notions of 'gang culture', 'gun culture' and 'knife culture' were cited in national newspapers, the report demonstrated that such discursive framings became established from 2000 onwards, with 'knife culture' emerging from 2003 onwards (Fig. 5.2).

Sveinsson argued that when the concept of 'culture' was used in the reporting of violent crime, it tended to skirt around what he called 'respectable forms of racism' whilst simultaneously negating the significance of structural analysis in the production of crime and violence:

'[S]tating that black people have a criminal nature' is not politically acceptable. Stating that 'black culture glorifies crime' is. Yet both statements are saying the same thing: crime is endemic within the black

---

[1] Refer to the discussion of the 1953 debate in the House of Commons in Chapter 1.

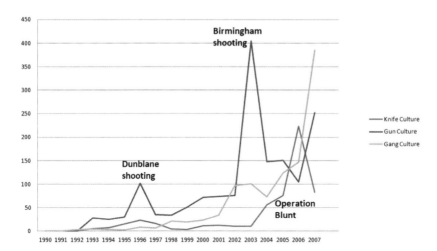

Fig. 5.2 Frequency of articles containing the terms *'gang crime'*, *'gun crime'* or *'knife crime'* in National Newspapers 1990–2007. Data from Lexis-Nexis (Graph reconstructed from Sveinsson, 2008: 6)

population, and is unrelated to the structure of British society and the experience of black people within it. (Sveinsson, 2008: 6, 7)

The attachment of 'knife crime' to a supposed 'knife culture' since its inception has enabled the concept to perform a dual function very effectively. Adopting a narrative of 'culture' largely excludes the white population; 'Culture' and 'community' are seldom evoked when speaking about white Britons. Except in the most bland and general terms, white middle-class England is not thought of as a 'community' in itself,[2] and to be English is not considered a 'cultural' trait' (Sveinsson, 2008: 3). Thus 'Knife crime', through a rhetoric of 'culture', inherently excludes white children from its implied meaning—negating societal responsibility for interpersonal youth violence by blaming Black children for

---

[2] Notwithstanding a number of recent attempts to construct such an identity, often around iconic moments in British, or English, history. O'Toole (2019) for instance argues that the symbolism of Dunkirk has often underpinned such an ideal, often connected to distant dreams of Empire (Trafford, 2021) a symbolism revived in the context of Brexit, and regurgitated every now and again in the propaganda of English nationalism (Gilroy, 1987) and most recently the politics of the English Defence League (Winlow et al., 2017).

their own disadvantage; 'Fascinating tales of gangs, murder and mayhem become part of insisting that culture is once again the key to seeing how blacks have been the primary authors of their own urban misfortune' (Gilroy, 2010: 22). Examining the concept of 'knife culture' in Sveinsson's work, we can see how the appearance and flourishing of this concept directly reflects the social history of 'knife crime' we have traced in previous chapters. This was a concept first employed publicly in around 2003 becoming prominent in 2006. In 2007 'gun culture' and 'gang culture' appear to eclipse 'knife culture' in news reporting, although this is far from being the end of the story. Applying similar analysis to news coverage beyond 2007 we have produced two further graphs. Figure 5.3 shows that the incidence of "knife culture" in news reports peaked again in 2008 reflecting the substantial surge in "knife crime" news as depicted in Fig. 5.4.

As the media responded to the increase in youth violence in 2007 and 2008 the interpretation of the problem through the lens of 'knife crime' also becomes its own justification. Once publicly recognised as an established crime category, 'knife crime' became an entirely self-contained phenomenon—the labelling standing as both description and explanation of the violence. The significance of reporting the increased violence

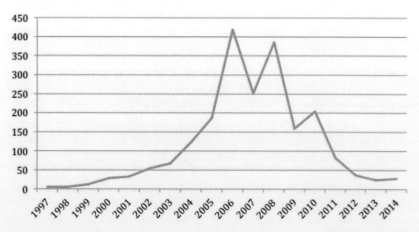

Fig. 5.3 Frequency of articles with the term 'knife culture' included 1997–2014 (Graph prepared using data from ProQuest—National and regional papers in England and Wales)

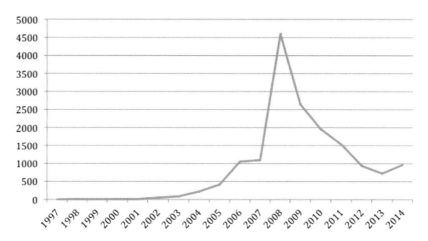

Fig. 5.4 Frequency of articles with the term 'knife crime' included 1997–2014 (Graph prepared using data from ProQuest—National and regional papers in England and Wales)

as 'knife crime' in 2007 was not limited to the realm of representation. The power and influence of the language of 'knife crime' shaped both public perception and, in turn, government policy. Furthermore, as the events of 2008 demonstrated, cultural racism through 'knife crime' became a fundamental component of the 'state of exception', providing public consent for the extension of police powers.

The War on 'Knife Crime'

Following reports of increasing teenage deaths in 2007 and early 2008 the societal reaction to 'knife crime' took a significant turn when Conservative MP Boris Johnson became Mayor of London in May 2008. Elected on a clear law and order manifesto, just ten days into his appointment, the Metropolitan Police and the new mayor declared a 'war on knife crime gangs' (Edwards et al., 2008) and promised 'a fight-back against knife crime' (ibid.). Using additional funding from the Mayor's budget, the Met police launched 'Operation Blunt 2'. This response included the formation of a specialist taskforce of one hundred and fifty uniformed officers, working in ten units of fifteen officers, targeting ten boroughs to conduct unlimited stop and search operations through Section 60 ('no suspicion') searches. The deployment of this particular power to target 'knife crime' represented a significant political development with lasting and destructive consequences on police-community relations. As we have seen, there are a variety of powers enabling the police to undertake a search of persons, premises and vehicles, most of them requiring that 'the officer has reasonable grounds for suspecting that stolen or prohibited articles will be found' (MPA, 2004: 17). However, Section 60 of the Criminal Justice and Public Order Act 1994 (along with Section 44 of the Terrorism Act 2000—now repealed), were distinctly different in that they do not require 'reasonable grounds' for searches. Prior to 2008 Section 60 searches were rare,[3] as they required preauthorisation by a senior officer who had to designate a particular area for such search activity. The legislation had primarily been used to police football matches to combat 'hooliganism' where the date and location of the Section 60 could be planned in advance. As a reinvention of this policing power the Met police assigned Section 60 as a 'knife crime' reduction tactic in 2008 to be used across all of London with authorisation for a rolling, blanket coverage.

At the launch of Operation Blunt 2, Assistant Commissioner Tim Goodwin admitted that the use of Section 60 in this way was a 'sensitive issue' describing it as 'not politically correct' amounting to a kind of 'in your face policing' (Edwards et al., 2008). But he went on to confirm the Met's commitment to it by saying, 'I see this going on for the long term because we really, really have to do something about it' (Edwards et al., 2008; Murphy, 2019). Comparing Metropolitan police stop and search rates from twelve months before, and twelve months after the declaration of 'war on knife crime', the prominence of Section 60 in this response is evident. Section 60 searches underwent a six-fold increase to over 121,000, whilst section one searches only doubled. The total number of searches in London increased by 292% in 2008 with the proportion of Section 60 searches increasing from 26 to 59% of *weapon related* searches. At the same time, however, the arrest rate halved from

---

[3] Refer to Chapter 4, Fig. 4.11.

4 to 2% per cent and stayed at 2% for the three years that the Operation Blunt 2 was in action (McCandless et al., 2016).

The arrest rate for dangerous weapons was lower still, retrieving less than one 'offensive weapon' per two hundred searches (Shiner, 2015). The claim that this intensive police search tactic was urgently required in order to reduce 'knife crime' was entirely undermined when it was revealed that the police actions undertaken during the 'war on knife crime' had no apparent impact on rates of recorded knife-involved offending or crime figures in general. One report on the effectiveness of Operation Blunt 2 compared statistics from London boroughs that were not targeted with those that were and found increased search rates had no effect on recorded crime—in fact, ambulance calls were found to have fallen faster in boroughs with smaller increases in search rates (McCandless et al., 2016).

In a comprehensive statistical study of ten years of police stop and search data in London Tiratelli et al. (2018) scrutinised and tested for evidence of significant correlations between each type of search power, specific offences and general recorded crime rates. This included particular attention to the impact of the dramatic increase in Section 60 searches in 2008 in relation to recorded crime before and after Operation Blunt 2. In summarising their findings Tiratelli et al. (2018) state; 'We struggled to find evidence of an effect of S&S on violent crime' (Tiratelli et al., 2018: 12). Whilst there is no evidence that the increase in stop and search impacted on violent crime or knife offences (a conclusion also reached by the Home Affairs Select Committee in 2009 (para 35), there is strong evidence that the extension of this power significantly increased racial discrimination. Around 120 black people were searched per 1000 in 2008–2009, a significant increase from the 78 per thousand the previous year (see Fig. 4.12). By contrast the white rate of stop and search showed very little change throughout the 'war on knife crime', increasing only slightly in 2008 from 15.5 to 17.3 out of every 1000 of the population (Home Office, 2017). Stop and search disproportionality between whites and blacks more than doubled during this time. In 2007 Black people were 4.1 times more likely to be searched in London than White people, but by 2008 they were 9.7 times more likely to be stopped

(EHRC, 2012: 24, 25). We have already referred to the need to understand disproportionality in stop and search through a proper assessment of the 'available population' (Miller et al., 2002; Waddington, 2004). And police commentators have frequently defended their tactics in these terms, but whilst the availability analysis makes an important point, the police can only stop and search those people who are out and about, the analysis still raises important questions. Firstly, the argument does not account for why stop and search disproportionality rates would fluctuate so dramatically (almost doubling between 2006 and 2008) or why arrest rates, following stops, should fall by half over the same period. Secondly, there is a paradox of crime amplification evidenced by the targeting of stop and search operations; the claim that prevalent areas of stop and search are racially proportionate because the available population is less white, is also a tacit acknowledgement that less white areas are disproportionately policed.

The idea that Operation Blunt 2 rested primarily upon the intensive policing of particular *criminal areas* is reflected in the strategic designation of specified areas for S.60 operations—sometimes, however, entire London Boroughs[4]—but at street-level, the claim is not supported by research. As Tiratelli et al. (2018) noted: 'we have no reason to believe that S&S activity was actively being targeted towards crime hotspots in a systematic and consistent manner across the police force area. Indeed, evidence suggests that it is *people, not places*, that are most commonly 'targeted' by officers for S&S (Tiratelli et al., 2018: 5, emphasis added). Whilst Operation Blunt 2 was justified by reference to a targeting of areas that police had identified as 'knife crime hot spots', the evidence suggests the real target was young Black people. The public argument to justify this disproportionality had been established for some time and stop and search rates had been increasing gradually since 2002. Even so there are particular characteristics of policing powers in 2008 that set this period apart.

The 2008 'war on knife crime' announced by the Metropolitan police in response to the increase in teenage homicides represented a distinct shift in policing. Not only in terms of the frequency of stop and search in

---

[4] Leroy Logan, former Superintendent Metropolitan Police, personal communication, 8.11.18.

the capital, but also regarding the dramatic uplift in police powers being regularly exercised in the street. Section 60 both legally and symbolically authorized the confrontational policing of young black people, the overwhelming majority of whom were found to be carrying nothing offensive. The blanket authorization, increased disproportionality and the coercive nature of this tactic, resulting in thousands of children experiencing the indignity, affront and distrust of being publicly searched. The continuation of Operation Blunt 2 for three years, despite its negative impact on arrest rates and its inability to reduce knife offences, suggest that this display of police power and its extension of force was not just a pragmatic response to 'knife crime'.

On the contrary, the lessons of *Policing the Crisis* (Hall et al., 1978) suggest that the articulation of law and order and the exceptional use of force underpinned by race and racism were a direct response to a series of tensions impacting first upon policing but which reflected a deeper hegemonic crisis, growing political and economic disorder and the attempted refashioning of political consent. The three years from 2008 that were marked by extended stop and search powers and increased police mobilisation in London's streets were also defined by a global economic event that anticipated the 'austerity to come' whilst threatening to expose the deep contradictions of neoliberal corporate capitalism. Whilst the global economic crisis, initially referred to as the 'credit crunch', had certainly pushed knife crime from the front pages of the newspapers (Squires, 2009: 1), it still served as an important justification for the tough law and order agenda. Later, especially when the Conservative-led coalition government's austerity measures began, robust policing continued to make important contributions to the management of crisis. As in earlier periods of neo-liberal governance, economic priorities prevailed over social ones; inequality was regarded as a major incentive: 'What the poorest needed most' it was argued, 'was not welfare, but order, discipline and a healthy respect for the work ethic' (Squires, 2016: 290). Drawing a direct parallel between the Thatcher governments, beginning in 1979 and the Conservative-led coalition in 2010, Farrall and Hay have noted how the neo-liberal social and economic policies adopted had a profoundly self-fulfilling aspect to them, ultimately 'demanding a more punitive response to crime' (Farrell & Hay, 2010: 566). In this fashion,

2010 represented a clear reworking of the 'free economy – strong state' relationship familiar to neo-liberalism (Gamble, 1988).

From the Crisis of the Banks to the Crisis on the Streets

To help contextualize the use of excessive force in the streets during this period it is important to review briefly the events and political decisions that took place in the aftermath of the global crash and how the ideological reworking of a national deficit came to disproportionately impact on young people and their day-to-day safety. Having inherited the £500 billion additional debt, the price of bailing out the UK banking system, the incoming coalition government of 2010 went on to implement a prolonged period of 'austerity measures'—a brutal rolling back of the state including devastating cuts to public services and welfare, deepening conditions of deprivation and increasing inequality. The politics of austerity after 2010 involved a distinctly ideological reworking of neoliberal crisis into a social responsibility agenda. Whilst in opposition in 2009 the Conservatives had begun began to construct a moralistic argument for austerity. Talking of 'broken Britain' and evoking post-war nostalgia around 'tightening our belts' and 'living within our means', the deficit resulting from the decision to support the banks was translated into an issue of irresponsible public spending (Berry, 2016). Reinforcing the neoliberal ideology of economic nationalism, sacrifice and restraint became a form of social cohesion, encapsulated by David Cameron's austerity catch phrase: "We're all in this together" (Brady & Dugan, 2012).

Yet even as this dubious claim still resonated, its falsehood was exposed by the announcement of a major package of cuts to welfare and public services. Most notably these included; a social security benefit cap (a maximum total of social security benefits received by one household, generally set at £26,000), the 'bedroom tax' (a withdrawal of benefits for people with unused bedrooms in their homes) cuts and increased scrutiny of disability benefits including the use of out-of work 'sanctions' (withholding benefits from those claiming Job Seekers Allowance for failing to meet increasingly more rigorous entitlement conditions). In terms of expenditure reduction, the hostile treatment and punishment of individual benefit recipients (including the introduction of the benefit fraud hotline) had a relatively small budget impact (Berry, 2016). The effect was arguably more symbolic than fiscal; linking the national economy to the culture and responsibility of the individual within an ideology of austerity. At the same time it divided and ruled: distinguishing 'shirkers' from 'strivers', law abiding citizens from criminal minorities, us from them. A more subtle way in which these juxtapositions were expressed might be discerned in the 2010 Conservative Party Manifesto. Tacking close to the party's familiar law and order agenda, the manifesto went on to claim that 'our communities are shattered by crime and abuse', before moving on to announce a major reorientation of criminal justice policy around the needs of *victims*, the silent, long-suffering majority. As we have already seen, white middle-England is seldom addressed explicitly *as a culture* (Sveinsson, 2008), but in law and order terms, recycling notions of 'white victimhood' might just be one of the ways. And indeed, if we recall the significant white victims who have punctuated our knife crime story—Philip Lawrence, Ben Kinsella, Tom ap Rhys Pryce—this picture holds. Despite the disproportionate exposure of young black males to criminal violence, contemporary victimhood by 'imputing crime to blackness' retains a fearful white outlook (Gilroy, 1982; Goodman & Ruggiero, 2008).

Yet even as we reflect upon the violence that has become almost entirely defined by the acts of knife wielding young people, it is nevertheless significant how the consequences of austerity impacted on young people themselves with particular ferocity, before translating full circle into the tabloid fears of middle England. For youth services, schools and early years provision suffered some of the most severe reductions of state funding—with many services left struggling to function under the rapid withdrawal of the local council budgets that sustained their work (Roberts, 2021: 51). In six years youth services lost £387 million, forcing 603 youth centres to close and with a loss of 3652 youth workers in the UK (Figs. 5.5 and 5.6).

More recent data collated by the YMCA shows that between 2011 and 2017 some £750 million was cut from local authority youth service

Total cuts in youth service spending, 2010-2016

2010/11	2011/12	2012/13	2013/14	2014/15	2015/16	TOTAL
£62m	£137m	£41m	£24m	£85m	£38m	£387m

Fig. 5.5   Cuts in youth service spending 2010–2016 (*Source* Unison, 2016: 4)

The collapse of youth services in the UK

	2012-14	2014-16	Total 2012-16
Youth work jobs lost	1,991	1,661	3,652
Youth centres closed	359	244	603
Places for young people cut	40,989	97,909	138,898

Fig. 5.6   The collapse of youth services in the UK (*Source* Unison, 2016: 5)

budgets reflecting percentage changes, per region, of between minus 53% (east of England) to 71% (West Midlands) and an average of 62% for the country as a whole (YMCA, 2018). Although the Coalition government had suggested that schools themselves would be protected from the cuts, consequences were inevitable. Many school-based initiatives such as, one-to-one teaching programmes, breakfast clubs, outdoor education, music services, school psychologists and speech therapists were funded through local council welfare support and services. Schools either had to cut these provisions or reallocate money from the pupil premium causing a knock-on effect on other budgets (Granoulhac, 2017: 437). The Education Maintenance Allowance (EMA) was also axed—a scheme that provided £30 a week to help college students from low-income families. Finally, in a decision with profound consequences for students, the Liberal Democrat party back-tracked on an election pledge not to increase tuition fees, prompting major demonstrations and violent confrontations with the police during the latter part of 2010.

The removal of the EMA and the cutting of many of the support schemes helping keep many poorer children in school had a significant impact upon Black and mixed ethnicity pupils. It has long been recognised that Black and mixed ethnicity pupils had the highest rates of both temporary and permanent exclusions, with black Caribbean pupils permanently excluded at nearly 3 times the rate of white British pupils (Gill et al., 2017; Perera, 2020; Timpson, 2019). Whilst young people living in disadvantaged areas had already demonstrated an increased exposure to violence by 2008, the Government's austerity response to that was to actively further exclude and marginalise the groups most at risk of everyday violence. The removal of the EMA and increase in permanent exclusions reduced access to education and employment, whilst the collapse of youth services and early years provisions removed the some of the limited safeguards and supports available to those young people experiencing the most extreme marginalisation. Austerity was an ideological project that mobilised public consent for a substantial rolling back of state welfare and dramatic increases in deprivation and inequality and further reinforced by an implication that Britain's real problems were its 'enemies' within and without. It is within this familiar context that the established racism of 'knife crime' is put to work within the management of hegemony, providing consent for increased police powers at a time of potential social unrest. As in the 1980s, this toxic combination of extreme deprivation, increased marginalization and excessive policing led to widespread discontent and, subsequently, the riots of 2011. Comparing the social and political response to the 'youth riots' of early 2011 with the reaction to the 'race riots' of the early 1980s, although drugs, mugging and 'street crime' were certainly a central part of a justification for the heavy-handed policing operations which prompted the 1980 and 1981 riots,[5] by 2010 the intensification of cultural racism and concerns about gangs and knife crime made the law and order arguments seem all the more compelling. Nevertheless, despite initially attempting to lay responsibility for the 2011 riots upon gangs (Cameron, 2011; HM Government, 2011), however, this claim was subsequently much discredited (Hallsworth & Brotherton, 2011; Lewis et al., 2011b; Newburn et al., 2011).

---

[5] The Brixton Riots are frequently reported to have been triggered by the Metropolitan Police 'Operation Swamp' in Brixton, the riot in St. Pauls, Bristol, a year earlier, following a police raid on a drinking club, is often overlooked.

Political Response and Public Resistance

By 2010 the intensive street policing underpinned by Operation Blunt 2 was attracting increasing criticism from organised groups and communities. The return to pre-Macpherson policing was described by Liberty 'as if Lawrence never happened' (Liberty, 2010) whilst evidence was even emerging of police being told to discriminate in stop and search (ibid.). A review by the Equality and Human Rights Commission (EHRC) in 2010 concluded that stop and search powers were being used in a 'discriminatory and unlawful way' (EHRC, 2010: 58), whilst the European Court found that the Metropolitan Police were 'violating individual freedoms and acting illegally' by employing Section 44 searches ('Terror Stop…', 2010). As we have seen (Fig. 4.11) increasing legal scrutiny forced the scaling back of stop and search after 2010 (Dodd, 2012). During the same period Section 60 Searches fell by almost two thirds (ibid.). A leaked letter from the Deputy Met Police Commissioner later revealed that this reduction was made in anticipation of a similar legal challenge to the 'no suspicion' powers entailed by Section 60 (ibid.). The Metropolitan Police reputation suffered further reputational damage in 2009 when a police public order officer, used unwarranted and excessive force against a bystander during the 2009 G-20 summit protests in London. The man fell, hitting his head and shortly thereafter died. Unknown to the police, the incident was caught on video exposing the falsity of a number of unofficial police briefings to the media (Lewis, 2009). In due course, a police officer was charged with manslaughter and, although acquitted, he was dismissed from the police. In the wake of this event and a series of running criticisms of an overzealous and confrontational policing of public order incidents,[6] the Chief Inspector of Constabulary, Dennis O'Connor, undertook an inquiry, later publishing a report entitled *Adapting to Protest* (HMIC,

---

[6] Complaints especially included police 'kettling' (surrounding protestors with ranks of police and only releasing people much later, slowly and in small numbers at a time); using powers under s.50 of the Police Reform Act to require the names and addresses of protestors, intensive photographing of protestors; and inconsistent police tactics, equipment and use of powers; and poor communication with protest organisers.

2009) intended to restore a tradition of 'consent based' policing which sought to 'facilitate' lawful protest.

Although not long in place, and the retraining of police public order teams and responses still incomplete, the new police public order strategies soon faced a stern test. In controversial and contested circumstances, on the 4 August 2011, the Metropolitan police shot and killed 29-year-old Mark Duggan in North London following a hard vehicle stop manoeuvre. It became the spark which ignited a tinderbox of discontent amongst young people. Angry that the police had failed to release details of the shooting or communicate with bereaved family members, a protesting crowd gathered at Tottenham Police station. The situation deteriorated, confrontation turned into conflict, and a full-scale riot broke out. Over the next three days riots accompanied by arson and looting occurred in several cities with upwards of 15,000 young people involved, some £300 million in property damages and five deaths. Film footage was reminiscent of the 1981 riots with large numbers of young people challenging the symbolic power of the police; cars and buildings were set alight, shops smashed and looted, and police cordons attacked. Important parallels have been drawn between the two sets of riots almost thirty years apart, but, whereas in 1980, Lord Scarman undertook a judicial inquiry seeking to explain the incident and make recommendations, no such analysis was deemed necessary in 2011. On the contrary, Prime Minister Cameron suggested he knew all he needed to know. 'This was not political protest, or a riot about politics. It was common or garden thieving, robbing and looting… This is not about poverty; it is about culture—a culture that glorifies violence, shows disrespect to authority' (Cameron, BBC, 2011). He contrasted the violent and criminal with the 'law-abiding majority' of 'innocent victims' and claimed that 'at the heart of all the violence sits the issue of the street gangs…' (ibid.), whilst promising 'a concerted, all-out war on gangs and gang culture'.

In contrast to Cameron's 'simple criminality' remark (Cooper, 2012; Scrase, 2017; Squires, 2011), a great deal of research, commentary and analysis, representing different schools of thought in social science and criminology explored many aspects of the riots (see for example Briggs, 2012; Flint & Powell, 2012; Lightowlers, 2015; Newburn, 2015; Slater, 2016; Solomos, 2011; Stott & Reicher, 2011; Stott et al., 2017;

Treadwell et al., 2013; Winlow & Hall, 2012). This is not the place to pursue these analyses in any depth although one of the most notable was the *Reading the Riots* collaboration between academics at the LSE and journalists at the *Guardian*. Findings from this survey of 270 people who had been directly involved in rioting confirmed that 'widespread anger and frustration at people's everyday treatment by the police was a significant factor in the riots in every major city where rioting took place' (Lewis et al., 2011a; Roberts et al., 2011: 4). Overall fully 85% of interviews claimed that policing was a major factor in the riots, second only to Poverty (86%), with Government Policy, third (80%). Fully 73% of those interviewed in the study had been stopped and searched at least once in the past year and participants across the country described their experiences of harassment, and of physical and verbal assault by police officers. Research from several sources found clear connections between stop and search, deprivation and anger towards the politics of recent economic decisions. The *Riots, Communities and Victims Panel*, established by the Deputy Prime Minister, concluded that 'stop and search was a major factor' in the cause of the unrest, with many young people frequently citing a 'lack of courtesy' during stop and search in the explanation of their actions (RCVP, 2012). Keeling likewise detailed his extensive focus group findings with young people who had been accosted by police and subjected to aggressive and humiliating weapons searches. He continued, 'the effect that negative experiences can have on the likelihood that a young person might call the police for assistance or be cooperative with the police in the future... is particularly concerning' suggesting both a lack of professionalism and impunity (Keeling, 2017). Whilst police commentators have often poured scorn on the idea that young people might carry knives 'for protection', a combination of fear with mistrust and a lack of confidence in the police seem likely to prompt that very behaviour (Brennan, 2019; Squires, 2009: 11–14). In Croydon, South London, one of the centres of the rioting, an Independent Review Panel was established to investigate the causes and consequences of the riot. It drew attention to a 'melting pot of tensions... unemployment and lack of opportunities... overcrowding, the physical environment, levels of crime and poverty' but singled out rates of stop and search, and emphasised the need for a review of police stop and search policy and practice (Croydon ILRP, 2012: 29).

The uprisings (Kettle & Hodges, 1982) of 1981 were widely referred to as 'race riots' although the events of 2011 were described as 'London riots' or 'youth riots' although both sets of events had similar multi racial representation (Gilroy, 2013). Despite the shift to non-racial language the construction of race and racism remained formative in the interpretation of events in 2011 (Solomos, 2011). Language and stereotypes that had come to stand in place of race were put to work. Pre-constructed racialised notions of criminality, such as 'gangs', 'youth culture', 'absent fathers', 'dysfunctional families' and 'knife crime', reproduced forms of implicit racism in the discussions of and responses to the riots that were often hard to pin down as racist. As Solomos has noted, 'media coverage and public debate about the events shifted away from issues about race and policing to a wider set of social and cultural symbols. Yet it is important that we do not lose sight of the role that race and ethnicity may have played in both the riots themselves and in shaping some of the underlying conditions in the areas at the heart of the violence' (Solomos, 2011). He went on to illustrate this implicit racialising of the disorders by reference to historian David Starkey's appearance on *Newsnight* where he argued that British youth culture had become 'black' and that the riots were 'a sign that a 'nihilistic gangster culture' had become a dominant norm in Britain', this was perhaps the most egregious example of such taken-for-granted racialised discourses being absorbed into a broader social and political explanations of the riots (Solomos, 2011).

The subtlety of contemporary racism—'new racism'—enabled a crucial contradiction; the 2011 riots could simultaneously be depicted as not *about race* even whilst 'black criminality' was constantly inferred. The utility of the concept 'knife crime' to represent high levels of everyday urban violence in deprived communities as 'cultural deficits', now enabled political violence (rioting) to be discredited through a perceptions of 'youth criminality' as 'culture'. This redesignation proved to be very effective, with the LSE research finding that 86% of the general public thought the two leading causes of the unrest were 'poor parenting and criminality' (Lewis et al., 2011a). Perhaps predictably the state response to the uprising was especially punitive and potentially violent. There were calls for the deployment of water cannons, rubber bullets and curfews (Bates, 2011).[7] In the weeks following the riots over 1000 cases were rushed through the magistrates courts with an unusually high proportion (70%) remanded in custody pending their hearings. Sentences awarded were regarded as unusually harsh (Lightowlers & Quirk, 2015; Pina Sanchez et al., 2017). There were reports of young people in their early 20s receiving four-year sentences for Facebook posts that were deemed to incite rioting (Carter, 2011). The extreme sentencing caused a sudden swell in the youth custody system leading to many young people being sent across the country, hundreds of miles from their families for often minor first time offences (ibid.).

The strange case of the way the English Riots of 2011 were interpreted, riots in which racism, race discrimination and racialisation was ever present but never instrumental, there but not there, provides a fine parallel for our knife crime story. We have encountered it before. In *Policing the Crisis* (1978) Stuart Hall and his colleagues described how urban violence, coded as 'black' via the mugging label, obscured the wider socio-economic conditions—poverty, disadvantage and racialised exclusion—which were themselves the underlying causes of the violence. So too with the riots. The dominant narratives, sometimes supported by criminological accounts emphasising the hedonistic and cultural aspects of the riotous actions: 'shopping with violence' (Newburn, 2015; Treadwell et al., 2013), at times completely overlooked the racial aspects which had animated the rioters, hostility to the police and anger about the perceived misuse of police powers (Jeffrey & Tufail, 2015). Neoliberalism itself frames a basic incapacity to perceive or understand the collective 'moral economy' of the disorders. Instead a common-sense individualism relegates group action to selfish opportunism. Without a sense or possibility of collective political culture the events in 2011 were construed as 'a brisk sequence of criminal events and transgressions that could be intelligible only when seen on the scale of personal

---

[7] In 2014, in anticipation of further disorders London Mayor, Boris Johnson, purchased three second-hand water cannon vehicles from the German Police incurring a total cost (including modification to make them roadworthy and compliant with the capital's low exhaust emission standards) of £322,000. Home Secretary Theresa May prohibited their use on British streets and the Metropolitan Police declared no desire to use them. In 2018 they were scrapped for a net loss of £300,000 (Weaver, 2018).

conduct' (Gilroy, 2013: n.p.). In essence, this is precisely the same analysis as we have developed in respect of 'knife crime'. For, focusing primarily upon the visceral, bloody and brutal act itself, rather than the broader context in which it occurs, 'knife crime', along with other transformed expressions of cultural racism, has produced major blind spots in our appreciation of the crimogenic power of racism. Broad theoretical research and debates often fail to connect with the detailed and specific forms that race and racism take in national and local contexts (Solomos & Back, 1996: 203). And we are left with simple 'crimes' which offer opportunity and justification to the police and authorities more than they address causes of poverty and violence. They called for the crisis, above all, to be *policed*, and so it was. We will return to these themes in our final chapter.

The End Game? 'Knife Crime' Normalisation

Before addressing this final phase of our 'knife crime' story it is worth reminding ourselves, as indicated in the final years of the knife crime time-line reproduced as Fig. 5.1, that it was only in 2011 that the Office for National Statistics (ONS) recorded data on knife-enabled violence became fully year-on-year compatible at the national level, and thereby capable of supporting national trend analysis. Until 2011 there had been plenty of anecdotal evidence, but the statistical data which had sustained so much public, political and media commentary had often been highly selective, partial and short-term, except in London where year on year comparable data became available in 2004. It is important recognise this aspect of the knife crime moral panic, especially because, with the popular commentary outrunning the data to such a degree, it was possible for any number of interpretations, assumptions and distortions to find themselves inserted into the narrative, often driven as much by the preoccupations of the speaker as the evidence before them. As we reach the final section of our timeline, however, the dominant discourse on knife crime had largely been established, its meaning and significance substantially settled. As we have sought to show, this was not the entirety of knife-enabled crime, there were still gaps, absences and silences, but the dominant narrative had firmly settled on young people, especially young black people, so as we explore the governmental and policing initiatives during this final phase, these groups remain the policy targets at the heart of knife crime discourse.

In the wake of the riots, the then Home Secretary, Theresa May, announced a national review of stop and search powers (Ball & Taylor, 2011), and the tactic remained somewhat out of favour for several years. Alongside the attempted reform of public order policing, and accelerating the launch of its *Tackling Gang and Youth Violence* programme (HM Government, 2011), the Coalition Government set out upon what it had described as a 'radical reform of our Criminal Justice system' (Cabinet Office, 2010: 13). Part of this was driven by the roll-out of the Government austerity measures which projected a reduction in Home Office spending by 24.9% between 2011 and 2015, and a 34.3% cut for the Ministry of Justice (Crawford & Keynes, 2015). The police were not to be exempted from these financial constraints, but they were on the defensive facing the new government in other ways too. A wide range of separate issues were involved,[8] but the prospect of major policing cuts generated the greatest controversy. The Home Secretary's regular visits to the Police Federation annual conference during these years saw her speeches met either with a stony silence or interrupted by angry heckling.

Although careful distinctions were attempted between 'back office' staff and 'frontline police' when discussions of policing cuts were raised by politicians, many policing commentators argued that it was precisely the 'back office' activities that kept frontline policing effective. More specifically, the stripping back of police support staff also contributed to the abrupt termination of the National Neighbourhood Policing Strategy (NPS) currently still being implemented. The NPS was an

---

[8] Issues included the reform of the Police Federation, changes to police pay, conditions of service and pensions, the containment of the powers of ACPO and its replacement by the more limited NPCC, the proposed abolition of elected Police Authorities in favour of Police and Crime Commissioners, the 'Plebgate' affair, the Leveson Inquiry, the publication of a final report into the Hillsborough disaster, which referred to police failings and a 'cover up', the dismissal of a Chief Constable for 'gross misconduct' and several investigations into the behaviour of senior officers, as well as suggestions that recorded crime statistics were being altered by target sensitive police forces (Squires, 2016: 288).

outcome of the Flanagan Review of Policing (2008) which had advocated the adoption of a stronger joined up partnership approach to community policing centred upon neighbourhoods. Overall the strategy was intended to deliver closer partnership working in neighbourhood management, joined up policy-making, better intelligence and information sharing, leading to more proactive problem-solving (Turley et al., 2012). The strategy was, in some respects, premised upon winning 'hearts and minds' drawing loosely upon the kind of thinking that had been developed in the reform of policing in Northern Ireland as part of the 'Peace Process'. Neighbourhood policing was also a reflection of a return to a form of 'policing by consent' considered to have the most to offer in high crime neighbourhoods where consent to policing was hardest to find (Longstaff et al., 2015; Myhill & Quinton, 2010). If neighbourhood policing was a potential solution to urban disorder, police legitimacy and violent crime—and an alternative to hard-nosed enforcement and dragnet style stop and search however, it had relatively little opportunity to embed and prove itself. Home Secretary Theresa May pulled a central plank from the NPS as early as June 2010 when she told delegates to the annual ACPO conference that the NPS commitment to police officers spending 80% of their time on active reassurance patrol in neighbourhoods was being scrapped, as unaffordable, with immediate effect (Travis, 2010). May went on to warn the assembled police chiefs of deep cuts to follow. Over the next five years police budgets fell by almost a fifth with the loss of 17,000 police officers nationally. Many Chief Constables voiced their concerns about the impact of the funding cuts on their ability to keep the public safe (Halliday, 2015) although amongst the most outspoken was Metropolitan Police Commissioner Bernard Hogan-Howe who talked of the police having to 'prioritise' and 'ration' the service they provided (Dodd, 2015). Sir Hugh Orde, the president of ACPO described the measures as the deepest cuts he had ever known, and suggested that a further 20% reduction in Home Office funding 'would inflict much greater damage on frontline policing than seen so far' (Halliday, 2015). In the West Midlands, Chief Constable Dave Thompson, commented that much routine police work, 'such as general neighbourhood patrols, were likely to be reduced as the force is forced to do more with less' and that this was likely to impact upon the force's efforts to keep a lid on gun crime and gang violence.

One of the ironies of the austerity inspired reforms pioneered by the Coalition Government in their ambition to 'cut crime' and restore the 'primary crime fighting role' of the police[9] lay in the fact that the NPS, with its close policing of troubled communities, combined with surveillance and intelligence-sharing, was precisely intended to keep a lid on youthful crime, disorder and violence. Police chiefs, politicians and a range of crime control commentators debated and researched at length the presumed relationship between police numbers and crime rates (by no means a new or simple question), although often drawing few definitive conclusions (Chivers, 2019; Draca & Langela, 2020). A particularly intriguing interchange was the Prime Minister's assertion on March 4, 2019, that there was no 'direct correlation' relationship between knife crime rates and police numbers (Weaver & Pidd, 2019), only for this to be contradicted the following day by the new Metropolitan Police Commissioner, Cressida Dick (Quinn, 2019) reiterating comments she had made a year earlier following a series of stabbings (Dearden, 2018c). However, there was no dispute that once the Neighbourhood Policing Teams were withdrawn and high visibility policing scaled back as cuts and competing police priorities began to take effect, gun crime, knife crime and gang-related violence all appeared to tick upwards once again.

Figure 5.7 depicts the resurgence of recorded knife crime after 2014. Over the same period homicides by sharp instrument increased by 35% and hospital A&E admissions arising from knife injuries increased 27.5% (Allen & Kirk-Wade, 2020). Firearm homicides increased by 34% and firearm offences overall grew by 39% (Allen et al., 2020). Noting the close relationship between the reductions in police numbers and rising violence is not to suggest that the former are the only, or even the most important, cause of the latter. On the contrary, as Draca and Langela (2020) have suggested rather more is involved, including the impact of austerity more generally, particularly unemployment, poverty, and cuts

[9] In her speech to the Conservative Party Conference on October 5, 2010, May said 'We will free police officers to become the crime fighters they signed up to be… cutting crime is the only test of a police force and catching criminals is their job.' Theresa May: A plan to fight crime: Conservative Party Speeches.

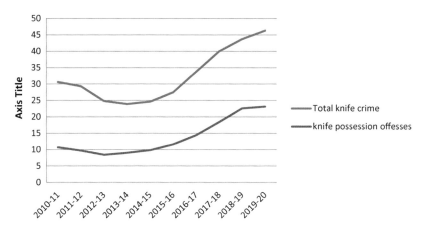

Fig. 5.7 Rising Knife Crime after 2014: England and Wales/Thousands (*Source* Allen & Kirk-Wade, 2020, and Crime in England and Wales: Appendix Tables. Table A4, Police Recorded Crime 2008–2009 to 2019–2020)

to local services (notably community mental health support), as well as school exclusions and educational and youth service provision. The Home Office's *Serious Violence Strategy* (HM Government, 2018) played down the impact of budget cuts and police effectiveness (loosely alluded to as 'criminal justice system effectiveness') (Buchan, 2018), noting that 'most academics agree that big shifts in crime trends tend to be driven by factors outside of the police's control—like drug trends and markets' before drawing a further, rather more particular, observation: 'some have questioned whether the reduction in the use of stop and search is driving the increase. The data do not support such a conclusion' (HM Govt., 2018: 24).[10] If anything, however, the evidence pointed another way,

---

[10] On launching the *Serious Violence Strategy document* the Home Secretary faced criticism for omitting from it any reference to a Home Office internal report that suggested that budget cuts had "likely contributed" to rising violence and "encouraged" offenders (Dearden, 2018b). Police officers appearing before the Home Affairs Select Committee in May 2018 returned to the question of police effectiveness. Garry Shewan, the retired assistant chief constable of Greater Manchester Police, argued that 'there had been a "degradation in the commitment to a neighbourhood policing model", which sees officers dedicated to small local areas… To reduce [crime] you have to have a close working relationship not just with the community but with all partners to understand why crime happens and come up with solutions… neighbourhood officers are best placed to solve problems and gather intelligence, including on gangs and extremism, at an early stage to prevent and disrupt crime' (ibid.).

for research had shown that poorly targeted Operation Blunt 2 stop and search exercises had had very little effect in crime or violence *reduction* (McCandless et al., 2016), not whether a diminished police presence might embolden offenders and increase crime and violence.

As the preceding discussion has made clear, 'knife crime' began to rise once again after 2014, with an apparent surge in youth homicides in London in 2017 and 2018. Some commentators were quick to link the rise in knife violence to the policing cuts, John Sutherland, a retired borough commander in the Metropolitan Police, argued that the 'plummeting number of police officers' and stretched resources were having a major impact. He said, 'in England and Wales there are 21,000 fewer police officers now than there were in 2010 and that's the lowest number since comparable record keeping began … You can't take that number of police officers off the streets and not expect it to have consequence'. He added that 'neighbourhood policing had been "decimated" across the country as a result of the cuts' (Dearden, 2018c). But notwithstanding the thorny question of police numbers, following the election of the coalition government and throughout the term of its successor there was no let-up in knife crime initiatives, even pre-dating the up-tick in knife violence. In 2010–2011, Sentencing Guidelines Council proposals for increasing, to a 25 year minimum, the severity 'tariff' for knife murder were implemented (Crewe et al., 2020: 8). The increase was justified in terms of the rate of increase of knife homicides and, although it was recognised that many such killings involved relatively young perpetrators (who would be receiving de facto 'life' sentences) it was felt important to seek to deter the 'gang violence' of which knife crime was presumed a part.

Following the controversy over police numbers and the effectiveness—or not—of stop and search in reducing violence, in April 2014 the Home Office published the results of a consultation exercise on the future of stop and search (Home Office, 2014). The choice of a consultation exercise meant that people's *perceptions* about the effectiveness of police stops would be recorded rather than any evidence-based assessment of what actually worked. Thus, of almost 5000 respondents, 46% said that they strongly agreed 'that the use of police powers of stop and search is effective in preventing and detecting crime and anti social behaviour' and a further 15% 'tended to agree' (Home Office, 2014: 7). There was no attempt to ascertain why respondents believed stop and search to be 'effective', what people thought, seemed more important than what worked. Having said that, a significant minority of respondents (27%) recognised that stop and search gave rise to complaints of discrimination and 'unfairness' (2014: 22). Moving on, searches for weapons (just over one thousand responses) and secondly for drugs (976) were judged to represent the best use of stop and search powers. On the back of this consultation Home Secretary Theresa May went on to announce a new 'Best Use of Stop and Search' Policy which would attempt to tighten up on the grounds for 'reasonable suspicion', limit s.60 ('no suspicion') powers to periods of 15 hours only and require more communication with the communities in which the powers were being employed. Somewhat generously, the new policy came to be known as 'evidence-led stop and search' and as Fig. 4.11 in Chapter 4 showed, during 2016 the rate of stop and search turned sharply upwards once again.

In Chapter 3 we discussed the first emergence of the 'knife crime' phenomenon. Our central point there concerned a series of 'pre-public' developments which were necessary to the emergence of knife crime and upon which, eventually, the fully fledged category of 'knife crime' came to stand. We likened the process to the police 'pre-mobilisation' around mugging and street crime in the 1970s and described by Hall et al. (1978). A similar sequence of developments can be detected in 2012–2015. In 2014 before 'knife crime' rates had begun to rise once more, and the former intensity of stop and search operations had been scaled back, there was a further recalibration of the seriousness of knife crime offences. Government passed the Legal Aid Sentencing and Punishment of Offenders (LASPO) Act 2012. Section 142 amended the 1953 Prevention of Crime Act (discussed in Chapter 1) by introducing a new offence of 'aggravated possession' with mandatory custodial sentences for a second knife possession offence; 6 months for adults, 4 months for 16 and 17 year olds. From April 2015 statutory restrictions were introduced relating to the use of cautions, in particular their use with those found in illegal possession of a knife (Ministry of Justice, 2016: 13).

The new offence also brought a significant change to knife crime recording. In the first place the 'aggravated' aspect of the knife possession (in a public place or school) rested upon a presumption of intention—that the knife was to be used to threaten or injure—thereby giving police a degree of leverage when considering a charge. In the second place 'aggravated knife possession' became a *recorded offence* in a way that 'simple illegal possession' never had been. It had long been one of the anomalies of weapon-involved crime recording in England and Wales that only 'weapon-enabled' offences—that is, when a weapon is *used* to commit another offence, such as an assault or a robbery—are recorded in the national crime statistics. Simply being *in possession* of the illegal weapon, presumably a precursor to its illegal use, has not been so recorded. It has been estimated that if simple possession were included in the crime figures, then gun or knife crime might appear to increase overall by some 50–60% (Squires, 2014), and it had been suggested that this was not an increase that any government would wish to see during its term of office (Barrett, 2008). Aggravated knife possession added another knife offence to the 'knife crime' count and, in particular, one that was particularly susceptible to stop and search activity. Indeed, recording knife possession offences was also a useful way of showing that stop and search exercises were 'productive'. In a very real sense, therefore, after 2014–2015, stop and search activities directly produced higher rates of knife crime as is indicated in the lower trend line (knife possession) in Fig. 5.7, and contributing significantly to the increased knife crime totals.

During 2014–2015 a 2% overall increase in knife crime, included a 10% increase in knife possession offences (Travis, 2015)—this was the first period during which behaviours that hitherto might have led to cautions were now mandatorily 'crimed'. There had been some resistance to the change from some Liberal Democrats and Labour MPs who argued that the proposed change was merely a populist move to appear 'tough on crime' ahead of the general election in 2015 (Wintour, 2014). But none drew out the potential of the new arrangements to appear to increase rates of knife crime. Nevertheless, the new measures resulted in the number of people imprisoned for knife offences more than doubling within twelve months (Ministry of Justice, 2016: 11).

In due course, in 2017–2018, both responding to the perceived increase in 'knife crime' and capitalising on the new powers, the Home

Office launched a number of s.60 stop and search 'pilot projects' in the seven police force areas with the worst knife crime statistics. This resulted in two and a half thousand additional searches during the year. The new 'intelligence-led' stops were credited with increasing the search success rate—more weapon finds and more arrests—with officers claiming many thousands of weapons had been taken off the streets. In 2019 Home Secretary Priti Patel announced an extension of the s.60 enhanced search project to all 43 police forces, lowering the rank of police officer empowered to authorise area-based s.60 searches to that of police inspector, lowering the degree of certainty required by a police officer in making an authorisation and extending the duration of such a designation to 24 and even 48 hours (Home Office Press Release, 11.8.19). In effect, the knife crime stop and search debate had now travelled full circle for a second time, the official caution that had surrounded stop and search since the Macpherson report, sidelined first during the 2007–2008 spike in knife crime but reappearing after the 2011 riots, was once again being set aside. In its new guise as 'intelligence-led' and 'best use', stop and search was back with a vengeance amongst the repertoire of police powers. To enable police to perform these searches safely, increasing numbers of frontline officers were to be equipped with Tasers; subsequently, Taser use increased 5.5 times throughout the decade 2009–2019 (Home Office, 2020).[11] Eighty-four per cent of 'less lethal' weapon use by police officers in 2020 involved officers protecting themselves (Home Office, 2020: 16). Citing the dangers facing frontline officers an NPCC spokesman urged that all officers should be equipped with Tasers (Press Association, 2018) although evidence was also emerging of a pattern of disproportionate Taser impact on Black and minority ethnic groups (Gayle, 2019; Noor, 2018). Nevertheless, looking forwards to a proposed new Offensive Weapons Act, and a proposed Knife Crime Prevention Order, the

---

[11] Taser use can involve a variety of actions, from drawing and pointing the weapon, engaging the 'red dot' targeting system or firing the taser, either remotely or in the full contact 'drive stun' mode (Dymond, 2020).

Home Secretary declared her full support for the police, 'we are experiencing a knife crime epidemic and I am determined to put a stop to it', she said (Home Office, 2019).[12]

Violent crime overall was reported to have increased by 24% in 2016 but the Office of National Statistics warned this was largely due to improvements in recording practices, more incidents being reported as crimes and increased confidence in the reporting incidents of rape (Travis, 2016). Teenage homicide rates remained relatively stable but by 2016–2017 public concerns were reignited once again, by a rash of knife attacks and murders involving young men, including incidents involving the use of 'zombie knives' in brutal assaults (Davis, 2016; Iles, 2016; Samuelson, 2016). In 2016 passing the Criminal Justice Act (Offensive Weapons) (Amendment) Order the Government legislated to ban such knives. The following year, Guardian journalist Gary Younge launched his 'Beyond the Blade' project, challenging a number of assumptions regarding the 'knife crime' label as it returned to the headlines. The project reported on the individual circumstances of every teenage or child knife homicide in England and Wales in 2017 and collected historical knife homicide data that had never before been collated by governments or the police despite their claims of prioritising 'knife crime' (Younge, 2017). Younge's analysis broadly substantiates our own, demonstrating enduring injustices in the label's evolution, use and definition. Looking at the inconsistencies of 'knife crime' reporting Younge (2018) found that in all national press other than *The Guardian* use of the label 'knife crime' was confined to incidents the victim was a black teen or child in London—with one exception, the case of Sait Mboob, a black 18-year-old stabbed in Manchester: 'So the term is not used to describe all crimes committed with knives' he noted, 'just those where young black men in London are involved' (Younge, 2018). Of the thirty-nine teenagers and children killed in knife attacks in England and Wales in 2017; twenty died in London, twenty-two were black, fourteen were white and three

---

[12] Using the language of 'epidemic' to describe patterns and trends in violence gained added significance with the Covid lockdown arrangements using police powers to help restrict virus transmission. Against this development, in our final chapter we explore the contrasting question of using public health interventions measures to respond to and prevent knife violence.

were Asian. Yet in the analysis of historical knife homicide data spanning forty years, roughly half of all teen and child deaths occur outside of London and the 'overwhelmingly majority… are not black' (ibid.). Analysis of where in London the deaths of children and teenagers by knives are concentrated reveals a compelling correlation. 'Very few stabbings take place in central London, with most occurring in the outer ring – travel zones three and beyond' (ibid.). This spatial relationship between teen deaths is still widely ignored, although the temporal fixation upon homicide 'clusters' continues to provoke 'flurries of media interest' (ibid.).

Likewise, when several knife homicides of young Black men occur in a relatively short space of time this creates urgency, news value and generates public attention. But the label that links such deaths also defines the response, thus the assumption of a 'criminal Black culture' obscures the common socio-economic context of the individual events. The four knife homicides on New Year's Eve prompted the heightened concerns about 'knife crime' throughout early 2018. The total fatalities throughout the year are compared to the earlier knife crime 'spike'; 'It is the highest number of teenage homicides in the city since 2008' (Dearden, 2018a). In March 2018 a cluster of unrelated murders in the capital accelerated the moral panic further and there were increasing demands for a proactive law and order response targeting young people (Drewett, 2018). The distinction between murders, knife murders and teen knife murders became increasingly blurred, as homicide figures including infants and adults (many in domestic violence contexts) are used to sensationalise 'knife crime' news in 2018. And when, as a result of this sensationalist aggregation of knife murders, it was reported that London's homicide rate in February exceeded that of New York's apparently sending 'sent shockwaves around Britain' (Buck, 2018). In fact the majority of the stabbing victims in London in February were adults, ten of the fifteen killed were over nineteen years old and two were women in their fifties, but the shock value of the figure as originally reported lay in its ability to drive a targeted response aimed solely at young people.

In February 2018, London Mayor Sadiq Khan released additional funding for the Metropolitan Police to 'combat knife crime' (Gov.uk, 2018a). In April The Metropolitan Police announced that this money will fund a *Violent Crime Task Force*, a dedicated team of 150 officers taking robust measures in targeted areas of the city. Yet this initiative involved precisely the same number of officers and exactly the same tactics which had comprised Operation Blunt 2 in 2008. As we have seen, rates of stop and search had already been taking off again, whilst S.60 authorisations had increased fourfold by 2017/2018 (Grierson, 2018). In the first month of the Violent Crime Task Force stop and search rates increased across London by 10% on average ('London Murder Rates…', 2018). The authorisation of s.60 search areas to stop 'knife crime' increased again by 219% during 2018–2019, the number of 'no reasonable grounds searches' increasing fivefold in London, 'from 1,836 in 2017–18 to 9,599 in 2018–19' (Murphy, 2019).

The sensational representation of crime data and the exceptional use of force from 2016 onwards have all the hallmarks of a second wave of moral panic over 'knife crime'. However, the proportion of all homicides involving a knife remained largely consistent throughout the period, as they did for the entire decade (Edgington, 2018), but as violent crime rates in general have increased in recent years so too have murder rates—including knife homicides. Knives or stabbing weapons were involved in 7% of all recorded violent attacks in the year ending March 2016, whereas 77% involved no weapons at all (Shaw, 2019). Of the 19,243 recorded knife possession offences in 2017, persons under eighteen accounted for only 4148, or 22% of all knife possession recorded despite the 15–19 age group being the most searched age category in London throughout the year (ibid.).

As knives make up a small proportion of violent crime, and young people with knives a smaller proportion still, it remains highly significant that this narrowly defined demographic is still the dominant concern even as violent crime and homicide rates appeared to rise once again. This youthful focus is very evident in the Offensive Weapons Act passed in 2019 which contained provisions dealing with 'corrosive substances' (acid attacks), certain classes of firearms and knives. Part two of the act (Sections 14–33) introduced the new Knife Crime Prevention Orders (KCPOs) and later sections dealt with the sale, delivery and possession of such weapons (including in private) and threatening any person with such a weapon whether in public, private or on school premises. Guidance surrounding the new legislation, also drawing on earlier acts from 1953 and 1988, partially resurrected an earlier Offensive Weapons Order relating to possession of hand-held weapons such as knuckle-dusters, hand claws, butterfly knives or 'push daggers'. The KCPO was substantially modelled upon the original Anti-Social Behaviour Order (ASBO) and came in three formats, a stand-alone order (based upon information provided to the court), an order made 'on conviction' of another relevant offence, and an 'interim order' (made on the basis of information supplied, deemed sufficiently urgent by the court, and without the knowledge of the person against whom the order is sought). Lasting for a fixed period of 6 months to two years, the KCPO was intended to protect the public by preventing knife enabled offending by either requiring a person to abide by a range of conditions (be at a certain place at a given time, report to certain persons or participate in certain activities) or, alternatively, to avoid certain places, persons or activities, or have in their possession certain items, or use the internet 'to facilitate or encourage crime involving bladed articles'. This last provision intended to address the goading and insulting thought to be associated with 'gang-related' drill music (Fatsis, 2019; Lynes et al., 2020). Breach of an order could involve imprisonment for between 12 months to 2 years.

Reflecting the largely youthful targeting of the first generation ASBOs (Squires & Stephen, 2005), the KCPO procedure, outlined in the 2019 legislation, makes repeated reference to schools and school premises, 'academies' and FE colleges and the Youth Court, at least anticipating a proportion of the KCPO target group will be of an age to use such institutions. Likewise, Section 15(4) makes it a requirement that anyone (for example a senior police officer) seeking a KCPO in relation to a person aged under 18 consult first with a relevant youth offending team (YOT) and Sections 19–20 (KCPO 'on conviction') refers to such orders made in respect of defendants aged 12 or over, or under 18, following liaison with a YOT. Finally, Section 21 requires that the conditions of an order do not interfere with school or college attendance. Several of the provisions of the KCPO procedure anticipate that young people will continue to be the focal point of knife crime enforcement. From around 2017 police forces had also begun running their week long, twice-yearly 'Operation Sceptre' exercises. The operation, run separately in each police force area combined a series of high-profile 'knife awareness' activities including what GMP referred to as 'educational talks in schools and colleges, stop and search activity—where appropriate, knife sweeps, high visibility patrols, warrants, and visits to habitual knife carriers' (GMP, 2020) as well as 'knife amnesty bins' in which people could anonymously dump unwanted knives. Amnesty bins—tackling violence one blade at a time—are never likely to make much of a dent in knife supply, although each police force participating in the scheme dutifully reported the numbers of knives 'removed from the streets'. Nevertheless, senior police officers and Police and Crime Commissioners reiterated the point that raising 'awareness' and 'sending messages'—in other words, communication—via a wide range of media, rather than arrests and weapon recovery, were the most important features of the campaign. We return to these images and their use by the police in Chapter 6, an important issue concerns the types of images being recycled and repurposed. It is especially important to examine the message being communicated. Press coverage featuring the week sponsored by various police forces around the country often comprised pictures of table tops displaying assorted knives recovered, or bins full of them. One of the logos used for Operation Sceptre reflected this idea, knives and a couple of swords arranged to resemble a knife (although rather less kitchen knives than one might expect, and rather too many specialist 'fighting knives', but perhaps this is to quibble). Rather more concerning are many of the other images deployed to underpin Operation Sceptre, in the first place a young man of indiscernible ethnic background, wearing a hoodie, thrusting a knife to the camera. The only part of the photograph in focus is the tip of the knife; behind every knife a hoodie. Lurking behind the knife man are two more grey-clad hoodies, this is clearly a gang. The gang connection is further strengthened with the Trident Gang Crime Command image of the crossed knives grave: 'knives take lives', an image, and strapline, reflected on the Operation Sceptre poster (Fig. 5.8).

Fig. 5.8   Images of and from Operation Sceptre 2017–2021 (*Source* Screen grabs from *Operation Sceptre* Police Publicity web-pages)

It is difficult, from this imagery, to conclude anything other, than that the message that police are seeking to convey about knife crime is that it primarily concerns young, gang-involved, youth. As we have seen, this has always been a misleadingly selective interpretation. Furthermore from the very earliest research, even in the very early days of 'knife crime', we have repeatedly been advised that information about knife carrying, especially that which plays into young people's fears, or suggests that knife carrying is in some way being 'normalised' amongst the youth peer group, or which implies that police will take a 'zero tolerance' stance as regards knife carrying, may struggle to elicit the desired responses from those young people considered most 'at risk'. At worst it may merely convince them that many of their peers are 'strapped' and dangerous, suggesting that knife carrying makes sense 'for protection'. In other words, enforcement alone is no solution.

Reaching such a conclusion about the most recent legislation, and other recent initiatives to address the perceived 'knife crime crisis' refers us back to our core questions. Why, despite the evidence, do young people, especially young black people in public continue to feature at the centre of the knife crime moral panic? Secondly, why does the UK with a relatively low homicide rate, and an internationally low knife violence rate, appear so preoccupied by knife violence? And thirdly it raises the question about how and why this political mobilisation around such racially defined crimes interacts with particular moments of social and political crisis. What can we say about the socio-political dynamics through which such crime mobilisation occurs?

In the first place, we return to the way in which knife crime represents the very latest in a long line of urban violence and disorder disproportionately and misleadingly associated with young black people and 'black culture', from mugging in the 1970s to gun crime, and gang-related violence from the 1990s, riots and disorder and finally knife crime. Secondly, it appears that contemporary preoccupations about knife violence are largely perceived through a white metropolitan 'civilisation thesis'. In Carter-Wood's terms (2015), knife violence is indeed part of the 'shadow of our modernity', part of a world we hoped we had lost, escaped or excluded, but which continues to haunt and challenge the expectations of our peaceful modern amnesia. And yet, in several ways, like most criminality, and a particularly atavistic, visceral and horrendous criminality at that, 'knife crime' remains, in Foucauldian (Foucault, 1977) terms eminently *useful,* and as Marx might have added, even *profitable* for some.[13] It reaffirms a distinction between the supposedly 'law-abiding' majority and an alien criminal sub-class. By endlessly recycling the appalling consequences of interpersonal violence and asserting the amorality of the criminal perpetrator it distances and absolves our responsibility whilst sustaining our righteous indignation and its power to punish. Perpetually misrepresenting the knife criminal as characteristically young, black and 'other' it confines and externalises the problem. Furthermore, as gang researchers have recurrently noted, even as heavy enforcement action is generally ineffective, often exacerbating problems of disorder, violence and division, it continues to be popular.

And finally, just as 'mugging' played this role in the 1970s, 'knife crime' provided a profound distraction and mitigation of the social impacts of austerity. In 2008 the 'knife crime epidemic' mobilising racist stereotypes and both fear and anger regarding alien violence ensured public consent for increased police on the street and the extension of search powers, manufacturing cohesion through outrage at a time of global financial and ideological crisis. 'Knife crime' and the popular reaction to it have also been employed in the management of social cohesion during the past decade; through intolerance directed at a 'criminal Other', drawing attention away from Britain's difficulties and divisions,

---

[13] Marx made the point about crime being profitable for locksmiths (*Theories of Surplus Value I,* pp. 387–388) by the same token; the makers of stab-proof vests and slash-proof clothing have seen a similar opportunity in recent years. Safeguard clothing (https://www.safeguardclothing.com/uk/) offers a full range of stab-proof and bullet-proof clothing, including newly fashionable urban combat gear (along with advice regarding where in the world such apparel is legal).

and justifying increasing police powers on the street. During the 'war on knife crime' economically deprived young people were increasingly subjected to humiliating displays of social exclusion, racial profiling and police hostility—whilst their collective resistance to both austerity and over-policing was branded 'mindless criminality' during the riots of 2011. Our analysis has demonstrated the unique ability of indirect forms of cultural racism to mitigate structural critique, as pre-established categories such as 'gangs' 'anti-social youths' and 'knife crime' contributed to a deep-set neoliberal logic of individual responsibility that deemed unnecessary any official inquiry into the causes of the riots in 2011. Nevertheless, the latest resurgence of concern regarding 'knife crime' has ensured that the scrutiny of violent acts by young people far outweighs the attention given to the marginal circumstances of many young people. The devastating cuts to youth services, the removal of the EMA, barriers to education and training, lack of opportunity and the compounding conditions of crime-inducing deprivation have vastly increased the harms endured by young people. And yet, the same racially selective application of 'knife culture' in 2007 is evident in the reporting of 'knife crime' twelve years later, obscuring the austerity context of a perceived intensification of violence. Our research emphasises the profound similarities between the 'moment of 1978' and the present, and the powerful historical continuities between 'mugging' and 'knife crime'. Above all, perhaps, it affirms the continuing significance of 'policing' in the neo-liberal management of social and political crisis.

Just as 1979's 'law and order election' heralded powerful changes to come, so the appointment of Boris Johnson as Prime Minister in 2019, a politician renowned for his brusquely racist language (Bienkov, 2019) and strong commitment to an ideology of law and order marked an important turning point ('Crime: What Has…', 2019; Walker, 2019). Within the first month of his premiership Johnson appeared to abandon austerity in law and order, announcing 20,000 more police officers, 10,000 more prison places, increased prison security and an expansion of stop and search powers ('Crime: What Has…', 2019). With immediate effect the Home Office changed the way in which Section 60 areas were approved, even at a time of political tension and high risk of social unrest.

Once again, knife crime was re-mobilised, leaked police documents in September 2018 even suggested a 'real possibility' that the military may be required to keep peace on the streets in the event of Britain leaving the EU (Khan, 2018); and six months later the Secretary of State, Gavin Williamson announces that 'UK armed forces "stand ready" to intervene in the knife crime epidemic' (Sharman, 2019). During the Covid crisis the enormous expansion of police powers to manage the viral pandemic suggested just how quickly citizenship rights might evaporate under the pressure of events and loosely drafted legislation. In March 2021 the Police, Crime, Sentencing and Courts bill, proposing major changes to the police ability to prohibit lawful protest passed its second reading in the House of Commons.

> **Learning Exercise 13: Knife Crime Rising Again**
>
> Referring to Fig. 5.7 and the surrounding discussion, explain why 'knife crime' began to rise, once more, after 2014–2015 and consider the impact and significance of this.
>   In what ways were developments in policing, new laws and police interventions implicated in the rising violence?

References

Allen, G., Audickas, L., & Loft, P. (2020). *Firearm crime statistics: England & Wales*. House of Commons Briefing paper, Number CBP 7654.

Allen, G., & Kirk-Wade, E. (2020, October 6). *Knife crime in England and Wales*. House of Commons Briefing Paper Number SN4304.

Ball, J., & Taylor, M. (2011, December 14). Theresa May to review stop and search in wake of Reading the Riots study. *The Guardian*.

Barker, M. (1981/2017). *The New Racism*. Junction Books Barr.

Barr, C. (2017, November 28). Child knife deaths in England and Wales set for nine-year peak. *The Guardian*.

Barrett, D. (2008, October 19). Gun crime 60% higher than official figures. *Daily Telegraph*.

Bates, S. (2011, August 9). Use of water cannon on rioters backed across political divide. *The Guardian.*

Bellis, M. A., Hughes, K., Wood, S., Wyke, S., & Perkins, C. (2011). National five year examination of inequalities and trends in emergency hospital admission for violence across England. *Injury Prevention, 17*, 319–325.

Berry, C. (2016). *Austerity politics and UK economic policy.* Palgrave Macmillan.

Bienkov, A. (2019, November 22). Boris Johnson called gay men 'tank-topped bumboys' and black people 'piccaninnies' with 'watermelon smiles'. *Business Insider.*

Blair, T. (2007). *Callaghan Memorial Speech.* UKPOL (online). Available at: http://www.ukpol.co.uk/tony-blair-2007-callaghan-memorial-speech

Brady, B., & Dugan, E. (2012, January 29). We're all in this together, says PM. Really, Mr. Cameron? *The Independent.*

Brennan, I. (2019). Weapon-carrying and the Reduction of Violent Harm. *The British Journal of Criminology, 59*(3), 571–593.

Briggs, D. (Ed.). (2012). *The English Riots of 2011: A summer of discontent.* Waterside Press.

Buchan, L. (2018, April 9). Home Office fails to mention police cuts in 114 page violent crime strategy. *The Independent.*

Buck, K. (2018). New York murder rate is much higher than London's, new figures show. *Metro.* Available at: https://metro.co.uk/2018/07/15/new-york-murder-rate-is-much-higher-than-londons-new-figures-show-7717873/

Cabinet Office. (2010). *The coalition: Our programme for government.* Cabinet Office.

Cameron, D. (2011, August 15). (a), PM's speech on the fightback after the riots. *Gov.UK.* Oxfordshire. https://www.gov.uk/government/speeches/pms-speech-on-the-fightback-after-the-riots

Cameron Attacks Radio 1's Hip-Hop'. (2008, June 7). BBC News (online). Available at: http://news.bbc.co.uk/1/hi/uk_politics/5055724.stm

Carter, H. (2011, August 16). England riots: Pair jailed for four years for using Facebook to incite disorder. *The Guardian.*

Carter-Wood, J. (2015). *Violence and crime in nineteenth century England: The shadow of our refinement.* Routledge.

Chivers, T. (2019, March 6). Do Police numbers really affect knife crime? Unherd. Do police numbers really affect knife crime?—UnHerd

Cohen, S. (1972). *Folk devils and moral panics: The creation of the Mods and Rockers.* Routledge.

Cooper, C. (2012). September). Understanding the English 'riots' of 2011: 'Mindless criminality' or youth 'Mekin Histri' in austerity Britain? *Youth and Policy, 109,* 6–26.

Crawford, R., & Keynes, R. (2015). Options for further departmental spending cuts. In C. Emmerson, P. Johnson, & R. Joyce (Eds.), *Institute for fiscal studies: Green budget 2015* (pp. 151–175). IFS.

Crewe, B., Hulley, S., & Wright, S. (2020). *Life imprisonment from young adulthood: Adaptation, identity and time.* Palgrave Macmillan.

Crime: What Has Boris Johnson Promised on Law and Order?. (2019, October 14). *BBC News Online.* https://www.bbc.co.uk/news/uk-49318400

Croydon Independent Local Review Panel Report. (2012). *Report into the Rioting in Croydon on 8th and 9th August 2011.* http://www.kinetic-foundation.org.uk/wp-content/uploads/2013/11/Croydon-Riot-report-1.pdf

Davis, B. (2016, August 18). Machete murder victim's family appeal to young to 'stop this war'. *Evening Standard.*

Dearden, L. (2018a, April 22). Why is knife crime increasing in England and Wales. *The Independent.*

Dearden, L. (2018b, May 2). Victims of violent crime 'dying in the streets' as police lobby for more government money, officer says. *The Independent.*

Dearden, L. (2018c, May 19). Police budget cuts are driving violent crime, Met Chief Says after fatal stabbings. *The Independent.*

Dodd, V. (2012, January 12). Metropolitan police to scale back stop and search operation. *The Guardian.* https://www.theguardian.com/uk/2012/jan/12/met-police-stop-search-suspicion

Dodd, V. (2015, March 12). The Police will have to pick and choose what they prioritise, warns Britain's top officer. *The Guardian.*

Draca, M., & Langela, M. (2020, Summer). Law, order and austerity: Police numbers and crime in the 2010s. Advantage Magazine: Austerity, 10th Anniversary Special

Drewett, Z. (2018, August 28). Return to stop and search to tackle London's knife crime problem. *The Metro.* Available at: https://metro.co.uk/2018/08/28/return-to-stop-and-search-to-tackle-londons-knife-crime-problem-7888564

Dymond, A. (2020). 'Taser, Taser'! Exploring factors associated with police use of taser in England and Wales. *Policing and Society, 30*(4), 396–411.

Eades, C. (2007). The year of the Knife. *Criminal Justice Matters.* No. 66 Centre for Crime and Justice Studies.

Edgington, T. (2018). Reality check: Are England and Wales experiencing a crime wave? *BBC News*. Available at: https://www.bbc.com/news/uk-443 97532

Edwards, R., Farmer, B., & Allen, N. (2008). Met declares war on knife crime gangs. *The Telegraph* [online]. http://www.telegraph.co.uk/news/majornews/1953088/Met-declares-war-on-knife-crime-gangs.html

EHRC. (2010). *Stop and think: A critical review of the use of stop and search powers in England and Wales*. Equality and Human Rights Commission.

EHRC. (2012). *Race disproportionality in stops and searches under Section 60 of the Criminal Justice and Public Order Act 1994*. Research Briefing Paper 5. Great Britain: Equality and Human Rights Commission.

Elliott-Cooper, A. (2021). *Black resistance to British policing*. Manchester University Press.

Farrell and Hay. (2010). Not so tough on Crime? Why weren't the Thatcher governments more radicalin reforming the criminal justice system? *British Journal of Criminology, 50*, 1–20.

Fatsis, L. (2019). Policing the beats: The criminalisation of UK drill and grime music by the London Metropolitan Police. *Sociological Review, 76*(6), 1300–1316.

Fatsis, L. (2020). Does drill kill? Moral panics, race and culture. *Sociology Review, 2*.

Flanagan, R. (2008). *The review of policing: Final report*. Justice Inspectorate.

Flint, J. F., & Powell, R. (2012). The English city riots of 2011, "Broken Britain" and the retreat into the present. *Sociological Research Online, 17*(3), 20.

Foucault, M. (1977). *Discipline and punish: The birth of the prison*. Allen Lane, Penguin books.

Gamble, A. (1988). *The free economy and the strong state: The politics of thatcherism*. Macmillan.

Gayle, D. (2019, March 12). Half of children shot by Tasers are from BAME groups. *The Guardian*.

Gill, K., Quilter-Pinner, H., & Swift, D. (2017). *Making the difference: Breaking the link between school exclusion and social exclusion*. IPPR.

Gilroy, P. (1982). The myth of black criminality. In M. Eve & D. Musson (Eds.), *Socialist register* (Vol. 19, pp. 7–56). Merlin Press.

Gilroy, P. (1987). *There ain't no black in the Union Jack*. Unwin Hyman.

Gilroy, P. (2010). Fanon and Amery: Theory, torture and the prospect of humanism. *Theory, Culture & Society, 27*(7–8), 16–32 (Sage).

Gilroy, P. (2013). 1981 and 2011: From social democratic to neoliberal rioting—Paul Gilroy. *libcom.org*. Available at: http://libcom.org/library/1981-2011-social-democratic-neoliberal-rioting-paul-gilroy

GMP (Greater Manchester Police). (2020). *Knife crime prevention campaign results*. https://www.gmp.police.uk/news/greater-manchester/news/news/2020/november/gmp-knife-crime-prevention-campaign-results

Goodman, A., & Ruggiero, V. (2008). Crime, punishment and ethnic minorities in England and Wales. *Race/Ethnicity: Multidisciplinary Global Contexts, 2*(1), 53–68.

Gov.uk. (2018a). Extra £110 million this year for Metropolitan Police in Mayor's Budget. *London City Hall*. https://www.london.gov.uk//city-hall-blog/extra-ps110-million-year-metropolitan-police-mayors-budget

Gov.uk. (2018b). *People living in deprived neighbourhoods*, found in UK population by ethnicity, ethnicity facts and figures. Published 16 March (online). https://www.ethnicity-facts-figures.service.gov.uk/uk-population-by-ethnicity/demographics/people-living-in-deprived-neighbourhoods/latest

Granoulhac, F. (2017). Excellence at what cost? Austerity and the reform of the school system in England (2010–2016). *The Political Quarterly, 88*(3), 434–442.

Grierson, J. (2018, April 13). Met Chief Defends Fourfold Rise in Use of Stop-and-search'. *The Guardian*. https://www.theguardian.com/uk-news/2018/apr/13/met-chief-cressida-dick-stop-and-search-london

Grosfoguel, R. (1999). Introduction: "Cultural Racism" and colonial Caribbean migrants in core zones of the capitalist world-economy. *Review (ferdinand Braudel Center), 22*(4), 409–434.

Hall, M. (2007, April 12). Black kids to blame for knife crime says Blair. *Daily Express*.

Hall, S., Roberts, B., Clarke, J., Jefferson, T., & Critcher, C. (1978). *Policing the crisis: Mugging, the state, and law and order*. Macmillan.

Halliday, J. (2015, February 22). West Midlands police face swingeing cuts. *The Guardian*.

Hallsworth, S., & Brotherton, D. (2011). *Urban disorder and gangs: A critique and a warning*. Runnymede Trust. https://www.runnymedetrust.org/uploads/publications/pdfs/UrbanDisorderandGangs-2011.pdf

Hayward, K., & Yar, M. (2006). The 'chav' phenomenon: Consumption, media and the construction of a new. *Crime, Media Culture, 2*(1), 9–28.

HM Government. (2011). *Ending gang and youth violence: A cross government report*. The stationery Office.

HM Government. (2018). *Serious violence strategy*. HMSO.

HMIC. (2009). *Adapting to protest: Nurturing the British model of policing*. Her Majesty's Inspectorate of Constabulary, Central Office of Information.

Home Office. (2014). *Police powers of stop and search summary of consultation responses and conclusions*. Home Office.

Home Office. (2017, February 15). *Stop and search*. Crime Justice and the law: Ethnicity Facts and Figures (online). Available at: https://www.ethnicity-facts-figures.service.gov.uk/crime-justice-and-the-law/policing/stop-and-search/latest

Home Office. (2019). Press release 'Government lifts emergency stop and search restrictions: A stop and search pilot has today been rolled out to all 43 forces in England and Wales. Home Office Press Office: Government lifts emergency stop and search restrictions—GOV.UK (www.gov.uk)

Home Office. (2020). *Police use of force statistics, England and Wales: April 2019 to March 2020*. Home Office.

Iles, W. (2016, August 22). How do we beat youth violence? Switch focus away from punishment. *The Guardian*, Opinion.

Jeffrey, B., & Tufail W. (2015). The riots were where the police were: Deconstructing the Pendleton riot. *Contention: The Multi-disciplinary Journal of Social Protest, 2*(2), 37–55.

Jeffs, T., & Smith, M. (1996). 'Getting the dirtbags off the streets'—Curfews and other solutions to juvenile crime. *Youth and Policy, 52*, 1–14.

Jones, T., & Newburn, T. (2002). The transformation of policing: Understanding current trends in Policing systems. *British Journal of Criminology, 42*, 129–146.

Keeling, P. (2017). *No respect: Young BAME men, the police and stop and search*. The Criminal Justice Alliance. https://www.barrowcadbury.org.uk/wp-content/uploads/2017/06/No-Respect-CJA-June-2017.pdf

Kehily, M. J. (2017). Pramface girls: Early motherhood, marginalisation and the management of stigma. In S. Blackman & R. Rogers (Ed.), *Youth marginality in Britain: Contemporary studies in austerity*. Policy Press.

Kettle, M., & Hodges, L. (1982). *Uprising: Police, the people and the riots in Britain's cities*. Macmillan.

Khan, S. (2018, September 9). No-deal Brexit could lead to 'real possibility' of the military on the streets, leaked police document says. *The Independent*. Available at: https://www.independent.co.uk/news/uk/politics/no-deal-brexit-military-police-leaked-document-a8529401.html

Lewis, P. (2009, November 25). How Ian Tomlinson's death at the G20 protests changed policing. *The Guardian*.

Lewis, P., Newburn, T., Taylor, M., & Ball, J. (2011a, December 5). Rioters say anger with police fuelled summer unrest. *The Guardian.*

Lewis, P., Newburn, T., Taylor, M., Mcgillivray, C., Greenhill, A., Frayman, H., & Proctor, R. (2011b). *Reading the riots: Investigating England's summer of disorder.* The London School of Economics and Political Science and The Guardian.

Liberty. (2010, October 16). Police told to discriminate in stop and search—As if Lawrence never happened. *Liberty Human Rights.*

Lightowlers, C. (2015). Let's get real about the 'riots': Exploring the relationship between deprivation and the English summer disturbances of 2011. *Critical Social Policy, 35*(1), 89–109.

Lightowlers, C., & Quirk, H. (2015). The 2011 English 'riots': Prosecutorial zeal and judicial abandon. *British Journal of Criminology, 55*(1), 65–85.

London Murder Rates 'Stabilising', Says Met Deputy. (2018, May 15). BBC News (online). https://www.bbc.co.uk/news/uk-england-london-44124666

Longstaff, A., Willer, J., Chapman, J., Czarnomski, S., & Graham, J. (2015). *Neighbourhood policing: Past present and future.* The Police Foundation.

Lynes, A., Kelly, C., & Kelly, E. (2020). Thug life: Drill music as a periscope into urban violence in the consumer age. *British Journal of Criminology, 60*(5), 1201–1219.

MacInnes, T., & Kenway, P. (2009). London's poverty profile. New Policy Institute. https://www.npi.org.uk/publications/income-and-poverty/londons-poverty-profile-2009

McCandless, R., Feist, A., Allan, J., & Morgan, N. (2016). *Do initiatives involving substantial increases in stop and search reduce crime? Assessing the impact of Operation BLUNT 2.* Home Office.

McMahon, W., & Roberts, R. (2011). Truth and lies about 'race' and 'crime.' *Criminal Justice Matters, 83*, 20–21.

Metropolitan Police Autrhority (MPA). (2004). *Report of the MPA scrutiny on MPS stop and search.* Metropolitan Police Authority, UK

Miller, L. (2008). *Perils of federalism: Race, poverty, and the politics of crime control.* Oxford University Press.

Miller, J., Bland, N., & Quinton, P. (2002). Measuring stops and searches: Lessons from U.K. Home Office Research. *Justice Research and Policy, 4*(1–2), 143–156

Ministry of Justice. (2016, 8 December). *Knife possession sentencing quarterly, England and Wales, July to September 2016.* Statistics bulletin: Crown Copyright Murphy, 2017.

Murphy, S. (2019, 4 June). Stop and searches in London up fivefold under controversial powers. *The Guardian*. https://www.theguardian.com/law/2019/jun/04/stop-and-searches-in-london-soar-after-police-powers-widened

Myhill, A., & Quinton, P. (2010). Confidence, neighbourhood policing and contact: Drawing together the evidence. *Policing: A Journal of Policy and Practice, 4*(3), 273–281.

Newburn, T. (2015). The 2011 English riots in recent historical perspective. *British Journal of Criminology, 55*(1), 375–392.

Newburn, T., Topping, A., Ferguson, B., & Taylor, M. (2011, December 6). The four-day truce: Gangs suspended hostilities during English riots. *The Guardian*.

Noor, P. (2018, December 5). Met use Tasers and restraints more often against black people. *The Guardian*.

O'Toole, F. (2019). *Heroic failure: Brexit and the politics of pain*. Apollo Books.

Perera, J. (2020). *How black working-class youth are criminalised and excluded in the English school system: A London case study*. Institute for Race Relations

Pina Sanchez, J., Lightowlers, C., & Roberts, J. (2017). Exploring the punitive surge: Crown Court sentencing practices before and after the 2011 English riots. *Criminology and Criminal Justice, 17*(3), 319–339.

Press Association. (2018, March 18). All UK Police should be allowed stun guns, says firearms chief. *The Guardian*.

Quinn, B. (2019, March 5). Met Police Chief says rising violent crime and officer cuts are linked. *The Guardian*.

Riots Communities and Victims Panel (RCVP). (2012). After the riots: The final report of the riots communities and victims panel. http://webarchive.nationalarchives.gov.uk/20121003195935/http://riotspanel.independent.gov.uk/evidence/

Roberts, D., Lewis, P., & Newburn, T. (2011). *Reading the riots: Investigating England's summer of disorder*. Guardian Shorts.

Roberts, S. (2021). *Solutions to knife crime: A path through the red sea*. Vernon Press.

Rodger, J. (2008). *Criminalising social policy: Anti-social behaviour and welfare in a de-civilised society*. Willan

Samuelson, K. (2016, April 1). Pictured: The horrifying 'Zombie Killer' knife that teenager used to kill 17 year old boy in fron to terrified families in children's playground. *Daily Mail*.

Scrase, S. (2017). *'Criminality pure and simple': An analysis of violent opposition to the police in the 2011 Riots*. Exeter University.

Sharman, J. (2019, March 6). Defence secretary Gavin Williamson says military 'ready to respond' to knife crime crisis. *Independent*.

Shaw, D. (2019, July 18). Ten charts on the rise of knife crime in England and Wales. *BBC News*.

Shiner, M. (2015, October 19). Stop and search: The police must not revive this discredited tactic. *The Guardian*.

Slater, T. (2016). The neoliberal state and the 2011 English riots: A class analysis. In H. Thörn, M. Mayer, O. Sernhede, & C. Thörn (Eds.), *Understanding urban uprisings, protests and movements* (pp. 121–148). Palgrave Macmillan.

Solomos, J. (2011). Race, rumours and riots: Past, present and future. *Sociological Research Online, 16*. https://doi.org/10.5153/sro.2547

Solomos, J., & Back, L. (1996). *Racism and society*. Palgrave Macmillan.

Squires, P. (2009). The knife crime 'epidemic' and British politics. *British Politics, 4*(1), 127–157.

Squires, P. (2011). There's nothing simple about simple criminality. *UC2 Online* (2), 2–6. uc.web.ucu.org.uk/files/2011/10/UC2Online.pdf (petersquires.net)

Squires, P. (2014). *Gun crime in global contexts*. Routledge.

Squires, P. (2016). The coalition and criminal justice. In H. Bochel & M. Powell (Ed.), *The Coalition Government and Social Policy*. The Policy Press.

Squires, P., & Stephen, D. E. (2005). *Rougher justice: Anti-social behaviour and young people*. Cullompton: Willan.

Stott, C., & Reicher, S. (2011). *Mad mobs and Englishmen: Myths and realities of the 2011 riots*. Constable and Robinson.

Stott, C., Drury, J., & Reicher, S. (2017). On the role of a social identity analysis in articulating structure and collective action: The 2011 riots in Tottenham and Hackney. *British Journal of Criminology, 57*(4), 964–981.

Sveinsson, K. P. (2008). *A tale of two Englands: 'Race' and violent crime in the press*. Runnymede Trust.

Tendler, S., & Ford, R. (2007, February 16). Armed Police sent out in force to reclaim the badlands. *The Times*.

Terror Stop and Search Police Statistics. (2010, June 10). *The Guardian* (online). Available at: https://www.theguardian.com/news/datablog/2010/jun/10/stop-and-search-terror-police-statistics. Accessed 12 Mar 2020.

Timpson, E. (2019). *Timpson review of school exclusion*. CP 92. London, HMSO.

Tiratelli, M., Quinton, P., & Bradford, B. (2018). Does stop and search deter crime? Evidence from ten years of London-wide data. *The British Journal of Criminology, 58*(5), 1212–1231.

Trafford, J. (2021). *The empire at home: Internal colonies and the end of Britain.* Pluto Press.

Travis, A. (2010, June 29). Theresa May scraps Labour police beat pledge. *The Guardian.*

Travis, A. (2015). Knife crime in England and Wales up for first time in four years. *The Guardian.*

Travis, A. (2016, October 20). Violent crime in England and Wales is up 24%, police figures show. *The Guardian.*

Treadwell, J., Briggs, D., Winlow, S., & Hall, S. (2013). Shopocalypse now: Consumer culture and the English riots of 2011. *British Journal of Criminology, 53*(1), 1–17.

Turley, C., Ranns, H., Callanan, M., Blackwell, A., & Newburn, T. (2012). *Delivering neighbourhood policing in partnership.* Home Office Research Report 61.

Tyler, I. (2013). *Revolting subjects: Social abjection and resistance in neo-liberal Britain.* Zed books.

Unison. (2016). *A future at risk: Cuts in youth services.* Unison: Unison Centre.

Wacquant, L. (2004). *Urban outcasts: A comparative sociology of advanced marginality.* Polity Press.

Wacquant, L. (2009). *Punishing the poor: The neo-liberal governance of social insecurity.* Duke University Press.

Waddington, P. A. J. (2004). In proportion: Race, and police stop and search. *British Journal of Criminology, 44*(6), 889–914.

Walker, P. (2019, August 11). Tories unveil law and order policy blitz amid election speculation. *The Guardian.* https://www.theguardian.com/society/2019/aug/11/tories-unveil-law-and-order-policy-blitz-amid-election-speculation

Weathers, H. (2005, April 26). A knife to our hearts. *Daily Mail.*

Weaver, M. (2018, November 19). Boris Johnson's unused water-cannon sold for scrap at £300,000 loss. *The Guardian.*

Weaver, M., & Pidd, H. (2019, March 4). No link between Knife crime and police cuts says Theresa May. *The Guardian.*

Winlow, S., & Hall, S. (2012). A predictably obedient riot: Postpolitics, consumer culture, and the English riots of 2011. *Cultural Politics, 8*(3), 465–488.

Winlow, S., Hall, S., & Treadwell, J. (2017). *Rise of the right, english nationalism and the transformation of working-class politics.* Bristol: Policy Press.

Winlow, S., Hall, S., Treadwell, J., & Briggs, D. (2015). *Riots and political protests: Notes from a post political present.* Routledge.

Wintour, P. (2014, June 17). Knife crime clampdown wins commons backing, leaving Lib Dems isolated. *The Guardian.*

Wintour, P., Watt, N., & Topping, A. (2008, July 16). Cameron: Absent black fathers must meet responsibilities. *The Guardian.*

Wood, R. (2010). UK: The reality behind the 'knife crime' debate. *Race & Class, 52*(2), 97–103.

Yardley, E. (2008). Teenage mothers' experiences of stigma. *Journal of Youth Studies, 11*(6), 671–684.

YMCA. (2018). *Youth and consequences: A report examining Local Authority expenditure on youth services in England and Wales.* YMCA. https://www.ymca.org.uk/wp-content/uploads/2018/04/Youth-Consequences-v0.2.pdf

Younge, G. (2017, November 28). Beyond the blade: We finally know how many youths are killed by knives. *The Guardian.*

Younge, G. (2018, June 21). The radical lessons of a year reporting on knife crime. *The Guardian.*

6

The 'Knife Crime Industry': Knife Fetish and the Commodification of Violence Prevention

The criminal produces an impression, partly moral and partly tragic, as the case may be, and in this way renders a "service" by arousing the moral and aesthetic feelings of the public... he produces criminal laws, penal codes, art, novels, plays and tragedies.... [In this fashion] The criminal breaks the monotony and everyday security of life....
Karl Marx (*Theories of Surplus Value I*, pp. 387–388)

Introduction

In previous chapters we have discussed in detail the interaction between police, news media and politics that came to define the 'knife crime' category as we know it today. However, there is an additional group of influential actors contributing to this discourse that has so far received little attention, both in this book and in wider society. From 2009 onwards we begin to see an increasing amount of targeted knife crime prevention work and the emergence of organisations dedicated to knife crime intervention as the sector became financially incentivised as a funding priority within criminal justice practice. This chapter considers the

© The Author(s), under exclusive license to Springer Nature Switzerland AG 2021
E. Williams and P. Squires, *Rethinking Knife Crime*,
https://doi.org/10.1007/978-3-030-83742-6_6

influence of actors within these networks extending across and beyond criminal justice agencies and including privatised services, creative arts and entertainment organisations and even commercial advertising businesses. Recognising how some commentators have begun to describe the emergence of a 'gang intervention industry' (Densley, 2011; Hallsworth, 2011), we will explore how these various agencies can be described as a 'knife crime industry', a concept that we use here to represent an interconnected network of public services and private enterprises that have come to benefit from the value bestowed on the label 'knife crime' in various ways. It will be argued here that the industry consistently fetishizes knives and knife crime work in their communications; capitalising in a number of ways from the symbolism and exoticisation associated with this label and its associated imagery.

It is by no means a new idea to suppose that individuals and groups stand to benefit from a magnified and sensationalised understanding of crime and deviance. Indeed, the concept of 'moral entrepreneurs' was central to Cohen's seminal work on moral panic in the 1970s. However, the expansion of communication through technology and social media since then presents a distinctly new landscape for crime discourse. This chapter draws heavily from examples of promotional content on Twitter. com, a micro-blogging social media website that in 2013 had around 317–328 million active users, of which around 16 million were in the UK (LSE, 2017). As a platform renowned for its concise and immediate response to events and current affairs, it has become common practice for organisations, charities and educational institutions to maintain Twitter accounts, posting and sharing relevant news and opinions for their followers and broader audiences. There are, for example, official police Twitter accounts for every borough in London and for each force across the UK, whilst the Home Office and members of Parliament tweet their events, activities and responses daily. This wide representation and frequency of communication have led to the increasing use of Twitter in social research representing a new public space for analysis (Carney, 2016). In this chapter examples of knife crime communications on Twitter are used to demonstrate the forms of communication that contribute to the knife crime industry, in order to explore the shifting meaning of the label in contemporary discourse.

The Shape of the Industry

The earliest knife-focused campaign group, 'Mothers Against Knives', was founded in 2005 to petition for a restriction on the sale of bladed weapons after a 31-year-old man was killed with an ornamental samurai sword in Middlesbrough in 2003. In 2008, during the heightened phase of knife crime concern, this campaign achieved success and replica samurai swords were added to the list of banned weapons for sale, import or hire in England and Wales (Criminal Justice Act, 1988). This was to be the first of many knife crime campaign groups that emerged from 2007 onwards with the intention to raise awareness or toughen criminal justice responses to knife offences. Others include: *Lives not Knives*— Founded 2007 (livesnotknives.org), *Communities Against Gun and Knife Crime*—founded 2007 (cagk.co.uk), *Say No 2 Knives*—Launched 2008 (sayno2knives.co.uk), *Solve This On-going Problem: 'STOP'*—founded 2008 (facebook.com/pg/Solve-This-Ongoing-Problem), *It Doesn't Have to Happen* 'IDHTH'—Launched 2009 (Hoskins, 2010), *No Knives, Better Lives*—launched 2009 (noknivesbetterlives.com), *I don't Carry a Knife*—Founded in 2010 (Channel 4 project Battlefront).

Victim charities and trusts such as The Ben Kinsella Trust (2008), The Rob Knox Foundation (2008), and the Tom Kirwan Trust (2013) mobilise as pressure groups for policy developments such as harsher sentencing, enhanced interventions in schools and increased police stop and search. They become an active link between government, the press, policing and schools, by developing 'knife crime' workshops, raising money and 'awareness', writing reports and organising events such as *The People's March Against Gun and Knife Crime* in October 2008. The Ben Kinsella Trust in particular demonstrates the influence such groups can have—with their founder and chair, Brooke Kinsella, publicly backing the Conservative party in the 2010 elections as the only party that would 'make our streets safe again' (BBC, 2010) and later becoming an advisor for knife crime funding allocations and tasked with assessing the effectiveness of interventions (Kinsella, 2011).

In interaction with such campaign groups and organisations, consecutive governments establish multiple legislative Acts that identify 'knife crime' as a distinct form of criminality for the first time and provide policy for 'knife crime' work in the sector. 'Knife crime' is specifically identified in: The Violent Crime reduction Act (2006), Tackling Gangs Action Programme (2007), Tackling Violence Action Plan; Saving Lives, Reducing Harm, Protecting the Public (2008), Tackling Knives Action Plan (2008), Youth Crime Action Plan (2008) and Count Me In; Together we can Stop Knife Crime (2010), and Tackling Knives together (2011).

Many of these developments and the policy initiatives they promote emphasise 'joined up' collaborative work to 'tackle knife crime', particularly between the Department for Children, Schools and Families, the Home Office and policing. For example, expanding the reach of the 'knife crime' response by providing step by step teaching resources and lesson plans for schools to 'raise awareness' and teach young people about 'knife crime' (Count Me In, 2010; Rogers, 2021). Additional policing operations are also launched in collaboration with campaign groups, such as; *Drop the Weapon* (2008), *Bin It* (2009), and *No More Knives* (2009). The scale of the response to 'knife crime' developing during these years produces a growing market for 'knife crime work'. Opportunities for funding and employment incentivise knife crime interventions, providing face-to-face work with young people and administrative and fundraising roles, along with management positions in the sector.

The forms of 'knife crime work' that are now commonplace were first developed from 2008 onwards when targeted government funding began focusing on knives and 'knife crime' as a priority public issue. The first of this kind was the Tackling Knives Action Programme (TKAP) receiving £7 million in 2008, a further £5 million in 2009 and a final £2 million in 2010. In 2011 this was replaced with the *Communities Against Gangs, Guns and Knives* project (CAGGK), which had received £4million in 2011 and a further £500,000 in 2012. The CAGGK fund was part of a total £18 million ring-fenced by the Conservative-led coalition for 'tackling knife crime' over two years. The news value of 'knife crime' was running at a comparative low in 2012 but the revenue for 'knife crime work' continued under the *End Gang and Youth Violence* (EGYV) post-riots funding that released £10 million for targeted intervention work and additional policing operations. As 'knife crime' news begins to regain prominence from 2016 onwards, the Mayor of London's office announced the *Anti-Knife Crime Community Fund* in 2017 with an initial £250,000 increasing to £1.4 million in 2018 and £15 million for policing 'knife crime' in London.

These knife focused government funds were accompanied by the shifting priorities of large funders such as the National Lottery and the Arts Council who provide long-term revenue in the sector. The Big Lottery fund, for example, provided a single grant of over £600,000 to ongoing anti-knife crime work at a south London church in 2009 and just under £500,000 to a theatre project aimed at reducing knife crime in 2010 (tnlcommunityfund.org.uk). These capital investments are relatively small compared to the hundreds of millions removed from statutory youth services since 2010 (Unison, 2016), but they represent a significant shift in priority funding at a time of resourcing scarcity in the youth sector.

It is clear the that 'knife crime work' since 2008 has developed into a multimillion-pound industry that is influential in leading policy change and cross-sector collaboration between the private, public and third sector. But beyond the financial market 'knife crime' projects emerging, there is also an ideological economy at work. In this chapter we consider both the direct beneficiaries of knife crime capital through services or goods, and the indirect beneficiaries that capitalise on the value and attention the label adds to their communications or content. Using examples of how the label is commonly used in online discourse, we wish to draw attention to the ways in which the meaning of the label is produced and reproduced through invested actors and the long-term impact of this dependency on our understanding and response to interpersonal youth violence.

Selling Knife Crime Work

Perhaps the most obvious 'work' within this industry are direct intervention projects with children and this contributes a large proportion of the promotion and advertising of services we see in online knife crime communications. However, the industry is much broader than this. There has been a great deal of innovation in the sector and it is now possible to find companies that provide anti-knife crime posters, t-shirts, stickers, magnets, educational packs, assemblies, teaching resources, knife deposit boxes and much more. Sometimes these are sponsored or associated with particularly fashionable market brands, celebrities or sports stars. The fact that these products are available is not in itself harmful but a closer look at their promotion and content suggests they often reproduce a particular understanding of the problem that encourages dissemination, affiliations and sales through a simplistic and often moralistic individualism.

In many instances such products reproduce the authority of the law and order response which, as previous chapters demonstrated, has rather limited evidence of success and merely perpetuates violence rather than reducing it. We can see this demonstrated in the posters advertised for use in schools (see Fig. 6.1) which claim to 'put an end to knife crime' through communicating hard hitting and attention-grabbing criminal justice facts and images. Information about the consequences of knife carrying is accompanied by the image of a large blade held in a clenched fist and a play on words: 'DON'T CUT YOUR TIME SHORT'.

The inclusion of the image of a knife is an aspect of the knife crime industry that we return to later in this chapter, but first the language adopted in such communications will be considered in more detail. The poster pictured has reproduced the common vernacular of responsibility adopted within the industry and the assumption that 'ending knife crime' can be achieved through educating children on the legal facts and personal risks. The consistent assumption that the solution to 'knife crime' is 'awareness' and information about potential punishments and consequences is frequently reproduced in knife crime communications across this industry with little or no opposition or critique.

Knife awareness projects and knife crime assemblies have become a regular feature in the lives of innercity young people. They reproduce defining narratives of the crime label in a variety of setting such as schools, youth clubs and pupil referral units and youth justice projects. By advertising and delivering 'behavioural change' interventions charities and organisations consistently reiterate for young people an individualised understanding of interpersonal violence; detaching criminal acts

Fig. 6.1   Don't cut your time short image branding (Accessed: Twitter.com, 12 March 2018)

from social or environmental conditions despite the evident connections. Furthermore, in communicating the need and justification for their work, these actors must constantly recycle this rhetoric through public discourse.

Take, for example, one London-based charity that frequently promotes its knife crime projects online as workshops designed for primary school children aged between seven and eleven years old. In its online fliers and adverts it repeatedly describes how the workshop focuses on 'decisions and consequences' in order to prevent 'knife crime'. In order to increase its visibility and position its advertisement more advantageously the charity actively participates in knife crime discussions online, particularly on Twitter. In one such instance the charity replies to a tweet from someone sharing terrible news that a family member had been stabbed. In reply the charity tweets;

> Heartbreaking news, we all dread news like this…We are doing all we can to stop knife crime across London, maybe you would like to support us with our anti knife crime education programmes, we rely on donations to stop this evil? (@letsget_talking)

Beyond the ethical considerations of asking for donations in response to such news, describing knife crime as 'this evil' asserts a particular understanding of the problem as fundamentally a moral one: good versus evil. Reminiscent of the infamous 'folk devil' (Cohen, 1972), such understandings of interpersonal violence are not only inaccurate but potentially harmful—increasing the very fears that in themselves can lead to more widespread defensive knife carrying. A similar mythologising language was used by a company called 'Knifesafe Limited' on Twitter to encourage service contracts for its knife deposit boxes that can be installed and managed at youth venues. In June 2019 the company tweeted:

> As Edmund Burke once famously said "The only thing necessary for the triumph of evil is for good men to do nothing." We urge all security leaders to adopt Knifesafe and become an innovator in combating knife crime across the United Kingdom. #bepartofthesolution #saferstreets

In this example the moral pressure is on the consumer—that to do nothing is to let the 'evil' of knife crime triumph and instead 'good men' should sign long-term contracts with Knifesafe Ltd. to have knife boxes fitted and maintained at public venues.

The framing and language used to advertise services and products demonstrate the scale of an industry that is responding to a market as much as it is the criminality itself. The influence of promoting 'what will sell' is significant when we consider that these advertisements are representations of 'real' interventions that will physically engage with children (as young as 7 years old) and that the language used to promote funding or donations will carry over into practice. For many young people their first engagement with professionals communicating 'knife crime' will be during special assemblies or projects delivered at school or through posters and advertising campaigns. The language and approach promoted through these media will be formative in their understanding of violence.

What we find across this industry is very little variation in approach or discourse resulting in a remarkable uniformity or a standardisation of language in knife crime work that assumes and reinforces an individualist understanding of the problem. Take for example the 47 successful applicants for the £250,000 anti-knife crime community fund in 2017. In the short summary of their projects published online, 39 of these (83%) used a distinct language of knife crime prevention that has become normalised in knife crime work and rhetoric. Phrases such as 'involved in knife crime' or 'knife related crime' are used throughout despite lacking in specificity or having no clear meaning or definition.

Nineteen of the summaries (40%) used language to describe 'targeting' particular types of young people, described as 'at risk', 'on the cusp', 'challenging' or 'hard to reach'. Whilst 23 summaries (49%) confirmed an individualist approach including 'education', 'awareness' or building personal 'resilience' as their key methods of prevention. Within these successful funding bids, project names such as 'Aspire Higher', 'Aspire to Change' or 'New Choices' exemplify the primary responsibilisation of the individual within the industry. By suggesting that young people just need to be more aspirational or make better choices in order to counteract the structural, symbolic and physical violence of their daily lives these projects tacitly reinforce a law and order understanding of 'knife crime'.

There are some indications within the project descriptions for the *Anti-Knife Crime Community Fund* of potential subversion from the individualist approach; two include a 'holistic approach', one mentions criminal 'exploitation' and a further two include the context of deprivation in their targeted group. However, none of the summaries suggest that 'knife crime prevention' requires educating, challenging and mobilising against inequality, racism or structural violence. It may be that organisations don't consider this to be an effective approach or perhaps they feel that funding bids are more likely to be successful if they conform to the language of the industry. Once the funding is secured projects may well engage in more critical discussions in practice but it is clear in its wider framing that the dominance of a particular 'knife crime' language and an ethos of individualism is rewarded in the industry. Many of the same themes and issues can be detected in specialist knife crime publications, such as workbooks designed for teachers. Rogers' (2021) volume *Gangs, Guns and Knives* by Jessica Kingsley publishers is designed as a series of lesson plans intended to 'raise awareness' amongst young people regarding a host of issues including negotiating peer group pressures and gangs, 'risk taking', staying safe on the streets and 'decision-making' and consequences. The work is undoubtedly well-intentioned and important although it reproduces the familiar 'resilience and responsibility' paradigm of intervention favoured the Government's own Ending Gang and Youth Violence strategy (HM Government, 2011), a form of cognitive behavioural therapy-*lite*, hoping to equip young people to handle the dangerous street-worlds and the suspicious policing they may encounter, although without addressing at all the broader social and economic dilemmas they have to negotiate. Almost the only reference to race or racism in the whole volume can be found in the section on gang identity and stop and search, the author writes 'young black men are more likely to be stopped and searched' (Rogers, 2021: 69). The information is presented as if it were an irreversible fact of nature, something to be endured rather than challenged.

Other communication of knife crime products and services suggests that enterprises within the industry promote a positivist approach to knife crime work as standard. Posters, assemblies and projects emphasise individuality and reinforcing an individual responsibility agenda. This produces a culture of 'knife crime work' that communicates to the public and to young people themselves that 'knife crime' emanates from a flawed character or bad choices; a societal 'evil'. Notable examples demonstrate that the language employed within the knife crime industry has two important implications: In the first place, the actions that comprise this industry are producing and reproducing a common-knowledge meaning and interpretation of the knife crime label. Secondly, the communication of professionals within this network extends this interpretation into practice and material forms; functioning as the interface between an idea of crime and physical interventions in everyday life. Knife awareness projects, assemblies and campaigns are now an everyday feature in the lives of innercity young people and produce defining narratives of the crime label in formal spaces such as schools, colleges and training centres. By advertising and promoting a message of 'behavioural change' interventions, charities and organisations consistently push young people towards an individualised understanding of interpersonal violence, detaching criminal acts from social or environmental conditions and the contexts within which they take place.

Campaigning for Individual Change

On the 23 March 2018 the Home Office launched the advertising campaign '*Knife Free*' in England and Wales 'amid warnings of stabbing epidemic in London' (Grierson, 2018b). With a budget of £1.35 million the campaign was predominantly digital, aimed at directing young people to the 'knife free' website through sharing the hashtag trend *#knifefree*. The launch was widely reported and promoted through online endorsement from individuals, organisations and institutions who pledged their support for the campaign from a variety of social media accounts, including police, charities, local councils and politicians (Fig. 6.2).

The government-led *#knifefree* campaign received more funding than the entire budget allocated in February 2018 to charities delivering face-to-face knife crime prevention work. This commitment of money was spent on an advertising campaign containing real life testimonies and images of young people and featured on Twitter, Snapchat, On Demand TV and Spotify, along with posters displayed in 'English cities where knife crime is more prevalent' (Gov.uk, 2018a). The Home Office commissioned research to advise the campaign and consulted with a range of charities and victim families in its development. Home Secretary at the time, Amber Rudd, described the campaign in an official statement, saying;

> The emotional stories at the heart of the new Knife Free campaign bring home in powerful fashion just what a far-reaching impact it can have on a young person's life if they make the misguided decision to carry a knife. I hope any young person who is seriously thinking about carrying

Fig. 6.2 Promoting the new Home Office 'knife free' campaign, March 2018 (Accessed: Twitter.com, 23 March 2018)

a knife listens to what the implications can be and realises what options are available if they choose to live knife free. (Gov.uk, 2018a)

Here, yet again, we see a focus upon urging behaviour change through education, in the belief that the slick production of short advertisements will influence the actions of young people. As with other prevention work, the language of the campaign reasserts the individual responsibility of the young person to implement change, without mention of available opportunities, cultural pressures, structural inequality or the harm caused by social policies and the sometimes discriminatory actions of the police.

On the 14 August 2019 the Home Office announced the *#Knife-Free* campaign would be extended to include 'special chicken boxes warning young people about the dangers of carrying a knife' (Gov.uk, 2019). Costing £57,000 and distributed to 210 fried chicken shops across England and Wales, the 310,000 printed fast-food boxes did not receive the same public support as the online campaign had the year prior. In a sense the very absurdity of the campaign was laid bare by the bluntness of its approach; the move was seen by many as offensive, racist and a waste of money (Rahim, 2019). The exasperation voiced towards a government that would so crudely employ such racialised tropes in this way was expressed by Labour MP David Lammy, who tweeted: 'Is this some kind of joke?! Why have you chosen chicken shops? What's next, #knifefree watermelons?'.

In addition to this racialisation, the reduction of the complex causes of violence to 'misguided decisions' throughout the *#KnifeFree* campaign risked further marginalising young people. To tell children who fear for their safety each day that the solution is to click on a website and simply 'choose to live knife free' communicates to young people that outsiders do not understand and therefore cannot help. As early chapters detailed, the decisions made by young people within the violent contexts of current social conditions are neither irrational nor illogical.

Campaigns such as *#KnifeFree* seldom present any evidence that they effectively reduce violence, indeed they are seldom subject to any credible evaluation, and yet the investment in such branded campaigns and communication initiatives continues to be central to the government violence prevention project. Perhaps the intention has always been more symbolic than material, a visible gesture towards 'doing something' by those with more interest in defining a dominant narrative of intervention than actually making change. On the other hand, there can also be a sense of collective action, resolve and fulfilment within campaign responses to 'knife crime'—and not all of these are limited to digital engagement and chicken shop boxes. Many community campaigns are inspired by individual tragedies or led by victims' families and they focus an energy for direct action that can mobilise groups to take to the streets. One such event took place in March 2018, when families, young people and community members in Camden organised a silent march in response to two fatal stabbings in the borough. Photos of large crowds with emotional banners were shared on Twitter on the 22nd of March (Fig. 6.3).

Fig. 6.3 Community anti-knife campaigns, March 22, 2018 (Accessed: Twitter. com, 22 March 2018)

There is undoubtedly a powerful unity and incredible political potential when communities come together in displays of solidarity such as the Camden March Against Violence, this represents a genuinely motivated mobilisation for change. However, the photos shared during this march suggest this community intervention is still predominantly articulated through the existing language and conceptual framework of the knife crime industry.

Although a march against 'violence', the communication is directed at the label 'knife crime' with the event described as 'Camden's response to knife crime', and participants are described as a community who are 'ready to stand up for an end to knife crime that is taking the lives of so many young people'. Here the loss of lives through violence is understood as 'taken by knife crime', a popular rhetorical device that insinuates 'knife crime' as an autonomous force; an outside threat, abstracted from economic conditions. Several banners visible in photos reproduce popularised catch phrases elsewhere directed at young people themselves; 'drop the knife, get a life' and 'lives not knives'.

Whilst some of the placards reference austerity and the need for economic investment, the political demands and economic criticisms made by communities in response to violence are compromised by the summation of the march as 'against knife crime'. In this way, the language and common discourse of 'knife crime' can be seen to actively depoliticise community responses to violence. Vernacular and phrases which have been normalised by the communications of the knife crime industry now act to redirect collective action into the condemnation of *young people's choices* and not the state's austerity cuts and policy failings.

From government-funded digital advertising campaigns to community-led marches, the core problem and the onus for change is consistently located within individual children and the potential for community action in the aftermath of violence remains predominantly within the existing structures and discourses that harm young people. This not only protects the state from scrutiny, but further excludes vulnerable young people through the misrecognition of their everyday lived experiences as just 'bad choices'. Launching symbolic anti-knife crime campaigns provides opportunities for the industry to draw attention to their services through endorsement and for central government to be seen as 'doing something' but have little impact other than reproducing a dominant narrative of intervention across the sector. The same opportunistic co-opting of knife crime can be seen in the entertainment and event industries, where the label is used to add value to existing enterprises. This commodification of the concept is an aspect of the industry that we will now consider below.

Learning Exercise 14: Examining Knife Crime on Twitter

Conduct your own mini-content analysis on Twitter.com and/or social media by using the advanced search option to collect all tweets that contain the exact phrase 'knife crime' on a chosen day or over several days. Make sure you select 'see all' rather than the 'top' tweets. Read through these one by one and record the number of times each of the following occurs;

A. Reporting or commenting on a recent violent incident.
B. Mentions policing (either posted by a police account, about stop and search or reference to policing by a member of the public.
C. Promotes a knife crime service, project or product (including campaigns, interventions, assemblies etc.).

D. Contains or insinuates racism or anti-immigration rhetoric.
If a tweet contains more than one of these content categories you can
count it in both.

Reflection:
Looking at your results is there anything that surprises you? Was the
quantity of content in any of the categories significantly larger or smaller
than the others? Why do you think this might be?

The Commodification of 'Knife Crime'

Along with services that provide direct anti-knife crime work or products
there are indirect beneficiaries of the knife crime industry which capitalise on the label through association. Enterprises such as creative arts,
radio and television programming and educational events all indirectly
benefit from the urgency and interest that the label entails. It is not only
that these industries refer to 'knife crime'—this in itself is nothing significant—but the particular ways in which they interact with the concept
and further recycle it is our main interest in what follows.

Exploring three separate examples from Twitter in March 2018, it will
be argued here that the interactions between indirect beneficiaries and
the concept 'knife crime' constitute a commodification of the societal
reaction to violence for reasons of status, entertainment and consumption. The first of these was when the British Broadcasting Corporation
(BBC) announced on Twitter that its renowned soap opera, *EastEnders*, would be introducing a 'knife crime whodunnit' story line. This
news was received with great enthusiasm by its audiences and was shared
over a hundred times in March with only one member of the public
responding negatively. The overwhelming majority of tweets welcomed
the violent depiction of knife crime as entertainment in a popular TV
soap opera with many hoping it would highlight the 'realities' of the
issue and prevent future violence between young people (Fig. 6.4).

It is widely reported on Twitter over the following days that the BBC
had been advised on the storyline by Brooke Kinsella of the Ben Kinsella

Fig. 6.4 Eastenders 'knife crime' story line, and reaction, 2018 (Accessed: Twitter.com, 22 March 2018)

Trust (McIntosh, 2018), a prominent charity in the knife crime industry, as mentioned above. The interaction between two enterprises in the network at this moment can be interpreted as beneficial for the work of both; the Kinsella Trust receives publicity whilst the BBC appears responsibly engaged with the topic. However, the reporting of the storyline as a 'knife crime whodunnit', and comments from fans such as 'sooo excited for it' (@TeamEECarter, 2018) reinforces an idea that the consumption of 'knife crime' as entertainment is not without problems.

The transition of 'knife crime' from a crime category to a cultural object as a soap opera storyline can be seen as a process of commodification, in recognition that the label comes to stand for something quite different within this interaction. When 'knife crime' is attached to cultural objects and communicated as entertainment it becomes its own distinct 'thing'—viewers are not 'excited' for 'knife crime' the crime category, but 'knife crime' the representational theme, or drama story line. Communicating 'knife crime' in this way increasingly constructs the category as a consumable commodity in the marketplace of the industry. The value of 'knife crime' as a commodity is demonstrated once again in an exchange between academics under a promotional tweet advertising a 'Trauma Conference' on the 19 March 2018.

For academics who are striving to provide critical debate on issues around recent violence, the commodification of 'knife crime' and its added exchange value can be challenging. Academics are often keen to increase impact by appealing to broad and varied audiences and the urgency of the label can be used to attract new viewers or readers to engage with alternative perspectives. But to what extent are the politics of their approach compromised by adhering to the norms of 'knife crime's representation? This was a dilemma confronted during the advertising of an academic conference with the title 'Knife Crime Programme' (Fig. 6.5).

In reply to the advert one Twitter user questions the choice of images saying;

> Sounds like some great speakers but I think the poster advertising it is terrible. Everyone knows what a knife looks like. It's not saying violence

Fig. 6.5 Trauma care conference 'knife crime' rebranding, 2018 (Accessed: Twitter.com, 19 March 2018)

reduction… it says knife crime programme. Sorry, I'm generally always positive. (@Karenmcluskey 2019)[1]

One of the speakers at the event then responds to confirm the £35 ticketed event has been rebranded without their knowledge or agreement, saying:

> I agree entirely Karyn and [sic] didn't agree to this change in branding of the programme. This is not a "knife crime" programme. (@DuncanBew 2018)

Evidently the 'Trauma Care Conference', with speakers who are advocates of the 'public health approach', discovered that their event had been rebranded on Twitter as a 'knife crime programme' accompanied by an image of a clenched fist and a hunting knife. The motivation behind this marketing is clear—organisers are aware that such branding will increase their audience and add value to the event even if it directly contradicts the intention and approach of the intended. Similarities can be drawn here with the dilemma of the Eastenders story line; to what extent should 'knife crime' content be made consumable, even palatable, in order to reach as wide an audience as possible?

The final example discussed here is that of a particular creative response to 'knife crime' shared on Twitter that demonstrates the complex interactions between enterprises and professionals within the network of the industry. On the 18 March 2018, one Twitter user shared an image of twenty-six-foot high sculpture referred to as 'the knife angel'. In the caption with the image the user prompts discussion writing; '*The 100,000 knives forming the Knife Angel have either been confiscated or surrendered to UK Police. What's your thoughts? #knifeart #creativity #protectingvulnerablepeople #savinglifes [sic]*' (Fig. 6.6).

This artistic contribution to the response to knife crime has been welded together using knives that were surrendered in amnesty knife-bins

---

[1] Karyn McCluskey is a Scottish forensic psychologist; she was formerly the director of the Strathclyde Community Violence Reduction Unit, which we have earlier discussed, from 2016 she became Chief Executive of Community Justice Scotland.

Fig. 6.6 The knife angel sculpture (Accessed: Twitter.com, 18 March 2019)

nationally during 2015 and 2016. Described as a 'national monument against violence and aggression' (alfiebradley.com), the piece was commissioned by The British Iron Works Centre and is said to be 'a memorial to those whose lives have been affected by knife crime' (ibid.). Built in Shropshire the sculpture was moved to Liverpool in November 2018 and there are plans for it to tour the country 'to create awareness of the knife problem the UK has' (Drury, 2018). The concept is not especially original, many gun control campaigns have featured the melting and artistic repurposing of confiscated firearms (Ferda, 2015; Keiren, 2020; Rasmussen, 2021).

Looking into this interaction more closely it emerged that the artist Alfie Bradley had previously created a four metre tall gorilla made from 40,000 donated spoons. His website features a video about the knife angel that includes footage of the owner of the British Iron Works Centre, Clive Knowles, describing how the project came about. He says:

The knife campaign really was born out of brain storming sessions. Having finished the spoon gorilla and needing to really keep that energy going and to get the next project underway. Now I'd recently seen a documentary where the police were defending themselves against the media and they were under a little bit of crossfire over their success at collecting knives off the streets of the UK and their amnesties. So we thought, having seen that – knives had been mentioned previously with regards to cutlery, this was being knives with reference to violence – so we decided to adopt the collection of knives, create the sculpture out of knives, and at the same time do something good for society and help the police remove those knives from the streets of the UK. (Clive Knowles transcribed from www.alfiebradley.com)

This honest account of the knife angel's inception demonstrates the overlapping interests within the responses to 'knife crime' and how they come together in the enterprises and creative initiatives within the industry. Knowles acknowledges that the creators were looking for a new project to follow on from a previous sculpture made of spoons. Knives were already being considered in continuation of a cutlery theme so they 'adopted' the collection of knives as a way to support police work that was receiving criticism from the media. The benefit for the artist and the Iron Works was that the piece would undoubtedly receive greater attention by being incorporated into a knife crime campaign. Whilst the police, by supplying the knives, also increased support for knife amnesties and their work through the emotive and dramatic display of the blades surrendered.

The associated hash tags on the tweet that make reference to protecting vulnerable people and saving lives, connect the artwork with a pro-policing message despite widespread scepticism regarding the effectiveness of knife amnesties. A petition with nearly thirteen thousand signatures asks for the knife angel to tour the UK 'raising countrywide awareness of the epidemic that has now become knife crime' (change.org, 2018). But many victim's families have objected to the use of weapons in a sculpture, stating; '*maybe you have not lost a child so cannot see the deep rooted agony this will cause… we don't need even more awareness about knife crime in London – we experience it every day*' (Elgot, 2015). Whilst the accuracy of the representation of knife amnesties as 'saving lives' is questionable, and the insensitivity of using weapons as a tribute to victims is problematic, the sculpture is undoubtedly a powerful image that stands alone from the interactions of the industry that created it.

The explanation of motivation within this particular interaction is indicative of a broader relation that is also reflected in the EastEnders storyline and the ticketed 'knife crime' trauma conference. Underneath the decision to associate services with the label of 'knife crime' lies a pre-existing objective: A dramatic storyline, an academic conference, or an Iron Works sculpture. The adaptation of these underlying objectives to incorporate 'knife crime' occurs as a secondary process: Consulting the Kinsella Trust for 'knife crime' certification, rebranding the conference to a 'knife crime programme' and adding an image of a blade to the poster, or collaborating with police to use surrendered knives. The original intention remains the same—but through association with 'knife crime' the motivation becomes reinterpreted as an 'anti-knife crime' endeavour, adding value to the service or industry through this re-articulation. These processes of collaboration produce new manifestations of 'knife crime' as cultural objects, independent of the interests underpinning their creation. In many respects, these themes take us back to the deep ambiguities historically associated with knives that we addressed in Chapter 2. Knives have served many purposes in human history; they have been tools, weapons, cultural artefacts, signifiers of prestige and emblems of masculinity. At the top of the Old Bailey, the Central Criminal Court, a female figure holds aloft the sword of justice. We cannot ignore knives and blades, neither can we abolish them, so it follows that violence, rather than the knife itself, has to be the focus of our efforts. We will not overcome knife violence, one weapon at a time, one stabbing at a time, our attention must go towards understanding the contexts of violence in which weapons are so dangerously deployed.

The sharing of the 'Knife Angel' on Twitter, along with the advertising of a surgical trauma conference as a 'knife crime programme' and the EastEnders 'knife crime whodunnit story line' have drawn attention to the significant reiteration of the label in creative industries that commodify the idea of 'knife crime' attached to new industry objects for exchange and consumption. Within these interactions two inferences can be made concerning the cultural articulation of 'knife crime': Firstly, the concept 'knife crime' brings together public and private industries that interact with each other in mutually beneficial relationships—simultaneously promoting 'knife crime work', increasing its value and justifying its existence. And, secondly, whilst the outward portrayal of collaboration with the arts and creative industries appears well intended (to "increase awareness" etc.), the analysis presented here suggests the ways in which 'knife crime' is consumed as a cultural commodity within these practices is problematic. Narratives focus upon the knife and a sensationalist audience-driven representation of the phenomenon, maximising the added value the label brings to such representations. Further analysis of the visual representation of 'knife crime' on Twitter suggests that the particular ways in which value is added to 'knife crime' as a commodity is often via a particular 'fetishisation' of the knife. This is an aspect of the response that will now be considered in more detail, through examples of images shared by police services on Twitter.

Police Twitter and the Fetishised Knife

Since 2008 the UK Police have gradually increased their use of Twitter as a method of engaging with the public in order to improve public trust and confidence in policing (Crump, 2011). Throughout this time knife crime has featured regularly as a source of validation of police work and to promote their community engagement activities such as visiting schools, running workshops or speaking at events. In fact, a large proportion of police community engagement work is being articulated through 'knife crime' (even 'governing through knife crime'), particularly their work with young children in primary school settings.

A dominant characteristic of the police 'knife crime' tweets is the frequent use of images of bladed weapons and knives to advertise police events and services or to display their work. Images of knives have always been included in reports of 'knife crime' and Chapter 4 discussed the formative role of these images in constructing the label in the 2000s. In recent years on Twitter there is a similar importance given to the representation of 'knife crime' through images of knives; these include blades found or seized by police during searches or weapon sweeps, visual representations of knives in anti-knife crime posters, campaigns or event advertisements.

Looking closely at the style and content of knife imagery shared frequently by police, we argued that in many instances the portrayal of bladed weapons is often so excessive, lurid and deliberate that it constitutes a knife fetish, in which the object is bestowed value and meaning beyond that which is represented by its use. This fetishisation will be discussed in relation to professional accountability and the contradictory communications of value in knife crime prevention more generally.

Take for example the images (Fig. 6.7), the first, an attention-grabbing image representing an imposingly bloodied knife stabbing into a freshly dug grave, in a tweet promoting school assemblies with 600 children. The second is from an official police Twitter account, sharing a composition of thirty-two decorative bladed articles arranged into the shape of a large knife, accompanied by a caption that even including an emoji knife.

Fig. 6.7 Police tweeting of knife crime imagery to promote school presentations (Accessed: Twitter.com, 12 March 2018)

The number and range of a variety of blades depicted in the second image is excessive, aiming for high impact—emphasising the threat of such a variety of weapons contained by the label 'knife crime'. Yet they are arranged aesthetically to resemble a knife; there is a communication of order and design and the blades seem impressively ornamental in this context. All these blades and weapons, however, are primarily designed to shock the viewer, drawing the gaze in to gain attention. The caption expresses police concern that too many young people are hurting and killing each other and promotes the use of *Crimestoppers* for public information and intelligence purposes. But rather than a representation of fact, the image is a constructed reality—the quantity and range of blades imply both the scale of the problem, but then attaches them only to young people through the words in the caption. The post maximises its reach and impact by capitalising on the value and inherent reverence for the bladed weapon, but this can also be seen to bestow a rather ambiguous value on the knives both as weapons *and cultural artefacts* in the process. In Chapter 2 we discussed the symbolic and cultural meanings that are evoked by bladed weapons in their representation and use.

Police communications on Twitter demonstrate how certain selective narratives about knife violence are incorporated in widely circulated images, narratives that—at times—can almost be seen as a celebration of the variety and power of awesome blades; a kind of 'knife porn' one would not ordinarily expect to see in police communications. Nevertheless, the excitement and enthusiasm for decorative and offensive weapons in the images connected to 'knife crime' go beyond simple representation—collectively they constitute a fetishisation of knives that has real consequences within the industry.

In a Marxist sense the fetishized commodity is a misconception of value '*in which properties are attributed to objects that can correctly be attributed only to human beings*' (Dant, 1999: 41). This 'spirit' bestowed on objects produces an 'unreal' intrinsic value from a material character and is fundamental to the creation of value in the capitalist mode of production (Dant, 1999: 41). But the fetishized object is also a mediator of social values, the properties contained are translated through material culture and become influential on behaviours and actions.

> A fetish is created through the veneration or worship of the object that is attributed some power or capacity, independently of its manifestation of that capacity. However, through the very process of attribution the object may indeed manifest those powers; the specialness with which the object is treated makes it special. (Dant, 1999: 43)

The use of knife images and the primacy of the blade in the very concept of 'knife crime' has produced a power and capacity of the object independent of its original significance. There is a characteristic of 'knife crime' that is bestowed on bladed weapons through their photographic representation. The images constructed to represent 'knife crime' reflect the accumulated meaning of the crime category. The knives in these representations are bestowed with the spirit of a violent and criminal culture. Once this 'specialness' is attached to the object and it is treated as 'special' the object may indeed manifest the spirit with which it was bestowed—now the knife *is* special. In this way, as the police poster above demonstrates, even kitchen knives—an object used every day in mundane food preparation—are perceived as dangerous weapons when presented in the context of 'knife crime'.

On one occasion on Twitter this fetishising process became exposed when the capacity of the object to embrace the constructed meaning was stretched too far. In a tweet later deleted by the Hackney division of the Met Police, but captured and shared by other users, the result of a 'weapon sweep' received a degree of ridicule (Fig. 6.8).

The original police tweet contains a photo of a cutlery knife, it has a small serrated edge with no sharp blade and no point. Its potential as an offensive weapon is clearly rather limited. But held by a uniformed police officer in forensic style plastic gloves it is presented to the camera as a dangerous weapon and shared on social media in order to communicate both the prevalence of knives and the effectiveness of police work.

The presentation of this culinary object as a weapon by police can be interpreted in several ways. Firstly, it can be seen to demonstrate the eagerness and desperation of the police to prove their worth by scouring the streets and displaying anything that could be considered a successful weapon search. And secondly, it suggests they sincerely anticipated the public would receive it as if it was a weapon. And it is this perception that

Fig. 6.8   Butter knife—stretching the label too far? (Accessed: Twitter.com, 16 March 2018)

exposes the power of the knife fetish—even a butter knife with no blade or point had the potential to be bestowed the dangerous spirit of 'knife crime' and viewed as a potentially dangerous weapon in this context.

The removal of the original tweet based on the response from the public suggests this was a stretch too far. The comments of those who shared a screen grab of the post emphasise not only the innocuousness of the object photographed but also the distinct 'Britishness' of the attempt to present this as a weapon. These comments accompanying the re-tweets of the image, whilst different in intent, suggest a similar reaction to the original photo as a communication specific to the British police. They both see the attempt to represent a 'blunt piece of metal' as a dangerous weapon as a reflection of the particular relationship between the police and 'knife crime' in Britain—an observation supported by the analysis of previous chapters.

This fetishisation of mundane objects into dangerous weapons by police has serious implications for young people. There is a sense that the over-representation of offensive knives in displays of police work, and in advertising across the whole of the knife crime industry, is in part constitutive of the power within the object that increases its appeal to young people. Whilst the 'specialness' of the knife and its implied 'animate' character are endorsed in the 'knife crime' communications of the industry, the same belief in a spirit of the weapon is reprimanded and reproached in the actions of young people. Since the publication of *Fear and Fashion* (Lemos & Crane, 2004) the idea that one reason young people carry knives is for added self-value or 'style' has been commonly accepted and is a belief often targeted in intervention work and anti-knife crime campaigns (Kinsella, 2011). If it is true, that knives *are* being fetishized by young people as fashionable and desirable objects to make themselves feel powerful (and safer), then it must also be the case that the fetishized communication of 'knife crime' is part of the wider material culture that produces this social value. In other words, police photos of thirty-two knives arranged into the shape of a hunting knife, also contribute to the desire to possess one of these revered objects.

Although there are moments when the 'unreal' value falls down and the fetish is exposed—such as the 'butter knife' weapon—there is no sense of responsibility that an obsessive representation of knives as powerful weapons contributes to the value contained by the object and therefore their appeal to young people. The language of 'taking responsibility' and 'making good decisions', the foundational discourse of the knife crime industry, falls short of its application to the professionals within its own network. The police, just like other services, benefit from the added value that an association with 'knife crime' brings to their work, but the celebration of the object's 'specialness' in certain police communications only makes the object itself more desirable.

Furthermore, the cross-industry consensus on the discourse and imagery that defines the discussion, raises questions of accountability. The mutual interests between professionals in the industry has led to charities, campaign groups and organisations being far more likely to *collaborate* with the police, the government and entertainment industries than to hold them responsible for these problematic representations. This diffused responsibility and lack of accountability within the industry is particularly harmful given the tenacity of aggressive racism and anti-immigration content that is often inseparable from the knife crime label in many online communications. The dominance of categories of content on Twitter that contained 'knife crime' whilst promoting far-right political ideologies will be discussed below, considering the shifting articulation of racism through 'knife crime' as a floating signifier.

'Knife Crime' the Floating Signifier

If you spend a little time on Twitter searching for 'knife crime' content or reading the comments on knife crime tweets, it does not take long before you are confronted with overt and extreme racism. In recent years this racialization has taken on particular forms and has become routinely directed at a particular British public figure. For example, of the total 5983 tweets containing the exact phrase 'knife crime' with reference to crime in the UK in March 2018, 2578 refer to Labour Party's London Mayor, Sadiq Khan—this total represents fully 43% of all knife crime tweets appearing that month. Of these, 90% of the tweets mentioning Khan contained negative content—representing 2311 of the 'knife crime' tweets in March, with only 115 positive and 152 neutral throughout the month. The association of the London Mayor with 'knife crime' is a particularly significant trend considering that Khan's remit for policy change is far more limited than that of the national government. References to government responsibility, including mentions of Prime Minister Theresa May amounted to only 263 during March 2018; the Mayor of London was held responsible for knife crime almost nine times more frequently.

Exploring the context and content of anti-Khan knife crime tweets further reveals a persistent trend in the use of the term 'knife crime' with reference to broader right-wing values; anti-immigration, pro-law and order and White supremacism. It was also found that 'knife crime' was used to interrupt and minimise the importance of liberal initiatives by the Mayor during March 2018: Laws against hate speech, pollution reduction, gender-neutral toilets and the gender pay gap commonly receive reply tweets to the effect of; '*but what are you doing about knife crime?*' (see below) (Fig. 6.9).

The language of tweets that use 'knife crime' as a symbol of Khan's failures or flawed priorities were often openly racist and Islamaphobic.

Fig. 6.9 Critical tweets directed at London Mayor, Sadiq Khan (Accessed: Twitter.com, 2 March 2018; Accessed: Twitter.com, 20 March)

Common references to 'Londonistan', a play on words to describe what is seen as an over-representation of Asain migrants in the capital, accompanied these tweets. Along with abrasive, insulting and often overtly racist personal attacks on Khan, such as 'Guantanamo too good for that little shite' (Twitter.com, 13 March 2018).

The authenticity of the 'knife crime as priority' sentiment of anti-Khan tweets is undermined by the increase in racist and anti-Muslim hate speech in response to Khan speaking about or acting directly on 'knife crime'. For example, the highest frequency of negative Khan tweets in March 2018 took place when the #knifefree advertising campaign was launched by the Home Office with the Mayor's explicit backing (Fig. 6.10).

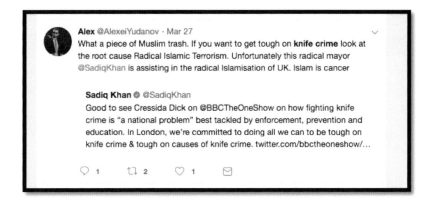

Fig. 6.10 Riding racist tweets on the back of knife crime problem (Accessed: Twitter.com, 27 March 2018; Accessed: Twitter.com, 25 March 2018)

Analysing the high frequency of tweets in this category the meaning that is conveyed through the communication of 'knife crime' is consistent in this context. For example, there is no attempt in anti-Khan tweets to really interrogate the issue of knives in London—the phrase is used symbolically rather than literally, to make quick reference to a broader political position. In this common use the phrase takes on a particular meaning; it represents a politically far-right belief that immigration leads to a 'loss of control' in British streets. 'Knife crime' within this rhetoric is used as a case in point, the long-established racialisation of the crime category provides a reliable signifier of violence and criminality as 'Other' that can be called upon to promote right-wing ideologies online. In many respects, these are precisely the themes we encountered, in Chapter 1, when parliament discussed the new offensive weapons Legislation during the 1950s.

Earlier chapters of this book have detailed the processes through which 'knife crime' came to be constructed as a criminality located amongst young, Black, innercity youths, and the political and social functions of this racialisation (see Chapters 3–5). However, the data analysed in this chapter suggests that the meaning of 'knife crime' is continuing to evolve through the communication of populist online politics. The references to Khan's Asian ethnicity and Muslim religion alongside and connected to 'knife crime' demonstrate the fluidity of the label's racism to incorporate contemporary right-wing ideologies. As previous chapters have detailed, the capacity of the label to perform this function has always been central to its existence. But the dominance of its use on Twitter as a tool to attack Khan is evidence of the agility of the label to adapt to the new political and ideological contours of contemporary racism.

This shifting meaning of the label and its continually adapting connotations to incorporate forms of racism suggest 'knife crime' functions, just as race itself, as a *floating signifier*. Floating Signifiers are seen to '*gain their meaning not because of what they contain in their essence, but in the shifting relations of difference which they establish with other concepts and ideas in a signifying field*' (Hall, 1997: 8). The concept of 'race' is described by Hall (1997) as a floating signifier in that ideas of racial difference function more as a language, or metaphor, rather than as any firm biological indicator. And because 'race' gains its meaning in shifting relations of difference, it can never be fixed but is 'subject to the constant process of redefinition and appropriation' (Hall, 1997: 8). 'Knife crime', as a signifier in the contested field of race, is also subject to the constitutive language that makes and remakes its meaning.

This is not to say that 'knife crime' doesn't mean anything, but rather that its meaning becomes fixed and re-fixed through the language and the 'making meaning practices' (Hall, 1997: 8) in the relations through which it is communicated. If Twitter represents a snap shot of the language that constructs 'knife crime' meaning at this time, then the hatred and vitriolic racism in tweets directed at Sadiq Khan make a significant contribution to the signifying field.

Recognising what 'knife crime' is made to mean through its consistent appropriation by far-right commentators should raise concern amongst a violence prevention industry that utilises the same signifier for their work with young people and vulnerable groups. The concept 'knife crime' cannot be separated from the racism and anti-immigration politics that are conceptually linked and constructive of its meaning in everyday language. Therefore, organising a response to violence through the language of 'knife crime' will inherently reiterate racist understandings of criminality. The analysis of the language of 'knife crime' in contemporary online use reveals the potential dangers entailed by intervention responses which reproduce a populist concept that has been appropriated by far-right politics in Britain.

Conclusion

Looking at the accumulation of charities, companies, organisations and campaign groups facilitated by the label, this chapter has discussed the commodification of knife crime as a cultural object that provides direct and indirect benefits to enterprises associated with the crime category. The professionals and enterprises within this network were seen to collaborate in mutually beneficial initiatives between government, policing, the third sector and the creative industries, producing a consensus on 'knife crime' as an individualistic, behavioural pathology.

Further analysis of particular collaborations shared on Twitter revealed the processes through which the value of 'knife crime' was added to existing projects to increase their relevancy and public appeal. This suggests that the idea of 'knife crime' has become commodified, produced and reproduced as a cultural object for exchange, entertainment and consumption within the extended knife crime industry. However, the same processes that establish value for knife crime as a commodity, were also seen to fetishise the concept for material gain and this presents a critical dilemma for ongoing knife crime work; how can preventative work seek to disarm a 'knife culture' whilst remaining dependant on its construction for their own legitimacy?

Along with the communication of the knife crime industry the inter-actions containing the label 'knife crime' in March were dominated by far-right politics online. Used as a signifier of lawlessness and the perceived threat of immigration on British civility, the concept was appropriated to endorse hateful and racist online abuse of London Mayor, Sadiq Khan. This symbolic and shifting racism has often been implicit in the concept of 'knife crime' and emphasises the urgency of rethinking the label's wide application.

Previous chapters have already established that 'knife crime' does not exist as an objective criminological *fact*, thus the processes through which the meaning of 'knife crime' as a floating signifier becomes pinned down are crucial to understanding the concept and its meaning and significance. This analysis of online communications reaches two fundamental conclusions on the contemporary construction of 'knife crime' meaning: Firstly, that the dependency and collaboration across an incentivised network of cross-sector industries greatly restricts the ability of professionals within this network to critique and challenge the harmful practices of commodification and fetishisation of 'knife crime'. Secondly, the re-appropriation of 'knife crime' by the far-right to fit with racist, especially anti-Muslim and anti-Asian, populism makes the uncritical position of the knife crime industry increasingly indefensible. The tension of working within these contradictions will be explored in greater detail in Chapter 7, where empirical research with practitioners and young people will examine the impact of knife crime discourse in everyday experiences of the label and its practices.

Learning Exercise 15: The Commodification of Knife Violence

Take a look at the following novelty 'knife block' widely available and advertised for sale in shops and on the internet. Can you see anything wrong in such an item? Sketch out your arguments for and against the sale of such an item.

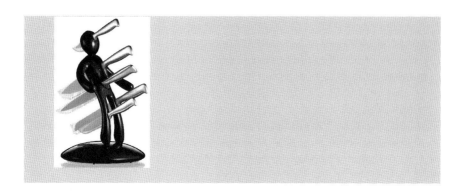

References

Bew, D. (2018, March 29). *Twitter*. Available at: https://twitter.com/duncan bew/status/979392749395902464. Accessed 11 June 2021.

Carney, N. (2016). All lives matter, but so does race: Black lives matter and the evolving role of social media. *Humanity & Society, 40*(2), 180–199. https://doi.org/10.1177/0160597616643868

Change.org. (2018). *Supporting the knife angel campaign* [online]. Available at: https://www.change.org/p/support-the-knife-angel-campaign-help-us-to-get-the-knife-angel-to-trafalgar-square-and-take-place-on-the-fourth-plinth-for-all-to-see. Accessed 11 June 2021.

Cohen, S. (1972). *Folk devils and moral panics: The creation of the mods and rockers*. Routledge.

Criminal Justice Act. (1988). *Offensive weapons, amendment no. 2, Order 2008*. Available at: https://www.legislation.gov.uk/ukdsi/2008/978011081 7774. Accessed 10 June 2021.

Crump, J. (2011). What are the police doing on Twitter? Social media, the police and the public. *Policy & Internet, 3*(4), Article 7.

Dant, T. (1999). *Material culture in the social world*. Open University Press.

Densley, J. (2011) Ganging up on gangs: Why the gang intervention industry needs an intervention. *The British Journal of Forensic Practice, 13*(1), 12–23.

Drury, J. (2018). *On the move: Knife Angel leaves Shropshire for Liverpool—With video and pictures*. Available at: https://www.shropshirestar.com/news/local-hubs/oswestry/2018/11/29/on-the-move-knife-angel-leaves-shropshire-for-liverpool-with-video/. Accessed 10 Dec 2018.

Elgot, J. (2015). 'Knife Angel' made from 100,000 seized blades divides opinion. *The Guardian*. Available at: https://www.theguardian.com/art anddesign/2015/dec/10/knife-angel-made-100000-seized-blades-mixed-rea ction-victims. Accessed 11 Dec 2018.

'Ex-EastEnder Brooke Kinsella backs Tories on crime'. (2010, April 27). *BBC News online*. UK. Available at: http://news.bbc.co.uk/1/hi/uk_politics/ele ction_2010/8646300.stm. Accessed 10 June 2021.

Ferda, L. (2015). In the line of fire: Using art to change opinions about gun control policy issues. *Carnegie Mellon Today* (cmu.edu).

Gov.uk. (2018). *Extra £110 million this year for metropolitan police in Mayor's budget*. London City Hall. Available at: https://www.london.gov.uk//city-hall-blog/extra-ps110-million-year-metropolitan-police-mayors-budget. Accessed 4 Sept 2018.

Gov.uk. (2019, August 14). *Special #knifefree chicken boxes launched across the country*. Home Office. Available at: https://www.gov.uk/government/news/special-knifefree-chicken-boxes-launched-across-the-country. Accessed 11 June 2021.

Grierson, J. (2018a, April 13). Met chief defends fourfold rise in use of stop-and-search. *The Guardian*. Available at: https://www.theguardian. com/uk-news/2018/apr/13/met-chief-cressida-dick-stop-and-search-london. Accessed 11 June 2021.

Grierson, J. (2018b, March 23). Home Office uses real-life cases in #knifefree ad campaign. *The Guardian*. Available at: https://www.theguardian.com/uk-news/2018/mar/23/uk-ad-campaign-to-reduce-knife-features-real-life-cases. Accessed 11 June 2021.

Hall, S. (1997). *Race, the floating signifier*. Media Education Foundation Film.

Hallsworth, S. (2011). Gangland Britain: Realites, fantasies and industry. In B. Goldson (Ed.), *Youth in crisis: Gangs terratory and violence*. London: Routledge.

HM Government. (2011). *Ending gang and youth violence: A cross government report*. London: The Stationery Office.

Home Office. (2010). *Count me in; Together we can stop knife crime*. The Department of Children, Schools and Families. Available at: http://www. knifecrimes.org/count_me_in.pdf. Accessed 10 June 2021.

Hoskins, P. (2010). *It doesn't have to happen in Alum Rock*. BBC Birmingham Website. Available at: http://news.bbc.co.uk/local/birmingham/hi/front_page/newsid_8522000/8522715.stm. Accessed 17 Sept 2019.

Keiren. (2020, October 22). Gun art. *Insteading*. Gun Art—Insteading.

Kinsella, B. (2011). *Tackling knife crime together—A review of local anti-knife crime projects*. The Home Office. Available at: https://www.gov.uk/govern ment/uploads/system/uploads/attachment_data/file/97776/kinsella-execut ive-summary.pdf. Accessed 12 Oct 2018.

Knifesafe. (2019, June 5). *Twitter*. Available at: https://twitter.com/knifesafe/ status/1136196910572888064. Accessed 11 June 2021.

Letsget_talking. (2018, March 12). *Twitter*. Available at: https://twitter.com/ letsget_talking/status/973164219565735937. Accessed 11 June 2021.

Lemos, G., & Crane. (2004). *Fear and fashion: The use of knives and other weapons by young people*. Lemos & Crane, Bridge House Trust, Corporation of London.

LSE. (2017). *Social media platforms and demographics: Digital communications*. The London School of Economics and Political Science. Available at: https://info.lse.ac.uk/staff/divisions/communications-division/digital-com munications-team/assets/documents/guides/A-Guide-To-Social-Media-Pla tforms-and-Demographics.pdf. Accessed 10 June 2021.

McIntosh, S. (2018, March 23). EastEnders: Actress Brooke Kinsella's hopes for knife crime storyline. *BBC News*. Available at: https://www.bbc.co.uk/ news/entertainment-arts-43422735. Accessed 17 Sept 2019.

Rahim, Z. (2019, August 14). 'Crude, offensive and probably expensive': Politicians attack government's anti-knife crime fried chicken boxes'. *The Independent*. Available at: https://www.independent.co.uk/news/uk/pol itics/fried-chicken-boxes-knife-crime-home-office-london-a9058936.html. Accessed 11 June 2021.

Rasmussen, E. (2021, May 28). A 64-foot angel is being made in downtown LA from confiscated and surrendered guns. *Long Beach Telegraph*.

Rogers, V. (2021). *Gangs, guns and knives: Activities and lesson plans to raise awareness with young people*. Jessica Kingsley.

TeamEECarter. (2018, March 22). *Twitter*. Available at: https://twitter.com/tea meecarter/status/966717082960981 0829. Accessed 17 Sept 2019.

Unison. (2016). *A future at risk; Cuts in youth services*. Unison: Unison Centre (@Karenmcluskey 2019).

7

The Realities of 'Knife Crime': Life Beneath the Label

Introduction

So far, in the book, we have explored the history, meaning and context of knife crime, challenging certain misunderstandings, ambiguities and fabrications wrapped up in the concept. Unpacking the 'knife crime' phenomenon we have drawn upon the theoretical tradition of social constructionism, we have deployed labelling theory (Becker, 1963), deviancy amplification, the notion of 'moral panic' (Cohen, 1972) and the theoretical insights of Policing the Crisis (Hall et al., 1978). Taken together this body of work has provided a framework through which the construction of 'knife crime' as a criminological fact has been challenged. However, some of the limitations of this approach are revealed in the questions that remain unanswered. Such as: how can we make sense of apparent increases in violence in the mid-2000s if not through the concept of a 'knife', 'gang' or 'violence' culture? And how can a critical understanding of 'knife crime' labelling account for or connect with the *real* experiences of practitioners and young people who are in direct contact with the actions defined by the label?

© The Author(s), under exclusive license to Springer Nature Switzerland AG 2021
E. Williams and P. Squires, *Rethinking Knife Crime*,
https://doi.org/10.1007/978-3-030-83742-6_7

Working beneath the political discourses and the pronouncements of policy makers there are professionals who confront the complex realities of interpersonal violence in everyday practices and actions. And there are also young people themselves. The experiences and insights of these groups are the focus of this chapter. Drawing on qualitative research with twenty youth justice practitioners and ten focus groups with a total of seventy-eight young people in southeast London, this chapter provides a grounded sociological understanding of the shifting experiences of youth that are concealed and obscured by assumptions contained within the 'knife crime' label.

The analysis in this chapter considers data from two sample groups with distinct empirical approaches; youth work practitioners were interviewed and asked to reflect on the transition into specialised 'knife crime work' in youth justice from 2008 onwards, whilst young people were presented with some of the core themes arising from earlier research and invited to discuss their meaning and significance. The themes emerging through analysis of the focus group and interview data are presented here along with a series of reflections upon what they tell us about alternative perceptions of and reactions to the knife crime phenomenon.

The purpose of this work has never been to explain or justify the actions of young people and the following points should not be considered as a positivist contribution to that end. Rather, it is intended that these interpretations, substantiated with supporting theory, extend rather than define an understanding of violence; identifying alternative 'knife crime' realities that have thus far not been represented by the label. For instance, chapter one detailed the ways in which a particular conception of 'knife crime' was fashioned drawing upon rather traditional, selective and judgemental ideas about what knife crime was, how it was evidenced and who was deemed responsible for it. This legally non-existent 'crime' was pre-loaded with such historical and xenophobic baggage that by the time mainstream social science (and administrative criminology) came to bear upon the issue it was thoroughly enclosed in a race-pathology narrative and simple reductionist cause and effect relationships. Our interview data firmly contradict these misunderstandings offering a fuller and richer rethinking of the daily realities of knife-involved violence.

Violent Sociological Shifts: The Moment of 2007–2008

The first line of inquiry during interviews with practitioners was to establish their first recollections of 'knife crime' becoming a concern within youth justice and their experiences of the initial adoption of the label within their work. Invariably this discussion would lead to practitioners describing an apparent intensification of violence between young people and recalling specific youth fatalities that immediately preceded the introduction of more targeted 'knife crime' work. Although our analysis of the label has sought to contextualise the moral panic over 'knife crime', the broadly shared accounts of practitioners do suggest that, at this time, beneath this label, there was a growing sense of unease about rising levels of interpersonal violence involving young people.

Whilst this agreement suggests the increased rates of violence reported in 2007 did signify an authentic crime concern amongst communities affected, there are significant differences between the accounts of this violence as reported in news media and the descriptions by practitioners working with young people. The reporting of 'knife crime' in 2007 and 2008 focussed heavily on homicides and knife injuries whereas youth justice practitioners recounted a much broader shift in the character of youth interactions towards increasing levels of anxiety, fear and violence. During the interviews there were several alternative practice-informed explanations provided for the changes witnessed during this period. The de-construction of 'knife crime' in previous chapters has sought to contextualise the policing response to the moral panic in 2008 in relation to the political and economic moment. The alternative accounts of the realities 'on the ground' presented here bring an additional level to the analysis. The ways in which tabloid understandings of 'knife crime' came to misidentify the changing landscapes of violence involving young people had particular implications that are explored here.

The following four themes emerging from the interview data, represent alternative perspectives on the causes of increased violence in 2007 and 2008, outside the restrictive explanations dictated by the label 'knife crime'. Observations and references that practitioners made to external forces or broader sociological changes are further investigated in the discussion which follows. The contribution of these accounts to the broader case study of 'knife crime' demonstrates not only that the construction of 'knife crime' has served systemic and structural interests, but that 'knife crime' discourse has suppressed the articulation of alternative explanations and understandings that are both important and urgently necessary for rethinking the problem and responses to it.

1. *The destabilising impact of proactive policing*

A reoccurring theme during interviews with Youth Justice Managers was that the structures of the informal drug economy had been destabilised in 2006 by a variety of proactive policing and immigration policies. It was repeatedly suggested that this contributed to increases in violence in subsequent years; the previously secure organised groups splintered into smaller and younger fractions, jostling for position and power in selling territories and the supply chain. As one former Intervention Manager described during interview:

> *They went hard on some of the top boys and they started deporting some people as well... 2006 police are coming harder putting people away and also some people are being deported you then suddenly had Black Mafia, you had Shower, Anti-Shower, Def and Rats all these types of gangs started coming through and suddenly every ward, if you like, in Lewisham had its own gang. Which made it even harder for us to deal with.* (Interview B 25.01.2018)

The term 'gang', like 'knife crime', has become synonymous with the idea of 'black criminality' and has facilitated discrimination in the Criminal Justice System by being a label disproportionately attached to Black offenders compared to White offenders (Amnesty International, 2018). However, whether attributed to American popular culture, UK media or organised crime, groups of young people in the 2000s were often self-defining as members of 'gangs'. These identified groups were not necessarily criminal, indeed many of them were friendship groups from school and neighbourhood (Densley, 2012), but they have been recognised as collectives with the potential to evolve into loosely affiliated crime networks (Hobbs, 2013: 126).

Previous research (Alexander, 2008; Densley, 2012; Hobbs, 2013; Smithson et al., 2012) has questioned the application of the 'gang' label to territorial disputes at the lower rungs of street drug markets (Kintrea et al., 2011), arguing that sensationalism over 'gangs' mythologizes petty criminality by progressively associating youth conflict with serious organised crime syndicates. However, there is no doubt that the multiple marginalisations experienced by young people in post-industrial London during the 2000s provided an endless supply of keen workers at the lower end of drug distribution structures—regardless of the accuracy of the 'gang' label:

> As legal alternatives have diminished, there is no shortage of potential labour for the complex overlapping urban networks that are located in a web of 'Multiple group-affiliations'… Whatever transgressional sobriquet is applied to them, these urban youth groups are part of the constellation of collaborations that constitute a community of practice responding to interpretations of global markets operationalized via local identities and sensibilities. (Hobbs, 2013: 136)

The accounts provided by practitioners in this research describe significant shifts in these networks in the mid 2000s, explaining how proactive policing created vacancies in crime networks and destabilised territorial monopolies at this time. It turns, these 'restructures' made it economically logical for aspirational young entrepreneurs to see these vacancies as lucrative opportunities worth fighting for.

Statistical evidence of increased rates of incarceration and deportation within the informal market in 2006 supports this idea, particularly the impact of the newly formed Serious Organised Crime Agency (SOCA) launched in April of that year. SOCA obtained 60% more funding in its first year than the organised crime division had previously received and increased its operations by 118% in 2006 with a 64% increase in arrests (Sproat, 2011: 344, 348). Corroborating this proactive policing dynamic to policing and the roll-out of the ASB 'respect agenda' data for 2006–2007, shows that the population of young people within the youth justice system reached its peak in 2006/2007 (Gov.uk, 2016), with youth custody returning to a new high the following year. The 'war' on knife crime had just begun and the Tackling Knives Action (TKAP) was gearing up whilst, in London, Operation Blunt 2 was being rolled out, with stop and search rates peaking (Fig. 4.11).

2. *Generational shifts*

Along with the incarceration and deportation of key figures in 2006, the murders of notorious 'olders' such as Eric Akinniranye (2004) and Andrew Wanogho (2006) marked for many the end of an era and a generational shift of power to emerging groups of 'youngers'. The word 'generational' is used here not in the sense of parent to child but more accurately from older sibling to younger sibling. Self-socialising youth peer groups with limited adult contact are known to organise into closely defined age-based micro-hierarchies (Densley, 2012), 'Olders' are often around 17–24 years old, whilst 'Youngers' are usually 12–16 years old (Densley, 2012: 53, 54), those younger than 12 are sometimes referred to as 'young youngers' or 'tinys' (Densley, 2012: 52). Although anxieties over youth subcultures often suggest that a new generation is distinctly more dangerous than those that went before (Cohen, 1972), data from interviews along with wider demographic and qualitative evidence (Thapar, 2021) suggesting that there were some distinct differences emerging amongst the youth groups arising in 2007 and 2008.

Interviews with YOT staff from this time produced clear evidence that they felt the youth offending service was ill-equipped and unprepared for the intensity of the trauma, fear and extreme violence young people were experiencing in 2007:

> And I definitely think this is related to the top tier of gang members, talking about the old school 28s, ghetto boys. What was happening was their younger brothers and sisters were now coming up and they had learnt about violence… there were murders like that across the whole of the UK, so when these guys are killed, across London, across specific areas of the UK it caused a split… I think maybe the first three to five children that died, stabbings had been going on, violence had been going on, but when the first of those children died, it definitely scared that generation. It traumatised them because they were now burying their friends. (Interview A: 21.02.2018)

In this account the generational shift is described as a 'split' resulting in children already exposed to the violence of their 'Older' taking a step up in the existing informal hierarchy whilst simultaneously traumatised by the death of their peers. Another YOS worker working with young offenders at this time also highlighted the impact on children of experiencing peer murder, the impact of blanket media coverage on knife-related crimes and how he recognised an increase in the severity of offending behaviours at this time:

> ...I started to notice around this time, 2007 to 2009 period, young people were turning up to the YOT in taxis, they stopped coming by bus and on foot because they were aware of their own mortality because so many children had been murdered. And what the media did negatively on this was they just publicised it everywhere and kids were like [sharp intake of breath] "I'm not walking on the street without a knife" ... I recognised that the boys and girls were talking to me in a completely different way... so I'm developing this whole new understanding. (Interview C 23.02.2018)

This observation of a direct impact between the media coverage of 'knife crime' at this time and the knife carrying behaviours of young people is especially significant when considering the multiple 'knife crime' realities that overlap. The tabloid interpretation of violence became the dominant representation, communicating an idea of 'knife crime' back to young people who came to reflect this understanding in their actions. There are strong echoes of Merton's 'self-fulfilling prophecy' in this reading of knife crime (Merton, 1948).

When interviewed, a former intervention officer from the Youth Offending Service expressed similar observations regarding the impact of the deaths of young people in 2006 and 2007. He cited disturbing developments in violence and how the statutory services neither understood the rapid changes and caseloads they were witnessing amongst the young people with whom they were attempting to work nor felt adequately trained and prepared to deal with the problems they presented:

> ...we were seeing some pretty bad youths come in, like, 'you lot are not a joke'... And I think if I recall, 2007, 2008 was a massive spike... So that's when things started looking a bit kind of like... well the question was

really "are we really equipped to be dealing with this as a YOS?"... But then the cases started coming in rapidly. And I just remember some stuff started happening where you were just like, I remember some sexual violence cases. I remember reading this kid had set a girl alight after raping her, and I remember thinking this has got nuts. (Interview B 25.01.2018)

Such accounts suggest that the increase in youth homicides around 2007 and 2008 was part of a broader generational shift of violence, including emerging younger groups of adolescents in London, drawn into the informal markets and conflicts prematurely by the instability caused by proactive policing or the death of respected 'olders'.

This interpretation of events by practitioners is corroborated by accounts of generational changes in recent ethnographic research in London (Clement, 2010; Hobbs, 2013). Social constructivist theories of deviance and subcultures often recycle a notion of a *transitional* youth criminality (Cohen, 1972: 228; Rutherford, 2002), emphasising that young people eventually mature into a working and conforming parent culture. However, research on young people's experience in London that spans the first 'spike' in 'knife crime' has demonstrated that this context is undoubtedly changing (Furlong & Cartmel, 1997). Echoing similar research findings in the USA, the point was made that 'growing out of crime' depended upon opportunities to do so, especially mainstream opportunities to learn, train and earn and community institutions to support and sustain lives (Hagedorn, 1988). In the USA, Wacquant and others (Alexander et al., 2014; Wacquant, 2008) have associated such changes with the rise of an economic neo-liberalism which turned the ghetto into the 'hyperghetto' from which there were few escapes. Without these opportunities (and compounded by skill-shortages, school exclusions, social marginality, racial discrimination and criminal records) young people could become trapped in low-paying and dangerous contraband economy roles—and, later, exploited in what became known as *County Lines* (Harding, 2020; Spicer, 2021). Such problems and the social divisions upon which they often rested may well have been far less widespread or acute in the UK but notions of 'precarity' (Standing, 2011), of 'youth marginality' and social division (Blackman & Rogers, 2017), of 'disconnected youth' (Macdonald & Marsh, 2001) or social mobility in reverse, the collapse of the unskilled youth labour market, the 'NEET generation'[1] and, as a consequence, the difficult transition to adulthood, all came to shape discussions on the 'state of youth today', culminating in the problems of anti-social behaviour, youth crime (Squires & Stephen, 2005), and finally gangs and violence.

Unlike working class teenagers in previous decades who may have demonstrated oppositional cultures 'as a means of reconciling themselves to their mapped-out future of low-status employment' (Clement, 2010: 444), it has been argued that working class young people growing up in neo-liberalism 'are deprived of such certainties; thus, their alienation and anomie are both greater and have become more real' (ibid.). Working class children under advanced neoliberal policies are both excluded from the core economy and increasingly ill-equipped for the 'service class' occupations at the periphery. Thus, it has been demonstrated in previous research, that the aspirational culture which once made 'respectable work' a desired destination in adulthood has been stripped away by generations of deindustrialisation and inherited worklessness (Hobbs, 2013: 122).

The observations made by youth work practitioners of an intensification of violence amongst a new emerging generation of teenagers in 2007 and 2008 are significant for several reasons. Firstly, they reiterate the findings of ethnographies in London at this time that recognise a distinct disconnection from formal work opportunities for a new generation of young people; thus supporting the argument that advanced neo-liberalism increases the individualist and entrepreneurial logic of working class children engaging in informal, risky and violent economies. Secondly, the consistency of such findings also highlight the need to take into account the accumulating impact of harms caused by advanced neo-liberalism. The long-term effects of consequences of deindustrialisation on young working class—especially black and mixed race young people—requires further interrogation, acknowledging that the shifting economies cause new challenges to which emerging generations must adapt. Thus grasping the 'realities' of 'knife crime' is not limited to opening out the processes of its (mis-)representation. Rather, beneath

---

[1] NEET—not in employment, education or training (Furlong, 2006; Rodger, 2008).

the headlines in 2007 and 2008 there were *real* and complex sociological shifts taking place in which the normalised brutalities of everyday life for many working class children created localised cultures of conflict and violence which many young people had to learn to negotiate.

3. Community Fragmentation.

Speaking with practitioners who grew up in the same south London areas as the young people with whom they work, several dimensions of the sociological shifts occurring were raised. Some drew attention to gentrification processes and the increasing visibility of social divisions and the strains of relative deprivation as formerly impoverished suburban areas came to be occupied by affluent residents and the businesses that serve them. Now aged in their forties the interviewees gestured to the streets where they grew up, describing them as 'unrecognisable' from their youth (see also Thapar, 2021: 136–161). One company director illustrated the different experience of a young person growing up in the divided economies of a London suburb saying; *'I can live on one road and I'm in absolute poverty and yet at the top of my road there's a coffee shop where cake, biscuit and a coffee is going to cost me £9 and I can see that there's people who can afford that and I can't'* (Interview L 01.05.2018).

The arrival of affluent neighbours was seen to change the sociological life of the suburbs and participants felt the disruption of their established communities had impacted young people's sense of belonging and strength of identity in the spaces earlier marked out as Caribbean and Black neighbourhoods. As one participant who grew up in Peckham described; *'we knew we were 'Other', you have to identify as 'Other', and we were all 'Other' together, you know? Even the African kids when they started coming they would pretend they were Jamaican because it was stronger to have our identity back then'* (Interview J 03.04.2018). There was a sense amongst those interviewed that there was a dispersion of the former 'black colony' that Hall et al. (1978) had described, as local economies changed, new migrant groups arrived and Black families themselves began to move out into the outer Suburbs.

Within these demographic changes (along with the economic shifts detailed above) practitioner interviewees suggested that the broader informal structures and youth-collective identities which had dominated everyday life for young people in the 1990s had became destabilised, leading local groups to fracture into smaller groupings located in more specific localities (even postcodes). It was generally agreed by those interviewed that these new, younger, more localised groups were significantly different to their predecessors:

> *I remember a time when then youngers got youngers but they were totally different to what the Peckham boys used to be. The original Peckham boys were older, it was different, and yeah they were on a few things, making money and that but they weren't crazy like these kids today. There's just too many of these little gangs now and no one can go anywhere.* (Interview J 03.04.2018)

Exploring the specifics of this example further, the interviewee was encouraged to say more about what the Peckham Boys were like and what areas this collective covered. His answers, along with corroborating accounts from others who grew up in the same area, provide an interesting case in point. The interviewee explained that the collaboration known as 'the Peckham boys' was originally a Southwark-wide group culture of collective pride and masculine identity to which temporal or permanent affiliation fostered a kind of loyalty to the area, safe movement in the home-borough, and a pastime of rivalry with outsiders. The biggest rivalry facing the original collective was with the 'Ghetto Boys', a name that primarily involved young people from the broad area of the neighbouring borough of Lewisham:

> *One of the things we used to do when we were around 14, 15, this would've been about 1995 or something, was we'd all sneak to Ghetto, which was Lewisham, and we'd spray paint 'Peckham Boys' on the bridges and they hated that, there was one at the end of Lewisham High Street we used to do. And that was dangerous because if we got caught it would be a serious fight.* (Interview J 03.04.2018)

Interviewees described how the instability of the group structures in the mid-2000s, due partly to the changing population and gentrification of the inner suburbs, caused a fragmentation of both the Peckham

Boys and Ghetto groups as restructuring created smaller collectives of more localised groups. The youth workers were asked if they could name the groups of young people they had worked with during the heightened violence of 2007 and 2008 and from their answers it was possible to piece together the following. The former collective known as 'Peckham Boys' in the 1990s had separated by the 2000s into; the Original Peckham Boys, Black Gang Ryders, Spare No-1, Shoot Instant, Pecknarm Young Gunners, Anti, Drugz Funz Armz, Pecknarm Killerz, Lettsom Gs, Crane Block, and Stick'em up klick. Meanwhilst Lewisham's 'Ghetto Boys' collective had divided into; Ghetto Boys, Shower, Anti-Shower, Catford Wildcats, Black Mafia, Brockley Mandem, Brocktown, Deptford Boys, Deptford Marlies, Hells Hustlerz, Monson Bloodset, Pepys Gang Bangers, Shankers and Gunners and the Money Makers.

From knowledge of the participants it can be surmised that within one generation the two collective identities that organised the movement of young people across all of Southwark and Lewisham had split into at least twenty-five rival groups. Analysing the self-defined labels of these groups there is a notable shift in discourse to reference violence, drugs and weapons as representative descriptors. The original name 'Peckham Boys' inferred the area and a sense of masculinity, and 'Ghetto Boys' added a sense of toughness and style, but those that followed are distinct in their provocation. Several of the new group names make direct reference to killing in the identification of their group, perhaps suggesting that a more aggressive and defensive form of territoriality defined this era.

The inference from interviews with practitioners is that in the mid-2000s the rivalry between Peckham and Lewisham had transformed into intense intra-borough fighting between closely situated smaller groups of young people. The realities of interpersonal violence (with or without knives) were that the changing maps of the city increased the likelihood of daily conflict greatly. For many young people living in these conditions, just going to school or visiting friends involved crossing invisible boundaries of fiercely defended areas.

The fear and daily anxiety of coming up against groups identifying themselves as 'killerz' and 'shankers' was one inescapable reality for young people at this time and accounts from practitioners suggest it severely limited young people's movement and access to London-wide opportunities. Whilst societal reaction to 'knife crime' draws attention to 'gangs' as a correlate of knife offending, it fails to see beyond the labels to recognise the sociological changes that caused the instability in the organisation of communities and increasing the essential vulnerability of young people moving through these divided and contested areas. This alternative reality of 'knife crime' suggests further research is required into the long-term impacts of gentrification and regeneration, especially its impact on marginalised groups which are precariously dependent on local resources and informal community relationships.

4. *Lucrative business and Pyramid schemes*

The last theme identified in interview data in relation to the critical years 2007 and 2008 was the consistent explanation of violence between young people as a symptom of heightened recruitment and new entrepreneurial practices in the informal economy and drug market of the 2000s. It was the opinion of many of the youth practitioners interviewed that the introduction of expensive mobile phone technology incentivised street robberies at this time, and that changing UK drug markets increased the recruitment of younger children by older teens and young people in their twenties. These ideas will be explored here in relation to existing research on informal markets, in order to assess, from the available interview data, the precise realities of 'knife crime' that young people were experiencing in London around 2007 and 2008.

Several ex-youth offending officers placed crucial significance to the advancement of mobile technologies in understanding increasing violence at this time. One described the increase in violence in 2007 as characterised by a shift 'from anti-social behaviour to street robberies' that was inspired by the release of iPods; '*Now people were walking around with 500, 600 or 1000 pounds gadgets in their pockets*' (Interview S 21.02.2018). The participant went on to point out that adults and organised crime networks were central in incentivising the 'quick cash' of mobile phone and iPod robberies but were not held accountable:

...adults are complicit in this, because there were so many shops locally - even now - who are allowing children to rob phones, walk in, exchange them for cash and send the phones abroad and have them re-chipped. And from an organised criminal perspective nobody was taking down these shops. (Interview S 21.02.2018)

The development of a lucrative industry relying on robbery that in turn increased knife carrying and use amongst young people, is an interesting observation by practitioners. It is true that the explosion of personal technologies in digital music players and mobile telephones is an aspect often overlooked in the discussion of knife crime in 2007/2008. The popular Blackberry smartphone was worth £400 when it was released in 2002, the first Apple iPod cost £300 in 2001 with a new generation produced every year, whilst the first Apple iPhone cost £500 in 2007. It is highly likely that the popularity of portable technologies and their high retail value incentivised street robberies at this time and that the ease of converting stolen phones and iPods into quick cash was a catalyst for violence amongst low-level criminal enterprises at this time.

Interviewees also drew attention to the deepening contradictions between the aspirations of young people looking to prosper in criminal syndicates and the realities of the limited opportunities available for success in these enterprises. Many felt that younger and more easily influenced young people were being targeted for recruitment into drug dealing enterprises at this time and being exploited by older (late teens and early twenties) young people who were themselves struggling to achieve success in these risky markets. Long before the label 'County Lines' emerged to define this form of devolved criminal enterprise, it was becoming the modus operandi of many drug dealing operations. One interviewee described the young people he worked with in 2007 as; *'hugely vulnerable! Easy pickings for the older lot'* (Interview N 03/04/2018).

Analysing such comments in the context of existing research (Clement, 2010; Densley, 2012; Hobbs, 2013) it can be inferred that the observed shift towards recruiting younger, more vulnerable children as 'easy pickings' at this time was one consequence of the stagnation of previously transient deviancy. As mentioned previously, the 'olders' with larger profit margins in the distribution chain, who traditionally left vacancies as they matured into the legitimate adult work culture (or were imprisoned, or died), increasingly began to continue occupying the higher 'gang' levels indefinitely. Applying the work of Densley (2012) on informal market structures, the conditions in 2007 and 2008 described by interviewees can be understood through the image of a drug dealing pyramid scheme; a multi-level marketing system that puts more emphasis upon the recruiting distributors than on the selling products (Densley, 2012: 55):

> If the basic idea is for sellers to recruit more sales persons, then rather than expanding the client base they are increasing internal competition. Only those who control the gang and supply the drugs at the top profit by having more Youngers trying to out-sell each other. For those at the bottom, the gang becomes an exercise in survival of the fittest… Gang structure serves a purpose: the rich get richer. (ibid.)

In relation to the comments made by interviewees in this research this suggests that *younger* young people came to be increasingly exploited by *older* young people within the drug market at this time. The implications of these realities in the intricate lives and interactions of young people provide alternative explanations for increased violence developing at this time. It has been previously argued that the frustration at the rigged systems of the drug economy is most commonly expressed as violence *between* low-end distributors—because 'Youngers climb the hierarchy in competition with their peers rather than their elders' (Densley, 2012: 56). The analysis of this interview data suggests that the intense recruitment of younger young people into competitive drug distribution networks, along with the robbery of mobile phones, provide lucrative incentives for criminal enterprises that increased the likelihood of knife carrying and knife violence in the everyday lives of young people throughout this period.

In summary, the analysis of interviews with youth work practitioners suggests several alternative realities to the context of violence in 2007 and 2008 that are not represented in the interpretation of acts as 'knife crime' at this time. Recognising the sociological shifts caused by; the death of iconic figures, the destabilising affects of proactive policing, structural changes in drug distribution, new criminal enterprises and the long-term impact of gentrification on inner-suburb communities—practitioners on the ground provide a 'realist' perspective on increased violence that goes beneath and beyond the knife crime label and its selectively constructed meaning.

The failure to identify and investigate these developments entailed a devastating neglect of vulnerable children in this moment. Instead, fatal stabbings in the mid-2000s were understood as distinct 'stand-alone' incidents of 'knife crime', an enduringly anachronistic form of interpersonal violence that 'spoke for itself' and the moral mileu occupied by its perpetrators and, more controversially, its victims. It was ultimately explained away through highly racialised processes of interpretation signalling notions of cultural deficit, racial pathology and social inferiority. The narrow focus on a deadly 'knife culture' itself negated any sense of societal obligation to evaluate the policies and social harm that had led to an emerging generation of actors who were younger, fragmented, further marginalised, increasingly vulnerable, exposed to extreme violence and at risk of exploitation. Furthermore, as earlier chapters have detailed, the response to 'knife crime' as it was understood in 2008 authorised excessive state force and discriminatory police practices targeted at young people in deprived areas. This issue was another aspect of the reality of 'knife crime' that young people themselves were asked about during the research. Their comments, reported in the next section, reflect often troubling experiences of stop and search and police power from 2008 onwards.

Confrontation and Hostility; Experiencing Exceptional Policing

In chapter five we examined the dramatic increase in stop and search in 2008 and the related extension of police powers in relation to ideas regarding *symbolic criminalisation* and the function of law and order at a time of economic uncertainty. Whilst we have addressed the broader social and economic context of policing at this time it is important to complement this analysis with a sense of what it felt like to experience those searches. Accordingly professionals working in the Youth Justice System in 2008 were asked about any significant changes in policing that they witnessed during the crucial phase of the 'war on knife crime'. It was abundantly clear that interviewees consistently recognised a distinct shift in the nature of police interactions with young people throughout this period.

In their responses practitioners described a new dynamic during the searches that they felt directly related to the authority and urgency that tackling 'knife crime' bestowed on searching officers. One YOS Intervention Officer described the new offences being processed by the Youth Offending Team in 2008 and how the speed of the government-to-policing reaction didn't allow time for training or education around legalities and rights:

Q: Did you notice an increase in stop and search in 2008 in response to Knife crime?

We definitely saw it in Triage, we saw more young people that had been stopped and searched. It was weird stuff like: "why are you here?" "Oh, I had a compass in my bag"… "right.. Did you pull that compass out on somebody?" "Nah, I just had a compass in my bag and I got stopped and searched and here I am"

Q: But you're allowed a compass for school right?

Well… yes… but this is it, 'bladed article' they would call it. So yeah, we started to see that as like, it was the new thing. Not that it was a new thing, but police were like "this is going to save everything" and you're like "oh ok, this is interesting". And I think what was happening was, not only were young people being stopped and searched but they didn't know their rights. And I think police were playing on that – you don't really understand your rights so we're just going to do it and that's where confrontation would come. Because what would happen was that, police would stop and search a young person, they wouldn't know how to articulate a simple question of "why?"

Q: What about the young person?

Yeh, "why am I being stopped and searched?" and "what is the process?" and "what am I allowed to carry and what am I not allowed to carry?". It

was almost like the government were like "we've got a knife crime problem"
– bang! (Interview F 29.01.2018)

The confusion over what was legal during this episode of blanket Section 60 searches exacerbated confrontation and heightened the tension in the interaction between police and adolescents. The speed of the response didn't allow time for young people to develop a sense of their rights, they were not equipped with the language or experience to communicate their frustrations and it was felt by practitioners that this inexperience was exploited by the police during searches.

The same question was put to a Youth Justice Resettlement Manager in 2018, and whilst pointing out that he felt there was some justification for increasing searches because 'the youths were carrying more weapons out of fear' (Interview D 16.02.2018) he also recognised a shift in the dynamic of the searches which began to connect the experiences of Black children with those of their parents.

> *...what they were doing was just stopping and just frisking, there was no communication. And officers weren't trained properly before they did it and then they're given this blanket responsibility and the authority to just go and pull up whoever they suspect to be somebody who is carrying something. And they're gripping these boys, getting their hands all over them. Its violent, its intrusive and if you really have done nothing wrong that is a tipping point for you which connects to what your fathers and mothers have told you about what police were like in the 70's and 80s and you say 'now I've had my experience.'* (Interview D 16.02.2018)

The frequency of searches increased, the powers used appeared more discriminatory and the dynamic of the interaction was more aggressive—and yet there was public consensus and support for it as a supposed urgent response to 'knife crime'. As discussed in chapter five, the renewed commitment to stop and search from 2016 onwards has produced similar experiences for contemporary young people. The following excerpts were comments from two young people during focus groups in 2018 talking about their own experiences of stop and search:

...one time I was at a party and someone had a comb in their back pocket and then five police pushed them against the wall and were like "what's that sharp object in your trousers?". I feel like they assaulted him kinda, just to get that comb out his pocket. And I didn't think that a comb - that's used to comb your hair - that the police would portray that like it was a knife. (FG 10 20.11.2018)

...at our school we had a 'stop and search' day thing, and they kind of covered it with "oh everyone's getting searched". At the beginning of the day they had that thing what you walk through [knife arch], so everybody had to walk through it. And you could basically see that they were basically stopping the Black children, the boys, they were basically stopping them and searching them when everybody else just had to walk through. It was like... even if you're coming into a school and seeing a bunch of Black children you'll still automatically think "oh they're bringing knives to school they're the ones causing the trouble." (FG2 26.11.2018)

The language young people used to describe how police 'portray' innocuous objects as knives (FG10 20.11.2018) or racial profiling in their deployment of knife arches (FG2 26.11.2018) suggests that contemporary stop and search continues to involve a sense of being taken advantage of and manipulated. These accounts demonstrate just a few of the practical realities of searching for knives; that the expectation of a knife provides justification for excessive force during searches and that the seemingly indiscriminate knife arches can be used as a cover for discriminatory search practices.

Beyond the arrest rates and measurements of disproportionality discussed in chapter five, the experiences of practitioners and young people reflect the realities of stop and search in connection to 'knife crime' that characterised police tactics. Emboldened by the political and public commitment to a proactive policing of 'knife crime', stop and search not only extends the consensus favouring forceful proactivity, but also facilitates the criminalisation of Black children in a number of ways. Beneath the generic function of 'policing the crisis', the deployment of 'knife crime' searches and the anticipation of knives in police work, represents an intensified reality of surveillance and criminalisation experienced especially by young black people.

Interviewing the young people it became apparent that these realities of 'knife crime' policing connected to the historic Black experiences of politics, policing and resistance in the UK (Elliott-Cooper, 2021), yet our young interviewees often had little access to these alternative narratives themselves. This issue, concerning the legacy of racism and anti-racist struggles and the consequences for young people today, is an issue developed next in the chapter.

Institutionalised Anti-Racism and Depoliticising 'knife Crime'

The focus group elements of the research with young people began with a presentation that included local histories of political struggle and Black activism, connecting the construction of 'knife crime' to a history of 'Othering' and the community resistance that was mobilised against racist and hostile policing of the community in the 1970s and 1980s. In the ten presentations delivered to 16–18 year- olds, the young people consistently commented that they enjoyed this aspect of the session. None of the seventy-eight young participants had heard about the 1980s riots or the developing Black resistance during the decade, despite many of them recognising the streets and landmarks in the black and white photos they were shown. In the discussions that followed many young people said they wished these histories were taught at school and wondered if it was being deliberately kept from them. When asked if they felt their current experiences related to the histories with which they had been presented, one group responded:

YP3:   *It looks different back then. Like, certain areas were more White then—it wasn't socially integrated.*

YP2:   *I think people don't tell us about what happened in the 70's and 80's because they're embarrassed.*

Researcher: That's interesting

YP2:   *Like, they had a political party that was being openly racist!*

YP1:   *Yeah…But they do that now!*

Researcher: Perhaps the language has changed so it seems different now.

YP3:   *I think that who they're racist to, as well, has changed too. Because at first they were racist to Black people more but now they've sort of shifted towards Muslim people - so the ways and who they're profiling has changed. And people can be acting like they're not racist in person but then get on social media and get together with other people and share stuff and say stuff that's very racist. And they can be like "I live in a multicultural area so how can I be racist?"* (FG1 31.10.18)

During this short interaction young people demonstrated that despite not having engaged with this type of material before, they were beginning to connect their histories and experiences to the changing influences of social integration, multiculturalism, social media and the shifting racisms they undoubtedly recognise. The comments made and their reflections upon critical political issues during the focus groups suggested that the young people welcomed the opportunity to explore these connections but that they had few opportunities to do so—certainly not within the formal educational curriculum.

Similarly, during focus groups young people were able to draw connections between broader aspects of racism and the heavy policing experienced by Black people. One participant described:

> *…Black people are always seen as second, or inferior to White people. So in terms of when they do stops and searches they're always quite firm and quite hostile – its to do with racism but I feel like the police are not really good at what they do… I feel like because Black people have that stereotype of being inferior to White people then they [police] use Black people as scapegoats and they use that for crime in order to impress and supposedly get their reputation up.* (FG9:20.11.2018)

In other words, knife crime provided police with an opportunity to assert themselves. Young people's responses suggested that, despite being exposed to the realities of a socially constructed 'Black criminality', and their underlying sense that these experiences were not appropriate, fair or right, critical anti-racist understandings to enable them to process these issues are not currently being made available to them through their formal or informal education systems. Recognising that young people are known to be disproportionately subjected to discriminatory stop and search and sometimes aggressive and hostile policing, and are likewise targeted by youth justice practitioners for intervention on the topic of 'knife crime' specifically,[2] it is significant that these themes, contexts and histories are not being presented to them by the adults who currently work and live around them. Exploring these aspects of young people's experiences through our original interview data with practitioners and young people themselves, it can be seen that the absence of critical anti-racist approaches in youth and community work is symptomatic of a broader discourse of race relations (Shukra, 1998) reflected in much official practice. Yet the professionals interviewed were primarily Black men (fifteen of the twenty interviewed), all of whom having worked in various roles seeking to impact young people's lives through the existing structures of the Youth Justice System. There was a reoccurring sense from their responses that they felt they were not only attempting to change young people but also the youth justice institutions themselves through their work. Yet many felt particularly constrained in this role. Nevertheless, many described their commitment to the institutions through an idea that '*change happens from the inside*' (D 16.02.2018), characterising themselves as '*the bridge between local initiatives and organisations*' (interview B 25.01.2018), '*a voice that will speak for the voiceless*' (Interview F 29.01.2018).

Some confessed that their best work was achieved when the structures were subverted or rules bent, but ultimately their job required professionalism and prioritised intervention on specific bureaucratic terms. Within these constraints, practitioners expressed their matter-of-fact acknowledgement of a flawed system, of an impenetrable 'police culture' that overshadowed their efforts of community and criminal justice cohesion, and a multifaceted institutional racism that was hindering their work at every level.

The difficulty and desperation of embodying this contradiction were expressed by one Company Director who recounted multiple times he

---

[2] These issues and the targeting of young black people for 'educational' and 'knife awareness' interventions are developed further in the next chapter on the 'knife crime industry'.

was aggressively stopped and searched in front of young people he worked with. On one such occasion he had just delivered a session on stop and search, defending police actions and encouraging cooperation, only to be aggressively searched in front of the young participants when leaving the youth centre. He concluded:

> *Its very hard to maintain your integrity, its very hard to keep pushing these key and positive messages because that is one of the only solutions we have... its very difficult.* (Interview L 01.05.2018)

Many of our research participants were highly skilled and experienced Black managers who had committed themselves to this frustrating tension of negotiating government machinery in order to reach young people and mediate interventions that were *at least* capable of achieving small, individual changes—knowing that without their contribution and compromise the youth work delivered would be inept and ineffective. But handling cases of severe child violence, within the inadequate structures of the institution, was often a difficult contradiction for genuine, caring leaders to resolve.

One participant spoke candidly of eventually leaving what he described as 'the frontline' of the Youth Offending Service, suicidal with Post Traumatic Stress Disorder. He attributed this to receiving no professional supervision and a persistent lack of recognition by his employers and managers of the intense social issues he confronted on a daily basis. Another manager described how he decided to redirect his commitment into pastoral Christianity with an understanding that the heavy case loads and the nearly exclusive focus on specific behavioural issues such as 'knife carrying' were restricting his potential to effect '*transformations of the heart*'.

Practitioners interviewed were socially and politically aware—often drawing on post-colonial interpretations of power and policing in the communication of their frustrations. For example, one former police officer who has worked in 'knife crime' prevention with young people for many years described his frustration with the institutional response to police racism thus:

...to get a good understanding of racism and police racism and personal racism you need to understand what it is – Really, I think it's got its roots in the British empire and colonialism... So if the diversity training of police officers doesn't touch on what the British Empire was, and meant and the vestiges of colonialism and neo-colonialism in today's world, then we're completely wasting our time. So it's just like, going through the motions and pretending that you're doing diversity training when you're not even beginning to touch on it. (Interview K 12.01.2018)

It is, perhaps, curious that practitioners experiencing the everyday confrontations, restrictions and frustrations of a legacy of imperialism and racism were not also organising to impart this knowledge onto young people facing the brunt of police brutality at this time. It is likely that between their existing occupational roles, the bureaucratic audit of youth justice processes and their heavy caseloads, such 'digressions' were both officially discouraged and allowed little time. It has been argued elsewhere that the movement towards Black representation in state institutions as a means of achieving equality, led to an increasing dependence on an official race-relations machinery for council grants, resources and facilities, and this integration restricted and shaped the way Black leaders responded to discriminatory institutional practices (Shukra, 1998: 62). During the 1980s, '*the movement against racism was bureaucratised through integration of black people into local government machinery... black people came to redefine their objectives such that small changes rather than social transformation became their concern*' (Shukra, 1998: 62).

Interpreting of feedback arising during the youth focus groups within this context of the institutionalisation of Black politics, whilst acknowledging the deep frustrations of Black practitioners working within these structures, several issues arise. Firstly, whilst the experiences of racial discrimination and police harassment have continued for emerging generations of young people, the political articulation of these interactions as racist and imperialist has, in many ways, become less accessible to those subjected to these practices. This has left contemporary youth alienated from the histories that contextualise their experiences and thereby restricting their capacity to organise in proactive resistance. The substantial jolt that the #*BlackLivesMatter* movement has brought to these arrangements has been substantial, although its sustainability is yet to be seen.

Secondly, the absence of significant anti-racist progress, due in part to the institutionalisation of race politics, has made it increasingly difficult for effective Black practitioners to sustain their work within the inherent contradictions of their practice. Accounts by practitioners in this research suggest that this untenable position has led to experienced Black leaders moving to different roles and away from direct and official youth work interventions. These dilemmas within the context of contemporary youth justice work were made particularly apparent during interviews with practitioners as they recalled the increasing specialisation of 'gang' and 'knife crime' intervention work with young people in the 2000s.

> **Learning Exercise 16: Analysis Activity—What Did Our Interviewees Think?**
> Looking at the results of interviews with youth work professionals, what do you think that they identify as the crucial social changes taking place over the years covered by the research?
> How do their explanations compare with your own sense of social change?
> Perhaps ask someone from an older generation—a parent or other family member—see how they account for the social changes under discussion. Compare and contrast the different explanations you encounter.

Specialisation in Youth Justice; 'Knife Crime Work'

Unlike traditional youth work, work with young people within the youth justice system has always been a targeted practice, structured around either punitive or preventative strategies and aimed at young offenders or young people 'at risk' of offending. However, interviews with youth justice managers and directors of organisations suggest there was a significant shift in the specialisation of crime prevention youth practice in the late 2000s. Participants described an increasing '*offence specific*' approach within the youth offending service in which 'knife crime' and 'gangs' became centrally organising features of their intervention practice and of the targeted project funding streams upon which they were increasingly reliant.

Many of the practitioners spoke fondly of a time when their work with young offenders was less structured and activities were organised around young people's interests and what they enjoyed doing. One former youth offending Manager reflected upon the work he did before the emergence of more targeted 'knife crime prevention':

Q: …So there was concern about street robberies when you started working there in 2005, at that point were there no knife crime prevention projects?

S: *No, what we had was 'RAP'; Resettlement Aftercare Provision. And the Resettlement Aftercare Provision was again, money that got released by New Labour - it was to bring a more creative approach to working with young people who were either at risk of offending or young people that were involved. We were working with the children who were offending. When we first started we were taking children to Alton Towers and my manager would say "Just book!" and I would say what's the budget? And there was no budget. Book me a nice 12-seater [minibus] and then what about food? What do you think they'd like? I think they would love West Indian. Cool. So we'll drop 200 for the West Indian. Where do you want to go? Alton Towers. We'll take them all the Alton Towers and spend a 1000… Just do it. Do whatever you want. And I do believe that was some of the best work we did. Because the children stopped coming to the YOT just for their order it became like the new youth club. Which is difficult to say because it is an institution about the management of children who have committed criminal acts so you shouldn't be enticing children in who haven't committed crime to start coming* (Interview S 21.02.2018).

Although reluctant to equate the punitive or intervention strategies of 2005 to the open access approach of a 'youth club' this practitioner described this as 'some of the best work' they did and went on to explain his efforts to recreate this delivery style in projects later developed for 'gang intervention'. When discussing why he thought provision had subsequently shifted to a more offence-related approach he suggested this was part of a new model influenced by wider policy changes:

> *They started to look at risk, need and responsivity around interventions - The RNR principle. And that basically means that any intervention delivered to a young person or an offender, you have to understand the risks that they present, you have to fully understand their needs and the programme has to be responsive to who they are... you can't just provide 'Alton Towers' you now need to be specific about particular offences, you need to provide an intervention that matches that.'* (S 21.02.2018)

This shift towards offence specific interventions described by participants created a demand for specially tailored 'knife crime prevention' programmes within the youth justice system. Practitioners described that from around 2009 'knife crime prevention' projects began to emerge and were delivered by both youth offending practitioners and external privately contracted companies. Devising services in response to the growing demand and the availability of earmarked funding made available for 'knife crime' work (often supplemented by branded 'anti-knife crime' merchandising) was described by participants as an 'attractive market' for entrepreneurial organisations. As one Company Director described:

> *...Everyone suddenly wanted to open a business "I run a youth organisation" "I do this, I do this" oh really? , ok no problem... It was like, yeah, anyone can work with gangs. Anyone can work in knife crime. Forget what you know, forget your understanding, forget anything - you go and grab a few trustees set up a committee, apply to the Big Lottery, make it sound great, a bit of funding – we now do gang work. Great!... So there's a whole economy being built around this problem now. There's millions of organisations that have been set up, there's heads of services now set up for this, special this, special that, trauma informed workers - you just name it – if you suddenly stop the problem, you've now got an unemployment problem for all of these other people!* (Interview O 10.05.2018)

It is significant that participants drew attention to the financial dependency that developed around the valorisation of work that directly responded to and specialised in 'knife crime'. In terms of how the construction of 'knife crime' was experienced on the ground, this specialisation of practice was influential for young people. The priority status of 'knife crime' funding at this time can be seen to transport the crime label from tabloid news and into institutional practice with very little adaptation or scrutiny. The work functioning under the same title as the moral panic itself came to dictate the content of projects working with young people, influencing the realities of children in contact with youth services, youth justice and mainstream education.

During an interview, one former Youth Offending Service manager who had been responsible for developing knife crime prevention and probation courses, ventured his opinion on the effectiveness of this shift towards specialisation. He replied:

> [*the knife crime prevention project*] *worked but we need to change it up a little bit because actually we're focusing on the - We're not focusing on the causes we're focusing on the issue. "you're here because of knife crime, but really we wanna talk about why you carried the knife in the first place"*

Q: You think that's what it was or what it should've been?

> *I think that's what it should've been. It wasn't that. It was more like "right let's bring in [ex 'gang member'] to tell you his experience and shock you, let me bring in the ambulance staff to shock you, lets bring in the police so they can tell you what's going down" instead of actually saying "you know what, why are you here in the first place and lets work backwards". Yeah, I think we dealt with the 'issue'... The problem with all these interventions is they focus on the behaviour, that's the problem.*

Q: Maybe that's the impact the 'knife crime' label had?

Well that's what the money was for, and that's what we were called to do (Interview N 03/04/2018).

This assessment of the design of prevention projects reveals several realities regarding how 'knife crime' came to impact on young people and practitioners at this time. Firstly, it demonstrates how the re-articulation of intervention work as 'offence specific' in reality grouped together the various offences of individual young people through the idea of a generic crime type socially constructed by a problematic and stigmatised label. Secondly, it describes a set template for 'knife crime' intervention work drawing upon shock and fear as the method of behaviour change, influencing the content of discussion and imagery that young people were exposed to through these interventions. And finally, crucially, it revealed the restrictive impact the label and its response had on effective practice. These comments suggest that even when practitioners felt they were not following the most effective approach to the problems they perceived amongst young people, they were tied to the inappropriate methods dictated by the social construction of 'knife crime' because '*that's what the money was for*'.

The continued prosperity of industries functioning under the banner of 'knife crime' is a reality of the response that will be returned to in the following chapter, whilst the final discussions of this chapter focus on an analysis of comments arising from the focus groups with the young people themselves. The consequences of the incorporation of 'knife crime' as a priority issue in policing, policy and youth practice, as discussed above, impacted on the lived realities of young people very significantly. Young people's responses during the focus groups reveal several crucial points for consideration, reminding us how these changes have been experienced in their lived realities.

Resilience and Retribution: Focus Group Analysis

During this stage of the research initial findings from the reinterpretation of the 'knife crime' phenomenon described in our early chapters were presented to ten groups of young people in both mainstream and informal youth work settings. In reflecting on this process and the findings of group discussions there are several important themes and observations to discuss. The first of these concerns the taken-for-granted familiarity that young people had with the language and methods of 'knife crime' interventions themselves. The knife crime 'industry' was well known territory for them.

Schools and youth centres were provided with a detailed description of the planned research and its aims and objectives in the initial stages of visits. However, by the time this was communicated to the young people, ahead of ahead of the actual sessions, it had all been abbreviated for them as: 'knife crime research'. As a result of this, young people had made certain judgments about what was to come and were already anticipating the content of presentations. As a result the sessions often began with a disinterested and indifferent audience who gradually engaged as the more critical content became apparent. On one occasion this growing enthusiasm led to a spontaneous round of applause by the young participants upon the completion of the presentation—a particular highlight of this research project. The difference between the expected and actual content of this 'knife crime' presentation was often one of the first things young participants commented on in the group discussions that followed. As one sixth-form student remarked; '*When they said you were coming to talk about knife crime we thought it was going to be like those police assemblies we get*' (FG9 20.11.2018).

Talking at length with groups about their previous interactions with 'knife crime' assemblies and projects there was consistent discontent with the delivery and assumptions contained within the usual presentations they received. Their experiences ranged from professionals who they found insulting and patronising in the simplistic advice they gave, to sickening feelings arising from being shown graphic photos of knife injuries. Young people's gloomy anticipation of the presentation they expected demonstrates not only a familiarity with the concept 'knife crime' but also profound dissatisfaction with the prevailing approaches of existing interventions. This consistent theme was one of many that emerged across the variety of settings and contexts of the focus groups.

Although the presentation focused on the labelling processes and responses to 'knife crime', young people invariably also wanted to discuss causes and solutions to violence between young people in the discussions that followed. Economic causes were frequently offered; with young people able to explain with depth and clarity the accessibility and attraction of 'fast money' compared to the low wages or high tuition fees of 'slow money'. As one young person suggested, *'you can be a rich criminal or a poor graduate'* (FG5 13.11.2018).

Young people described with insight the processes through which they were groomed into drug dealing by 'olders', the increased likelihood of contact with predatory dealers in densely populated, deprived housing estates, and the absence of supervision as parents worked long hours on low pay to provide for their families. In contrast, participants never suggested economic or structural solutions to the issues they discussed. Variations on comments such as *'more activities for young people'* (FG6 13.11.2018), *'more education on the risks'* (FG9 20.11.2018) or *'move away from dangerous areas'* (FG10 20.11.2018) were common during discussions, centring the importance of the individual's responsibility to access reformative provisions or to remove themselves from harm.

During one focus group a participant explained the aspect of himself that he felt had kept him from becoming violent. Tapping his finger on the side of his head he said; *'I'm very strong up here, mentally. Some people are more resilient than others'* (FG5 13.11.2018). The use of the word 'resilient' is particularly interesting considering its prominence in the language of 'knife crime' prevention and intervention. Even when structural solutions were hinted at, young people repeatedly returned to a discourse of individual responsibility (see Furlong & Cartmel, 1997), with one group suggesting *'the government haven't got any money to help'* (FG9 20.11.2018). Demonstrating the extension of a fatalistic individualism into the understanding of proximal violence one participant described the recent deaths of local young people saying; *'when they die, although it's deep yeah, but, they had it coming'* (FG2 26.11.2018). Other members of the group concurred.

This assertion of a particular type of young person that willingly engaged in extreme violence and thus deserving of retribution was a consistent theme during focus groups. Sometimes referred to by participants as 'gang bangers' or 'nutters', they were spoken about as a small minority, often with references to poor mental health and impulsive violent behaviours, and were seen to pose a great threat to the majority of young people. When focus group members were asked whether they would ever approach the police to remove the threat of this identified minority or to refer them to mental health services, the suggestion was met with laughter. One young person explained it as follows: '*but the police treat me like dirt and then I'm going to basically put my life in their hands because I've snitched? Nah, how can they protect me? Do they even want to protect me? That's nuts!*' (FG 9 20.11.2018).

This reaction, in line with previous research (Bowling & Phillips, 2002; Densley, 2012; Kushnick, 1999), suggests that the over-policing of young people, particularly Black children, has had lasting implications for their accessing of protection through legal routes. Five of the ten focus groups were conducted with young people within mainstream educational settings. Their shared experiences of stop and search and the suspicion and humiliation that often crosses school gates highlighted the continuing dilemma of a 'non-intelligence led' proactive policing that cannot differentiate between young people who are 'high risk' and young people who are 'at risk'.

Overall the focus groups provided an essential contextualisation of the findings of this research. They reaffirmed how the multiple realities of 'knife crime' as both a tangible threat and a societal response are navigated in the everyday lives of young people. Living with the threat of extreme violence and with little trust or faith in the ability of the police to enforce justice, it is staggering—although not surprising—that many young people have come to understand the deaths of children as self determined or 'deserved'. This reality, as described by young people, acts as an urgent reminder of the still recurring and self-defeating material impacts of our *policing* [of] *the crisis*.

Conclusion

The first hand data analysed in this chapter has presented an empirical case establishing the alternative understandings of 'knife crime'. Interviews and focus groups provided a crucial context for the acts defined as 'knife crime' presenting multiple realities that have typically been obscured by the dominant tabloid (mis-)representations of a youth phenomenon. In this phase of the research, it is suggested that beneath the headlines of the late 2000s there were *real* and complex sociological shifts taking place during which the normalised brutalities of everyday life for many working class children became more intense.

The practitioners recalled with ease and specificity the developments in the informal economy, which fragmented affiliations as well as generational shifts which redefined the experiences of young people during this period. The changes in youth justice work that increasingly focused on knife offending were also discussed, along with young people's troubling experiences of increasing rates of stop and search.

Interpreting these findings it is evident that the multiple, overlapping realities of knife crime are not equally represented by the label. The dominant representation of 'knife crime' is that defined by the tabloid press throughout the moral panic, and it is this version of reality that dictates the specialisation of youth work intervention practices and the hostile attitude of the police. The discussions during focus groups suggested that young people were still navigating the contradictions between lived realities and 'knife crime' representations, tasked with trying to keep themselves safe from normalised everyday violence in deprived areas of the city, whilst being subjected to discriminatory and confrontational policing in the name of 'knife crime prevention'.

Practitioners who were aware of the contradictions of 'knife crime' work at this time were seen to remain committed through necessity and lack of alternatives. They described their positions as '*the only solutions we have*' and '*what the money was for*'. The empirical phase of this research has emphasised the importance of radical approaches that look beyond constructed categories of criminality, to the realities of both the acts *and* the responses that define them. It is only this endeavour that reveals the very *real* harm caused by the label 'knife crime' and the responses that it validates; exposing the true costs and consequences of this moral panic.

References

Alexander, C. (2008, June). (Re)thinking gangs. The Runnymede Trust.

Alexander, K., Entwisle, D., & Olson, L. (2014). The Long shadow. Sage.

Amnesty International. (2018, May). Trapped in the matrix: Secrecy, stigma, and bias in the Met's gangs database. Amnesty International.

Becker, H. S. (1963). The other side: Perspectives on deviance. The Free Press of Glencoe.

Blackman, S., & Rogers, R. (Eds.). (2017). Youth marginality in Britain: Contemporary studies of austerity. The Policy Press.

Bowling, B., & Phillips, C. (2002). Racism, crime and justice. Pearson.

Clement, M. (2010). Teenagers under the knife: A decivilising process. Journal of Youth Studies, 13(4), 439–451.

Cohen, S. (1972). Folk devils and moral panics: The creation of the Mods and Rockers. Oxon and Routledge.

Densley, J. A. (2012). The organisation of London's street gangs. Global Crime, 13(1), 42–64.

Furlong, A. (2006). Not a very NEET solution: Representing problematic labour market transitions among early school-leavers. Work, Employment and Society, 20(3), 553–569.

Furlong, A., & Cartmel, F. (1997). Young people and social change: Individualisation and risk in late modernity. Open University Press.

Gov.uk (2016). Lowest ever number of young people in custody. GOV.UK; Youth Justice Board Press. (online). Available at: https://www.gov.uk/government/news/lowest-ever-number-of-young-of-people-in-custody. Accessed 22 May 2018.

Hagedorn, J. (1988). People and folks: Gangs, crime and the underclass in Rustbelt city. Lakeview Press.

Hall, S., Roberts, B., Clarke, J., Jefferson, T., & Critcher, C. (1978). Policing the crisis: Mugging, the state, and law and order. MacMillan.

Harding, S. (2020). County lines: Exploitation and drug dealing among urban street gangs. Bristol University Press.

Hobbs, D. (2013). Lush life: Constructing organized crime in the UK (1st ed.). Oxford University Press.

Kintrea, K., Bannister, J., & Pickering, J. (2011). 'It's just an area—everybody represents it': Exploring young people's territorial behaviour in British cities. In B. Goldson (ed.), Youth in crisis: Gangs, territoriality and violence. Routledge.

Kushnick, L. (1999). 'Over policed and under protected': Stephen Lawrence, institutional and police practices. *Sociological Research Online, 4*(1), 156–166.

Macdonald, R., & Marsh, J. (2001). *Disconnected youth? Growing up in poor neighbourhoods.* Palgrave Macmillan.

Merton, R. K. (1948). The self-fulfilling prophecy. *The Antioch Review, 8*(2), 193–210.

Pitts, J. (2007). Americanization. In J. M. Hagedorn (Ed.), *Gangs in the global city: Alternatives to traditional criminology.* University of Illinois Press.

Rodger, J. (2008, December). The criminalisation of social policy. *Criminal Justice Matters, 74.*

Rutherford, A. (2002). *Growing out of crime: The new era?* Waterside Press.

Shukra, K. (1998). *The changing pattern of Black politics in Britain.* Pluto Press.

Smithson, H., Ralphs, R., & Williams, P. (2012). Used and abused: The problematic usage of gang terminology in the United Kingdom and its implications for ethnic minority youth. *British Journal of Criminology, 53,* 113–128. https://doi.org/10.1093/bjc/azs046

Spicer, J. (2021). *Policing county lines: Responses to evolving provincial drug markets.* Palgrave Macmillan.

Sproat, P. A. (2011). The serious and organised crime agency and the national crime squad: A comparison of their output from open source materials. *Policing and Society, 21*(3), 343–351.

Standing, G. (2011). *The precariat: The new dangerous class.* Bloomsbury.

Squires, P., & Stephen, D. (2005). *Rougher justice: Anti-social behaviour and young people.* Willan Publishing.

Thapar, C. (2021). *Cut short: Youth violence, loss and hope in the city.* Random House, Viking.

Wacquant, L. (2008). *Urban outcasts: A Comparative Sociology of urban marginality.* Polity Press.

8

A Joined-Up Approach to Sustainable Violence Prevention?

Knife Crime as a Public Health Issue

There has been much discussion, even advocacy, favouring a rebalancing of strategies for addressing knife-involved violence. Indeed, referring to the timeline that opened Chapter 5 (Fig. 5.1) almost two decades of 'knife crime' crisis, agitation, politicking, police action and criminal justice strategy have culminated in a new high-mark for knife violence, more knife murders, greater punitiveness (more people in prison and for longer sentences) but diminishing rates of cases cleared up (sanction-detections). To the timeline at the beginning of Chapter 5 (Fig. 5.1), as well as a declining commitment to neighbourhood crime prevention, rising crime and diminishing rates of crime detections, we could also add trends revealing increased custodial sentencing and for significantly longer periods (Allen & Kirk-Wade, 2020). Taken together these trends paint a picture of diminishing police effectiveness but increasing criminal justice punitiveness, a kind of 'ground zero' for reformers and the very antithesis of Waller's arguments in '*Less Law, More Order*' (2008), discussed later.

© The Author(s), under exclusive license to Springer Nature
Switzerland AG 2021
E. Williams and P. Squires, *Rethinking Knife Crime*,
https://doi.org/10.1007/978-3-030-83742-6_8

Clearly, despite all the enforcement-led action, something isn't working. Yet a complicating aspect associated with framing knife crime as a public health issue, in common with many related social problems, concerns the 'inverse care law' (Tudor Hart, 1971). Simply put, this 'law' argues that those most likely to be in need to health care support and resources are likely to be the least able or willing to access it (Appleby & Deeming, 2001). The people most likely to be involved in knife crime— either as perpetrators or victims—are the least likely to be engaged with health authorities, least likely to have trust and confidence in the police and, in both regards, are least likely to seek help (Pound, 2019). This is one of the reasons that care has to be taken not to erect barriers to health seeking (for example compromising confidentiality in data-sharing with law enforcement—an issue to which we will return).

In response, a variety of commentators have urged the adoption of a 'public health approach', dialling back the current emphasis on police enforcement-led interventions, which often appear to exacerbate problems, and instead they draw upon the insights of what is often referred to as 'the new' or 'critical public health' approaches (Peterson & Lupton, 1996). Advocacy on the part of 'public health' approaches to violence reflects a number of influences and has found support in many quarters, in particular the World Health Organisation (WHO), and the U.S. Centres for Disease Control (CDC) which have gained credibility and leverage (though not without criticism)[1] in helping address the phenomenon of gun violence as a public health issue in the USA. For many, the public health approach has the simple merit of shifting away from a predominantly police and enforcement driven or punitive perspective, and towards an approach that, whilst offering the promise of science, understands violence in a social context whilst establishing more progressive, evidence-based and, above all, *sustainable* solutions (Waller, 2019: xv). The fact that in the UK great success has been claimed for

---

[1] For a long time the CDC were Federally prevented in the USA from undertaking research into gun violence following legislation (the *Dickey Amendment*, 1996) backed by the NRA and a consortium of right-wing lobby groups which sought to prevent Federal budgets being used to advocate gun control—even though epidemiological work had already demonstrated how lower rates of gun violence could be achieved (Kellerman & Reay, 1986). Congress revised the law in 2018 and gun *safety* research became fundable once again in 2020 (Metzl, 2018).

the 'radically new' Public Health model adopted in Glasgow/Strathclyde further has recommended it to the violence prevention research and policy community (Astrup, 2019; Roberts, 2019: 98).

Superficially a focus on health is also reflected in the occasional references to knife crime and violence as an 'epidemic' (Gilligan, 1997; Squires, 2009; Haylock et al., 2020: 1453), indeed, 'our generation's epidemic' as the Youth Select Committee termed it (British Youth Council, 2019) with all that this might imply about its transmission, and epidemiology (Slutkin, 2013; Slutkin et al., 2018; Slutkin & Ransford, 2020). As Perry (2009) has argued, a distinctive advantage of health-based violence intervention strategies is that they are based upon scientific and evidence-based epidemiological modelling of 'causal' or influencing processes, and are thereby potentially *preventive* rather than merely reactive, triggered by the breach of given offence categories. For Haylock et al. (2020), the central contribution of a public health perspective would be 'a holistic approach and [strategic] leadership' (2020: 1453). And as Mitton (2019: 135) has argued, 'a reconceptualisation of the problem in health terms may help authorities avoid the damaging consequences of an almost reflexive default to securitised and draconian criminal justice responses, which at their extremes have tended to worsen rather than reduce violence'. Furthermore, a guilt and punishment based approach to violence has tended to individualise the phenomenon whilst losing focus on the wide range of influences which appear to make certain people, places and situations more violent than others. Mitton again, 'where an approach puts *exclusive* focus upon the individual or a specific community in isolation, to the degree that broader structural causes are marginalised or obscured, the picture of what drives violence (and therefore what may work to prevent it) is left drastically incomplete' (2019). On the other hand, of course, if violence is understood entirely as the result of structural causes, situational influences and behavioural norms we lose sight of the human agency and decision-making which goes into the performance of a violent act. In either case, the scope for making policy changes is diminished. The especial contribution of a 'critical public health' or broadly 'epidemiological' focus is its ability to widen our perspective on the problem of violence, to bring more ideas than law and deterrence alone to the table, without losing sight that choices, however misguided they may be, that are involved. Just as the Covid 19 pandemic has shown how various social, cultural and behavioural practices can have a profound effect on viral infection rates (virology, biology), or, simply put, how behaviour impacts health, so social structures, processes and divisions can shape patterns, cycles and vectors of violence.

Of course, staying with the public health angle, there is the point that episodes of interpersonal violence are often concluded by at least some of the participants ending up in hospital emergency rooms or, more worryingly, in the morgue, where medical practitioners of various specialisms might ply their particular trades. Yet dissatisfactions with what has often been termed a 'patch 'em up and send 'em home' approach to injury care has caused many doctors to seek more preventive and longer terms forms of intervention. This is so even though a great deal of the medical research on knife violence injuries in the UK and elsewhere has not necessarily been part of a wider prevention strategy but more a question of the effectiveness of different surgical techniques (Meer et al., 2010; Khan et al., 2018), trauma case control (Webster & Tai, 2015; Wilkinson, 2019) or the assessment of the most effective entry points for knife crime education (Wells, 2008). Although, undoubtedly other medical interventions have undoubtedly involved wider problem scoping (see Maxwell et al., 2007). In other contexts, policy makers have advocated for health assessment 'triage techniques' to determine violence prevention priorities (Abt, 2019). We will return to this issue later.

Patient attendances at accident and emergency have also generated a database of knife injury incidents which might complement—or rival—police recorded knife crime incidents, either confirming or challenging available data on knife violence trends. As we have noted, for a time during earlier phases of the emerging UK knife crime moral panic, hospital knife injury trends and police recorded knife crime trends, did not always coincide. Even the Home Affairs Select Committee in 2009 discussed the difficulty of determining clearly whether knife crime was 'going up or going down' (HASC, 2009: 10, para. 15) and, in earlier chapters, we have discussed some of the reasons for this. Perhaps the most important caveat here involves the need to understand how data is *produced* prior to reaching any determination of its explanatory value.

This is basic social science—'facts' don't speak for themselves. In the later phases of the knife crime crisis, the requirement that A&E departments notify the police of apparent knife injuries may well have deterred all but the most seriously injured from attending A&E and thereby lowering the assaultive injury figures. Accordingly, as we have insisted throughout this book, understanding the production of crime and injury data is vital in making sense of it, even so, plenty of uncertainty remains. Something of this uncertainty was reflected in a 2007 ACPO/Home Office guide on 'knife crime'. 'Perhaps surprisingly', the report noted, 'the available data indicates that the proportion of violent offences involving the use of a knife has remained relatively stable in recent years. This fact is certainly contrary to public perceptions that knife crime is rising. There may also be an element of underreporting' (ACPO/Home Office, 2007: 4). In this case, the available data, suggesting a 'relatively stable' trend in knife violence is explained away because it fails to correspond with public perceptions which themselves are often a product of media reporting and may well be way off the mark. Yet no attempt was made to explain how these public perceptions may have been formed or, indeed, regarding the role that the police—primary definers of crime, after all—may have played in helping establish them. The knife crime story comprises many instances where the statistical evidence is selectively deployed, or discarded altogether, depending upon the story it appears to tell. Thus far, knife crime interventions seldom reflect a case of 'evidence-led' policy making, but often rather more a form of rather selective, policy-led, evidence chasing. Where the evidence cannot be found, 'public perceptions' have frequently been drafted in to bolster the case. As we will show, these points have a direct bearing upon the debate about 'public health' approaches to knife crime.

One of the most direct and immediate influences upon the development of public health thinking about knife crime has been the perceived success of the approach pioneered in Scotland and which we touched upon in chapter two. The Scottish model of violence prevention grew out of a number of police-led initiatives designed to address gang involved youth violence in the Glasgow/Strathclyde area. Operation Reclaim (2004) was initially focussed upon the reopening of sport and recreational areas, long abandoned as a result of youth violence, and providing safe, supervised spaces for educational, recreational and diversionary youth activities, safe opportunities for sport and recreation. Rolled out across the north of the city, the initiative was attributed with contributing to significant reductions in crime and disorder. Subsequently this was combined with Operation Phoenix, bringing together teenagers from 17 areas of the city to participate in sport and recreation projects, whilst also attempting to foster positive relationships with the police. Over the duration of the projects, gang fighting was recorded as having diminished by between 70 and 40 per cent (Nicolson, 2010). However developments in Scotland did not arise from nowhere, a number of international developments helped lay the foundations of a new approach. In Boston, Massachusetts, the much heralded Operation Ceasefire (designed to address gun violence between rival gangs) was gaining attention as a new, long-term, approach to prevention and 'targeted deterrence' (Kennedy, 2011) and, as noted earlier, in Chicago, Gary Slutkin and his colleagues were pioneering a new epidemiological approach to 'cure violence'. This involved adapting a number of tried and tested intervention strategies more usually associated with disease control, such as detecting and interrupting transmission (in this case by interrupting emerging conflicts),[2] identifying and treating those individuals considered to be at highest risk and changing the social norms to which they adhered (attitudes centred on hostility to 'outsiders', low self-esteem, 'angry masculinity' and enduring commitments to grudges, vendettas and feuding in feedback loops of retaliatory behaviour: see for example, in a US context, Gilligan, 1997; Jacobs & Wright, 2002; Mullins et al., 2004; Mullins, 2006; Stewart et al., 2006) and the environments in which such norms and behaviours have prevailed (Slutkin, 2013).

Slutkin and his colleagues have made their case in a wide variety of publications (Slutkin, 2013, 2016; Slutkin et al., 2018; Slutkin &

---

[2] A powerful and inspiring award-winning documentary film, *The Interrupters* (2011), featured a year in the work of the project's 'violence interrupters' or community mediators as they sought to negotiate, persuade, cajole and beseech their clients to either avoid resorting to violence in the first place, or discouraging retaliation.

Ransford, 2020),[3] describing the evolution their approach in Chicago where medical practitioners contemplated the relentless daily toll of gang-related gun violence and sought ways to address it more effectively. It appeared, to Slutkin and his colleagues that there were broadly two flawed approaches currently advocated, a punitive approach founded upon attempts to 'suppress' the problem (Hoffman et al., 2011) and what he characterised as a 'solve everything' response (2016: 45). The former approach tended to be popular ('highly overrated in the public mind') but seldom very effective, whilst most health care professionals had, on the whole, long ago given up the idea that punishment could contribute very much to cure. 'Solve everything', however, demanded that solutions be found for every problem that was going wrong in chronically violent communities—poor schools, dysfunctional families, poverty, racism and drugs—before any meaningful attempt could be made to tackle the violence. Slutkin and his colleagues did not dispute the scale of the problems endured by the poorest and most victimised communities, but simply insisted that it was not necessary to wait until every other problem was resolved before anything could be done about the violence. Indeed, they argued, it was often violence which was inhibiting the development of other initiatives targeting poverty, job creation or school improvements. When they looked at the data using insights from epidemiology, researchers found that it occurred in 'wave forms', it clustered and spread as a result of the types and patterns of human interaction (Abt, 2019). In other words, Slutkin and his colleagues argued, violence behaved as a disease and from all their other work; they knew that disease processes could be reversed (Ransford & Slutkin, 2017: 604). On this basis, medical researchers went on to develop a broad-based 'cure violence' initiative drawing upon what the available data told them about the

---

[3] There are many more contributors to the debate about whether violence can be understood and responded to as if it were a disease process, including the contributions of critics who reject such an approach (for example Greene, 2018). Although we will draw out certain issues, this is not the place for a full rehearsal of the argument except to note that we are discussing the issue because there is substantial evidence of the approach having positive effects (in both the USA and Scotland, for starters: Waller, 2019) and a great deal of debate about the merits of adopting such an approach in the rest of the UK. Furthermore, the public health approach is regarded as the major alternative to punitive/deterrence enforcement interventions which have tended to prevail in the UK, so merits some discussion here, although whether such interventions are best pursued *instead of* or *in conjunction with* policing initiatives still prompts much argument.

contexts in which it was most likely to erupt, the underlying risks and the triggering events, the behavioural norms, the expectations and what they called the 'situationally adaptive responses' which facilitated its spread (Slutkin et al., 2018). Cure violence projects employed outreach workers, youth workers and other 'interrupters' to engage with communities, victims and perpetrators (recognising that often, only time and chance distinguished victims from perpetrators). According to Hoffman et al. (2011) a cumulative impact of this work, often coordinated by the WHO, has been to shift, somewhat, certain behavioural assumptions about youth violence as a 'rite of passage' towards recognising it as a serious social problem (especially in parts of the world, including major regions of the global South, where young people had access to military grade weaponry) resulting in many needless deaths and injuries.

The 2002 WHO Report, *World Report on Violence and Health* which is often regarded as being critically instrumental in shifting the analysis of violence towards a more public health informed discourse (Perry, 2009) was instrumental in prompting the establishment of the Strathclyde Violence Reduction unit. Strathclyde had one of the highest rates of knife crime in the world, over five times the rate of England and Wales (Carnochan & McCluskey, 2010: 400), and appeared to present an especially challenging problem. Furthermore, research conducted in three Glasgow Hospitals had suggested that violence was significantly under-reported, with serious assaults under recorded by the police by between some 50 and 70% (Squires et al., 2008). The point underscores our earlier remark regarding the non-correspondence between police and hospital injury data, but the 'Cure Violence' initiative established the importance of having the hospital at the centre of the violence reduction programme. More than that, it was 'critical' that 'highly trusted community-based health workers provide services in a confidential way, *so as not to dissuade people from seeking care*' (Ransford & Slutkin, 2017: 607, emphasis added). Unfortunately when the public health approach to violence reduction was proposed for adoption in London hospitals this approach to confidentiality was rejected in favour of A&E personnel directly reporting stabbings to the police and, under constant pressure from both Government and police,[4] the debate has persisted about this issue ever since (Cole, 2010; Thornton, 2019; Timmis et al., 2019; Morris, 2019). As we have shown, the practice of reporting named individual victims to the police has several self-defeating consequences: in Scotland, A&E data was only released in aggregated form in order to allow researchers to accurately assess risks, plot clusters of violence ('hot spots'), establish relationships and follow the patterns of retaliation and recurring conflict across the city, in order to make *strategic and community* based interventions, but no personal data was revealed. In London individual details *were* reported to the police so that only the most seriously injured went to the hospital, implying that the database of knife-involved violence was incomplete and therefore fairly useless as the central intelligence tool intended to underpin the entire public health approach.[5]

Discussing this issue in the BMJ in 2008 Shepherd and Brennan noted that many victims of violence were pressurised into not reporting violence, 'many violent incidents that result in medical treatment are not reported to the police because patients are afraid of reprisals, they are unable to identify assailants, or they are unwilling to have their own conduct scrutinised'. Despite this, they argued, 'emergency departments can help by collecting *anonymised* data on the locations and times that violent events occur and the types of weapons used, and by sharing these data with crime reduction agencies. Clearly unless violence hotspots are identified, they cannot be targeted. It is not safe to assume that the most serious violence, including knife and gun violence, will have

---

[4] As Morris noted, in the *Lancet* (2019): ' The new guidance from the General Medical Council (GMC), which came into force on Oct 12, extends the previous policy of mandatory reporting of gunshot wounds… Pressure to change the guidance has come from the UK Government for several years, but recently the Association of Chief Police Officers has also advocated increased reporting by doctors and other sectors such as social services'.

[5] The Home Affairs Select Committee Report on *Knife Crime* in 2009 gave a good deal of consideration to this issue, receiving evidence both for and against the mandatory reporting, by A&E departments, of knife injuries to the police. In the end they rather fudged the issue, referring to the sharing of 'anonymous data' but then urging that the police be informed when *an individual* arrived at A&E with a knife wound. On the one hand the Committee noted that the General Medical Council were themselves currently debating the issue and, whilst accepting that 'the first duty of doctors is to their patients' they nevertheless resolved that 'it is in the public interest that the police are informed when a person arrives at hospital with a wound inflicted in a violent attack' (HASC, 2009: para. 189 and recommendation 41, and page 90).

been reported' (Shepherd & Brennan, 2008, emphasis added). They continued to advocate for NHS emergency departments making strategic inputs to crime and violence reduction initiatives. This call was taken up in the British Medical Journal, (Ponsford et al., 2019), some ten years later, still reiterating the point that, for all the talk and advocacy on behalf of a strategic public health reduction strategy, rather little had so far been delivered:

> 'there have been longstanding calls to take a public health stance to tackling serious violence … such an approach involves treating violence as a disease: quantifying and monitoring it, identifying drivers and risk factors and using evidence based approaches to stem its spread and to address the conditions from which it emerges and propagates. This shifts attention away from seeing violence solely as a criminal justice problem amenable to a criminal justice solution.

Ponsford et al., continued, addressing such violence.

> requires more complex responses. These involve whole-system, multi-agency synergies between criminal justice systems, schools, health care services, industry, third sector organisations and communities that focus on primary prevention at a population level as well as 'treating the symptoms' of the disease... Yet to date, the dominant public policy conversation has remained firmly focussed on improving policing strategies and 'securitising' neighbourhoods where there is perceived to be a high risk of knife crime. (Ponsford et al., 2019)

In moving south, however, the public health approach to violence shifted from being a quantitative, aggregated intelligence tool designed to support community interventions and *prevent and disrupt* violence, into an individualised, investigative measure to help apprehend and prosecute perpetrators and, in this way, support an *enforcement* approach. As Carnochan and McCluskey noted, 'the first step in a public health model is to define the extent of the problem of violence … yet police officers are expected to prevent and detect violence based upon a fraction of the necessary information. Gaining a true picture of the levels of violence is imperative to enable us to evaluate the effectiveness of deployment of resources and to develop different and more effective ways of operating across policing, health and education' (2010: 405). As they went on to note, the new health strategy involved a multidisciplinary approach 'involving medicine, epidemiology, education, economics and other disciplines… allowing for the framing of the problem in a way that is consistent with, and supported by, research and evidence-based principles' (ibid.). By disregarding the role of research and evidence, the public health model as exported to London and, later, England, was fatally flawed, a mere adjunct to an enforcement approach rather than a thorough-going alternative. Scotland was the first European country to define violence as a primary public health issue and it remains at the forefront of tackling the issue. In England, by contrast, the public health approach was found to be seriously lacking, as a brief discussion reported in the Home Affairs Select Committee deliberations on Serious Youth Violence, revealed:

> The evidence we received suggested that the Government's rhetoric on public health has not yet been reflected in its actions. Chief Constable Dave Thompson criticised the Home Office for producing "quite a crime-based strategy. If you look at the document, it alludes to a public health based strategy, but it is not yet a public health based strategy".

Other witnesses agreed, arguing that there had been 'insufficient coordination across Government at a national level … Last year, the interim report of the Youth Violence Commission warned of "an increasing risk that the term 'public health model' is being used without a proper understanding of what is actually required to affect lasting change"' (HASC, 2019: paragraph 53). It appears there had been little real progress in ten years, after all the Home Affairs Select Committee in 2009 had begun to outline the key elements of a 'public health' approach to violence drawing upon guidance from the World Health Organisation. Four stages in such an approach were identified:

- Appropriately defining the problem through the systematic collection of information about the magnitude, scope, characteristics and consequences of violence;
- Establishing why violence occurs using research to determine the causes and correlates of violence, the factors that increase or decrease the risk for violence, and the factors that could be modified through interventions;
- To find out what works to prevent violence by designing, implementing and evaluating interventions, and
- To implement effective and promising interventions in a wide range of settings. (HASC: 67, para. 187; Krug et al., 2002; WHO, 2014)[6]

In the light of these precisely defined stages, it is clear that very little resembling a public health *strategy* for addressing serious youth violence, including knife crime has been progressed very far in the UK. Despite a clear starting point, the systematic collection of information and investment in research, the UK experience has primarily comprised assessments of a variety of police-led law enforcement actions. As the WHO report noted, strategies are often insufficiently underpinned by research and adequate data and police leadership of interventions is widespread although these seldom extend beyond familiar 'community policing' activities, often insufficiently connected to wider agencies and supports. In England and Wales, by contrast, the rolling back of a national new neighbourhood policing strategy was widely interpreted as the catalyst for a resurgence of youth violence, gang activity and knife crime. On the other hand, the simple fact that a number of research initiatives have been undertaken by clinicians, within trauma centres, and centred upon knife injury victims, does not, of itself, qualify the work as a public health approach to violence prevention, even though health professionals are clearly dealing with the consequences of violence.

---

[6] The 2014 WHO Report, *Global Status Report on Violence Prevention*, represents the most complete and final version of a document which had many previous iterations. It provides a useful outline of the necessary components of public health-led violence reduction programmes whilst assessing the weaknesses in many existing programmes. It has subsequently been complemented by further work such as the UN ODC *Global Homicide Report* 2019.

Learning Exercise 17: A Public Health Strategy—Checking your Understanding

What are claimed to be the chief advantages of a joined-up, health-led (epidemiological, evidence-based) approach to tackling violence?

If Scotland was able to develop such a project, what was holding back the development of similar initiatives in England?

As we have seen, young people, especially younger male members of black and minority ethnic groups are far from being the majority perpetrators of knife violence, therefore interventions exclusive to certain demographics or focusing only upon the misuse of certain weapons lack the breadth to represent genuine public health strategies. By the same token, just as Slutkin rejected the 'do everything' approach there is equally no 'one size fits all' solution. As Thomas Abt (2019: 6) has noted, different kinds of violence require different responses, even as they may have a good deal in common. A deprived community background is key, especially poverty, compounded by racism and blocked opportunities, deprivation is a prolific incubator of violence, although violence 'is not just a manifestation of poverty; it is a force that perpetuates poverty as well' (Abt, 2019: 13). As Bellis et al. (2011, 2012: 29) have demonstrated, emergency hospital admission rates for assaultive violence are four times higher in the 'most deprived communities' as compared with the most affluent. Yet whilst the evidence gathering practices may be similar, building risk profiles and patterns of victimisation, the targeting of risks and the precise interventions necessary will differ significantly if the objective is to address knife violence between youth gangs as opposed to patterns of intimate partner violence in the home. As we have already shown, the tendency of 'knife crime' strategies to ignore the latter *almost entirely*, even though knives are the weapon most frequently employed in domestic homicides (Cook & Walklate, 2020) points to the lack of purchase that evidence has thus far secured in these policy circles.

Thus far in this chapter we have suggested that the involvement of health professionals in responses to knife violence does not, in and of itself, imply that a health strategy is in place. For example health involvement might be confined to the paramedic recovery of victims and the treatment of serious knife wounds in Accident and Emergency centres, in other words '*treat 'em and street 'em*', the short-term medical equivalent of an arrest-based enforcement approach delivered by the police. At the same time, a strategic health approach that simply accepted the conventional public framing of knife crime as a problem that is overwhelmingly youthful and predominantly black would likely involve resurrecting the race-pathology myth which has long surrounded populist conceptions of urban violence (Gilroy, 1982). Haylock et al. drawing upon a systematic review of British knife crime studies as recently as 2020 (sixteen articles), have noted that understanding the complex of relations involving ethnicity, risk and weapon use is underdeveloped for 'minimal research has investigated these risk factors within a UK setting… [which] has led to misleading media reporting and no consistent or strategic approach [adopted] to tackle this growing problem' (2020: 1453). Despite a great deal of superficial commentary, Haylock et al. concluded that, when controlling for other factors (such as socio-economic status, adverse childhood experiences and mental health) research results 'did not identify a strong relationship between ethnicity and youth violence'. Certain ethnic minority groups and especially recently arrived migrants and refugees did experience more acute forms of community deprivation as well as higher rates of violence victimisation, whilst gang involvements typically 'mirror the demography of the community' in which they arise. In part, this will account for the 'over-representation of ethnic minorities as perpetrators and victims of weapon-related crime within police-recorded data' (Haylock et al., 2020: 1462). The authors concluded by addressing the policy implications of their work: 'As no clear association was found between gender, ethnicity and weapon-related crime, policy makers should *avoid targeting individuals based on stereotypes* in these areas. This may also reduce discrimination within policy efforts, ensuring a holistic approach to mitigate youth violence' (2020: 1463, emphasis added).

By contrast, a more recent study by Coid et al. (2021), despite its many positive and original features as a study seeking to unearth the epidemiology of knife violence, focused entirely upon a sample of young, disproportionately black, young men, asking them:

have you been in a physical fight, assaulted, or deliberately hit anyone in the past 5 years, [or] if they had carried a knife. [Respondents] were asked about outcomes of violence, victims, number of incidents, whether violence … involved gang fights, whether they were gang members, … They were asked whether violence was instrumental (to obtain money, drugs or sex), [or if] they had deliberately looked for a fight, often ruminated about violence, found violence exciting, easily lost their temper, became violent if disrespected, or would typically obtain a weapon and look for someone who had threatened them. (Coid et al., 2021)

It is not that these are *necessarily* improper research questions simply that they tend to consolidate a widely shared perception that the phenomenon known as 'knife crime', standing for all knife-enabled violence, begins and ends on the streets, forever the preserve of our usual, youthful black, suspects. It becomes increasingly clear that, so long as responses to knife crime remain trapped within such misleading and highly racialised—though no doubt widely shared—misperceptions, they will continue to perpetuate the largely self-fulfilling but otherwise ineffectually punitive and stigmatisingly pathological responses we have witnessed thus far. It is here, then, when we turn to policy responses that the strongest case for *rethinking knife crime* emerges.

As we have already suggested and as a good deal of the literature affirms (Abt, 2019; Roberts, 2021; Waller, 2019) it is to wider contexts: families, relationships, networks and communities that we need to turn in order to develop an appropriately strategic, joined-up and sustainable approach to violence.

Sustainable Violence Reduction Strategy: Prioritising Without Stigmatising?

Drawing upon WHO Reports published in 2002 and 2004 (Krug et al., 2002) many public health violence prevention strategies have based their interventions upon what they refer to as an 'integrated understanding' drawing out the 'cross cutting risk factors' for violence as reflected in

Fig. 8.1. Sometimes referred to as an ecological model for public health intervention, versions of this model can be found widely in the public health strategy literature (for example, Sethi & WHO, 2007; Donnelly & Ward, 2014; Haylock et al., 2020).

As the diagram shows, the model, sometimes also regarded as an 'ecological' model for understanding and responding to violence (Coid et al., 2021; Fagan & Wilkinson, 2000; Ward, 2015) draws out four sets of factors: individual, relational, communal and societal and specifies the problematic elements, or risks, at each level which can be conducive to violence. Because we have adapted the model from several pre-existing ones, and have tried to tailor it to a British context—and knife crime, in particular, some of the risks and responses in earlier versions have been altered. For instance, in American versions of the model (Rutherford et al., 2007), addressing illegal firearm supply is marked out as a critical risk requiring attention. In regards to knife crime in the UK, as we have seen, supply side interventions regarding

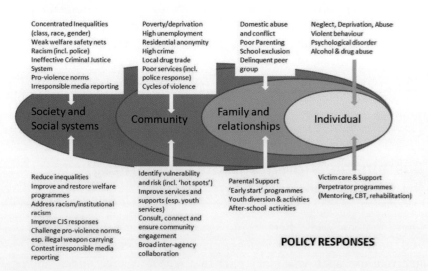

Fig. 8.1 Cross cutting risk factors for violence (*Source* Adapted from WHO, 2002, 2014; Rutherford et al., 2007; Bellis et al., 2012: 27; Ward, 2015; Coid et al., 2021)

knives seem unlikely to bear fruit. Instead, contesting illegal weapon carrying especially in known violence 'hot spots' seems more likely to yield positive outcomes—but seldom on its own. Without wider and longer term measures to achieve community trust and confidence and support for the most vulnerable (and, crucially, 'buy in'), contesting weapon carrying by the few might look rather like a short-term s.60 stop and search action, disruptive of community consent and resented by many. Furthermore for the UK knife crime version of the model, because we have been centrally concerned by the often misleading, stigmatising and broadly racist reporting of much knife crime our concern is that this largely counter-productive framing of the problem be more effectively contested. As we emphasise later, a critical criminological response requires that equal attention be paid, not just to the crime or the violent event itself, but also to the way in which this is *reacted* to. In 'rethinking knife crime' it is essential that reactions to knife crime are themselves scrutinised and deconstructed, that the 'power to criminalise' is not deployed in a discriminatory fashion and that the misidentification of risk is not itself part of the problem. Taken together, this is broadly what Abt is suggesting when he insists that violence prevention interventions must be both 'evidence informed' and 'community informed' (2019: 9). Broad inter-agency collaboration is also essential, but at the *strategic* level as practised in the Strathclyde violence prevention initiative, not simply requiring A&E departments to refer the names of stabbing victims to the police, which, as we have seen, lends itself chiefly to an individualised enforcement approach.

The model marks a significant step forward in seeing violence as the outcome of several layers of influence although the overwhelming focus for interventions thus far adopted, despite much talk of 'strategic health promotion', has typically been the individual, especially the criminal behaviour of individuals. The thinking behind the public health 'cross cutting risk factors' model has somewhat influenced the development of strategic thinking for tackling youth violence policy in the UK, in the first place the influential report *Dying to Belong*, produced by the Centre for Social Justice (CSJ, 2009) and second the Government's Gang Strategy Report which appeared shortly after the 2011 riots (HM Government, 2011). Whilst *Dying to Belong* set a context it called 'broken Britain'[7] to describe the conditions in which street gang violence was plaguing many urban areas, and recognised poverty, deprivation and racism as contributory factors, it made no suggestions for policies to address these issues at all, still less showing any kind of willingness to acknowledge that austerity policies would be likely to make such problems worse.

Similar issues were apparent with the Government's 'gang strategy' report *Ending Gang and Youth Violence* (HM Government, 2011). On the one hand, in a series of revealing diagrams (2011: pages 13–17) the strategy document depicted the wide range of agencies which had a potentially supportive role to play in the life of a growing child, although the extent to which many of these agencies were depleted, over-worked, understaffed and struggling to cope with the consequences of austerity went entirely overlooked (see Roberts, 2021). In an ideal world these several agencies might well have provided wrap-around support, guidance and resources, providing a framework for a public health violence prevention strategy, but this was austerity Britain, there were holes in the safety net and gaps in provision. In another compelling diagram, the 'life cycle of a gang member' was depicted; his pathway, from birth to adulthood, negotiated a jungle of risks and traps as well as opportunities both good and bad. The document even went so far as to invent 'Boy X' as the unfortunate youngster on this pathway towards gang life. The life-course depicted certainly connected with the kind of thinking reflected in the risk factors diagram but everything depicted on this hypothetical 'gang pathway' was understood entirely from the point of view of the individual, *his* risks and *his* choices, *his* engagements, or not, with local agencies and *his* eventual succumbing to the peer pressure of delinquent friends and associates. Always, the focus was with the individual, in common with *Dying to Belong*, the Government gang strategy report discussed many of the wider social factors which influenced individuals 'at risk' of becoming involved in violent gang networks and weapon use but seldom proposed doing anything about them. In common with

---

[7] 'Broken Britain' became one of the central elements of Conservative commentary in the run-up to the 2010 general election, seemingly connecting the idea that not only was Britain 'broke' financially following Labour's banking crisis bailouts, but also that the country was social and morally broken (see Squires, 2016).

many 'social capital' approaches to youth crime prevention (Halpern, 2005) the focus rested upon strengthening individual resilience in the face of crimogenic risks and social stresses (for example HM Government, 2018: 57) rather than addressing the risks themselves directly, the contrast with a broad-based and strategic public health response is clear to see. Both of these documents, each of which has centrally underpinned contemporary government responses to gang and youth violence reveal the limitations of a half-hearted and essentially 'cherry-picking' response to violence prevention. For example, both Kennedy (2011) and Abt (2019) have described the ways in which the highly successful Boston *Ceasefire* project was both cannibalised and adjusted when implemented in a variety of American cities according to the whims, political preferences and interests there prevailing. As we've noted this is a fairly familiar aspect of policy transfer and project implementation, bearing out the vital importance of *social reactions* in shaping understandings of, and solutions for, crime and violence. Adopting only those elements of a strategy which correspond to an a priori ideological and political preference and broadly populist media is never likely to break the cycle of inappropriate problem definition and ineffective response which has brought us to where we are.

The levels of explanation built into the *cross cutting risk factors* model are, in many respects, closely related to those developed by Taylor, Walton and Young (1973) as their foundation for the '*New Criminology*' launched in 1973. The explanatory framework they developed specified the need for a 'society level' explanation (or what they referred to as 'the wider origins of the "deviant" act' which they termed "a *political economy of crime*"); next came the 'more immediate origins of the act', the 'relational' aspects, and finally came the situational context of the act (the situated social dynamics of the actual act/violence). But this was where conventional criminology, and for that matter, public health violence strategies, have tended to part ways. For the *New Criminology* went further to insist that attention be given to the circumstances in which different kinds of public *reactions* to deviant acts (in our case, forms of violence) were mobilised. In the first place were the 'immediate origins of social reaction' (shock, fear or outrage—although in some cases, pleasure, humour or tolerance—recognising how violence is also consumed, enjoyed and commodified[8]). Then followed the wider contexts of social reaction, shaped by society's dominant values, beliefs or a variety of overlapping prejudices; reactions might be shaped by punitive, racist, or homophobic attitudes, or religious conceptions of 'desert'). Finally, for the *New Criminology*, there were the consequences of (recurring) social reaction; social divisions, exclusions, such as the consolidation of criminal careers and identities, deepening hostilities and discriminations and the entire infrastructure of selective criminalisation and deviance amplification.

The important difference between these different perspectives, as we have sought to spell them out in this book concerns the tendency of traditional (or administrative) criminology and the conventional public health perspectives to take 'deviance', or in our case 'knife-enabled violence', largely as it finds it: an appalling crime that must be tackled. Any violence is attributed entirely to the characteristics of the individual perpetrator, nothing more needs to be said, and as black-letter criminology would have it, the perpetrator must be held accountable, apprehended and then punished. A more realist, public health informed, approach might go to some lengths to explain and contextualise the violence of the violent but in the end, whatever social causes and crimogenic environments there may be, as Abt (2019) puts it, the first and most immediate targets of prevention are the stabbed victim in the emergency room—who must be prevented from bleeding to death—and the guy with the knife (it usually is a man), who must be prevented from stabbing anyone else. The first task falls to the medics, the latter to the police, but whether working alone or working together, the contribution of these two groups fall some way short of a comprehensive public health strategy, for each only deals with individuals whereas a public health strategy must engage with relationships, communities and societies as well. This includes the shop that sold the knife, the group who brought the drugs, the school that excluded, the housing department

---

[8] As we have already seen, violence sells newspapers, it entertains - from Shakespeare to *Star Wars*; it is variously perceived, depending upon time, place and circumstance and who is inflicting violence upon whom, and as either the nadir of brutal inhumanity or bold, righteous and justified, a mark of 'manhood' or national character. As we have suggested, the social reaction—or the interpretation of violence—is central.

which presided over the sinking of the estate, the welfare budgets that were never enough, the youth centre that closed, the jobs and opportunities that disappeared, the police who had lost the trust and confidence of the community and persisted in a daily low-level racialised harassment of its young men and, finally, the youth who uttered the disrespect and the peer group who urged him on. Yet however wide a conventional public health approach looks to explain the wider determinants of knife-enabled violence or, more especially, in our account, the particular offence labelled 'knife crime', intervention still targets individual perpetrators (although recognising that there may be tremendous symmetry between perpetrators and victims, that it might only be time and chance which separate them; today's perpetrators might well be tomorrow's victims). This is undoubtedly because the very meaning and definition of 'knife crime' is locked within a precisely coded social reaction which essentialises by race, age and place, the meaning of the incident. Knife crime is formed in this reaction, without the reaction there is no 'knife crime', just a spectrum of immature and youthful violence. By contrast, 'knife crime' is so much darker, deeper and challenging, and so obviously a product of a racialised 'otherness'. It follows that a public health approach needs to be sensitive to these reactions which might endlessly throw up the same 'usual suspects'—young, poor, black—forever reinforcing a racialised understanding of the crime whenever knives are raised in violence. We know that many of our contemporary enforcement practices at best simply recycle the problem; and more often exacerbate it, whilst fixing its distorted impression in the minds of the watching public. Accordingly, analysis should guard against the kind of public health intervention that, oblivious to the significance of reaction, broadens the pathology of blade violence, finding its dangerous potential in virtually all difficult racialised settings and relationships, and especially those it is unable or unwilling to address. For instance, even research which has sought to get to grips with why so many young people feel worried by violence, that seeks to understand their fears and experiences whilst expressing horror and revulsion regarding the prevalence of stabbings on the streets can end, contrarily, by normalising weapon carrying as more and more young people feel they need to take their own precautions—carry weapons—whilst out in public (Marfleet, 2008;

YJB, 2013). Addressing the local and contextual factors which help to sustain a culture of knife possession, carrying and use are an indispensable component of a successful strategy, both by addressing the fears and insecurities promoting resort to weapons and providing support to the vulnerable.

So rather than build such a deep and self-fulfilling picture of knife crime and its central characters: the perpetrators and victims, a critical public health approach, even if it must necessarily *begin* with the most acute and urgent cases—the victim bleeding in A&E or the knife-wielding attacker—should not neglect the poverty, racism, fractured relationships, impoverished communities and broken societies of which it is so often a consequence. The issues need addressing from both ends at once in a joined-up evidence-led and community engaged fashion. And whilst, as we have shown in an earlier chapter, knife crime has spawned an entire industry of endeavour: think tanks, policy groups, commercial sponsorships, government information campaigns, youth outreach, educational projects and police 'campaigns', much reflecting the 'gang intervention industry' phenomenon described by Densley (2011), these initiatives are seldom sufficiently targeted on those most at risk in the most violence-prone areas nor embedded in local communities and complemented by the necessary long-term strategic problem-solving and community regeneration initiatives that can begin to make a violence reduction programme sustainable.

'Sustainability' was a central concern of witnesses before the Home Affairs Select Committee on 'serious youth violence' as they discussed the committee's question as to whether the Government strategy was 'fit for purpose'. Evidence from West Midlands Police and the West Midlands Police and Crime Commissioner, complained that consistency and sustainability were often lacking. Chief Constable Thompson remarked, 'I have been around policing a long while. I saw the TGAP [*Tacking Gangs Action*] programme; I was involved in the *Ending Gang and Youth Violence* programme; and here we are again. What happens is we do not drive forward a sustained, consistent approach'. His colleague, the PCC noted, 'both [the] EGYV and the Serious Violence Strategy suffer from being "short term", and that both "lack sustainability"' (HASC, 2019: 17). Voicing a familiar criticism which, to some extent a public health approach was intended to remedy, Sir Denis O'Connor, the former Chief Inspector of Constabulary criticised the 'really inadequate' data sources which underpinned the programme. Without evidence and clear targets, he suggested, it was difficult to see how the strategy could succeed. Dame Louise Casey, former head of the Troubled Families programme agreed, calling the strategy 'woefully inadequate' and adding that the strategy did not go far or wide enough, 'It is not a coherent, overall Government strategy that pushes forward into communities' (HASC, 2019: verbal evidence, 17–18). The committee signed off this discussion with a bold and critical conclusion:

> Although the strategy refers to risk factors for involvement in violence, … it is not underpinned by any attempt to collect data or gain a clear understanding of the number of people—particularly young people—at risk of serious violence. We fail to see how the Government can get a grip on this problem or pursue a public health approach without a clear understanding of the size and location of the populations most at risk, so that it can target resources effectively. …The strategy states that serious violence comes at "a huge cost to individuals, families and communities through loss of life, and the trauma caused through both the physical and psychological injuries suffered". We agree; but there is a serious mismatch between the Government's diagnosis of the problem and its proposed solutions. This is symptomatic of wider dysfunctions within the Government's response to this issue, and its approach to crime and disorder more broadly. (HASC, 2019: 18 paras 41–42)

Something of this rather piecemeal approach to interventions had been reflected in the earlier Kinsella Report, *Tackling Knife Crime Together* (2011).[9] It was ten years ago and still relatively early in the 'knife crime panic' (but as our overall timeline shows, we were already well into phase three of knife crime enforcement) and whilst the idea of getting a TV celebrity to convene a review of 'knife crime projects' and to encourage young people to engage may have been a laudable one, there is still something rather amateurish about such an approach. As

---

[9] Brooke Kinsella's brother, Ben, was stabbed to death in 2008 and she became an active campaigner against knife crime.

is usual the review focused entirely upon *youthful* knife violence, other dimensions of the issue went unexplored although the report did briefly mention lack of support for young women as victims. A start, perhaps. Yet evidence already existed, systematic reviews had been undertaken and the phenomenon of gangs and serious youth violence had been subject to a great deal of rigorous research (for example, Eades et al., 2007; Silvestri et al., 2009) suggesting that a whistle-stop tour of knife projects to assess 'what works' had a rather more presentational and symbolic aspect rather than anything to do with real evaluation. Many of the projects were run by youth workers in schools, youth clubs and the community. They were invariably local, small scale and isolated. Around this time, Prime Minister Cameron had been promoting the cause of something he had called the 'Big Society' (BBC News, 2010; Bochel, 2016: 62); he had in mind a flourishing of charitable endeavour to address the country's social problems, but if the review of knife crime projects revealed anything it was the patent inadequacy of isolated localism as a solution to these issues. Some of the projects visited were intended to break down barriers between police and youth, others were to support young people leaving care or custody and many had sport, diversionary or mentoring aspects. However, even if many of the 'findings' had a rather impressionistic feel to them, the report was not without merit, visiting a wide variety of projects and making observations on their work. Poverty, lack of opportunity and 'gang culture' were centred as the key drivers of knife violence and a lack of sustainable funding or agency collaboration were identified as barriers to progress. But having identified these broad social and economic influences, the report was rather short on fundamentals; neither race nor racism was even mentioned in the report and although the financial vulnerability of many projects caught in short-term funding cycles was commented on, no recommendations on this were forthcoming: an opportunity missed. The vital contribution of youth work with vulnerable young people was a key theme, but no mention was made of the way local authority youth work budgets had been slashed over recent decades, a process that was continuing apace in 'austerity Britain'. The report concluded by recommending more 'knife awareness' work in schools (in subjects such as PSHE), more effective data-sharing around individuals thought to be 'at risk' and more early intervention.

Taken as a whole, however, the suggestions appear tokenistic and the review is essentially superficial, reading between the lines it exposed how little the government understood the knife crime phenomenon and how inadequately prepared they were to deal effectively with it.

Taking up the point about delivering knife awareness projects in schools Gilbert and Sinclair (2019) describe a knife crime education intervention delivered to schools in London and Luton. Students were surveyed before and after the classroom sessions and the research claimed that the results showed that pupils were more 'knife aware' after the sessions, that they would be less likely to carry knives themselves and more likely to discourage or report others. On the other hand it is equally plausible the students were simply feeding back what *they thought* was expected of them. Citing this study is not intended to single it out but just to introduce certain caveats. For instance, nothing was known about the propensity of the particular cohort of students surveyed to carry knives in the first place. Secondly, in the absence of anything else changing in the lives of young people, it is at least optimistic to expect significant behaviour change to result from a solitary educational presentation. And finally, raising knife awareness has been shown to be something of a double edged sword, feeding the fears that prompt knife carrying in the first place.[10] Too often what we have labelled the 'knife crime industry' simply builds and recycles the problem, normalising it when it ought to be addressing the underlying conflicts, deprived communities, fractured relationships and hostile cultures which appear to foster illegal knife carrying and use.

Fortunately evaluations of other strategies suggest significantly more promising results. Canadian criminologist Irvin Waller has for many been advocating for what he calls 'Smarter Crime Control' (Waller,

---

[10] At least the Gilbert and Sinclair project (2019) did not make the mistakes that a Metropolitan Police Knife awareness schools presentation entailed. The aim of the police video, followed up by questions and discussion (described more fully in Squires, 2016), was to warn young people of the risks they faced carrying knives—or associating with friends (peer groups, gangs) who might carry knives. Not only did young people risk being stabbed, they also risked arrest and prosecution themselves (under the 'joint enterprise' principle), if a friend used a knife. Given an opportunity to convey a supportive message and engage with young people, the MPS seemed to prioritise scaring them, firstly about the dangers of knife violence and secondly about the dangers associated with police construing liability where none existed.

2014), a movement that includes no less an advocate than the current US Vice President, Kamala Harris, whose book, *Smart on Crime* (2009) drew upon her experiences as District Attorney of San Francisco. In his most recent work Waller (2019) catalogues the lessons to be drawn from the most successful violence prevention projects worldwide. He has particular praise for the Strathclyde Community Initiative to Reduce Violence (CIRV) which, as we have seen, has been so responsible for galvanising the momentum for health-led violence prevention strategy in the UK (Waller, 2019: 166). For Waller, however, the important thing is not what the strategy is called but what it does, how a range of agencies collaborate, how communities are engaged and political 'buy-in' for consistent sustainable funding is secured. For Waller, the importance of a health and epidemiological focus was primarily concerned with the scientific and evidential foundations which directed the appropriate targeting of a range of interventions; he also featured the Cardiff Violence Reduction Strategy which employed trauma centre data to understand violence trends and patterns and in order to target hotspots for alcohol-related violence (2019: 161). For Waller, however, some of the most important interventions could be educational, or based upon youth outreach work. One of his chief arguments being that, in preventing violence, policing interventions were often the least useful, an argument dating back to his book *Less Law, More Order* (2008), where the argument that many social problems were 'over-policed' and that violence prevention work could usefully be decriminalised, first took shape. In common with Vitale (2017), Waller has argued that 'the police have too much to do' (2019: 39).[11] Intriguingly, amongst several evaluations demonstrating the contribution of a variety of forms of youth outreach work to violence prevention, Waller refers to a College of Policing assessment suggesting that educational programmes, youth work schemes, and early intervention projects produce far greater violence reduction effects than

[11] During the height of the police cuts and austerity debates the then Commissioner of the Metropolitan Police Sir Bernard Hogan-Howe pointed out that reduced numbers of frontline police officers would require some reprioritising of policing tasks, there were simply too many Grade 1 'emergency' calls to deal with. Some 40% of emergency calls, he argued, involved persons with mental health issues and circumstances that the police were often ill-equipped or trained to deal with effectively (Dodd, 2015).

policing. Indeed the global evidence suggests that by far the least effective police initiative for tackling violence is 'stop and frisk' (Waller, 2019: 30, 47; see also Butts and Delgado, 2017). The fact that most British debates about tackling knife crime remain stuck at this point suggests that 'Smart Crime Control' may still have some way to go in the UK.

According to Foster, reporting from the Scottish Centre for Crime and Justice Research (2013) the important issue for effective interventions lay in understanding the various motivations that young people had for carrying knives in public, and this question demanded two kinds of data: evidence about *where* and *when* violent altercations took place (which could often be gained from trauma incident records), and evidence about *why* (which required trusted access to both perpetrators and victims). It followed that health, education and youth work outreach services gave a far better purchase on the violence problem than policing alone and her report went on to prioritise youth diversion and educational interventions. Another College of Policing endorsement for youth outreach work emerged in 2019 further crediting the crime prevention practice in Strathclyde which had brought recorded criminal violence down to a 41 year low, whilst drawing familiar lessons about scientific problem analysis and appropriate targeting, early and sustained multi-agency intervention and proper communication with affected communities, mentoring programmes and diversion work (McNeill & Wheller, 2019). Conversely, interventions involving only the police, or sentencing changes, had far less impact.

Finally, much as we have been advocating a rethinking of the knife, one recent researcher has urged the necessity for 'a new direction in tackling knife crime' (Roberts, 2021: 3) a new direction that draws especially upon many of the insights and innovations in violence reduction we have been discussing. Her five pronged solution echoes many of the points already made and draws upon the evidence we have been discussing:

re-engage with communities, especially those most which are deprived and divided and currently bearing the brunt of the violence problems; facilitate outreach work with people, sometimes called 'connectors', who are already part of the community, proving early warnings and interceding when conflict threatens;

Re-establish strong and supportive local partnerships;
Dial back on the police enforcement-led punitive interventions (such as 'stop and search');
Offer real opportunities to young people.

Roberts concurs with our own analysis, in that, whilst there has been much talk of learning lessons from Scotland's violence reduction strategy, the Government 'have not looked at the wider polic[ies] behind it or the connected services that work with [it]' (2021: 5). Instead punitive and populist 'law and order' responses have predominated as the community, youth and social services offering the better purchase on youth social problems have been drastically cut back and we have continued to '*over*police the crisis', recycling many of the institutionally racist features which have typically alienated many of the very groups most impacted by knife violence. The delivery of smarter crime control, indeed, smarter public policy, still seems a long way off.

> **Learning Exercise 18: Crime Prevention Propaganda? What Is It Saying?**
>
> Search for examples of all kinds of knife crime prevention publicity, knife crime safety information materials on the internet and across social media. What social values are being reflected—both explicitly and implicitly—in the examples you have found?
>
> How would you go about putting together your own violence reduction advertising or information providing campaign?

References

Abt, T. (2019). *Bleeding out: The devastating consequences of urban violence—and a bold new plan for peace in the streets.* Basic Books.

ACPO/Home Office. (2007). *Knife crime—Best practice guidelines.* London: ACPO and the HomeOffice.

Allen G., & Kirk-Wade, E. (2020, October 6). *Knife crime in England and Wales* (2nd ed.), House of Commons Briefing Paper, No. SN4304.

Appleby, C., & Deeming, C. (2001). The inverse care law. *Health Service Journal, 111*(5760), 37.

Astrup, J. (2019, July/August). Knife crime: Where's the public health approach? *Community Practitioner,* 14–17.

BBC News. (2010, July 19). David Cameron launches Tories' 'Big Society' plan. *BBC News.*

Bellis, M. A., Hughes, K., Wood, S., et al. (2011). National five-year examination of inequalities and trends in emergency hospital admission for violence across England. *Injury Prevention, 17,* 319–325.

Bellis, M. A., Hughes, K., Perkins, C., & Bennett, A. (2012). *Protecting people promoting health: A public health approach to violence prevention for England.* Centre for Public Health.

Bochel, C. (2016). The changing governance of social policy. In H. Bochel & M. Powell (Eds.), *The coalition and social policy.* Policy Press.

British Youth Council. (2019). *Our generation's epidemic: Knife crime.* Youth Select Committee Report, British Youth Council.

Butts, J. A., & Delgado, S. A. (2017). *Repairing trust: Young men in neighbourhoods with cure violence programs report growing confidence in police.* John Jay College of Criminal Justice. Available at https://johnjayrec.nyc/2017/10/02/repairing2017/. Accessed 11 Sept 2017.

Carnochan, J., & McCluskey, K. (2010). Violence, culture and policing in Scotland. In D. Donnelly & K. Scott (Ed.), *Policing Scotland.* Routledge.

Centre for Social Justice/Antrobus, S. (2009). *Dying to belong: An in-depth review of street Gangs in Britain.* CSJ.

Coid, J., Zhang, Y., Zhang, Y., Hu, J., Thomson, L., Bebbington, P., & Bhui, K. (2021, January). Epidemiology of knife carrying among young British men. *Social Psychiatry and Psychiatric Epidemiology* [Online first].

Cole, A. (2010, November 16). Surgeons call for identity of knife victims to be shared with police. *British Medical Journal, 341.*

Cook, E. A., & Walklate S. (2020, June 27). Gendered objects and gendered spaces: The invisibilities of 'knife' crime. *Current Sociology* [Online], 1–16.

Densley, J. (2011). Ganging up on gangs: Why the gang intervention industry needs an intervention. *British Journal of Forensic Practice, 13*(1), 12–23.

Dodd, V. (2015, March 12). Police will have to pick and choose what they prioritise, warns Britain's top officer. *The Guardian.*

Donnelly, P. D., & Ward, C. L. (Ed.). (2014). *Oxford textbook of violence prevention.* Oxford University Press.

Eades, C., Grimshaw, R., Silvestri, A., & Solomon, E. (2007). 'Knife crime' a review of evidence and policy (2nd ed.). London: Centre for Crime and Justice Studies.

Fagan, J., & Wilkinson, D. (2000). Situational contexts of gun use by young males in inner cities. Washington, DC: US Department of Justice, NCJRS.

Foster, R. (2013). Knife crime interventions: What works? The Scottish Centre for Crime and Justice Research, Scottish Government Social Research Report No. 04/2013

Gilbert, E., & Sinclair, P. (2019). Devastating after effects: Anti-knife crime sessions. The Flavasum Trust.

Gilligan, J. (1997). Violence: Reflections on our deadliest epidemic. Jessica Kingsley Books.

Gilroy, P. (1982). The myth of black criminality. Socialist register. London: Merlin.

Greene, M. B. (2018). Metaphorically or not, violence is not a disease. AMA Journal of Ethics, 20(5), 513–515.

Halpern, D. (2005). Social capital. Cambridge: Polity Press.

Harris, K. (2009). Smart on crime: A career prosecutor's plan to make us safer. Chronicle Books.

Haylock, S., Boshari, T., Alexander, E. C., Kumar, A., Manikam, L., & Pinder, R. (2020). 2020 Risk factors associated with knife-crime in United Kingdom among young people aged 10–24 years: A systematic review. BMC Public Health, 20, 1451–1470.

HM Government. (2011). Ending gang and youth violence: A cross government report. London: The Stationery Office.

HM Government. (2018, April). Serious violence strategy. London: The Stationery Office.

Hoffman, J. S., Knox, L. M., & Cohen, C. (Eds). (2011). Beyond suppression: Global perspectives on youth violence. Praeger Press.

Home Affairs Select Committee (HASC). (2009, June 2). Knife crime: Seventh report of session 2008–09. HC 112. London: The Stationery office.

Home Affairs Select Committee (HASC). (2019). Report: Serious youth violence. 16th Report of Session 2017–19. HC 1016. House of Commons.

Jacobs, B. A., & Wright, R. (2002). Street justice: Retaliation in the criminal underworld. Cambridge University Press.

Kellermann, A. L., & Reay, D. T. (1986). Protection or peril? An analysis of firearm-related deaths in the home. New England Journal of Medicine, 314(24), 1557–1560.

Kennedy, D. (2011). *Don't shoot: One man, a street fellowship and the end of violence in inner city America.* London: Bloomsbury.

Khan, A. M., Fleming, J. C., & Jeannon, J. P. (2018). Penetrating neck injuries. *British Journal of Hospital Medicine, 79*(2), 72–78.

Kinsella, B. (2011, February). *Tackling knife crime together: A review of local anti-knife crime projects.* Home Office.

Krug, E. G., Dahlberg, L. L., Mercy, J. A., Zwi, A. B., & Lozano, J. (2002). *World report on violence and health.* Geneva: WHO.

Marfleet, N. (2008). *Why carry a weapon?: A study of knife crime amongst 15–17 year old males in London.* London: Howard League for Penal Reform.

Maxwell, R., Trotter, C., Verne, J., Brown, P., & Gunnell, D. (2007). Trends in admissions to hospital involving an assault using a knife or other sharp instrument, 1997–2005. *Journal of Public Health, 29*(2), 186–190.

McNeill, A., & Wheller, L. (2019). *Knife crime: Evidence briefing.* Coventry: College of Policing.

Meer, M., Siddiqi, A., Morkel, J. A., van Rensberg, P. J. & Zafar, S. (2010). *Knife inflicted penetrating injuries of the maxillofacial region: A descriptive, record-based study.*

Metzl, J. (2018, October 2). *Social science and the future of gun research. Items: Insights from the social sciences.* Social Science and the Future of Gun Research-Items. https://items.ssrc.org/understanding-gun-violence/social-science-and-the-future-of-gun-research/.

Mitton, K. (2019). Public health and violence. *Critical Public Health, 29*(2), 135–137.

Morris, K. (2019, December 19). UK doctors begin reporting gun and knife crime. *The Lancet, 374*(9707), 2401–2402.

Mullins, C. W. (2006). *Holding your square: Masculinities, streetlife and violence.* Willan Publishing.

Mullins, C. W., Wright, R., & Jacobs, B. (2004). Gender, streetlife and criminal retaliation. *Criminology, 42*(4), 911–940.

Nicholson, J. (2010). Young people and the police in scotland. In D. Donnelly & K. Scott (Ed.), *Policing Scotland.* Routledge.

Perry, I. (2009). Violence: A public health perspective. *Global Crime, 10*(4), 368–395.

Peterson, & Lupton, D. (1996). *The new public health: Health and self in the age of risk.* London: Sage.

Ponsford, R., Thompson, C., & Paparini S. (2019, April 1). We need a renewed focus on primary prevention to tackle youth knife violence in the longer term. *British Medical Journal: Opinion, 365.*

Pound, N. (2019, October 1). Those most at risk of involvement in knife crime are the least likely to have any interactions with a GP. *British Medical Journal, 367.*

Ransford, C., & Slutkin, G. (2017). Seeing and treating violence as a health issue. In F. Brookman, E. R. Maguire, & M. Maguire (Eds.), *The handbook of homicide* (pp. 601–625). Wiley-Blackwell.

Roberts, S. (2019). The London killings of 2018: The story behind the numbers and some proposed solution. *Crime Prevention and Community Safety, 21,* 94–115.

Roberts, S. (2021). *Solutions to knife crime: A path through the Red Sea?* Vernon Press.

Rutherford, A., Zwi, A. B., Grove, N. J., & Butchart, A. (2007). Violence: A priority for public health. *Journal of Epidemiology and Community Health, 61*(9), 764–770.

Sethi, S., & World Health Organization. (Ed.). (2007). *European report on preventing violence and knife crime among young people.* Copenhagen, Denmark: World Health Organization.

Shepherd, J., & Brennan, I. (2008, July 26). Tackling knife violence: Emergency departments should contribute to local crime reduction partnerships. *British Medical Journal: Editorial, 337,* 187–88.

Silvestri, A., Oldfield, Squires, P., & Grimshaw, R. (2009). *Young people, knives and guns: A comprehensive review, analysis and critique of gun and knife crime strategies.* London: Centre for Crime and Justice Studies.

Slutkin, G. (2013). *Violence is a contagious disease. The contagion of violence.* Institute of Medicine. Available at: www.cureviolence.org/wp-content/upl oads/2014/01/iom.pdf.

Slutkin, G. (2016). Is violence 'Senseless'? Not according to science. Let's make sense of it and treat it like a disease. *Health Progress, 97*(4), 5–8.

Slutkin, G., & Ransford, C. (2020). Violence is a contagious disease: Theory and practice in the USA and abroad, In M. Siegler & S.D. Rogers (Eds.), *Violence, trauma and trauma surgery.* Springer.

Slutkin, G., Ransford, C., & Zvetina, F. (2018, January). How the health sector can reduce violence by treating it as a contagion. *AMA journal of Ethics.*

Squires, P. (2009). The knife crime 'epidemic' and British politics. *British Politics, 4*(1), 127–157.

Squires, P. (2016). Voodoo liability: Joint enterprise prosecution as an aspect of intensified criminalisation. *Oñati Socio-legal Series, 6*(4), 937–956. https://ssrn.com/abstract=2871266

Squires, P., Silvestri, A., Grimshaw, R., & Solomon, E. (2008). *The street weapons commission evidence: Guns, knives and street violence*. London: CCJS, Kings College.

Stewart, E. A., Schreck, C. J., & Simons, R. L. (2006). 'I ain't gonna let no-one disrespect me': Does the code of the street reduce or increase violent victimisation among African American adolescents? *Journal of Research in Crime and Delinquency, 43*(4), 427–458.

Taylor, I., Walton, P., & Young, J. (1973). *The new criminoogy: For a social theory of deviance*. Routledge.

Thornton, J. (2019, April 1). Doctors could be obliged to report youths at risk of knife crime, says Home Secretary. *The British Medical Journal: Research, 365*.

Timmis, S. et al. (2019, May 8). Doctors should not be legally obliged to report youths at risk of knife crime. *The British Medical Journal: Research, 365*.

Tudor Hart, J. (1971, February). The inverse care law. *The Lancet, 7696*: 405–412.

Vitale, A. (2017). *The end of policing*. Verso.

Waller, I. (2008). *Less law, more order: The truth about reducing crime*. Manor House Publishing.

Waller, I. (2014). *Smarter crime control: A guide to a safer future for citizens, communities and politicians*. Rowman & Littlefield.

Waller, I. (2019). *Science and secrets of ending violent crime*. Rowman & Littlefield.

Ward, C. (2015). Youth violence. In P. Donnelly & C. Ward (Eds.), *The Oxford textbook for violence prevention: Epidemiology, evidence and policy*. Oxford University Press.

Webster, C., & Tai, N. (2015). The management of knife injuries. In I. Taylor (Ed.), *Recent advances in surgery*. JayPee Publishers.

Wells, J. (2008). Knife crime education. *Emergency Nurse, 16*(7), 30–32.

Wilkinson, E. (2019, February 5). How medical teams are coping with rising knife crime. *British Medical Journal, 364*.

World Health Organisation (WHO). (2002). *World report on violence and health*. WHO.

World Health Organisation (WHO). (2014). *Global status report on violence prevention*. Geneva: WHO.

YJB. (2013). *The knife crime prevention programme: A process evaluation*. Youth Justice Board for England and Wales.

9

Conclusion: Still Policing the Crisis?

We began our research on this question at different times and, initially, exploring different phases of the 'knife crime' phenomenon. As is now fairly well known, there was a peak in rates of knife violence around 2007—over 5000 hospital admissions and 272 knife-related homicides—the highest number recorded in a single year (Thapar, 2021: 12–13). This apparent 'epidemic' of interpersonal violence appeared to buck a falling crime trend that had begun to manifest itself in the mid-1990s (British Youth Council, 2019; Britton et al., 2012; Squires, 2009). Subsequently, rates of so-called 'knife crime' began to fall away, only to rise again after 2015 amidst high-profile debates about the extent to which austerity, policing cuts and police stop and search practices had impacted upon the issue (see Chapter 5). By 2015, however, the country had entered a full-blown moral panic about 'knife crime', establishing a depressingly familiar circular debate about safety on the streets, the state of youth, trust and confidence in the police, institutional racism in criminal justice and the most effective way(s) to establish sustainable forms of violence prevention. The questions arising here form the substance of this book and unpacking the socially constructed concept, or label, of 'knife crime' was, at the outset, a central objective.

© The Author(s), under exclusive license to Springer Nature
Switzerland AG 2021
E. Williams and P. Squires, *Rethinking Knife Crime*,
https://doi.org/10.1007/978-3-030-83742-6_9

It is perhaps obvious, now, that knife violence is both an old and a new problem. Knives are amongst the world's oldest weapons and have been used for millennia to kill prey for food, to defend self, family and friends, from enemies, and to fight in warfare. Whether it be Julius Caesar, stabbed in the back by his associates, Abraham about to sacrifice his son to demonstrate his faith in God (Genesis, 22: 9–12), the knife fight in *West Side Story*, the serial killer, *Mack the Knife*, celebrated in song by performers such as Louis Armstrong, Bobby Darin and Frank Sinatra, or the superhero *Blade*, played by Wesley Snipes. Knives, swords and daggers seem ever present throughout our violent past. Indeed, many parts of early modern Europe experienced 'knife fighting cultures', where a lower class of man emulated members of the more honourable and aristocratic classes who engaged in elitist duelling practices, by street-fighting with knives, responding to threats and slights to their own sense of masculinity, or defending the honour of loved ones. When duelling fell into decline, suppressed in turn by church and state and civilised opinion, public knife fighting still persisted, engaged largely by younger men and gangs, in the darker corners of society, sometimes well into the twentieth century. And throughout history, the knife's widespread availability has often brought an increasing lethality to domestic and intimate violence, the 'invisible victims of knife crime' according to some commentators (Mackintosh & Swann, 2019).

And yet, contemporary 'knife crime' is also something quite new, and different again. The use of the actual label 'knife crime' as a crime category in England and Wales has a relatively recent history. Originally it became a descriptor of particular forms of violence in Scotland in the 1990s, yet the label first appeared south of the border, in the early 2000s, refering to a perceived new crime phenomenon emerging in England and Wales. In the first place, the conception of knife crime that began circulating in police and media circles around 2002—when it was first mentioned in a news report—referred to no actual legally defined offence. Bamber's report in the *Daily Telegraph* instead commented on how 'Rising Knife Crime Deals Further Blow to Blunkett' (Bamber, 2002), telling how rising rates of knife crime appeared to be frustrating New Labour's crime reduction plans. But this referred to no particular crime—just any and all crimes recorded which were committed either with the *use of* (to assault or intimidate), or *in possession of*, a knife deemed illegal. As Elliott-Cooper (2021: 31) has argued knife crime is not an offence, in and of itself, but by grouping a range of such offences together, the police, politicians and media can create impression that this type of crime was *new*, that it was *rising fast* and that it represented *a particular set of dangers* to society. We have certainly been here before.

As we have argued, 'knife crime' is one of the most commonly used and least understood crime labels in contemporary usage. As Cook and Walklate (2020) have noted, it renders a substantial number of knife crime incidents—and their victims—largely invisible. This tendency of the police and media (and subsequently politicians and public opinion too) to refer collectively to a type of crime that does not correspond directly to any particular range of counted offences has been noted on many previous occasions by criminologists. This reporting practice allowed the speaker or journalist a form of 'evidential leeway' when describing certain types of crime as either rising or falling—although usually rising. Rising crime typically *is* the story. The evidence goes back to Cohen's (1972) work on moral panics, but is most clearly demonstrated by Hall et al., in *Policing the Crisis* (1978). Hall and his colleagues focussed upon the supposed crime of 'mugging'—a highly racialised notion inherited from American street crime—but which could not be found on any British statute book. Given that it is not possible to count what is not (legally) defined, commentators came to apply the label 'mugging' to any number of different types of offence (assaults, robberies, thefts) which occurred on the streets and where 'race' was claimed, identified or inferred, as regards the description of the alleged perpetrator or based upon where and when the offence was said to have been committed. By including or excluding any given category of crime from the trend being described, the alleged 'crime rate' could be significantly altered—usually increased. Similar observations have likewise been remarked upon in relation to the notion of 'gang related' offending—for instance, how closely related does the offending have to be to the gang in order to qualify as 'gang related'? Research has suggested that this need not be very close at all; in fact, the use of the label 'gang related' has tended to reveal rather more about the perceptions of the viewer than the actions of the viewed (Smithson et al., 2013).

Recent discussions of 'moped crime' or 'scooter crime' betray similarly ambiguous foundations. It is hardly new for offenders to travel to their crimes on bikes or motor-scooters, but until recently no-one ever took much notice or counted the numbers. Yet subsequently 'moped crime' became a new crime type—so serious was it perceived to be, so dramatically was it said to be rising, and such impunity was said to be demonstrated by the audacious, bag-snatching, moped offenders, that the MPS devised a quite exceptional, not to mention very dangerous, tactical protocol for ramming the get-away vehicles and causing them to crash, in order to apprehend offenders.

It is our argument here that the 'knife crime' phenomenon has been subject to essentially similar amplification processes. The timeline we presented in Chapter 1 (Fig. 1.4) reveals how this crime category came to be concocted, piece by piece. First, the Knives Act 1977 was passed, this defined a range of knives as 'especially dangerous' and banned their sale or marketing, and also empowered the police to add 'knife crime searches' to their s.60 ('without suspicion') stop and search activities. This gave the whole 'knives issue' a higher police profile. In time, an 'institutional' definition of 'knife crime' began to emerge, and later the police introduced a crime recording code to identify the occasions upon which a knife had been used, employed or was simply carried in a number of other recorded offences. This aggregated data established a number for 'knife crimes' recorded, providing a spurious empirical foundation for the establishment of supposed 'knife crime trends'—but it related to no particular offences and was largely dependent upon the discretion of the police in recognising and applying the code. Yet once there is a number, there can become a trend, although it was not until 2011 that year-on-year compatible figures were available nationally. Two years earlier the Home Affairs Select Committee (HASC, 2009) examining the emerging 'knife crime' question, had voiced its concerns about the reliability of the available data and whether the knife-involved crime numbers were rising or falling, remarking rather pointedly that 'there is no Home Office definition of knife crime' (HASC, 2009: 6). Even so, the label 'knife crime' has continued to be unstable, for, in 2014, the Government passed the Legal Aid Sentencing and Punishment of Offenders (LASPO) Act 2012.

Section 142 of the Act introduced a new offence of 'aggravated possession' with mandatory custodial sentences for a second knife possession offence. Hitherto, mere possession of a knife' had not been recorded as a 'knife crime' but with 'aggravated possession' now added to the category and stop and search operations being widely rolled out again, police pro-activity was itself likely to have a significant impact upon rates of recorded 'knife crime'. And from around 2015, as we have seen, knife crime began to rise once more. Knife homicides and stabbings increased, it was not as if the measures introduced since 1997 and the considerable efforts, both policing and political, could be shown to be working—quite the contrary.

And as the knife crime crisis rolled on, we come to another of the central concerns of our book. None of our research and nothing we have written should be thought to suggest that knife violence, or 'knife crime', is not a serious modern problem, that the private tragedies represented by stabbings, occurring with an unacceptable frequency, represent major issues for the safety, cohesion and security of communities and hugely important public challenges for health, development and (social and criminal) justice. And yet, precisely because the existing strategies of police and government appear not to be effective, the criticisms we raise the point to major problems in the way that knife crime is currently understood and responded to. Our analysis tells us that the way in which 'knife crime' is currently understood ensures that it is responded to in a rather ad hoc, short-term and ineffective fashion, both punitive and enforcement-led, and in ways which largely perpetuate and exacerbate the problem. Our central argument urges a profound rethinking of knife crime.

Looking for a way in which to engage that 'rethinking' process, we drew inspiration from the work of Stuart Hall and his colleagues in 1978. However, much as in the case of the 'mugging' story told by Hall et al., the significance of the ambiguously evidenced 'knife crime' category was not confined to the statistical aspects. There was already a significant historical legacy in which knife violence was understood as both 'uncivilised' and 'brutal', a visceral and violent throwback to a moral dark age. In particular it was (incorrectly and often patronisingly) associated with primitive and 'alien cultures' or 'foreign-ness'. We have

seen how, during the parliamentary debates on the 1953 Prevention of
Crime Act and the Offensive Weapons Act, 1959, various politicians had
drawn connections between 'certain classes of offenders', race and knife
violence, noting a supposed affinity between 'foreigners, …flick knives
and gangs' which has, unfortunately, many contemporary resonances. By
contrast, Olden (2011) describes racially motivated violence culminating
in a gang murder in Notting Hill in 1959, an incident involving a gang
of white racists and a stiletto knife. Even down to the police failure, in
1959, to arrest the culprits, the case was hugely reminiscent of the killing,
some thirty-four years later, of Stephen Lawrence. The historical record
rather puts paid to the theory of knife-involved crime fitting any kind of
selective racial profile—other than, of course, the one imposed upon it by
police constructions and media reporting. In these respects, the debates
of the 1950s have a great deal in common with those arising during our
more recent 'knife crime' crisis.

Accordingly, our argument is that the *new* 'knife crime' represents,
like mugging in the 1970s, a highly racialised and predominantly youth-
centred crime category, even though this flawed depiction of the problem
and its associated misdirection fails to address the greater proportion
of the problem of knife violence in contemporary Britain. In turn,
the distorted focus upon such a partial aspect of contemporary knife
violence contributes to a profound misunderstanding of violence and its
aetiology, neglect of violence and victimisation processes, the complete
betrayal of many victims, whilst performing a disservice to many others.
It conveys the erroneous impression that violence might be addressed
one incident, one weapon, at a time and without sustained investment
and social change, by implying that the police and public enforcement-
led interventions will remain in the driving seat of violence reduction
strategy. By contrast, as we have seen, the police have, for some long
time, been deeply implicated in the reproduction and political recycling
of the *new* 'knife crime' problem. And although this is not intended as
a blanket condemnation of policing's a potential contribution to public
safety, profound cuts to police staffing after 2010 and the axing of the
National Neighbourhood policing strategy, certainly undermined police
capacity to address emerging youth and gang violence. For example the

British Youth Council Report of 2019 is full of references to the impact of policing cuts on police performance:

> We acknowledge the cuts in police numbers over the recent years, and the impact that this has had on police forces across the country. This significantly reduces the capacity of the police to engage in their communities in a positive way, building a constructive relationship with young people in schools and on the streets. Instead of being able to work to prevent knife crime, it forces them to work reactively once a knife crime offence has already taken place. (British Youth Council, 2019: paras. 74–77)

Nevertheless, there remain profound institutional issues with regard to policing's equal and accountable delivery of safety and security. Particular policing interventions (such as stop and search, and surveillance) still evoke much criticism, whilst 'trust and confidence' in the police still register great concern within BAME communities—especially their younger members—and more insistently since the #*BlackLivesMatter* mobilisations.

Following the academic approach of Hall and his colleagues in 1978, we have sought to capture something of the 'conjunctural' context in which the 'knife crime' phenomenon first arose and assumed its familiar shape and character. This involved delving into the 'pre-history' of knife crime and grasping the criminological 'precursors' to the problem—the emergence of the highly racialised contemporary gang question and the related question of 'gun culture'—another form of 'weapon-identified' criminality which shared a number of the social and criminological characteristic that, later, were to be identified with 'knife crime' (Eades et al., 2007; Squires et al., 2008). Whilst the very unique and supposedly 'alien'—and 'unBritish' (Squires, 2000)—character of gun crime may have caused it to overshadow, for a while the far more prevalent violence involving knives, this was to change. When rates of gun crime appeared to fall significantly after 2004, knife crime surfaced, only temporarily pushed from the front pages by the 'credit crunch' and austerity crisis of 'Broken Britain' after 2008. It later returned around 2015, with a lethal vengeance, significantly exacerbated by the spending cuts which had so 'hollowed out' front line policing (Thapar, 2021: 247), decimated youth services and blighted the opportunities of so many already disadvantaged young people (Roberts, 2021; Thapar, 2021: 257) who became, in due course, knife crime's 'usual suspects' and over-represented victims (McAra & McVie, 2005; Medina Ariza, 2014; Quinton, 2011).

Setting such a context for the emergence of 'knife crime' represents the essence of our conjunctural analysis of the emergence and recycling of the knife crime problem. However, as the timeline we have drawn to help describe the developing phenomenon has shown, knife crime remained at the centre of an exceptional, constantly moving, law and order storm. Through 'total policing' a new knife code and symbolic homicides the face of knife crime evolved and racialised. Below command levels, the police had expressed their own misgivings about the Macpherson verdict on 'institutional racism' (Foster, 2006), and even though Stephen Lawrence had been killed by a knife-wielding white racist gang, the reporting of knife crime began to acquire an increasingly racialised aspect. A form of ideological push back against Macpherson emerged. The full force of law and order Britain, surreptitiously allying itself to a supposed police point of view insisted that only tough policing, intensified stop and search and punitive sentencing could end the knife crime crisis. Pushed into action the Metropolitan Police produced its own knife crime report which had a significant impact on subsequent reports as journalists picked over the data for headlines: '*Increase in Knife Crime Led by Young*', and '*a knife crime every 25 minutes in the capital*' (Davenport, 2004). Despite a number of exceptional killings of white victims, each generating columns of condemnation in the national and local press, news reporting focused increasingly upon black victims—and implicitly—on black perpetrators. And by 2006 'knife crime' began to be regularly and openly defined through ethnicity and a number of sometimes subtle, sometimes explicit, racial signifiers. By the end of 2006, as with the implicit coding of 'gang talk' there were increasing references made to 'knife crime' and particular references to 'Black communities'. Reviewing the national reporting of knife crime, some ten years later for, his 'Beyond the Blade' project, Gary Younge found that use of the label 'knife crime' was confined to incidents where the victim was a black teen or child in London. The label was not used to describe all crimes committed with knives, his research showed, 'just those where young black men in London were involved' (Younge, 2018). This, even though roughly fifty per cent of teenage and child homicides occurred outside London, and the overwhelming majority were not black.

Partly as a consequence of this highly slanted and selective reporting of the 'knife crime' problem, increasing levels of support came to be voiced in favour of the reinstatement of police stop and search to its pre-Macpherson proportions. Furthermore, comments, findings and conclusions such as those referred to above also reaffirmed the cyclical relationships between crime reporting, police activity, police outcomes, political utterances and further reporting, all the time recycling and refreshing the 'knife crime' phenomenon for its intended audience. The example we presented in Chapter 4 (Figs. 4.4–4.10), involving the continual recycling of a photograph of a dangerous array of confiscated knives, which was used in any and every knife crime story, irrespective of context or relevance and clearly indicating the capacity for media agendas to be manipulated, and harnessed to political and institutional bandwagons. In this case it involved endorsing a return to supposed 'tough' law and order strategies and high-profile stop and search practices (despite the consequences) and despite the fact that the research evidence suggested deep scepticism about the crime reduction effectiveness of such policies (McCandless et al., 2016).

The media chorus supporting the return to robust policing approaches subsequently became associated with a growing acknowledgement that, in fact, policing alone might not be enough to tackle the *underlying* causes of knife crime. Although this idea had arrived early—evidenced by WHO approaches to violence (WHO, 2002), the seemingly successful Strathclyde Community initiative to Reduce Violence (CIRV) and other articulations of so-called 'Smarter Criminal Justice' (Waller, 2014, 2019), initially failed to gain much actual traction in England and Wales, or London more specifically. The supposed 'public health led approach' pioneered successfully in Glasgow and Strathclyde, Scotland, found many 'in principle' supporters south of the border, but practice was a different matter. Members of the Home Affairs Select Committee (HASC, 2019) concurred with the view that, whilst there had been much *talk* of a sustainable public health approach, clarity about what it would entail on the ground, what it would do, what it would look like and how it might be funded, was rather harder to find. Eventually, however, new Violence Reduction Units (VRUs) were established in 2019, in the eighteen police force areas considered to have the worst 'serious violence' problems, supported by a Home Office 'Central Violence Fund' of £100 million. Roughly two-thirds of this (not all of it 'new money') was earmarked for policing enhancements and the remainder was for 'community initiatives' intended to:

> build capacity in local areas to tackle the root causes of serious violence...
> bring[ing] together police, local government, health and education profes-
> sionals, community leaders and other key partners to ensure a multi-
> agency response to the identification of local drivers of serious violence
> and ... to take necessary action to tackle these. This includes being
> responsible for driving local strategy and embedding cultural change
> alongside their commissioning role as a means to make the VRU
> sustainable. (Home Office, 2020: 4)

Given the arrival of the Covid pandemic and the disruptions this has caused, it is perhaps rather early to judge the impact of the new VRUs, although the omens may not be so good, there were more stabbings in the first part of 2021, leaving London on track towards a new record in teenage knife fatalities (Davis, 2021; Jackson, 2021). The final report of the Youth Violence Commission (YVC) (Irwin-Rogers et al., 2020) looks cautiously towards the VRUs, insisting they need 'long term funding' as they develop 'expansive and ambitious roles at the local and national level… [and] collaborate as a network' (Foreword, YVC, 2018: 8). Yet, at the time of writing, the VRUs are still little more than 'architecture', maybe only the 'scaffolding' of a response, for as Vicky Foxcroft MP, chair of the YVC, acknowledged 'young people continue to lose their lives, *and the real work is yet to be done*' (ibid. emphasis added). 'The long-term success of the VRUs, however, is far from certain', the report noted (Irwin-Rogers et al., 2020: 16).

Yet the VRU money hardly makes a dent in the funding deficits caused by well over a decade of youth service funding cuts—another issue raised repeatedly by the 'youth select committee' (British Youth Council, 2019) and the Youth Violence Commission: 'Youth services, decimated by recent cuts, require a far greater injection of investment to begin what will undoubtedly be a long and difficult process of recovery' (YVC, 2020: 17). Thapar likewise notes that between 2011 and 2019 spending cuts removed fully 46% of London's youth services budget, closing over a hundred youth centres in the process and axing hundreds of youth worker jobs. By the end of the decade, 'at least £35 million less *per year* was being spent on the city's youth services compared with pre-austerity levels' (2021: 257). And yet, £35 million was the *total* allocation for 18 VRUs in 18 cities across the country as a whole. Research by the *YMCA* and *Action for Children* showed that some £260 million had been withdrawn from local authority children's services budgets between 2011 and 2017, with the loss of over a thousand children's centres and 760 youth centres, some major cities losing close to 90% of their youth services budgets (ibid., 257; YMCA, 2018). In effect, little of the current planning for preventing or reducing 'knife crime' goes anyway towards addressing the kinds of deep and broad-based intergenerational concerns expressed by the youth workers and young people who were interviewed for this research. With relatively few exceptions, rather few recent explorations of knife crime engage very meaningfully with the people most directly involved and most directly affected by the risks and disadvantages of city life, the fear and danger occasioned by knife crime and their ambiguous relationship policing and authority. This suggests a less than auspicious background from which to launch a new 'violence reduction' initiative.

In place of statutory and universal youth services we have seen the emergence of what we have called a new 'knife crime industry' (see Chapter 6). In many respects, this new adjunct to the 'crime prevention industry' or, perhaps, extension to the 'gang industry' (Densley, 2011) is but the culmination of a much longer trend in the increasingly selective targeting of youth service funding. More and more, youth service resourcing became competition based, short term and increasingly selective, geared around specified 'health, safety or crime reduction' targets—such as substance abuse education, teenage pregnancy prevention and violence reduction. As the YVC put it:

The Commission found serious problems with the provision of youth services. An extraordinary number of third sector organisations are being forced to compete for small pots of short-term project funding, leading to the closure of many organisations and a toxic climate of inadequate and ineffective services. The sector requires wholesale change that will facilitate the development of long-term strategies, sufficient and stable funding arrangements, and high quality services on which young people can rely. (Irwin-Rogers et al., 2020: 10)

In contrast, the 'knife crime' intervention models adopted often included public/private partnerships, advertising, media campaigns and broad-based behaviour change promotional activities, even commercial marketing strategies. Nothing in our argument is intended to disparage the hard work and commitment invested by many people deeply concerned by knife-involved violence and who, perhaps touched directly by the problem themselves, now work tirelessly to address the problem in whatever ways they can: mentoring young people, raising funds, supporting families and victims. Yet taken together, we have suggested, such efforts have at times amounted to a troubling commodification of 'knife crime' which, whilst it might bring benefits and political advantages to some simply replicates the tragedy for many more. In stark contrast to the notion that crime does not pay, the new 'knife crime' has brought many direct and indirect benefits to enterprises, entrepreneurs, politicians and commentators in the process of constructing a problematic, essentially neoliberal, consensus on 'knife crime' as an individualistic, racialised, behavioural pathology. In this process 'knife crime' has become commodified, produced and reproduced as a cultural object for exchange, entertainment and consumption within today's extended knife crime industry. We have questioned, in particular, how a preventative strategy that is so positioned and ideologically oriented can expect to disarm a 'knife culture' upon which it is so dependent for its own legitimacy? As we have argued, what we have labelled the 'knife crime industry', allied with a punitive law and order politics, simply serves to build and recycle the problem, normalising it when it ought to be addressing the underlying issues: deprived communities, fractured relationships and hostile cultures which intensify social exclusion increasing feelings of insecurity, and ultimately, self-defeatingly, prompting further illegal knife carrying and use. Above all, we are still building the problem, seemingly and endlessly, still '*policing the* [knife crime] *crisis*'. And that, finally, is why 'knife crime' needs such a fundamental rethinking.

Learning Exercise 19: Exploring Violence Reduction Units
What are they for, what will they do, how will they work?
Read the guidance prepared for VRUs, Violence Reduction Unit interim guidance (publishing.service.gov.uk), how are they expected to make an impact on levels of serious youth violence? How confident are you that they will meet their objectives?
    How will we find out if these VRUs are successful? How are the VRUs positioned to address issues of deprivation, lack of opportunity, trust and confidence in authority, and racism and discrimination which we have identified as important underlying drivers of knife crime?

References

Bamber, D. (2002, March 10). Rising knife crime deals further blow to Blunkett. *The Sunday Telegraph*.

British Youth Council. (2019). *Our generation's epidemic: Knife crime*. Youth Select Committee Report, British Youth Council.

Britton, A., Kershaw, C., Osborne, S., & Smith, K. (2012). Underlying patterns within the England and Wales crime drop. In J. Van Dijk, A. Tseloni, & G. Farrell (Ed.), *The international crime drop: New directions in research*. Palgrave Macmillan.

Cohen, S. (1972). *Folk devils and moral panics: The creation of the Mods and Rockers*. Abingdon, Oxon.

Cook, E. A., & Walklate S. (2020, June 27). Gendered objects and gendered spaces: The invisibilities of 'knife' crime. *Current Sociology* [Online]: 1–16.

Davenport, J. (2004, September 30). Increase in knife crime led by young. *Evening Standard*, UK.

Davis, R. (2021, June 18). A quarter more stabbings so far in 2021 as capital could have worst year for killings on record. *MyLondon.*

Densley, J. (2011). Ganging up on gangs: Why the gang intervention industry needs an intervention. *British Journal of Forensic Practice, 13*(1), 12–23.

Eades, C., Grimshaw, R., Silvestri, A., & Solomon, E. (2007). *'Knife crime' a review of evidence and policy* (2nd ed.). Centre for Crime and Justice Studies.

Elliott-Cooper, A. (2021). *Black resistance to british policing.* Manchester University Press.

Foster, J. (2008). 'It might have been incompetent, but it wasn't racist': Murder detectives' perceptions of the Lawrence Inquiry and its impact on homicide investigation in London. *Policing and Society, 18*(2), 89–112.

Hall, S., Roberts, B., Clarke, J., Jefferson, T., & Critcher, C. (1978). *Policing the crisis: Mugging, the state, and law and order.* Macmillan.

Home Affairs Select Committee (HASC). (2009). *Knife crime: Seventh Report of Session 2008–09.* HC 112, 2 June 2009. London: The Stationery office.

Home Office. (2020). Violence reduction unit interim guidance. Crown Copyright.

Irwin-Rogers, K., Muthoo, A., & Billingham, L. (2020, July). *Youth Violence Commission, Final Report.* YVC.

Jackson, S. (2021, June 17). London is on track for worst year of teenage killings since 2008, Metropolitan Police warns. *SkyNews.*

Mackintosh, T., & Swann, S. (2019, September 13). Domestic violence killings reach five year high. *BBC News Website.*

McAra, & and McVie. (2005). The usual suspects? Street-life, young people and the police. *Criminology and Criminal Justice, 5*(1), 5–36.

McCandless, R., Feist, A., Allan, J., & Morgan, N. (2016). *Do initiatives involving substantial increases in stop and search reduce crime? Assessing the impact of Operation BLUNT 2.* Published March 2016, Home Office.

Medina Ariza, J. J. (2014). Police-initiated contacts: young people, ethnicity, and the 'usual suspects'. *Policing and Society, 24*(2), 208–223.

Olden, M. (2011). *Murder in Notting Hill.* Zero Books.

Quinton, P. (2011). The formation of suspicions: Police stop and search practices in England and Wales. *Policing and Society, 21*(4), 357–368.

Roberts, S. (2021). *Solutions to knife crime: A path through the Red Sea?* Vernon Press.

Smithson, H., Ralphs, R., & Williams, P. (2013). Used and abused: The problematic usage of gang terminology in the United Kingdom and its implications for ethnic minority youth. *British Journal of Criminology, 53*(1), 113–128.

Squires, P. (2000). *Gun culture or gun control? Firearms, violence and society.* Routledge.

Squires, P. (2009). The knife crime 'epidemic' and British politics. *British Politics, 4*(1), 127–157.

Squires, P. with Solomon, E., & Grimshaw, R. (2008). *'Gun Crime': A review of evidence and policy.* Centre for Crime and Justice Studies.

Thapar, C. (2021). *Cut short: Youth violence, loss and hope in the city.* Penguin Random House.

Waller, I. (2014). *Smarter crime control: A guide to a safer future for citizens, communities and politicians.* Lanham, MD: Rowman & Littlefield.

Waller, I. (2019). *Science and secrets of ending violent crime.* Lanham, MD: Rowman & Littlefield.

World Health Organisation (WHO). (2002). *World report on violence and health.* WHO.

YMCA. (2018). *Youth and consequences: A report examining Local Authority expenditure on youth services in England and Wales.* YMCA. https://www.ymca.org.uk/wp-content/uploads/2018/04/Youth-Consequences-v0.2.pdf

Younge, G. (2018, June 21). The radical lessons of a year reporting on knife crime. *The Guardian.*

Youth Violence Commission. (2018, July). *Interim report.*

Youth Violence Commission. (2020, July). *Final report* (Co-authored by K. Irwin-Rogers, A. Muthoo, & L. Billingham).

Index

Printed in Great Britain
by Amazon

16264575R10226